M000167298

In his Contours of Pauline Theology Dr Holland argues forcefully that the main contours of Paul's thought can only be understood when we understand Paul as an exegete and theologian of the Old Testament, with the hoped-for New Exodus, now fulfilled in Christ, at the centre of his reading strategy. This approach finds corporate and covenantal themes to lie at the very heart of Paul's concerns. In constant critical engagement with the whole range of contemporary scholarship Holland maps out for himself and his readers new ways of understanding Paul and offers new insights into a range of absolutely vital issues from justification to Christology, and new insights into Pauline texts from Romans to Colossians. Challenging, unsettling and infuriating Dr Holland's tour de force cannot be ignored.

Dr Peter Head
Lecturer in New Testament, University of Cambridge

It is refreshing to read something radically new in such a popular area as Pauline studies. So often what promised new perspectives, new insights, turns out not to be essentially different. Tom Holland's original and creative approach to Paul does not fall into this category. Here Paul is not the innovator of Christian doctrine - he received his theological model from his Jewish upbringing in which he was taught that Yahweh would bring about the promised New Exodus. Paul came to realize that this had been inaugurated by the paschal death of Christ. Thus Holland maintains that there existed a common hermeneutical model for both Judaism and the New Testament church i.e the New Exodus. Justification is not a declaration of being in the covenant, but refers back to the creation of a covenant between Yahweh and His people. This view of justification fits in with Paul's doctrine of corporate baptism, the washing of the believing community accomplished by the Spirit through the death of Christ. Paul's theology is not individualistic, but corporate, so it is believers collectively as the church and not the believer's individual body which comprise the temple of the Holy Spirit. I anticipate that if it finds acceptance, the proposals of this book should provide a timely and fruitful alternative to some of the theological emphases that have guided the church for too long.

Dr. William S. Campbell
Department of Theology and Religious Studies
University of Wales

Having watched Dr Holland developing his ideas over a period of several years, I am thrilled that his work is now available to a wider public. All who are interested in Paul's theology will discover much that is stimulating and provocative here. He develops in detail his view that the Exodus events provide the vocabulary and imagery for much of what the apostle wishes to say about Christ, his salvation and his people. Apart from his novel interaction with the so-called "new perspective", many will be fascinated by his work showing the influence of Passover themes in Paul's understanding of Christ as "first born", and in his theology of justification, covenant inclusion, baptism, etc. I warmly commend this work.

Ven. Dr. Paul D. Gardner
(Archdeacon of Exeter)

Dr. Tom Holland of the Evangelical Theological College of Wales has produced a significant contribution to the discussion of Pauline theology. He presents a Paul whose thinking is rooted in the Old Testament scriptures and developed within the framework of covenantal relationship. The two major lenses through which Paul's letters must be viewed are a "New Exodus" paradigm and a corporate reading of the texts. When these lenses are used, it is clear that Paul's theology is in full agreement with the teachings of Jesus and the other New Testament authors. Along the way, many of the new vectors in Pauline theology are explored and critiqued. Whether or not everyone will agree with Dr. Holland's conclusions, all serious New Testament scholars must engage his evidence and his arguments in considering The Contours of Pauline Theology.

Dr. John D. Harvey
Associate Professor of New Testament and Greek
Columbia Biblical Seminary & School of Missions, USA

CONTOURS OF PAULINE THEOLOGY

A RADICAL NEW SURVEY OF THE INFLUENCES ON PAUL'S BIBLICAL WRITINGS

TOM HOLLAND

MENTOR

For Barbara,
who God gave to me –
my joy, my love, my strength

Copyright © Tom Holland 2004

ISBN 1-85792-469-X

Published in 2004
in the
Mentor Imprint
by
Christian Focus Publications,
Geanies House, Fearn, Ross-shire,
IV20 1TW, Scotland, UK

www.christianfocus.com

Cover design by Alister MacInnes

Printed and bound by
WS Bookwell, Finland

Fuller versions of the chapters in this book are available at
www.tomholland.instant.org.uk

All rights reserved. No part of this publication may be reproduced, stored in a retrieval system, or transmitted, in any form, by any means, electronic, mechanical, photocopying, recording or otherwise without the prior permission of the publisher or a license permitting restricted copying. In the U.K. such licenses are issued by the Copyright Licensing Agency, 90 Tottenham Court Road, London W1P 9HE.

Contents

Key of Cited Abbreviations

ALW	Archis Für Liturgiewissenschaft, Rengensburg
BT	Banner of Truth
CBQ	Catholic Biblical Quarterly
Con	Concilium
DPL	*Dictionary of Paul and his Letters* ed. G.F. Hawthorne, et al. (Leicester: Inter Varsity/ Downers Grove; Intervarsity, 1993)
EQ	Evangelical Quarterly
ExpT	Expository Times
HTR	Harvard Theological Review
Interp	Interpretation
JBL	Journal of Biblical Literature
JETS	Journal of the Evangelical Theological Society
JJS	Journal of Jewish Studies
JSOT	Journal for the Study of the Old Testament
JTS	Journal of Theological Studies
JSNT	Journal for the Study of the New Testament
NovT	Novum Testamentum
NICNT	New International Commentary on the New Testament
NTS	New Testament Studies
REJ	Revue des études juives
RHPR	Revue d'histoire et de philosophie religieuses
PCB	Peake's Commentary on the Bible
SBT	Studies in Biblical Theology
SJTh	Scottish Journal of Theology
TrinJ	Trinity Journal
TDNT	Theological Dictionary of the New Testament G.Kittel and G Friedrich, eds., Theological Dictionary of the New Testament (ET 10 vols.; Grand Rapids: Edermans :1964-76)
Them	Themelios
Theol Rev	Theologische Revue
TynB	Tyndale Bulletin
Stud Theol	Studia theologica
VT	Vetus Testamentum
WTJ	Westminster Theological Journal

Acknowledgements

To mention those who have helped me in my research would be a task that would take a book in itself! Often it has been a chance remark made which directed my thoughts in a totally different direction. There have been others who have patiently listened and encouraged, without, I suspect, understanding what drove me to spend what seemed to them a lifetime to undo a knot in Pauline or wider biblical thought. Others have had to bear with me as I have preached another sermon that yet again made reference to things which did not fit into the traditions of interpretation that they had been more comfortable with, but kindly allowed me space to explore what I increasingly felt was the substructure of New Testament thinking. I hope that these and others, if they do me the favour of reading these pages, will understand what it was that I was struggling with. To those who bore with me and encouraged me, I want to express my sincere thanks.

But there are others who have had a more immediate and direct influence. Those who have read parts of the text at various stages and given their comments. They have saved me from far more mistakes than those which will become apparent to the reader. None, of course, bear any responsibility for what is written. I want to thank Prof. Don Carson for reading a draft of one of the chapters in its early stages, and Dr. Douglas de Lacey, Dr. Tom Wright, Dr. John Balchin, Dr. Eryl Davies, Dr. Gwyn Davies, Rev. Clifford Taylor, Rev. Peter Seccomb, Rev. Bendor Samuel, Rev. John Bugden, Rev. Brian Edwards, Rev. Philip Eveson and Mark Mattison, the editor of the Paul Page on the Internet, for reading and interacting at different stages in the long journey. Obviously none of these good men is responsible for the contents of what has now been committed to print. I have tried to evaluate their comments, but have finally gone in the direction that I believe the evidence has led me.

Special mention must be made of my two supervisors, both very busy men who kindly read and interacted with my ideas to sharpen and challenge them, Prof. D.P. Davies of St David's College, University of Wales, and Dr. Paul Gardner, now Archdeacon of Exeter, England. I am grateful for the care that these men gave to the task and for the gracious guidance that they have given.

I also want to thank Malcolm Maclean of Christian Focus Publications for his expertly executed editorial skills that have made the book more readable. I also want to thank Mr Victor Perry for his help in proof-reading an earlier version of the text.

I want to thank Dr. Eryl Davies, the principal of The Evangelical Theological College of Wales for his forbearance and encouragement. I am one of many whose personal development owes so much to this wise and kind man. I must thank also the staff of ETCW who have discussed and challenged my ideas, and for their graciousness for continuing to accept me even when they have not been sure of the proposals that I have made. Thirdly, I want to thank the students, both past and present, at ETCW who have discussed and challenged my thinking in a way that only students seem to be able to do!

There are four men who have during the years of this research been a source of invaluable encouragement. None of them are academics, but each of them displayed such love for Christ and his truth that they constantly inspired me. Ted Whomes and Bob Gentle, members of the congregation I pastored and whose love and encouragement continues to be a source of immense encouragement, even though they have received their reward in Christ's presence. Their widows know how much their fellowship meant. Also Allan Maynard and Jack Ploughman, men who as members of the local congregation, accompanied me on visits to Romania and encouraged me in my preaching. I cannot tell how much the encouragement and fellowship of these four men has meant.

At a more personal level there is my family. I have been blessed with two sisters, Anita and Norma, who through the long years have prayed and expressed their love to me in ways that few brothers can possibly experience. And more immediate, Lois, Elisabeth and Abigail, my three daughters who cannot remember a time in their lives when their father was not poring over books looking for clues that would point him in a direction that would make better sense.

And, especially, to Barbara. She has been to me what Katie was to Luther. Time and again she has kept my eyes on the big picture and the issues that are the foundations to the work of God in this world. Barbara has borne so much that I could make this long journey. I owe her more than can ever be expressed.

Section One

Explorations of Heritage

Chapter One

Paul, Jesus and the Old Testament Promises

For generations scholars have claimed that Paul was the creator of Christianity. According to them Paul changed the original message of Jesus and what emerged was something that Jesus himself would never have recognised as what he had taught. Such a claim is a massive attack on the authority of the Christian gospel. If the greatest teacher of the early church left his Master's teaching, then there is a question that must be asked, Do Christians follow Jesus, or do they follow Paul? The claim of this book is that Paul never left the religion of the Old Testament. In fact, it will be argued that he never departed from the teaching of Jesus.

This is a very different position from that of most New Testament scholars in the past hundred years who have not only claimed that Paul Hellenised the Jewish message, but have also argued that the Gospels were written by Christian communities who invented stories and sayings about Jesus to teach the Gentile believers what Jesus would have taught concerning various issues if he had lived among them. The Gentiles faced issues that the Palestinian Jews would have known nothing about. The church gave its approval, it is claimed, to the composition of stories, attributed to Jesus, that would be the vehicle of instruction for the new believers. These stories, it is argued, became part of the source out of which the four Evangelists composed their Gospels.

But if these records do not accurately record Jesus' teaching, then we cannot possibly ask if Paul is teaching the same thing as Jesus. If they are not reliable records, then we can only guess at what Jesus actually taught. It would therefore be foolish to say that Paul did not follow Jesus' teaching if we have no reliable record of it. This illustrates the folly of much New Testament research. To argue that we do not have the original teaching of Jesus, and then to say that Paul rejected it, is blind prejudice. Of course, the answer from some will be that we know Jesus taught as a Jew and Paul taught as a Greek, and this justifies the assertion that Paul left the teaching of Jesus. But this claim concerning Paul being Hellenistic, as we shall soon see, can no

11

longer be sustained. If however we can demonstrate that the Gospels
are a faithful record of Jesus' teaching, then we can compare Paul's
teaching with that of his Master. Once we have considered Paul's
commitment to the teaching of Jesus, we can go on to examine the
contours of Pauline Theology.

The structure of the book

To help the reader navigate this book we will briefly outline its
structure. First, in chapter 1, we will consider whether the Old
Testament Scriptures were significant for Jesus and Paul. We will
also examine the claim that the Gospels are not a reliable record of
the teaching of Jesus. Then in chapter 2 we will examine the sources
that Paul based his teaching on. Did he really depart from Jesus, was
he really a Hellenist teacher, or has he been misunderstood? In chapter
3 we will pause to consider the way scholars are using ancient Jewish
literature known as the pseudepigrapha. These are considered
important documents for understanding both the Gospels and Paul.
We need to ask if this material is relevant to the study of the New
Testament. In chapter 4 we consider Paul's thinking when he speaks
about believers being slaves. Studying this particular example will
help us to decide if Paul stayed within his preconversion Jewish
theological framework, the setting that most scholars see as Jesus'
natural conceptual home. If we conclude that he did, then it will give
grounds for seeking to interpret him from within this spiritual and
intellectual framework. Having done this necessary groundwork we
will explore, in chapters 5–12, particular subjects that are key themes
in the theology of Paul. These studies will seek to focus on an Old
Testament framework for understanding the mindset of Paul. The
themes chosen centre on the way God saves a people through the
death of Jesus.

It will become clear that the evidence powerfully suggests that the
teaching of both Jesus and Paul has clear links with the Old Testament.
Only by appreciating the nature of these links can we really discover
the nature of Paul's theology. We will discover that Paul's theology
has its roots in the model of the Passover and the Exodus which he
sees to have been a type of the work of Jesus. This, we will discover,
was the very model used by Jesus himself. The conclusion reached is
that Paul departed neither from the Old Testament Scriptures nor the
teaching of Jesus.

Difficulties to understanding

The New Testament presents its own set of difficulties for the reader who wants to understand its message. It was written almost two thousand years ago. We know that the meaning of words and the ideas they contain can change in a matter of years. We use the term 'generation gap' to speak of the cultural gap between older and younger generations living at the same time. The older generation struggles with the new ideas and values of the younger generation. Old words are given new meanings and new words are coined, both of which confuse the older generation. The cultural/generation gap between modern society and the New Testament world is immense and is an obstacle to a clear understanding of the New Testament.

It is hard enough to understand properly an earlier generation of our own nationality. The meaning of words has changed, the significance of customs has altered and the passage of time has rejected earlier beliefs so that they are no longer held or even understood. How much more difficult it is to understand the New Testament! Not only is there the massive cultural gap that makes study of the New Testament difficult, there is also the complication of mixed alien cultures. The New Testament is dealing with more than one people group. It is interacting with the culture of a range of peoples and assumes that the reader is aware of their significance for particular statements. While all of the New Testament writers, apart from Luke, were Jews, most of the New Testament writers wrote for both Jews and Gentiles. So in what culture did they set their writings? Was it Jewish, Greek, or a lost variant? Perhaps culture did not really matter. Many modern people switch without thought between their own and American culture. Were the New Testament writers doing the same? How do we decide on the imagery used by the New Testament writers and what culture it was from?

New Testament scholars have struggled with these obstacles for years. Most modern scholars think that the early church sacrificed its Jewish inheritance. This, they argue, was inevitable, so that its missionaries could effectively communicate its message to the Gentile world. This has led the majority of scholars to assume that the New Testament is made up of layers of traditions that reflect these early stages of change.

For most New Testament scholars there are three layers of tradition that make up the New Testament documents. The first is

Jewish material that comes from the life and teaching of Jesus in Palestine. After Pentecost the church took its message concerning Jesus to the Jews of the Diaspora. These Jews lacked much of the social background of the Palestinian Jews. To communicate with them the message was simplified. Imagery that would have been easily understood in Palestine, but meaningless in other parts of the world, was dropped. In its place was put imagery that the Diaspora Jews would have been familiar with. Local Palestinian customs were explained, Jesus was portrayed as a universally significant figure, and demands that could only be met in Palestine were dropped. Thus a second layer of tradition emerged.

The third layer of tradition came when the church began to proclaim its message to the Gentiles. These knew even less of the Palestinian background of Jesus' life and teaching than did the Diaspora Jews. Furthermore, the Gentiles lacked the knowledge of the Old Testament that the Diaspora Jews shared with the Palestinian Jews. At this point, most scholars believe, the original Jewish message was all but abandoned as the Christian community tried to win the Gentile world. Teaching that was essential to the Jewish understanding, but that was offensive to Gentiles, was dropped. New imagery to explain the church's teaching was developed. So, for example, redemption was described as being purchased as a slave in the market, and Jesus was deified.

These three stages of evolution, from a Jewish message to a fully Gentile (Hellenistic) religion with Jewish origins, are assumed to be part of the historical development of the New Testament writings. Much New Testament scholarship is an attempt to identify these layers in the New Testament documents. Scholars spend much of their professional lives trying to identify the stage in this development that a particular text has come from.

But this practice raises a very important question: How do we know the meaning of the New Testament documents? If they are the response to changing cultures, then which culture(s) are we expected to read them against? The impossibility of answering this question means the collapse of objective biblical truth. This is at the core of most modern thinking which has led many to abandon all hope of discovering such a thing as the authoritative Biblical message.

The process described above assumes that the beliefs of the early church evolved. Jesus 'became' the eternal Son of God as a result of the church's missionary work. It was essential that Jesus was shown to be superior to the pagan gods, so he was given the status of divinity. This inevitably implies that Jesus never thought of himself as being God. The belief that Jesus is the eternal Son of God, it is argued, was the product of the early church developing its missionary message, a product of their interaction with Greek philosophy and religion. Jesus was not the source of the church's distinctive teaching, Hellenism was! Such claims cannot but shake the foundations of traditional understanding and leave us with the question, 'Do we have the right Jesus?'

We have got into this crisis of belief because we have accepted the argument that the Christian message changed from one level of understanding to another. Each level or layer, while supposedly making it easier for the newly evangelised group to accept the gospel, actually made Jesus progressively into something he was not. All this rests on the belief that the New Testament is largely the product of the Gentile church.

Now if this is a true account of how the New Testament writings developed, then it ought to be obvious that the apostles have left an example for all future generations of Christians. Whenever the gospel is taken into a new culture, whatever is offensive or unclear to the people being evangelised should be abandoned. Missionaries, to be biblical, must rewrite the gospel using culturally acceptable symbols that help the people they seek to evangelise. The legitimacy of this contextualising process is so widely accepted that it is hardly ever commented on.

Changing attitudes

Despite the widespread acceptance of the explanation outlined above, the assumption that the Christian message changed from a Jewish to a Gentile message is now being seriously challenged. For example, New Testament scholar Mark Nanos has recently asserted: 'Where New Testament scholarship is concerned, the literature can now be read as Jewish correspondence, written by and for Jews and Gentiles concerned with the Jewish context of their faith in Jesus as the Jewish Messiah. Simply put, we can now read the New Testament as a Jewish book.'[1]

Scholars are recognising that the New Testament documents do

[1] Nanos, *Mystery*, 7.

not reflect the transition described above, which has been at the heart of liberal theology. The evidence suggests that this process never took place when the New Testament was being written. They are Jewish documents that must be read in the cultural and religious context of pre-AD 70 Judaism. It is increasingly being recognised that during the writing of the New Testament the church remained faithful to its Jewish heritage. It was in the second century AD that Greek influence began to pervade the thinking of the church, after the New Testament documents had been written.

Thus, the evolutionary model certainly applies to the teaching of the church in the second century and beyond, but not to the early community. In other words, the transition to a Hellenistic church was much later than has been assumed. It happened after the completion of the New Testament documents and did not affect their content. This second-century process of Hellenisation was the result of two momentous events. The first was the division that took place between the church and Judaism. This separation happened in the latter part of the first century. The second was the emergence in the second century of Gentile leaders within the church. These men brought their Hellenistic intellectual training with them and they unwittingly read it into the Christian Scriptures. They used the Greek text of the Old Testament along with the emerging New Testament canon that was also written in Greek. Rather than appreciating the Hebraic mindset that lay behind these writings, they treated them as 'authentic' Greek literature, the same as the Greek texts by which they had been educated. They soon began to lose sight of the Old Testament background to the New Testament writings and in its place inserted a Hellenistic scheme of thought. It thus follows that the Hellenisation of the Christian gospel was in the second century, much later than New Testament scholars had assumed.

The setting of the New Testament

With the realisation that the early church never abandoned its Jewish message there emerges a much better way of explaining how the apostles communicated the gospel of Jesus. Instead of adapting the message of Jesus to the ideas of the people it was being taken to, these people were taught the Jewish Scriptures. This gave them the key to understand Jesus' message and work. By understanding this Old Testament background, the converts were helped to appreciate the life and teaching of Jesus in all of its Jewish significance. The responsibility of the church's teachers was to apply the principles of the Old Testament, as interpreted by Jesus, to the life of the churches that were made up of both Jews and Gentiles. That this did happen is clear. The first missionaries were Jews. They first went with their message to the synagogue (Acts 13:14; 14:1; 17:2, 10, 17; 18:4; 19:8). In the synagogues were not only Jews who shared their acceptance of the Old Testament Scriptures but also people known as 'God-fearers'. These were Gentiles who were offended by the corruption and teaching of the Gentile religions. These God-fearers sought the God of the Jews because they respected the high moral standards of Judaism. They attended the synagogue services, but few converted to Judaism. Most God-fearers found the initiation ceremony of circumcision a major obstacle to conversion.

It was to these Jews and Gentiles in the synagogue that the good news about Jesus was first taken. They had the Old Testament background. They did not need to be taught Israel's history and Scriptures, they already shared in them. After only a short time of instruction they were able to understand the message of Jesus in almost its entirety. The God-fearers enthusiastically welcomed the apostles' message that God accepted them without circumcision. They were told that God's concern was their hearts, not their flesh. Physical circumcision did not matter, it was the change of heart that really counted, this is what circumcision was intended to symbolise (Rom. 2:28-29; Eph. 2:11-18; Phil. 3:3).

This explains how the early church not only survived, but grew. Often the apostles were driven out of the communities they had preached to, leaving behind a handful of believers. Sometimes these believers had been converted for only a matter of days (Acts 13:40–14:7). How could they survive without the help of the apostles? They were able to grow in their faith because they had the Old Testament. It was these Scriptures that taught them all that God was going to do. They gave them a framework to understand their past and hope to face the future.

But how did the Jews understand these Scriptures in the first century? Were the apostles imposing some new meaning on these sacred writings or was their message plainly supported by these texts? To understand why it was so natural for Jews and God-fearers to accept the teaching of the apostles we need to understand what the

Jews had been waiting for. This expectation was the result of their history, the experiences that made them who they were. Within Judaism were many groupings and they certainly differed from each other in understanding. Their own particular history determined how they interpreted the details. Nevertheless, all of these groups shared the common history of Israel and this common history gave them a large measure of agreement over the big picture that the Old Testament gave. Most, like the community at Qumran, thought that other groups were excluded from the events that were foretold. To understand how the Jews interpreted their Scriptures, and to understand the big picture that united them, we need to review briefly their history.

Redemptive history
The following outline is basic but necessary for a proper understanding of Jewish identity. Most readers will be familiar with it and may want to proceed to the next section, 'The promise of restoration.'

The Jews boast that they have a unique history. Their claim is that the only true and living God, the creator of all things, chose Abraham and promised him the land of Canaan as his inheritance. A promise was given to Abraham regarding his descendants. This promise was formalised by a covenant or agreement between God and Abraham that was to be the basis of all that happened to Abraham's offspring.

After many trials and setbacks, Abraham and his family eventually settled in the land of Canaan and prospered. But as with all families there were difficult times. A major setback came some hundreds of years later when the family, now very large, had to migrate to Egypt to survive a famine that was ravaging Canaan. Here they had plenty of food. However, as time went by, the government of the land changed and took a hard line against immigrants. The Jews became the object of ferocious persecution and they were forced to work as slaves. For a period their male babies were put to death at birth.

It was at this point that another great Jewish figure came on the scene of history: Moses. As a baby his life was spared when an Egyptian princess found him. She adopted him as her son and so he entered into the royal family. Eventually, as an adult, he transferred his allegiance to his own people. After forty years in exile he returned to lead his people to freedom. Pharaoh did everything possible to stop them leaving. Moses warned him that if he did not let the people go, then his firstborn son, and those of all the other Egyptian families, would be struck dead. The warning was ignored. However, the Jews obeyed what they were told to do. Taking the blood of a slain lamb, they smeared it on the doorposts of their homes and stayed indoors. That night the angel of death came through the land of Egypt. Where he saw the blood, he passed over the home. Where the angel found no blood, he killed the firstborn male child. This was the night of the Passover that Jews celebrate to this very day. It is still the greatest event in Jewish history.

The story of the Exodus is well known. Moses led the Jews out of Egypt. However, instead of immediately possessing the land their ancestors had left, because of disobedience they journeyed in the wilderness for forty years. Eventually, the Jews settled back in the Promised Land. Their history continued to have its highs and lows.

Thinking that the success of the surrounding nations was because they had kings, they became a monarchy. Their first king was Saul. He was succeeded by another important figure in Jewish history, King David. The Bible presents David as a man of great integrity who strove to do what he knew God wanted of him. Under his leadership the nation was made secure and prosperous. Despite this he was denied the one thing that he wanted to do. He longed to build a temple for God to dwell in. God would not allow this because David as a military commander had shed much blood. However, God was pleased with David's desire and promised that rather than David building a house for God, God would build a house for him. The family of David would become the Jewish royal dynasty. David was promised that one of his descendants would always rule over the chosen people.

Tragically David's son, Solomon, was not the king that the nation needed. Although he was known for his wisdom, he could not apply his wisdom to his own life. He demanded far too much tax from the people in order to finance fabulous building programmes. But worse still, he abandoned the clear instruction of Israel's God that forbade marrying foreign wives. This was commanded because of the fear that the gods of the other nations would gain a foothold in the nation. This is exactly what happened. Solomon's foreign wives brought their entourages with them. Soon there were thousands of foreigners living in Jerusalem as part of the extended royal family, and their gods were being worshipped. Monotheism was abandoned and paganism, which they had suffered so much to overcome, was now being practised. All this took place in the very temple of Israel's God.

With the worship of these foreign gods came the lifestyles of the surrounding nations. The Jewish people imitated them and in doing so broke the moral commands that God had given them. This act of flirting with the gods of the surrounding nations was described as adultery. Israel's God was described as a husband and Israel was depicted as his bride. When they had left Egypt under Moses' leadership they had entered into a solemn agreement, a covenant. They had promised to be faithful to their God and he in return promised that he would be faithful to them as a nation. In that covenant agreement was the warning that God would not accept other gods sharing Israel's life. If they did, God would put her away.

As Israel's national life declined, God sent prophets to warn her of the consequences of turning away from him. The nation had divided under two kings. The kings rejected the prophets' message and the divided nation declined further into moral chaos. Eventually God acted against his people. First the Assyrians invaded the breakaway northern kingdom. Its cities were destroyed and the people were taken into exile. Later, the Babylonians came against Judah, the part of the original twelve tribes that had stayed faithful to the house of David. They destroyed its towns and villages. They then laid siege to the capital, Jerusalem, and eventually overthrew it. They destroyed the entire city including the sacred temple. The royal family were either put to death or taken into captivity along with almost the entire population. It was the beginning of one of the darkest periods of ancient Israel's history.

The Promise of Restoration

Understandably the morale of the nation collapsed. They had never thought God would allow this to happen to them. They saw the exile as God's punishment for their sins and found great difficulty in thinking that there could be a new start. But this is the very thing that the prophets had promised.[2] In spite of the collapse of the royal family, they predicted that a descendant of David would be raised up (Isa. 11:1). He would lead the people from their captivity back to the Promised Land (Isa. 11:11). He would be anointed with the Spirit of the Lord for this task (Isa. 61:1-2). He would lead the people through the wilderness (Hos. 2:14); it would be just like when the Jews left

---

[2]For each of the following details I provide one Old Testament reference, although several references could have been given for each detail.

Egypt, for it would be a Second Exodus. The pilgrimage through the desert would be under the protection of the Holy Spirit (Isa. 44:3), just as the pilgrimage from Egypt had been. There would be miracles (Mic. 7:15) like when they came out of Egypt, and the desert would be transformed as nature shared in the re-creation of the nation (Isa. 55.13). The returning exiles would return telling of the salvation of God (Isa. 52:7-10). There would be a new covenant established which would be centred on the Davidic prince (Isa. 9:6-7) and, unlike when the people came out of Egypt when their flesh was circumcised, this time the hearts of the people would be circumcised (Jer. 31:31-34). This return from exile would be their return to Eden (Isa. 51:3). Once the people arrived back at Jerusalem they would build a magnificent temple that the descendant of David would dedicate (Ezek. 44–45). Into this temple all the nations would come to worship Israel's God (Isa. 2:1-5). The Lord would come into his temple (Isa 4:2-6) and, finally, the wedding between God and his people would be celebrated with a great cosmic banquet (Isa. 54:1-8).

We find the history of the return of the Jews from exile in the books of Ezra and Nehemiah and the minor prophets such as Haggai, Zechariah and Malachi. What these books show is that while the people attempted to build a temple, it was a poor pathetic attempt compared with that which had been destroyed by the Babylonians. They constantly looked for the coming of the descendant of King David, but he did not come, and for four hundred years they groaned in their sense of failure, guilt and disappointment.

This period of four hundred years saw no significant change for the Jews. They were always effectively under the control of another nation. They longed for their exile to end. They had returned to their own land but they were as far from God as they had ever been, for he had not fulfilled his promises. Not until they had complete freedom could they accept that their punishment was over. The literature of the Jews during this period, known as the intertestamental period or the second temple period, clearly shows the faith that they had. They clung to the hope that God would yet fulfill the promises he had made to them through the prophets. The Scriptures, which we have surveyed above, became their light throughout the long dark years of shame under the domination of the Greeks and then the Romans. The following examples illustrate this hope.

The Dead Sea Scrolls

The *Damascus Document* provides clear evidence of the expectation of a coming Davidic Messiah who would fulfil the Isaianic prophecies. He was called both the Root and the Branch, titles familiar in New Testament Christology as well as in the prophetic expectations of the seventh and eighth centuries BC:

> A ruler shall [no]t depart from the tribe of Judah when Israel has dominion. [And] the one who sits on the throne of David [shall never] be cut off, because the "rulers staff" is the covenant of the kingdom, [and the thous]ands of Israel are "the feet," until the Righteous Messiah, the Branch of David, has come. For to him and to his seed the covenant of the kingdom of His people has been given for the eternal generations, because he has kept [...] the Law with the men of Yahad. For [...the "obedience of the people]s" is the assembly of the men of [...] he gave[3]

Another document from Qumran known as *Joshua Apocryphon* gives further information about the community's expectation as to what the descendant of David would achieve:

> He will not [abandon Zion], to make His name dwell there, the Tent of Meeting....[to the end] of time, for, look, as a son is born to Jesse son of Peretz son of Ju[dah...he will choose] the rock of Zion and drive out from there all the Amorites from Jeru[salem...] to build the temple for the Lord, God of Israel, gold and silver [...] cedar and pine shall he bring from Lebenon to build it; and his younger son [shall build the temple...and Zadok] shall serve as priest there first[...] [....]from heaven [...] the Lord's beloved will dwell there securely [....for a long] time and his people will dwell for ever. But now, the Amorite is there, and the Canaanite [and the Jebusite and all the] inhabitants who have committed sin, whom I have not sought [...] from you. As for the Shilonites, I have made them servants [...][4]

Other texts from the scrolls tell of how the Davidic Messiah would complete his work by establishing a spiritual temple (a building of holiness). It was not a physical building that he was going to construct, it was a spiritual one. It would be made up of the Community Council in conjunction with the 'sons of Heaven'.

---

[3] *A Genesis Florilegium* (4Q252) Fragment 1 Column 5, translated by Wise, Abegg and Cook, *Scrolls*, 277.

[4] *Joshua Apocryphon* (4Q522) Fragment 1 Column 2, translated by Wise, Abegg and Cook, *Scrolls*, 422-23.

...He gave you authority, O ye (4) this was how He glorified it when you sanctified yourself to Him, when He made you a Holy of Holies...for all.[5]

In the book of Ezekiel there was the expectation of an eschatological temple; so in Qumran. This expectation was in fact based on Ezekiel's vision in chapters 40–48.[6] The Qumran community used the imagery of the Old Testament to describe their relationship with Yahweh. As the Jews saw themselves to have become the bride of Yahweh in the wilderness, so they believed they had been called into the wilderness for this unique relationship. It would be at this time, when Yahweh took her as his bride, that the Gentiles would enter the blessings of the covenant community:

Like one whose mother comforts him, so He will comfort them in Jerusalem (Isa 66:13) [and He will rejoice as a bridegroom] over his bride. His [presence] will rest upon it for ever, for His throne will last forever and ever, and His glory [...] and all Gentiles [...] for beauty [...] I will bless the [Lord...] Blessed is the name of the Most High [...] [...] Bless, [O my soul....You have placed] Your mercies upon me [...] You have established it on the Law [...] the book of Your statutes [...][7]

The Exodus certainly formed the pattern of expectation for the Qumran community. In the War Scroll document it sees God to be involved in history in the same way that Isaiah had spoken of. The Messiah's eschatological victory over Belial and his forces would be a repetition of God's triumph over the armies of Pharaoh.

By the hand of Thine anointed, who discerned Thy testimonies. Thou hast revealed to us the [times] of the battles of Thy hands that Thou mayest glorify Thyself in our enemies by levelling the hordes of Satan, the seven nations of vanity, by the hand of Thy poor whom Thou hast redeemed [by Thy might] and by fulness of thy marvelous power. [Thou hast opened] the door of hope to the melting heart: Thou wilt do to them as Thou didst to Pharaoh, and to the captains of his chariots in the Red Sea.[8]

[5] *The Children of Salvation* (Yeshaʻ) and the *Mystery of Existence* (4Q416, 418). Fragment 1.

[6] cf. *The Words of Michael* (4Q529) and *The New Jerusalem* (4Q554).

[7] *Hymns of the Poor* (4Q434, 436) Fragment 1 column 1, translated by Wise, Abegg and Cook, *Scrolls*, 394-95.

[8] 1QM 11:7c-10a, translated by Vermes, *Scrolls*, 136.

A major difference between the understanding of Qumran and the New Testament is that the former looked for two Messiahs. One was to be a king from the tribe of Judah and the other a priest from the tribe of Levi. For the Christian community there was only one Messiah. He comes from the tribe of Judah and is the son of David. He fulfils both offices of king and priest in his own person.[9]

Thus, in the expectations of Qumran, there was the ongoing hope that the prophecies of the exilic period would yet be fulfilled. They looked for two Messiahs who would fulfil all that the prophets had predicted.

Josephus

Josephus tells us how Theudas promised that the Jordan would divide once again, and how another prophet predicted the repetition of the miracle of Jericho on the walls of Jerusalem. Josephus also tells how the weaver Jonathan foretold of miracles in the wilderness.[10] He repeatedly tells how the messianic pretenders called their followers to the desert,[11] the location that popular opinion associated with the coming of eschatological salvation. This practice was founded on the historical fact that the Jews came from the wilderness following their Exodus, to claim their inheritance.

Psalms of Solomon

The Psalms of Solomon, of Pharisaic composition, show how the prophetic expectation of the New Exodus was flourishing in the first century BC. Psalm 17 gathers all the main threads of the prophetic predictions together and cultivates an expectation of a coming Davidic Messiah. The Psalm speaks of God's promise that David's kingdom will never end (v. 4) and then appeals to God to fulfil his promises and give Israel her king. Lohse summarises the Psalmist's expectations:

> This king will throw off alien dominion, seize the holy city from the foe, purge it of the heathen, subdue the peoples, judge the tribes of Israel, and rule the land in purity and righteousness, so that nations will come

[9]Eisenmann, *Uncovered*, 225, against the common consensus, claims that the recently published texts show that the Qumran community's expectation of one Messiah, who was a king and a priest, was the origin of the New Testament doctrine. The New Testament writers are more likely to have got their model from Zecheriah 6:13.

[10]Josephus, *Ant*.20.5.1;20.8.6 and *B.J.* 7.9.1; *Ant* 20.8.6 respectively.

[11]*Ant* 20.97-99,167f,188.

from the ends of the earth to see his glory and look on the glory of the Lord vv21-46. He will rule as a righteous king who is taught by God Himself. In his days no wrong will be done, for all are holy and their king is the servant, the Lord's anointed v32.[12]

The Book of Tobit

The involvement of the Gentiles in the eschatological salvation is discussed in the book of Tobit. The author says:

> After this they will return from the places of their captivity, and will rebuild Jerusalem in splendour. And the house of God will be rebuilt there with a glorious building for all generations for ever, just as the prophets said of it. Then all the Gentiles will turn to fear the Lord God in truth, and they will bury their idols. All the Gentiles will praise the Lord, and his people will give thanks to God, and the Lord will exalt his people. And all who love the Lord God in truth and righteousness will rejoice, showing mercy to our brethren.[13]

The Book of Baruch

Baruch also refers to the Exodus when it says:

> Arise; Jerusalem, stand on the heights and turn your eyes to the east;
> see your sons reassembled from the west and the east at the command of the Holy One,
> jubilant that God has remembered them.
> Though they left you on foot,
> with enemies as an escort,
> now God brings them back to you like royal princes carried back in glory.
> For God has decreed the flattening of each high mountain,
> of the everlasting hills, the filling of the valleys to make the ground level,
> so that Israel can walk in safety under the glory of God.
> And the forests and every fragrant tree will provide shade for Israel at the command of God;
> for God will guide Israel in joy by the light of his glory with his mercy and integrity for escort.[14]

---

[12]Lohse, *TDNT* 8:480.
[13]Tobit 14:4-7.
[14]Baruch 5:5-9.

The Rabbinic Writings

We find in the Rabbinic literature repeated references to the Exodus as a model of final redemption.[15] There was widespread expectation of a repetition of the signs of the Exodus[16] and the expectation of once again being taken into the wilderness to meet with God.[17] This would happen on the night of the Passover.[18] It was believed that a new Moses would lead the people, a new Moses who was identified with the promised descendant of David.[19] It was expected that once again the people would be fed miraculously with manna. Ben-Sira, in his extended prayer for deliverance, prays for a repetition of 'signs and wonders' in a final redemption constructed on Exodus categories.[20] On the analogy of the Exodus, the end time glory would be revealed on the 14th of Nisan.

Another strand of the Rabbinic material relates to the offering of Isaac by Abraham (the *Aqedah*). In this material, the Passover, the 14th of Nisan, becomes the crucial date that marks the anniversary of all other major historical events. It celebrates the creation of the world, the offering of Isaac, the fall of Jericho and the coming of the Messiah who will appear in Jerusalem on the last Passover. Some strongly contest the date of this material. However, the objections can be shown to be misdirected. If the earlier dating is accepted then there is certainly significant evidence that Judaism in the New Testament period linked the final redemption with the Passover. This final celebration in the presence of the Messiah is inevitably seen to fulfil the New Exodus expectations.

The New Testament

We have seen a strong expectation of a New Exodus within the Old Testament and throughout the intertestamental literature. Clearly this hope was powerful and sustained Israel throughout her suffering. What we need to establish is whether this hope of a New Exodus had

[15]Str.-B, 1:68ff, 85ff; 2: 284f, 293; 4: 55f.

[16]Str.-B, 1:85, 4: 954.

[17]Str.-B, 4: 939f.

[18]Jeremias, *TWNT* 4: 857, note 111.

[19]*Mekilta* on Exodus 12:42, *R. Johhua b. Hananiah*, c 90; cf. *Tg. Yerus* 1 Ex 21:42; *Tg. Yerus* 11 Ex 15:18 cf. 12:42), and later, Ex R.18.12 on 12:24; 'Let this sign be in our hands on the day when I wrought salvation for you, on that very night know that I will redeem you.' cf. Ex R.51:1 on Ex 12:2; Jeremias, *Eucharistic,* 207.

[20]*The Book of Wisdom* is an Alexandrian Passover Haggadah, so Buckley, *Phrase,* 53.

any significant influence on the writers of the New Testament.

There are a number of scholars who are strongly supportive of there being a 'New Exodus' pattern in the Gospels of Mark and Luke.[21] They claim to have identified the presence of highly developed theological insights, which could be triggered off by Old Testament texts. The mere quotation of a short text had the effect of alerting the reader to the Old Testament passage from which it had been taken. In this way these texts had a far greater significance for the first readers of the New Testament than is normal today. Their knowledge of these passages meant that they automatically understood the passage of the New Testament that they were reading in the light of the Old Testament passage out of which the quotation had been drawn.

The generally recognised New Exodus material in the New Testament is Acts 26:17-18, Galatians 1:3, Colossians 1:12-14 and Revelation 1:5-6. Luke 1–2 reflects the expectations of a group of devout Jews at the time of the birth of Jesus. These were aware of the same traditions that are reflected in the *Damascus Document* found at Qumran.

It is the longing for the fulfilment of these New Exodus promises that is the background to the New Testament. All four Gospels open with John the Baptist saying that he is 'the voice of one crying in the wilderness, "Prepare the way of the Lord."' The importance of this text is clear in that it is one of the few passages that all four Gospels preserve. John took the words from the prophecy of Isaiah that announced the coming of the descendant of David to fulfil God's promises. When Jesus stood up in the synagogue, he said that the Spirit of the Lord was upon him to preach the good news to the poor (Luke 4:18-19). He was claiming to be the one who had come to bring freedom from captivity. He was claiming to be the son of David, the promised king.

The fact that both John the Baptist and Jesus began their ministries by quoting Isaiah is very significant, the former citing Isaiah 40:3-5 (Luke 3:4-6) and the latter citing Isaiah 61:1-2 (Luke 4:18-19), both passages being New Exodus based. By using these texts they were declaring that the eschatological salvation that Isaiah had predicted was at long last breaking into human history. This understanding is

[21]Mánek, 'Luke', 8-23; Bowman, *Mark*, *passim*; Watts, *Isaiah*, *passim*; Klijn, 'Origins', 7; Daube, 'Structures', 174-87; Piper, 'Unchanging', 16; Wright, *Victory*, *passim* and Stahlin, 'Exodus', 82.

confirmed by the question John asked when he sent messengers to Jesus to ask if he was the Christ. Jesus replied by pointing to the signs of Isaiah (Luke 7:21-22). These were the very signs that Isaiah wrote of that would accompany the New Exodus when it finally happened. Jesus also commended John saying that he fulfilled the prophecy of the one sent before the Lord to prepare his way (Luke 7:27). Clearly both the Baptist and Jesus set their ministries in the context of the Isaianic predictions of the New Exodus.

At Jesus' baptism, the voice from heaven said, 'This is my beloved son, in whom I am well pleased.' This is widely recognised to be based on Isaiah 42:1ff. In other words, God was identifying Jesus as the Servant who would bring about the New Exodus. Indeed, on the mount of Transfiguration, a key incident in the Gospel, Jesus talked with Moses and Elijah about 'his coming *Exodus*', not the much weaker rendering, 'departure' as in the NIV.[22] This Exodus theme is stressed even more by the way Jesus took his disciples to the upper room to celebrate the Passover. There can be no doubt that he wanted his death to be understood as a Paschal offering. His death was for his disciples and was the means of their redemption. Without it there could be no Exodus for them.

David replaces Moses

Among the expectations that were commonly shared relating to the New Exodus was a belief in the identity of the new Moses. He was not to be of the tribe of Levi, like Moses, but of the tribe of Judah. He was to be none other than the promised descendant of David whom Yahweh had declared would have an everlasting throne.[23] Jesus' fulfilment of the promises relating to the predicted Davidic deliverer is crucial for appreciating the early church's understanding of the person and work of its Saviour. It is no coincidence that the evidence brought against Jesus, evidence that secured his crucifixion, related to his claims to kingship (John 18:33-39). Nor is it more of a coincidence that Jesus denied claims to an earthly kingdom, while asserting his claim to a spiritual one (John 18:36).

The New Testament writers did not need to keep using the term

---

[22] οἳ ὀφθέντες ἐν δόξῃ ἔλεγον τὴν ἔξοδον αὐτοῦ, ἣν ἤμελλεν πληροῦν ἐν Ἰερουσαλήμ (Luke 9:31).

[23] See 2 Samuel 7:16. Ellis, *Prophecy,* 195 says that 2 Samuel 7 is used in Acts 13:6-14 in a midrashic manner. He also points out that 2 Corinthians 6:7 and Hebrews 1:5 show that a Christian reference to the text is assumed.

'son of David'. They could choose from a range of related titles that to the first-century believer meant exactly the same thing. Many scholars say that Matthew's Gospel shows Jesus is the second Moses. This misses the fact that Moses is rarely mentioned in direct contrast to Jesus, whereas David is repeatedly recalled. Matthew clearly has an Exodus structure, but it is not Moses who brings this deliverance about, it is the son of David. This is what the prophets had foretold. The significance of Jesus being the son of David would be clear to any Jewish believer. The fact that Jesus had died with the inscription 'the King of the Jews' above his head at Passover spoke of the Davidic prince offering Paschal sacrifices (Ezek. 45:25). This was something that Ezekiel had predicted and is a theme that we will investigate more fully later in our study. The king was establishing the kingdom into which his subjects were to be incorporated.

The importance of the prophets

If we bypass the eighth-century prophets and merely link the significance of Jesus' Davidic descent with the promise to David of an eternal throne, then we miss the New Exodus motif that is lurking beneath the surface of the title. This motif is not only in the Gospel narratives where Jesus is continually honoured as the long-awaited descendant of David. It is also in the preaching of the early church, as recorded in Acts. The reference to the raising again of the tent of David (Acts 15:15-17) is particularly significant. It demonstrates that it was not merely the role of the Davidic descendant that Jesus fulfilled, but that the early church clearly saw that all aspects of the Davidic covenant were being fulfilled in him. Because he had come, the Gentiles could now be welcomed into the covenant community. Coupled with the title 'son of David' is the title 'the Christ', which is used regularly throughout the Epistles. This title carried with it all the messianic associations of the son of David.

New Exodus themes

Other New Exodus themes are widely dispersed throughout the New Testament. The New Covenant, circumcision of the heart, gift of the Spirit, pilgrimage, the return to Eden, the eschatological temple, the conversion of the nations, and their inclusion in the covenant community and the eschatological marriage, are further examples of Old Testament expectations that overflow into the aspirations and understanding of the early church. They saw that it was Jesus who had brought these promises to fulfilment. It was Jesus who had brought about the New Exodus and with it its resultant blessings.

Behind these widely recognised themes there is a whole substructure of allusions. Once the paradigm has been identified, this substructure lights up with a clarity that is compelling.

Conclusion

This survey demonstrates the level of saturation that the expectation of a New Exodus had reached at the time of Jesus' ministry. What is abundantly clear is that the hope of these promises one day being fulfilled did not die. In all of the Jewish literature that we have of the period there is clear evidence that the hope of the New Exodus sustained the nation as a whole. They waited for the day when these promises would finally be fulfilled. To ignore this expectation in any attempt to understand the New Testament message would be folly.

Returning to the question that was asked at the beginning of this chapter, are the Gospels reliable records of the teaching of Jesus? The answer must be that there is no reason to reject them as not being so. Scholarship has failed until recently to appreciate the essential Jewishness of these writings and has read them through a lens that has seriously distorted their message. Given the correct lens, that of the fulfilment of the prophets' promises of a New Exodus, the Gospels are saying nothing that requires a later date or a different religious background from first-century Judaism to make sense. In the next chapter we will examine if Paul shared this same expectation.

Chapter Two

Paul and the Prophets

We have seen that the prophets' predictions of a New Exodus had a powerful influence on the New Testament writers. Both Jesus and John the Baptist understood their own ministries in the light of this expectation. The material listed in chapter 1 concerning the predictions of a New Exodus shows that the major contributor to this expectation was the prophet Isaiah. In this chapter I will seek to show that Paul was immersed in this Old Testament stream of expectations and that it was a powerful influence on how he interpreted the life, death and resurrection of Jesus. Indeed, it can be shown that many of the major doctrines of Paul are found in embryonic form in the book of Isaiah.

Paul not only quoted from Isaiah many more times than all of the other prophets put together, but he actually used the prophet's writings as the skeleton of his gospel. He took the quotations and arranged them in such a way as to outline the history of salvation, from the Fall of man to the eventual establishment of the messianic kingdom. Around these quotations he built his argument. The full import of this fact is only appreciated when the quotations are listed in the order they are used and read in that same sequence. What it shows is that if the letter to the Romans was laid out as a continuous papyrus, and the citations from Isaiah were raised out of the text and suspended at their point of use, those texts, in that order, would summarise salvation history. Such a pattern could not be anything but intentional.

The cited texts of Romans

We follow the Isaianic texts Paul cited in the order that he used them:

"As it is written, 'God's name is blasphemed among the Gentiles because of you'" (Romans 2:24; Isaiah 52:5, LXX).

"Their feet are swift to shed blood: ruin and misery mark their paths and the way of peace they have not known"(Romans 3:15-17; Isaiah 59:7-8).

"Isaiah cries out concerning Israel: 'Though the number of the Israelites should be like the sand by the sea, only the remnant will be saved. For the Lord will carry out his sentence on earth with speed and finality'. It is just as Isaiah had said previously" (Romans 9:27-28; Isaiah 10:22-23, LXX).

"Just as Isaiah said previously, 'Unless the Lord Almighty had left us descendants, we would have become like Sodom, and we would have been like Gomorrah'" (Romans 9:29; Isaiah 1:9, LXX).

"As it is written, 'See, I lay in Zion a stone that causes men to stumble and a rock that makes them fall' " (Romans 9:33a; Isaiah 8:14).

"and 'the one who trusts in him will never be put to shame'" (Romans 9:33; Isaiah 28:16, LXX).

"As the Scripture says, 'He who believes in him will not be disappointed' " (Romans 10:11; Isaiah 52:7, LXX).

"As it is written, 'How beautiful are the feet of those who bring good news!'" (Romans 10:15; Isaiah 52:7).

"For Isaiah says, 'Lord, who has believed our message?'" (Romans 10.16; Isaiah 53:1, LXX).

"And Isaiah boldly says, 'I was found by those who did not seek me, I revealed myself to those who did not ask for me'" (Romans 10:20; Isaiah 29:10, LXX).

"What then? What Israel sought so earnestly it did not attain, but the elect did. The others were hardened as it is written: 'God gave them a spirit of stupor, eyes so that they could not see and ears so that they could not hear, to this very day'" (Romans 11:7-8; Isaiah 29:10, LXX).

"And so all Israel shall be saved: as it is written, 'there shall come out of Zion the Deliverer, and he shall turn away ungodliness from Jacob; for this is my covenant unto them when I shall take away their sins'" (Romans 11:26-27; Isaiah 59:20-21, LXX).

"Who has known the mind of the Lord? Or who has been his counsellor?" (Romans 11:34; Isaiah 40:13, LXX).

"For it is written, 'As I live, sayeth the Lord'" (Romans 14:11a; Isaiah 49:18).

"Every knee shall bow to me, and every tongue shall confess to God" (Romans 14:11b; Isaiah 45:23, LXX).

"And again, Isaiah says, 'The root of Jesse will spring up, one who will arise to rule over the nations; the Gentiles will hope in him'" (Romans 15:12; Isaiah 11:10, LXX).

"Rather, as it is written, 'Those who were not told about him will see, and those who have not heard will understand'" (Romans 15:21; Isaiah 52:15, LXX).

These passages show the perspective that Paul had in regard to salvation history. It was that of the evangelical prophet. The quotations work systematically through the various stages of the development of the purposes of God in the salvation of mankind.

Israel has not responded to her calling, she has acted like the other nations (Romans 2:24: Isaiah 52:5; Romans 3:15-17: Isaiah 59:7-8).

God's purpose is to show his faithfulness to his promises by saving a remnant (Romans 9:27-29; Isaiah 10:22-23).

God will appoint a saviour, for both Jews and Gentiles (Romans 9:33; Isaiah 8:14; 28:16; Romans 10:11: Isaiah 8:16). Notice how Paul stresses the universality of Christ's salvation as he follows up the quotation of Isaiah 28:16 with: "For there is no difference between Jew and Gentile – the same Lord is Lord of all and richly blesses all who call on him, for 'Everyone who calls on the name of the Lord will be saved'."

Paul then goes on to speak of the church's responsibility to declare the salvation of God, as it had been fulfilled by the remnant in the previous age (Romans 10:15; Isaiah 52:7).

But there would be the same response of unbelief to the gospel message (Romans 10:16; Isaiah 53:1).

Even so, the electing purposes of God would not be overturned by the sinfulness of man. What God purposes he will achieve (Romans 10:22: Isaiah 65:1; Romans 10:21: Isaiah 65:2; Romans 11:8: Isaiah 29:10).

God's purposes will be fulfilled, and all Israel, as Paul has already defined her (Rom. 4:11-12), will be saved (Romans 11:26-27; Isaiah 59:20-21).

All of this is beyond man's design, it is of God alone (Romans 11:33-34; Isaiah 40:13).

The salvation promised to Abraham, in which the nations are to share in the covenant blessings, will finally be fulfilled. Those who were never part of the people of God have come into the eschatological community (Romans 15:21; Isaiah 52:15).

Interdependence

This dependency upon Isaiah must not obscure the fact that the New Exodus theme was not the sole possession of 'the evangelical prophet'.

It was shared widely by pre-exilic, exilic and post-exilic prophets. Because of this, themes which are more prominent in other prophets could be interwoven into the material received from Isaiah without in any way reducing the perspective of the New Exodus.

We can see from the above analysis of the use of Isaiah in Romans that there is no haphazard use of the prophet's writings. It is beyond reason to reject that they were deliberately used by Paul as his structure. In other words, Paul does not simply use the prophecy of Isaiah, he depends on it. His reasoning and exposition of the good news of Jesus is arranged around this structure. This is for the simple reason that Jesus is the fulfilment of all that the prophets had been saying. Jesus is the son of David, he is the deliverer of his people. We are going to see that this is the foundation of all that Paul argues for.

The context of Paul's letters

It is not enough to gather related texts on a particular subject to understand Paul's teaching on a particular matter. The circumstances of each letter will determine how it was read. If Paul was responding to a crisis situation, then his style and content would no doubt be different than if he wrote on the same subject to a church not facing the same crisis. In a crisis situation he might stress details that ordinarily would only be one of a number of threads in the understanding. Galatians was clearly written in a theological crisis while the way that Romans was written suggests that Paul handles the same material in a more reflective way. Romans was written in a far less critical situation and this is reflected in the tone of its arguments. In interpreting a passage we need to be sensitive as to the way the congregation originally heard it and the significance that such statements would have had in the situation to which they were written. To overlook this can cause us to give prominence to statements that ought not to be given special attention.

There are many possible reasons for Paul writing to the churches. Normally it was because there were pastoral problems that had to be addressed. These problems had their root, as is so often the case, in theological confusion. Not until these theological problems had been unravelled could the pastoral difficulties be resolved. But what were these problems? Is it possible to discern them from the content of the letters? Indeed it needs to be asked how Paul came to be aware of problems in churches that he had never visited. Some of these congregations were on the other side of the world as far as the geography and the transportation of the day were concerned.

Obviously, it could be argued that the church or some of her members had informed Paul of the problems, as happened concerning the problems at Corinth (1 Cor. 1:11). In this case Paul could address the problems directly and knowledgeably. It would be convenient if we could assume Paul had similar knowledge about other congregations through the same means. However, unless the letter indicates that he had received this information, it is dangerous to make such a blind assumption. It assumes that Paul had details of the circumstances of the church's life that he might not have had. This in turn presupposes that the exact situation in the church is reflected in Paul's instructions.

Most scholars assume that Paul had detailed information about the churches to which he wrote. The themes of letters are carefully examined and traces of conflict are sought for what might give the clues needed for a proper understanding. What is so often overlooked is the wider church and the problems that it had. It is possible that Paul anticipated that the Romans, for example, would eventually be afflicted by the same problems that the Corinthians or the Galatians had experienced. This provides us with a realistic situation in which to read the letter. We are not presupposing exact prescriptions for existing problems, rather we are reading teaching that is intended to protect the readers from the 'infections' that would certainly visit them!

Naturally the wider problems of the church cannot be presumed to be those being dealt with by the letter to the Roman church, but they certainly should not be ignored. There were certainly opponents of Paul travelling around the churches trying to win converts to their legalistic understanding. Paul was acutely aware of this fact. What would be a sensible method is to see if the problems that are so readily identified in the wider church match the remedies that Paul prescribed in his letters to churches he did not know personally. If they do match, then a careful reading may tell us if Paul knew in detail, or if he is only anticipating their eventual experience of the problems. Whatever the situation, the prescription is in the form of theological debate and practical application. It is these issues that we must carefully examine.

Circumcision and the Gentiles

The problem of the Corinthian and Galatian churches, and indeed of
Gentile Christianity itself, was that they were having major difficulties
in their relationships with their Jewish Christian brothers. There were
many sincere Jewish believers in Christ who could not square
acceptance of the Gentiles into the covenant without them having to
go through the initiation of circumcision. This affected virtually every
church. Judaizers were roaming the empire to persuade the converts
of Paul's mission that there was a final step they still had to take.
This, they argued, was circumcision. They claimed that this alone
would bring Gentiles into the full grace of the covenant.

But there was also a far less noble side to this conflict. Many
Jewish believers were seriously intimidated by the growing number
of Gentiles entering the church. The presence of a few might have
been sufficient to make them feel good that the superiority of the
Jewish faith had at long last been recognised. But to see these numbers
growing, and especially in Rome where the Jewish numbers suddenly
dropped as a result of the edict by Nero, left the Jewish Messianic
believers a vulnerable minority. They could no longer set the agenda
and give the lead to the Gentile converts. It was increasingly these
'bastard' sons of Abraham that were claiming the right to discern the
will of God in key issues of faith and practice. There was only one
solution to this most serious situation, and that was to demand that the
Law required the Gentiles be circumcised. Such a master stroke gave
the power back to the 'pure' minority, but betrayed the very essence
of the gospel. Thus the circumcision issue was a later development
and came from a rearguard defensive manoeuvre to save the Jewish
veto in the church. We shall see in chapter 9 that some scholars have
failed to recognise the steps of this development and have finished up
wrongly saying that Saul's persecution of the Hellenists was over the
circumcision issue.

In other words, circumcision was the issue that was threatening to
split the young church. There was a real danger that the umbilical
cord would be cut and a permanent separation take place between
the Christian Gentile church and its Jewish 'Christian' mother. For
Paul this would have been disastrous. There was only one body and
only one Lord who dealt with all on the same grounds of grace. The
Pauline letters show Paul struggling to maintain the relationship
between the two communities, a relationship that was costly in the

extreme for Paul to advocate. The Acts of the Apostles documents the energy and time that Paul spent trying to keep the doors of communication and fellowship open (15:1-2; 21:17-26). Two time-consuming visits to Jerusalem, when he had many other pressing matters to attend to, are evidence of the importance of the relationship. His first visit was to allow the apostles to examine his ministry (Acts 15:1-4). The second was to take a gift from the Gentile churches to the poor in the Jerusalem church (Acts 21:17-19). There are scholars who see this substantial gift as an attempt at removing Jewish Christian suspicion of the Gentile churches. Others think the reason for the visit was that Paul wanted to lead a Gentile team with gifts into Jerusalem as a fulfilment of prophecy. Zechariah (14:16) had predicted that Gentiles would come to Jerusalem to offer their praise and sacrifices to God.

These two problems, both essentially about the Gentile/Jewish relationship as members of the covenant community, are found in Paul's theology of salvation. In the letter to the Romans we find a remarkable fit with this theology and practice that Paul advocates. The first eleven chapters are essentially about the way God has dealt with the Jews. It considers their privileges and how they were uncircumcised when God accepted them. So again, reasons Paul, God is following the same path in accepting uncircumcised Gentiles. In other words, Paul is stressing the biblical evidence that the Gentiles are being brought into the covenant in exactly the same way as the Jews had been. He spells out how their representative, their father Abraham, was accepted.

Paul regularly makes the point that the redemption from Egypt was only a type of the salvation that was going to be accomplished in the last days (Rom. 3:21ff; 8:1-3; 9:30-33; 11:25-27; 1 Cor. 10:1-4.). Being part of the original deliverance did not mean that their salvation was complete. It pointed to a far greater act of salvation. To claim superiority because of the deliverance from Egypt, and not to appreciate its 'trivialness' in comparison with the salvation which all believers, both Jews and Gentiles, now shared through Christ, was folly indeed.

This tension, of being treated as second-class citizens of the kingdom, provoked the Gentiles to respond to the Jews. Some Gentile believers were goading the Jews that they had displaced them and that God no longer had any purpose for his ancient people in his redemptive plans. Their argument was self-evident. The numbers of

Gentiles that were coming into the church was clearly shifting the balance of its composition.[1] Such tensions had to be resolved, because they were members of the one body and belonged to the same Lord.

Meat and idols

In the midst of these theological debates over who had priority was a very practical problem. This came from the society in which the Gentiles had been converted and in which they still lived. Before their conversion they had worshipped in the temples of the local gods. Often these temples were centres of social activity and the gods were seen as patrons of various trade guilds. When a person was converted, he naturally stopped attending the temple. Sometimes it cost him dearly, for he could no longer be involved in the guild his trade operated under. His conversion could literally cost him his livelihood.

But even though he no longer visited the temple, the snares of the temple met him on the very streets that he walked. After the temple sacrifices had been made, the meat was sold to local butchers for resale to the public. For the Jewish Christian this was no problem. With their strong background of monotheism they knew that the idols had no real existence (1 Cor. 8:4-7). They were merely the product of the darkened imaginations of men. They did not believe in the existence of the gods that were worshipped in the temple, so why should not they eat the meat, providing that it was *kosher*? The fact that it had been offered to a god that did not exist meant that the problem did not exist either. In practice few Jews would want or need to eat this meat. They would have continued to eat their *kosher* meat, which was probably outside the price range that most of the Gentile Christians could afford.

Christian freedom and responsibility

But such an example of indifference to the meat's origin was a real problem for those who had lived in the fear of the existence of these gods. While the Gentile converts knew these facts, they could not easily shake off the memory with its lingering influences of the things that had so deeply affected them. The sacrifices had been about involvement in something evil and Satanic. Even if the deities did not

---

[1]Cosgrove, 'Other', 621, says: 'Jewish Christians are also a minority within Gentile-dominated Roman Christianity and one can only conclude that whatever their prejudices toward the gentiles, these do not carry equal psycho-social weight with those of the gentile Christians toward them.'

exist, this did not change the fact that there was a kingdom of darkness and evil that had exploited their ignorance and fear. For the Gentile converts there was real concern of being linked with anything that happened in the pagan temples. It was a link that they feared would be the cause of compromise and the means that Satan would use to take control of them once again.

The meat had associations that they could not shake off and it caused them such deep distress. That some Gentile Christians were being won over to the Jewish argument and boasted in their superior knowledge made Jewish/Gentile tensions even worse. Such 'successes' by the Jewish section no doubt gave great satisfaction, but the cost of this power game was that some Gentile believers were overtaken with confusion and their faith was wrecked. We get insights into this happening at Corinth (1 Cor. 8:9-13), and in Colossae (Col. 2:16-19), as well as in other Asian churches (Rev. 2:20-22).

Now these issues were clearly the common problems of Jewish/Gentile relations in the churches. Indeed, because of the intense loyalty of the Jewish community to the law of Moses, it was inevitable that these problems would arise. Wherever the two communities were in coexistence, and they certainly coexisted in the church, these sorts of religious differences would be highlighted.

The letter to the Romans was not an attempt to guess at their problems, nor was it a mere opportunity that Paul took to explain his gospel. It was an attempt to keep the two communities together, bearing a common witness to the Lord who had saved them. The letter demonstrates Paul's keen theological and pastoral awareness as he writes a meaningful letter in which the Jewish/Gentile relationship is frankly faced. He exposes the pastoral problems that the integration of the two communities produced and deals with them head on.

It was only from a united church that Paul could effectively embark on his mission to Spain. He was only too aware of what it meant to be distracted from the task of evangelism. Existing divisions in his supporting churches had taught him these painful lessons. The gospel was not about casting the Jews off in favour of the Gentiles, but about bringing both into the eschatological covenant community. It was only as they accepted each other and lived as the new man that the nations would take note of what God was doing in Christ. They were to be living evidence that God was reconciling enemies to each other and to himself. Their unity was vital to the mission of Paul.

The corporate setting of Paul's letters

In attempting to locate the Jewish mindset of Paul, we need to be careful that he is not inadvertently isolated from the corporate mindset that is foundational to the whole Old Testament. It is all too easy to forget that Paul was a devout Jew long before he responded to the claims of Jesus to be the Messiah. But even then, after he responded, he neither deliberately nor subconsciously rejected his heritage. One of the features of that heritage was to gather to hear the Scriptures read to the congregation in the synagogue. These gatherings were an essential part of his experience from the earliest years of childhood. He continued meeting in the synagogue until he was finally denied access.

The significance of the synagogue experience was that it controlled the way Paul heard the Jewish Scriptures. Hearing them corporately was not a distorting influence, for the messages of the prophets were rarely delivered to individuals but were delivered to the people of the covenant collectively. The gathered congregation was therefore the ideal setting to hear the same word being delivered to another generation of the covenant people.

The same principle is being followed in Paul's letters. He expects the believers to gather together to hear them read. Indeed, the possibility of individuals having their own private copy could hardly have crossed the mind of the apostle. He wrote his letters to them to be read out loud and his arguments were therefore constructed with that setting in mind. In other words, the practice of interpreting letters written to churches as though they were to individuals causes serious distortion when it comes to interpreting their contents. The letters are not about what God has done or is doing for a Christian. They are about what God has done or is doing for his covenant people, the church. It is not permissible, despite the widespread practice, to read the details as though they describe the experience of the solitary believer. Such practice not only makes much of the individual, it in turn makes little of the covenant community. The privilege of individuals owning their own copy of the Scriptures for private reading is a blessing that believers have only recently, in historical terms, enjoyed. This private possession of the Scriptures is only possible because of the advance of printing technologies and the increase in personal private wealth.

The importance of the public reading of the letters is endorsed by Witherington. He recognises that they were read publicly and, he argues, this gave Paul the opportunity to maximise his argument and its effects. By carefully selecting who took and read the letter, he could have its contents delivered to their best advantage. All the skills of the public orator where used, according to Witherington, to deliver the content of the letter to the gathered congregation.[2]

Loss of responsibility?

If it is argued that this loses the individual perspective of the New Testament, then the reply must be made, 'What is meant by individual perspective?' Western individualism is certainly not the same as biblical individualism. That both the Old and New Testaments clearly recognise the responsibility of individuals to apply the Word of God to their own lives goes without saying. But that is not individualism in the sense that is normally meant in modern understanding. The biblical perspective is that every person is a member of a community and that membership determines his/her own self-identity. The individual believer is addressed through the message that is given to the people of God and its primary reference is to that covenant people. It necessarily has a secondary reference, to the individual as he/she is called to fulfil their obligations to the covenant. The Old Testament prophets reminded Israel of the unique relationship that existed between her and Yahweh. They called her, and by implication each individual Jew, to live out what they were. So Paul followed the same pattern. He constantly reminded the church of her calling and appealed to her that she live as the covenant community in the world. At times he applied his exhortations to specific groups of people, such as masters and slaves, spelling out the ramifications of what he has said for their daily living. Very occasionally he even addressed individuals,[3] but the undoubted thrust of the letters is that they are addressed by and large to the church. If this is lost sight of, they become texts that wrongfully endorse all manner of unbiblical individualistic understandings and behaviour.

In insisting that the letters are to the church we are not saying anything new. Most commentators say the same thing. I shall seek to keep this corporate perspective to the fore of our thinking as I attempt to interpret the letters. I shall seek to interpret the letters as describing the church's experience unless there is clear evidence that Paul is

---

[2]Witherington, *Corinthians,* 45.
[3]Romans 16:1ff; Philippians 4:2; Colossians 4:17

directing his teaching to a particular individual or group of people within the church such as the husbands or children.

Community and initiation

If these claims concerning the corporate nature of the letters are correct, then they inevitably raise questions concerning initiation. This is unavoidable because the passages that have been commonly seen to refer to the individual experience of being brought into the covenant community will, with this refocusing, be seen to be speaking of the historical creation of the covenant with the covenant community. The question that must therefore be answered is, 'where does the individual believer fit into this scheme of reading?'[4]

The question is a serious one. There are those who view salvation as universally applied to the whole of mankind, and such would see no problem. They would no doubt accept the corporate reading with enthusiasm. Such euphoria over having found a solution to their own problems of inclusion is however ill-founded. It will become clear that Paul insists that there is a fundamental division in the human race. It is no longer between Jew and Gentile, for a new division has come into existence. There are those who are in Adam and those who are in Christ. It is of course true that *in Christ* there are no ultimate divisions of status, but it is abuse of Paul's argument to say that he claims that this truth applies to all humanity. To ignore this fundamental premise of two separate communities under their respective heads, so clearly found in Pauline theology, is to destroy the very basis of his arguments. Whatever the doctrine of salvation that is developed, what can be certain is, if this fundamental division is ignored, then it is not corresponding accurately to the realities that the apostle taught.

Whatever the solution to this problem is, one thing is clear, the early church saw the absolute need for personal repentance and faith. There is no suggestion that man automatically benefits from Christ representing sinners before God. Whatever the theological structures that undergird the doctrine of salvation, God calls all people everywhere to repent and believe (Rom. 10:9-15). Any argument for the early church's understanding of the corporate nature of the letters

---

[4]See Wright, *Victory*, 256, for his understanding of individual conversion in a community setting. In *Testament*, 278, he says: 'It is important not to lose sight of the corporate nature of these ideas. In so far as individual Jews reflected on their own state before God, it was as members of the larger group, whether the nation or some particular sect.'

must respect this clear basic tenet of the early church's understanding which is expressed so clearly by her evangelistic ministry.

To suggest solutions to this problem at this stage is to anticipate the arguments that need to be made. Not until the relevant texts have been considered and a case has been made for their individual or corporate perspectives will it make sense to offer a solution.

Conclusion

We have noted Paul's dependence on Isaiah particularly but also on the Old Testament as a whole. He continually refers to the great themes of the promises made by the prophets when they spoke of a coming New Exodus. In this exposition of Paul I intend to take Paul's commitment to the Old Testament Scriptures seriously, and to attempt to understand him from that perspective; especially from within the New Exodus paradigm. I believe that it can be shown that his doctrinal system fits perfectly into this model and that it resolves many of the difficulties Pauline Theology has traditionally assumed to have existed. It is this perspective that allows him to argue that his gospel is according to the Scriptures and that they are the fulfilment of the promises that God has made to his people.

I am arguing that Paul was not the innovator of Christian doctrine. Instead, he is the faithful ambassador who conscientiously delivered his Master's message to the Gentiles. He stayed within the framework of Old Testament theology and stressed the promises that had been made regarding the acceptance of the Gentiles. Paul received his theological model from his Jewish upbringing, in which he was taught that Yahweh would bring about the promised New Exodus. He had come to realise that this had been inaugurated by the death of the only Son in his Paschal death. We shall see in chapter 4 that Paul saw himself to be called to the prophetic ministry of the New Covenant.

In the next chapter I am going to consider the relevance of the Pseudepigraphal literature for understanding Paul. I will argue that while it has uses in telling how widespread particular topics occupied the attention of different strands of Judaism, it is nevertheless not appropriate as a source for understanding the theological detail of Second Temple Judaism.

Excursus
Scholarly opinion concerning Paul's use of the Scriptures
Having considered the expectations of Judaism we need to ask how
the New Testament writers, and Paul in particular, used the Old
Testament in their arguments.

The apparently haphazard use of the Old Testament in the New
Testament has long been an embarrassment for Christians. The best
that could be claimed was that though it followed methods of
interpretation that are totally unacceptable in today's terms,
nevertheless these methods were consistent within the accepted
exegetical principles of Second Temple Judaism. Following Rabbinic
methodology for interpreting the Old Testament, the New Testament
writers were able to massage the text of the Old Testament in the
process of interacting with a series of vaguely related texts. By this
method, the desired meaning that was sought was demonstrated to
be in the original text.[5]

While this explanation disposed of some of the problems, it
nevertheless left a major disjunction. The methodology was still making
texts say something that the original Old Testament text was never
intended or able to say. Such an understanding inevitably led many to
conclude that there was no logical relationship between Old Testament
and New Testament theology.

As we have already seen in chapter 1, modern scholarship sees a
historical development of the message of the New Testament writings.
Most of its Jewish message is seen to have been lost in the process of
adapting to the needs of the growing Gentile church. Indeed, it is
claimed that material was produced by the Hellenistic Church and
read back into the ministry of Jesus. It is argued that the Christian
gospel absorbed parts of the outlook it was challenging, using its cultural
and religious practices as models for explaining its own message.
Thus it is not only the Gospels that are seen to have been moulded by
Hellenism, but the Epistles are also seen to have recast the original
kerygma into a form that the non-Jewish world could understand.
Bruce said that 'There are elements in the New Testament which
are essentially Jewish/Palestinian, and others which are equally
recognisable as Hellenistic, but there is no hard and fast line of
demarcation between the two: in the broad central band of the spectrum
they merge into each other'.[6] Bruce went on to say that the ability to

---

[5]see Longenecker, *Exegesis,* 19-50.

adapt was the genius of the gospel.[7] Much of the work of modern scholarship centres on identifying the units that emerged and placing them in their time location so as to map the progress of the development of the Christian message. However, what has increasingly been appreciated is that rather than drifting from his Jewish roots, Paul was anxious to show that his gospel was the same as that held in Jerusalem. He did not alter the primitive gospel to suit the Gentiles.[8] Alongside this recovery of the Jewish Paul, there has been a growing appreciation of Paul's faithfulness to the Old Testament Scriptures.

Lindars, while accepting that Paul was saturated in the Old Testament, denied any logic behind the selection of the texts and doubted that a New Testament theology based on the Old Testament ever existed in the early church.[9] He argued that such a claim demanded 'that items of gospel tradition were entirely evolved out of Old Testament prototypes'.[10] Lindars claimed that the actual provable use of the Old Testament in the New Testament does not support such a hypothesis. This is similar to Bultmann who claimed that the original meaning and context of the Old Testament sayings are entirely irrelevant.[11]

Grech saw the use of the Old Testament to be without reference to its original context, the text being interpreted not in the light of its original meaning, but of the Christ event: 'The interest of the readers was not that of knowing what happened of old but how the words of the law and the prophets illuminated the events which were taking place in their own days.'[12]

If this haphazard use of the Old Testament by the New Testament writers is true, then there is no possibility of a basic paradigm existing that guided the New Testament writers.

All of the views considered above undermined the earlier work by Dodd. He identified a possible solution to the problem. By analysing the use of the Old Testament in the New Testament, he concluded that the patterns that emerged suggested that the New Testament writers used the same Old Testament material. He claimed from this

[6]Bruce, 'Classical', 232.
[7]*op. cit.* 241.
[8]so Noack, 'Hellenistic', 51.
[9]Lindars, 'Place', 61.
[10]*op. cit.* 60.
[11]Bultmann, *Primitive*, 187.
[12]Grech, 'Testimonia', 319, 322.

evidence that there were books of testimonies which the early church had collated which related to various subjects. Dodd went beyond this observation to suggest that the texts cited were used as a pointer back to the passages out of which they had been taken. He argued that the early church would have known the Old Testament Scriptures so well that the mention of a few key words that were familiar would have had the effect of bringing to the readers'/hearers' minds all that the original Old Testament passage contained. In other words, the theology of the passage that the text was originally in was brought over into the passage in which it was now quoted. Dodd argued that the use of the quoted text could be shown to have followed careful exegetical principles in which there was no violation of the text's original meaning. In fact, the original Old Testament context was used to understand its significance in the New Testament.[13] Dodd's claims certainly avoided the scepticism that had developed, but as we have seen above, they were not widely received.

While many have rejected Dodd's thesis, there are those who have supported it. Beale, for example, has claimed that the New Testament hermeneutic was faithful to the meaning of the Old Testament text. What he was unable to say was what the paradigm was that guided their interpretation other than the general theme of redemptive history. Beale commented: 'Jesus and the apostles had an unparalleled redemptive historical perspective on the OT's relation to their own situation.' He further claimed that: New Testament Scripture interprets the Old Testament Scripture by expanding its meaning, seeing new implications in it and giving it new application. Therefore, the canon interprets the canon, later parts of the canon draw out and explain more clearly the earlier parts. He went on to claim that 'Of all the major Old Testament citations and allusions found in the New Testament only a very few plausible examples of non-contextual usages have been noted by critics'.[14]

Even the few examples that Beale has allowed to be non-contextual may in fact be found to be contextual once the paradigm has been correctly identified. Käsemann also saw that 'Paul found in the Old Testament the harbinger of what was to come and the criterion for a proper understanding of the present'.[15] Fischer saw this faithfulness

---

[13]Dodd, *According*, 1ff.

[14]Beale, 'Wrong Text', 91.

[15]Käsemann, *Romans*, 94. Longenecker, 'Exegesis', 3-38 disputes that we will ever reproduce the exegetical method of the New Testament.

to the meaning of earlier Scripture to have been characteristic of the Old Testament prophets themselves, for Jeremiah had argued that the new covenant would be nothing less than the true fulfilment of the teaching of Moses.[16]

Thus an increasing number of scholars are turning from the scepticism of previous generations.[17] Indeed, it is increasingly being recognised that Paul's gospel can only be understood in Jewish terms.[18] The unity of Old Testament and New Testament theology was emphasised by Hubbard, who wrote: 'Not only does the Old Testament prophecy lead into the New, but the New Testament appropriates the Old Testament promises and reads them as preparation for God's new beginning.'[19] Noack said that the time is past when Paul could be made responsible for having altered the primitive gospel to suit the requirements of the non-Jewish world and of having invented a whole Christology and doctrine of salvation by atonement in Christ.[20] Paul was anxious to stay in complete accord with the Jerusalem church and its leaders. Beker says that it was essential for Paul to maintain that the Jews still had priority in the gospel, otherwise God's faithfulness to his promises would be in doubt and faith in a God who went back on his promises would seriously weaken Christian confidence.[21] Similarly, any tampering with the plain meaning of Scripture would equally invalidate the authority of Scripture and by implication the covenant promises of God. Thus any theory of hermeneutics that does not take these factors into account should be viewed as being out of touch with the New Testament world. The historical context requires that the hermeneutic for understanding Paul respects Yahweh's promises in such a way that they are clearly, even to Gentile believers, fulfilled in Christ. The mind of the first century was no less

[16]Fischer, 'Fulfilment', 176.

[17]See Wright, *Messiah*, 171; Namos, *Mystery*, 7; Munck, 'Jewish', 203.

[18]Wright, *Messiah*, 321-2. Davies, 'People', 14, also sees things differently from the religio-historical perspective, but allows for some theological contextualization. He says: 'Paul, while he also exploits Hellenistic forms and literary genres, takes seriously the scriptures of his people and seeks to deal with the problem in their terms – employing rabbinical and other methods to do justice both to this new emergence, the Christian community, and its matrix, the Jewish people.' He goes on to say that Paul did not think in terms of moving into a new religion, 'For him the gospel was according to the scriptures' (p. 20).

[19]Hubbard, 'Hope', 58.

[20]Noack, 'Hellenistic', 51.

[21]Beker, 'Faithfulness', 11.

able to see flaws in arguments than is its twenty-first century counterpart. This Old Testament perspective for Paul's thinking was supported by Barrett, who said that 'Paul's Jewish heritage continued after his conversion. Indeed, Paul saw himself in the stream of Old Testament prophetic ministry.'[22] Hays says, 'We will have great difficulty understanding Paul, the pious first-century Jew, unless we seek to situate his discourse appropriately within what Hollander calls the "cave of resonant signification" that enveloped him: Scripture.'[23] Again, Hays says: 'To read Paul against this background of inner-biblical exegesis is to understand his place in the stream of tradition in a new way. He saw himself as a prophetic figure, carrying forward the proclamation of God's word as Israel's prophets and sages had always done, in a way that reactivated past revelation under new conditions.'[24]

Hays demonstrated that the New Testament writers used the original context of the Old Testament they cited as a 'resonance chamber', amplifying the significance of the quotation as it echoed in the theological context of the passage from which it was taken. Such usage obviously supposed that the readers were acquainted with the literary method in order for them to benefit from the skilfully constructed effects.[25]

Thus it is now being appreciated that Paul was anxious to underline the fact that his gospel was according to the Scriptures and to show that it was in complete harmony with what the church in Jerusalem taught. Indeed, this move toward reconciling Paul with his supposed abandoned roots has been accelerated by recent scholarship. It has come to recognise the essential Jewish nature of not only Paul's writings, but indeed of the whole of the New Testament. Nanos has recently written: 'Where New Testament scholarship is concerned, the literature can now be read as Jewish correspondence, written by and for Jews and gentiles concerned with the Jewish context of their

[22]Barrett, 'Sacrificed', 147-8.

[23]Hays, *Echoes*, 21.

[24]*op. cit.* 14.

[25]The author can testify to the feasibility of this hypothesis. When lecturing in communist Romania to Christian leaders who had no libraries apart from their Bible, the mention of an obscure Old Testament text would immediately produce a response in which they added the historical and theological significance of the passage quoted. They would immediately use the information to interpret the significance of the text as quoted in the New Testament.

faith in Jesus as the Jewish Messiah. Simply put, we can now read the New Testament as a Jewish book.'[26] Nanos further says: 'The very Jewish Paul whom Luke portrays in Acts can be seen also in Romans.'[27]

What Dodd's work, as well as most of those who followed his basic thesis, lacked was a paradigm to demonstrate what the guiding principle for quoting the Old Testament was. For a paradigm to be established, it is necessary to demonstrate that Judaism itself respected the context of the Old Testament texts it cited in its own writings. Also, it is necessary to demonstrate that the proposed paradigm was commonly held in Judaism in order that its inferences might be readily identified by the readers. Evidence has been presented for the widespread expectation of the New Exodus that naturally forms a common paradigm. Evidence that Judaism respected the context of Old Testament texts was provided recently by Brewer.[28] He has shown that the Rabbis prior to AD 70 paid careful attention to the origin of the passages they cited, and followed a method of exegesis that was faithful to the original context. Thus if the New Testament writers followed Rabbinic methodology in expounding Old Testament Scripture, then we might expect this methodology to be reflected in the New Testament use of the Old Testament. This practice ought at least to be found in Paul for he was trained in the rabbinic schools, as were many of the early converts from Judaism (Acts 6:7; 21:20). We have already seen that there was a common hermeneutical model for both Judaism and the New Testament church – the New Exodus.

What I am saying is that we ought to find in Paul's exegesis of the Old Testament (and indeed this inevitably applies to the rest of the New Testament writers!) respect for the original context and meaning of the cited texts, and that these citations should be examined for their associations with the theme of the New Exodus.

[26]Nanos, *Mystery*, 4.
[27]*op. cit.* 18.
[28]Brewer, *Techniques*, 1ff.

Chapter Three

Methodological Presuppositions

Throughout history biblical scholars have made simple mistakes which have had serious consequences. This chapter reviews some of the basic errors that have had massive influences on how academics have interpreted the texts of Scripture. The chapter aims to show how these errors have left a deeply flawed understanding. We will then examine a mistake that is currently being made and is having equally devastating influence.

Until recently scholars saw no difficulty in using etymology as the key to understanding the meaning of biblical words. Philologists would tell us what the roots of words were and it was naively assumed that the meaning was transferred across the centuries to the text that was being considered. It does not take a trained linguist to know that language is constantly changing. Thus to establish the meaning that a word had two thousand years earlier is of little help in understanding its meaning when used by a completely different generation. What determines any word's meaning is not how earlier generations understood the particular word, but how the generation that has produced the text under consideration interprets it. This can only be known through carefully reflecting on both its immediate and its wider context. In retrospect it is a mistake so simple that it matches the massive mistake of failing to design computer software to handle dates past the end of 1999.

Another mistake that should never have happened relates to the Greek language of the New Testament. The New Testament documents were written in the *Koiné* Greek that pervaded every level of the Hellenistic world. For centuries it was considered that the appropriate preparation for the study of New Testament theology was a thorough grounding in the Greek classics. Thus most New Testament scholars of previous generations followed this well tried and little questioned route into theology. Those who had this education were looked on as eminently suited to the task of New Testament exegesis. They had the great advantage of being able to fall back on the broad learning they had gained of the Hellenistic world, its thought patterns and its vocabulary.

Few saw that there was a flaw in this method, but there was. While the vocabulary of the New Testament could be found throughout the Hellenistic world, it did not have the same meaning when it was used in a religious sense within the Jewish community. Here the language had imbibed its own theological meaning as a result of the translation of the Hebrew Bible some two hundred years or so before Christ. The Hebrew meaning had been poured into the text of the Greek translation to produce a language that had its own particular lexicon. It was Greek in its alphabet and vocabulary, but Hebrew in its mindset and essential meaning. It was this very *language* that Judaism bequeathed to the infant church as she interpreted and proclaimed the message of the prophets.

Seen from this perspective, the classical method of training for theological study was fundamentally flawed. It was not from Athens that the writers of the New Testament had drawn their understanding, but from Jerusalem. Much theological literature that exists demonstrates this confusion. It is evidenced in the way that even those who assert the New Testament's dependence on the Old Testament still nevertheless give emphasis to the Hellenistic cultural and literary background that they presuppose the text draws on.

Bultmann is another example of how flawed practice totally spoiled the work of a world-renowned scholar. Bultmann's reliance on the Gnostic documents was misplaced trust. His argument was that the New Testament writers were fighting against the threatening mindset of Gnosticism. He argued that the early church borrowed its language and imagery from Gnosticism, using it to develop their claims for Jesus. These claims were, according to Bultmann, far greater than anything Jesus would have claimed for himself. Bultmann held that by studying the Gnostic documents the background of the theology of the New Testament could be identified and so its history could be plotted and understood. Out of this study he sought to demythologise the gospel. His mistake was to assume that the Gnostic texts on which he relied were evidence of the state of Gnosticism in the first century. Recent scholarship has demonstrated that this was not the case. Gnosticism was only in its embryonic stage in the first century. Rather than Christians borrowing from Gnosticism, it had been Gnosticism that had borrowed from Christians.

As we saw in chapter 1, the methods of liberal theology are increasingly being revealed to have been based on faulty presuppositions. During the closing decades of the 1800s Europe was caught up in an intellectual revolution that was to alter radically the way man viewed himself. This ranged from the natural sciences to religion. The history of mankind was no longer seen as static, but as dynamic and evolving. In politics this gave birth to communism, in theology to liberalism. The premise that liberal scholars embraced was that there was no unique divine revelation. All religions were the products of folklore or the borrowing from other religions, either directly or by adapting their opponents' arguments to promote their own worldviews.

This method struck at the heart of the traditional understanding of Christian revelation and the authority of the Bible in particular. It assumed that the New Testament was not historically reliable and that it was virtually all the product of the emerging Gentile churches as they used their own traditions to teach their new-found faith in Jesus of Nazareth. The thrust of much New Testament research since the advent of liberal scholarship has been to identify the points at which units of New Testament materials came into existence. It seeks to assign the material to its place in its evolution from being a message about a Jewish prophet to becoming the religion of Gentiles who claimed for Jesus a status comparable with the gods of the Hellenistic world.

After almost a century of liberal dominance, the method that it has developed is being seriously challenged from some of the leading academic institutions throughout the world. An important factor in this change was the discovery of the Dead Sea Scrolls. These have demonstrated that the language that had been assumed to have been borrowed from Hellenism had existed independently in Judaism itself.

Some are presenting their own alternatives to replace the method of liberalism, but what is clear is that liberalism is no longer the dominant attacking force that it once was. It is being asked far more searching questions than it has ever previously been asked in order to justify its claims. Alongside of this is the growing realisation that the New Testament is not a collection of Hellenistic writings, as argued by the liberal forefathers, for it is being increasingly recognised to be a collection of essentially, if not entirely, Jewish writings. If this is true, then it challenges at a fundamental level the presuppositions of theological liberalism. There was no radical Hellenistic development. The identification of the New Testament as a collection of Jewish writings means that we have to abandon, or at least radically restrict, the method that has prevailed for the last hundred years, and begin all over again.

The above examples indicate how serious it is to build on flawed assumptions. The fact is that presuppositions determine conclusions. It is for this reason that liberalism was almost inevitably going to win the debate while it set the agenda. It had effectively set the rules of the game and this determined that it would always win when appealing to people with open minds. It is always important in any debate, but in theology especially, that before engaging in the debate, the assumptions are examined and if necessary challenged. Like a carefully drawn up legal agreement, liberalism determined what evidence was permissible and established the laws of evidence. The hypothesis that it set forth as representing the historic facts of the New Testament meant that there could be only one conclusion, that liberalism was right.

What the above cases demonstrate is that no matter how gifted and able a scholar is, if his arguments are built on unsubstantiated assumptions, he cannot compensate by his learning. Until scholars are willing to acknowledge the mistakes they are making, their conclusions will always be flawed.

What is embarrassing for scholarship is that the major mistakes of the past should never have been made. It did not need exceptional academic ability to see that languages change their meaning. Nor does it take an academic genius to see that translations preserve something of the conceptual background of the original text. Indeed it ought to be obvious that failure to recognise this would not only miss conceptual riches, but if they are overlooked then their absence from the reading of the translated text will leave a far from adequate synthesis of ideas. These very simple mistakes had profound effects and brought serious confusion into biblical scholarship.

I now want to suggest that a research method that has recently found widespread acceptance in scholarly circles will be seen in years to come to have polluted the academic process and significantly distorted the conclusions of scholarship by imposing an extraneous and poorly constructed meaning on the New Testament text. This is being done by the modern use that is made of the pseudepigraphal writings.

Contemporary confusion – The Pseudepigrapha

The pseudepigrapha is a body of ancient literature that has become very influential in recent New Testament research. Before we consider and evaluate its influence, a brief look at the history of the literature and its study is appropriate.

Throughout the Christian era it has been generally known that writings whose authorship was not known have existed. This collection is known as the pseudepigrapha. The name reflects their false claims of authorship. They were attributed to important historical Jewish figures who clearly did not compose them.

Until recently, one of the problems in using this material has been that the Christian community preserved it. While there was little doubt that it was based on a Jewish genre and indeed probably had within it genuine Jewish material, there was no certainty as to how reliable it was as a guide to Jewish thought. It was widely regarded as mostly of Christian composition and therefore not representative in any significant way of intertestamental Judaism. Indeed, G. F. Moore pointed out that it is of a totally different genre from the Rabbinical material which, though later, was the only authentic Jewish literature of the period that existed outside of the New Testament. For Moore, this difference confirmed the necessity for caution in accepting the material as relevant for Jewish studies of the New Testament period.

Pseudepigraphal development

In fact there is ongoing debate as to what should be included in the pseudepigrapha collection. It is a corpus that has slowly expanded over the past century.

a. The Collection of Deane. A work published in 1891 by W. J. Deane listed the following works as making up the Pseudepigrapha:

Lyrical
  The Psalter of Solomon

Apocalyptical and Prophetical
  The Book of Enoch
  The Assumption of Moses
  The Apocalypse of Baruch
  The Testaments of the Twelve Patriarchs

Legendary
 The Book of Jubilees
 The Ascension of Isaiah

Mixed
 The Sibylline Oracles

b. The collection of Charles. R. H. Charles published in 1913 a two volume work called *The Apocrypha and Pseudepigrapha of the Old Testament*. In volume 1, *The Apocrypha of the Old Testament*, Charles listed the following:

Historical Books
  1 Esdras
  1 Maccabees
  2 Maccabees
  3 Maccabees
Quasi-Historical Books Written with a Moral Purpose
  Tobit
  Judith
Wisdom Literature
  Sirach
  Wisdom of Solomon
Additions to and Completion of the Canonical Books
  1 Baruch
  Epistle of Jeremy
  Prayer of Manasses
  Additions to Daniel
    Prayer of Azariah and Song of the Three
     Children
    Susanna
    Bel and the Dragon

The second volume of Charles' work was called *The Pseudepigrapha of the Old Testament*. In this volume he listed the following:

Primitive History Written from the Standpoint of the Law
  The Book of Jubilees
Sacred Legends
  The Letter of Aristeas
  The Book of Adam and Eve
  The Martydom of Isaiah

Apocalypses
> 1 Enoch
> The Testaments of the XII Patriarchs
> The Sibylline Oracles
> The Assumption of Moses
> 2 Enoch, or the Book of the Secrets of Enoch
> 2 Baruch or the Syriac Apocalypse of Baruch
> 3 Baruch or the Greek Apocalypse of Baruch
> 4 Ezra

Psalms
> The Psalms of Solomon.

Ethics and Wisdom Literature
> 4 Maccabees
> Pirke Aboth
> The Story Ahikar

History
> The Fragments of a Zadokite Work

c. The collections of Moore. By 1920 G. F. Moore listed the collection as follows:

Mekilta	Tanhuma
Mekilta De-R. Simeone. Yohai	Debarim Rabbah
Sifra	(Deuteronomy)
Sifrè on Numbers	Bemidbar Rabbah
Sifrè Zuta	(Numbers)
Sifrè on Deuteronomy	
Midrash Tannaim	Sirach
	Psalms of Solomon
The Mishnah	Gospels and Acts
Tosefta	Teaching of the Twelve Apostles
Pirkè Abot	
Abot De-R.Nathan	
Seder 'Olam	Testament of the Twelve Patriarchs
	Jubilees
Bereshit Rabbah (Genesis)	The Schismatic Sect in Damascus
Shemot Rabbah (Exodus)	
Ekah Rabbati (Lammentations)	1 Maccabees
Pesikta De R.Kahana	2 Maccabees
Pesikta Rabbati	Flavius Josephus
Wayyikra Rabbah (Leviticus)	Philo

d. The collection of Charlesworth. In 1985 Charlesworth expanded
the list:

Apocalyptic Literature and Related Works

1 Enoch   Questions of Ezra
2 Enoch   Revelation of Ezra
3 Enoch   Apocalypse of Sedrach
Sibylline Oracles   2 Baruch
Treatise of Shem   3 Baruch
Apocryphon of Ezekiel   Apocalypse of Abraham
Apocalypse of Zephaniah   Apocalypse of Adam
The Fourth Book of Ezra   Apocalypse of Elijah
Greek Apocalypse of Ezra   Apocalypse of Daniel
Vision of Ezra

Testaments (Often with Apocalyptic Sections)

Testaments of the Twelve Patriarchs   Testament of Moses
Testament of Job   Testament of Solomon
Testaments of the Three Patriarchs   Testament of Adam
(Abraham, Isaac and Jacob)

Expansions of the Old Testament and Legends

Letter of Aristeas   Ladder of Jacob
Jubilees   4 Baruch
Martyrdom and Ascension   Jannes and Jambres
of Isaiah   History of the Rechabites
Joseph and Aseneth
Life of Adam and Eve   Eldad and Modad
Pseudo-Philo   History of Joseph
Lives of the Prophets

Wisdom and Philosophical Literature

Ahiqar   Pseudo-Phocylides
3 Maccabees   Syriac-Manander
4 Maccabees

Prayers, Psalms and Odes

More Psalms of David	Prayer of Joseph
Prayer of Manasseh	Prayer of Jacob
Psalms of Solomon	Odes of Solomon
Hellenistic Synagogal Prayers	

Fragments of Judeo-Hellenistic Works

Philo the Epic Poet	Theodotus
Orphica	Ezekiel the Tragedian
Fragments of Pseudo-Greek Poets	Aristobulus
Demetrius the Chronographer	Aristeas the Exegete
Eupolemus	Pseudo-Eupolemus
Cleodemus Malchus	Artapanus
Pseudo-Hecataeus	

When Moore published his list in 1920 he urged great caution in embracing the material as a reliable source for New Testament studies. He expressed his concern over the way the pseudepigraphal writings were being used in New Testament research. His concern was that this literature, which was increasingly available to New Testament scholars because of translations, was not properly understood. One of Moore's concerns was that the material was being used by people who were ignorant of its diversity and its particular genre, which required careful use as a hermeneutic tool. Another of Moore's concerns, as mentioned already, was that there was no textual evidence to show that the material was truly Jewish.

Some of Moore's concerns were allayed with the discovery of the Dead Sea Scrolls, for amongst them were two of the works of the pseudepigrapha, the books of Jubilees and 1 Enoch, along with fragments from the book of the Testaments of the Twelve Patriarchs. Thus some of the material of the pseudepigrapha was genuinely early and Jewish, so making it relevant to the New Testament period. The discovery of this material resulted in the essentially Jewish nature of much of the New Testament being recognised. This in turn caused scholars to pull back from the previously held assumption that New Testament religious imagery reflected the Graeco-Roman world. Themes such as the Kingdom of God, the Son of Man and the Son of God have all been shown to have been part of Judaism and not the creation of the early church, as had been argued by liberal scholars.

The discovery of the Dead Sea Scrolls has produced a renewed confidence in the authenticity of the pseudepigraphal material. This has meant that New Testament scholars have embraced it as the key to understanding the mindset of Second Temple Judaism and the world of the New Testament.

While the mistakes of previous generations of scholars are slowly being rectified, the present generation is falling into its own traps. The mushrooming of intertestamental studies as a result of the discoveries at Qumran has produced another method of training for theologians. The pseudepigrapha has become the key for deciphering the New Testament message. There is no doubt that these writings give fascinating insights into this period of Judaism. They are an invaluable source for evidence of the extent to which particular theological topics were discussed throughout the different strands of Judaism. Nevertheless, the extent of their relevance for the New Testament message must be questioned. As we have seen, the mistake of the past was to assume that the Greek of the New Testament was the same as that used in secular society. This same sort of assumption is being made in another guise by many New Testament scholars. The assumption is that there was a strict equivalence in terminology or even themes found in these writings and in the New Testament. But this assumption cannot go unchallenged,[1] not least because it is radically changing the message of the New Testament documents.[2]

The pseudepigraphal texts are used as the key for understanding the meaning of the New Testament. This presupposes that they share the same theological outlook and that their meanings are transposable. But this is to ignore a fatal flaw. There were, and still are, many theologies within Judaism. The documents represent different Jewish perspectives many of which were distinctive from, and in contradiction to, the others. This is made clear by Charlesworth, who, when commenting on the pseudepigrapha, says: 'In these writings, as in the Dead Sea Scrolls, we are introduced to the ideas, symbols, perceptions, fears, and dreams of pre-AD 70 Jews. Since none of them can with assurance be assigned to Pharisees, Sadducees, Zealots or Essenes,

---

[1]So for example Davies, *Origins*, 172, and Barrett, *Corinthians*, 75, both challenge the parallels concerning the Spirit in Qumran as having any significance for understanding the New Testament doctrine of the Spirit.

[2]For example, interpreting the meaning of the death of Jesus in the light of Jewish martyr theology. For a discussion on this, see chapter 8.

it is wise not to describe early Judaism in terms of four such sects; rather we must now think of many groups and numerous subgroups.'[3] Not until those distinctives are understood and their relationship to the New Testament established can they be safely used. To dump these texts mindlessly into footnotes or text of commentaries in order to give supporting evidence is doing the very opposite to what is intended. Instead of moving New Testament studies on to more scholarly methods, it is taking a retrograde step. It is polluting the primary text from which New Testament theology can be safely done. As those who specialise in the intertestamental literature are fond of saying, we cannot speak of Judaism but of Judaisms. The method that has been adopted ignores the complexity of these sources and unwittingly reads a particular theology into the text and then in turn uses the pseudo-theological insight as the key to interpret the New Testament. The method is a circular one. Not recognising the differences in the meaning of the same terms within this range of literature, scholars have read their own meaning into the term, and then used that to show what the New Testament meant.

Perhaps it is Neusner who has been most vocal in declaring the complexity of Judaism. His concern is not the one that I am seeking to alert the reader to – care in using intertestamental literature for interpreting the New Testament. His concern is simply that Judaism has been reduced in the thinking of many scholars to a homogeneous system. His particular point is to establish that Judaism did not have common expectations concerning its coming Messiah, but many and sometimes conflicting expectations. Indeed, Israel did not look for a Messiah but for messiahs. Neusner says:

> What is wrong with the established view is simple. People join together books that do not speak the same language of thought, that refer to distinctive conceptions and doctrines of their own. If books so close in topic and sentiment as the four Gospels no longer yield harmonization, books so utterly remote from one another as the Mishnah and Philo and Fourth Ezra and Enoch should not contribute doctrines to the common pot: Judaism. But if we do not harmonize, then what we have to do is quite the opposite: analyse. In fact all we propose is to describe things item by item, and to postpone the work of searching for connections and even continuities until all the components have had their say, one by one. For, as we see throughout this book, each of the components – the distinct books – makes its own distinctive statement.[4]

---

[3]Charlesworth, 'Pseudepigrapha', 538-9.

Indeed, Charlesworth has himself given warning of the diversity of Judaism:

> The contradicting ideas should not be explained away or forced into an artificial system. Such ideas in the Pseudepigrapha witness to the fact that early Judaism was not a speculative philosophical movement or theological system, even though the Jews demonstrated impressive speculative fecundity. The Pseudepigrapha mirror a living religion in which the attempt was made to come to terms with the dynamic phenomena of history and experience.[5]

Indeed, my concerns are multiplied by Charlesworth's remark concerning the difficulty of locating the documents of the Pseudepigrapha in their original theological stable. He says that 'we cannot identify with certainty any author of the pseudepigraphon as being a Pharisee or an Essene or a member of another sect'.[6] In other words, we don't even know what theological school to assign the documents to! This makes it impossible to know the significance that should be given to the theological terminology the documents use, for the meaning given to terms differed from group to group.

What also needs to be recognised is the *limitation* of the documents which we have. As already indicated they represent a whole range of theological traditions but they convey very limited samples of the particular tradition that they come from. How much of Paul's theology would we appreciate if we had only 1 or 2 Thessalonians, or Philippians or even 1 Corinthians?[7] It is only the multiplicity of documents addressed to different congregations and dealing with a wide range of issues that gives us reasonable grounds to believe that we can attempt to produce a Pauline theology. Obviously documents such as the letters of John, Peter or James give us only a limited glimpse into the thinking of their authors. Although this may prove a major hurdle

---

[4]Neusner, *Judaisms*, xiii. See also the warning given by Bauckham, 'Apocalypses', 114, who says: 'Heavily influenced by apocalyptic as primitive Christianity undoubtedly was, it was also highly selective in the aspects of apocalyptic which it took over. This is a fact about the NT which can only be appreciated by diligent study of pseudepigraphal works which do not look at all relevant to the NT.'

[5]Charlesworth, *Pseudepigrapha*, 2 xxxiii.

[6]Charlesworth, *Pseudepigrapha*, 2:xxix.

[7]See Fee's warning, *Empowering*, 594, against assuming that we have Paul's pneumatology sewn up: 'A text like this one alerts us that Paul's understanding is too large for us to encompass by merely collecting particular texts and looking at them.'

for scholarship, for orthodox Christianity it is not a problem, for it believes in the unity and inspiration of the Scriptures as written by men under the direction of the Spirit of Truth. We do not, or should not, look to these individual writings for a full theology. However, being part of the Christian Scriptures and sharing a similar mindset and system of beliefs, they can be interpreted from that wider perspective to which they also contribute. Obviously such a claim would be invalid if they represented factions within the early church, but such suggestions are no longer acceptable in the light of the results of modern research.

Furthermore, De Jonge has raised other problems that add to the dangers of relying on these texts. Like Moore back in 1920, he points out that the transmission of these texts was in the hands of Christians and that they preserved them because they served their purposes. We have no idea of how much material was discarded because it did not serve the new movement's expectations. In addition there is the problem that these documents are almost entirely translations of the original texts, so we cannot be certain as to how faithful these translations are. We certainly know that the early 'Christians' were not averse to interpolating their own material into these texts in order to use them to support their views. It is difficult even to guess just how much tampering took place. However, since we know from textual evidence that they had been prepared to tamper with the New Testament documents, there is little doubt that at least the same amount of tampering would have taken place with the documents of the pseudepigrapha. It is no wonder that De Jonge warns of the need of specialists to guide New Testament theologians in the use of these texts.[8]

But even if it were possible to demonstrate theological equivalence between New Testament texts and the pseudepigrapha, what would it prove? For example, how widely were the pseudepigraphal writings known? How far had their message penetrated wider Judaism? Were they known beyond Palestine and how do we know that the population of Palestine knew them? How can we know that an apparent reference or even an echo from the Jewish pseudepigrapha, or later recorded Rabbinic tradition for that matter, could have been recognised by the readers of the New Testament? How do we decide each individual New Testament writer's knowledge of the pseudepigrapha? Indeed, Dunn claims that Luke as a Gentile shows no evidence of

[8]De Jonge, 'Pseudepigrapha', 61-63.

having been aware of intertestamental Judaism.[9] Yet it is these writings
that Turner and Menzies rely on – and incidentally, they come to
totally different conclusions![10] They are an example of the danger of
reading into the texts one's own preferences and then using the texts
for understanding Luke's mindset concerning the Spirit. Indeed, not
only does Luke fail to show that he is aware of these sources, but
even if he had been, what relevance would they have had? He wrote
his Gospel for Gentile readers who were scattered across the Roman
world and who could not possibly have known of their existence or
contents. No one can seriously suggest, or rather should not seriously
suggest, that the Gospel writers expected these so-called allusions to
be picked up by their readers. Such claims strain the evidence way
beyond the point of credibility.

But even if there are echoes of these documents, could it not be
that these extra-biblical writings are themselves echoing some other
source that both the pseudepigrapha and the New Testament writers
were familiar with? In other words, they could both be echoing an
unknown source. Are the pseudepigraphal writings in the same
theological stream or have they drifted even further from the
unrecognised source? The way the Dead Sea Scrolls and the New
Testament use the same Old Testament material in different ways is
a warning of the possibility of this three-way relationship. These are
all questions or possibilities that are dangerously ignored by most
scholars as they draw upon the texts for support for their interpretations.

Wright acknowledges the variety of beliefs in Judaism that makes
us speak of Judaisms. He correctly, in my judgement, claims that
despite this variety we can trace the outlines of a worldview and a
belief system which were shared by a large number of Jews at the
time.[11] What I think he fails to do is recognise that he imports details
into his own interpretation from these sources. He has given meanings
to these texts that are the basis for interpreting the New Testament
texts that he seeks to be faithful to. In fact, as indicated above, it is
not possible to have any certainty as to the detailed meaning of these
texts without knowing their original stable and without having a
substantial collection of texts from the same source dealing with the
themes they mention. In using this method, Wright, along with a growing
number of other scholars, builds his exegesis on foundations that are

[9]Dunn, 'Response', 21.
[10]Turner, *Spiritual*, *passim*. Menzies *Empowered*, *passim*.
[11]Wright, *Testament*, 338.

unreliable. So, for example, his Wisdom Christology relies on these texts. This is in spite of his own acknowledgements of the immense complexity of the material.[12]

The concern I am expressing may be appreciated if we imagine a contemporary situation. A visitor to the UK seeks to gain some understanding of the Scottish Presbyterian doctrine of the Spirit. The research begins with a survey of what the population thinks about the subject. Searches of past editions of newspapers give a variety of references to the Spirit. Then a search of the literature of other religious groupings within Scotland is made of their understanding of the Spirit. Spiritualists, Mormons, Jehovah's Witnesses, Unitarians, Baptists, Methodists, Roman Catholics, etc. are consulted. Within this contextual study, the writings of the Presbyterian divines are then considered.

Now if this method were followed, and the fruit of the wider study were the basis of understanding the primary texts, there would be virtually no possible chance of understanding the distinctive doctrines of Presbyterianism. It is the theological differences that are the important points of study, not the similarity of vocabulary. Much contemporary New Testament study is conducting its research in a similar way. The fact that terminology is similar or even identical is no guarantee that the meaning is the same. Failure to appreciate this results in eisegesis and not exegesis.

It might be thought that the above illustration makes the point, but it does not. The reason for saying this is that it does not actually fully match the situation in New Testament studies. To have a direct equivalence you would have to imagine that the researcher who has gathered all of this material on the Spirit from so many sources has a disastrous day. All of the search facilities he has employed fail. They are never available for anyone ever to use again. Better still for the illustration, his collection of material is the only collection in the world. And then, to add to this technological disaster, he is working in his study with the window open and a gale blows through the study window. Every top sheet of paper, with the details of the origin and theological background, is blown out of the window and lost forever. Added to this the pages are scattered all over the room and the

---

[12]Wright, *Testament*, 119, says: 'We have learned that we must not glibly pass over differences of setting and time, imagining continuity of thought between documents of different provenance.'

collections are completely mixed together so that it is impossible to know what page belonged to what group and therefore what the terminology on the individual sheets of paper conveyed to the original writer. The ability to locate the sources that they came from and therefore the views that they represent has also totally gone. There are now only piles of texts, which cannot be labelled for their origin and whose original meaning can only now be guessed at. And now the researcher begins his study of the Presbyterian doctrine of the Holy Spirit!

This is in fact the situation in New Testament studies as far as the use of the pseudepigraphal writings are concerned. We do not know their theological homes, we can only guess. Making any sense of these sources will demand incredible discipline and patience and they certainly must not be pulled across into the field of New Testament studies as evidence to show that the proposed exegesis is supported by these texts. To use this method is to disregard the rules of historical research for admissible evidence.

It might seem that the above conclusion is too harsh, that the pseudepigrapha must have more value than that limited use that has been conceded earlier. In fact what I have argued for is really not even accurate, because it is even more serious. Even within the one community that we can define, and whose literature we have access to, the Qumran community, variation stops the possibility of any certainty in drawing conclusions concerning its belief system. The following extract shows why this is the case:

> It is not possible to do a simple, homogenous Qumran messianic belief without doing violence to the nature of the evidence. Nor, however, is it acceptable to make this variety of concepts the basis for working out a pattern of systematic development in chronological order for messianic beliefs at Qumran. We simply do not have sufficient information to allow precise dating of the Qumran works (essential for the construction of this kind of chronological schema), nor do we know enough about the interrelationship of the various Qumran writings.[13]

If there is so much uncertainty in interpreting the documents of such a clearly defined community, what chance is there of understanding an array of texts that come from such diverse groupings (and whose identity and origin we do not even know) that existed

---

[13]Chester, 'Expectations,' 25.

within first-century Judaism? The complexity of the problem demands extreme caution in making any claims, and such caution is very rarely exercised, even by those who say they recognise its need.

But these observations are not meant to suggest that we languish in ignorance concerning the mindset of the early church. Paul's use of the Old Testament prophets shows without a shadow of doubt the dependence of the early church on these writings. Indeed, we know that the whole of Judaism fed off these Scriptures. Every member of the covenant community drank in from their streams of warning, comfort, encouragement and hope. They gathered at least weekly to hear them read and to be taught from their pages. The Psalms were used to express their worship to God. It is these writings that saturate the New Testament literature. To rely on texts, whose influence on the expectations of the covenant people is extremely doubtful, while the Old Testament Scriptures are being treated as though they had little formative influence, is an irrational procedure. Not only were the New Testament letters written to communities outside of Palestine and presumably outside of access to most pseudepigraphal writings; so were the Gospels themselves. In contrast the Old Testament Scriptures were influential not only throughout every form of Judaism within the Promised Land, but in every synagogue throughout the Roman Empire. Furthermore, it is these writings that Paul explicitly states are fulfilled in the person and work of Jesus the Son of David (Rom. 3:21f.; 1 Cor. 15:3). It is from these Scriptures that the apostles taught, not from a dubious Palestinian perspective, but from the perspective that Jesus himself had taught them.

The question of the significance of the influence of the rabbinic tradition on the New Testament writers has been widely discussed. There are scholars who point out that the traditions were not written down until the end of the second century and therefore the material that precedes this date has its own problems relating to authenticity. Other scholars reject what they see as undue scepticism and treat the records as accurately preserving the traditions of the rabbis who are quoted.

Conclusion
We have attempted to evaluate the pseudepigrapha for New Testament research. We have seen that while it points to a widely held set of expectations, the detail was interpreted by each group in

its own distinctive way. The common terminology is not evidence of a common theology and its literature is of limited value for New Testament research. What they do provide is evidence as to how widely different themes were discussed, but this evidence does not give us the details that we need to map the theology of these documents accurately. We have seen in chapters 1 and 2 that the key to the New Testament is the Old Testament. It is therefore the message of these writings that will be used as the theological key to Pauline thought.

Chapter Four

Isaiah and the Servant

We have seen that the prophecy of Isaiah is probably the major influence on Paul's thinking. The prophet clearly determined the apostle's theology of salvation. For Isaiah, the key figure in his message of hope was someone known as the Servant of the Lord. In this chapter I want to explore the extent to which Paul was influenced by the prophet's perspective of the Servant figure. The prophet's theological understanding on this issue was supreme amongst the Old Testament writers, especially his contribution to understanding Israel's call to servanthood. Porteous has noted that 'Isaiah is the theologian par excellence of the Old Testament, but his importance for theology lies, not so much in any abstract formulations he may have reached about the oneness and creative power of God, as in the way in which he seems to have given living embodiment to his understanding of Israel's call to be God's servant in the world.'[1]

The reason for choosing to examine this theme at this point in the study is that it illustrates how Hellenism has determined the way the New Testament is read. We will see that once the Greek control has been appreciated, previously unrecognised Old Testament theology breaks out of the New Testament text. This discovery ought then to give us confidence and hopefully appetite for exploring other strands of Old Testament theology in the writings of Paul.

Because Isaiah's understanding of the Servant of the Lord gives embodiment to the concept of Israel being God's servant in the Old Testament, I shall limit our investigation to that book. Furthermore Isaiah is the ideal place to begin for, as we have seen, it had a profound influence on the understanding of Paul's doctrine of salvation of which the Servant figure was an essential part.

An examination of the Old Testament Hebrew text of Isaiah shows that *ebed*, servant, was a title applied to a wide range of people. There were no alternative titles available for the Old Testament writers, so the variations in meaning had to be derived from the context in which the individual word was used. *Ebed* was used for kings (Isa. 37:24), prophets (Isa. 20:3), the nation of Israel (Isa. 41:8, 9), the

[1]Porteous, *Theology*, *PCB*, 157.

Messiah (Isa. 42:1) and even ordinary Israelites (Isa. 65:13-15). What can be said of *ebed* is that it spoke of someone who was subordinate in some way to another, whether to God or man, as master.

Confusion

Confusion arose when the Old Testament was translated into Greek. A study of the Hebrew text alongside the Greek (LXX) shows that there was no consistency in the minds of the translators as to the choice of an appropriate Greek word for a particular type of *ebed*. The two principal terms available were *doulos* and *pais*. The evidence shows that *pais* was used not only of the ideal servant, but also of Israel, and in such a way as to remind her of her unworthiness, for her 'unadopted' name 'Jacob' is used in parallel with this term.[2] *Pais* is also used of individual prophets (Isa. 20:3). The problem is rendered even more complex when we realise that this same term is applied to domestic servants or used generally as a title of anyone who is in an inferior position to another (Isa. 24:2; 36:11; 37:5). Confusion is even more compounded in that this same term, used in these various ways, is paralleled by the use of *doulos* in each respect. So we find *doulos* applied to the ideal servant (Isa. 53:11), the nation (Isa. 42:19) and to domestic servants (Isa. 14:2). In the Hebrew text the context was clearly the key to a proper understanding of the particular meaning of the term. The translators of the LXX evidently did not think it necessary to distinguish accurately between the various usages, and hence to designate one particular Greek word to correspond to each particular category of servant.

The apparently arbitrary use of *pais* and *doulos* is not limited to the LXX. We also find the same range of usages for both terms in the New Testament. We find *pais* used for a domestic servant (Matt. 8:6, 13), for Israel (Luke 1:54) and for David (Luke 1:69). We also find *doulos* being used with an equally wide range of meanings. It was used for a slave (Matt. 8:9), for a domestic help (John 18:10), for a prophet (Rev. 10:7), for Christians (Rom. 6:17), and for Christ himself (Phil. 2:7). It is evident that the arbitrary use of *pais* and *doulos* by the translators of the LXX influenced the practice of the New Testament writers and it would, therefore, be imprudent to attach any significance to the use of either term without deliberate reference to the context. It is thus the context alone that must determine how a

[2]cf. Isaiah 42:19; 44:1-2; 44:21; 45:4.

particular use of a word should be understood.

This confusion has obscured the significance of the repeated use Paul makes of the term *doulos*. It has normally been seen as a reference to a bondslave, someone without legal standing or personal claims, someone owned by another, since that is what the *doulos* was in Graeco-Roman society. This connection assumes two fundamental points. First, that the Roman idea of *doulos* was the same as Paul's concept, and secondly, that Paul's concept was the same as the Old Testament concept. This latter connection must be assumed to exist in Paul's thinking in that his understanding of *doulos* is normally understood to be the same as that of the *ebed/doulos* in the LXX. However, it is a point in dispute as to whether Israel ever experienced, amongst her own people, slavery in the classical Greek or Roman sense.

De Vaux summarises the general picture:

Certain writers, and especially Jewish scholars, have denied that real slavery ever existed in Israel; at least they maintain Israelites were never reduced to slavery. There is a semblance of justification for this view if we compare Israel with classical antiquity. In Israel and the neighbouring countries there never existed those enormous gangs of slaves which in Greece and Rome continually threatened the balance of social order. Nor was the position of the slave ever so low in Israel and the ancient East as in Republican Rome, where Varro could define a slave as 'a sort of talking tool', 'instrumenti genus vocale'. The flexibility of the vocabulary may also be deceptive. Strictly speaking *ebed* means slave, a man who is not his own master and is in the power of another. The king, however, had absolute power, and consequently the word *ebed* also means the King's subjects, especially his mercenaries, officers and ministers; by joining his service they had broken off their social bonds. By a fresh extension of meaning, the word became a term of courtesy. We may compare it with the development of its equivalents 'servant' in English or 'serviteur' in French, both derive from *servus*, a slave. Moreover, because a man's relations with God are often conceived on the model of his relations with his earthly sovereign, it became a title for pious men, and was applied to Abraham, Moses, Joshua or David, and finally to the mysterious Servant of Yahweh. By 'slave' in the strict sense we mean a man who is deprived of his freedom, at least for a time, who is bought and sold, who is the property of a master, who makes use of him as he likes; in this sense there were slaves in Israel and some were Israelites.[3]

[3] de Vaux, *Israel*, 80.

De Vaux then proceeds to make comparison between the Semitic form of slavery and the Graeco-Roman form, to show how the former was much more controlled and humane.

However de Vaux fails to distinguish the essential difference between the Hebrew slave, who is sold into the possession of another, and the slave of Yahweh. It is not merely the status of the owner. The essential difference is one of covenant. The king was the *ebed* of Yahweh because he had been elected, called and appointed to that office, and not because of anything less.[4] The ministers of the king in turn represented Yahweh and fulfilled the purpose of the covenant, to establish righteousness. To fail to see this is to miss the whole point of the *ebed* of Yahweh. In social terms it would be equivalent to seeing little difference between the role of a housekeeper and the role of a housewife in Western society today. It would also be foolish to think that the role of the housekeeper could simply evolve into the role of the housewife. Language may evolve, but a covenant relationship does not; it requires a decisive act of commitment and acceptance.

Ambiguity in Old Testament theology inevitably leads to ambiguity in New Testament theology, and indeed this is the very thing we find. For example, Barrett notes an aspect of the problem when, in commenting on Romans 1:1, he says:

> Paul describes himself in the first instance as a slave of Jesus Christ. This is a common term with him (cf especially Gal. i.10; Phil. i.1), imitated also by other New Testament writers (James i.1; 2 Pet. i.1; Jude i). It is particularly appropriate to an apostle, but can be used of any Christian (cf. vi.22); that is, Paul begins by describing himself as a Christian before he goes on to mention his special status and vocation. The description is more striking in a Greek work, such as this epistle, than in Semitic literature. A Greek did not think of himself as a slave (δουλος) of his ruler or king, nor did he think of himself as the slave of his divine king, or god, or speak of his service to the god as slavery. The Semitic king, however, was a slave owner, and the highest of his ministers could be regarded as his slave (e.g. 1 Sam. viii.17; 2 Sam. xiv.22). The king in turn is God's slave (e.g. 2 Sam. vii.19). Other distinguished members of the theocracy are described in the same terms (e.g. Ps. cv.26, 42; Amos iii.7). Thus Paul, as the slave of Christ, appears to be a member – as the context will show, an outstanding and privileged member – of a people of God analogous with the People of God in the Old Testament.[5]

---

[4]1 Samuel 10:1; 15:1; 2 Samuel 7:8,9.
[5]Barrett, *Romans*, 15-16.

Barrett is suggesting that the Old Testament concept of the servant of Yahweh was based on the analogy of slavery, only elevated from a human situation. But this is not so, as we have seen. Barrett does however move in the right direction when he goes on to say that Paul 'appears as a member of a people of God analogous with the people of God in the Old Testament', but as we have seen, Barrett misunderstands the Old Testament theology of the Servant of God.

If we follow the trend of de Vaux's and Barrett's arguments, and seek to work out a slave concept in the New Testament, there are important questions that must be raised. Are we to conclude that Paul not only claims that he has no rights of his own because he is in bondage to Christ, but also that he is serving Christ against his own will? If Paul is saying he has no rights, how can he look forward to a reward or payment for his labour – 'a crown of life'? The slave concept totally precludes such a possibility. Furthermore, when Paul's use of the term in Romans 6 is examined we come up against these same problems in specific statements. 'Do you know,' he says, 'that when you offer yourselves to someone to obey him as slaves, you are slaves to the one you obey – whether you are slaves to sin, which leads to death, or obedience, which leads to righteousness' (Rom. 6:16). This slavery begins in an act of offering to someone, and the slave is clearly choosing which master he will serve, something that would never arise in the practice of slavery. It may be argued that this is a reference to the Old Testament practice of the slave choosing to stay with his master when the year of jubilee arrives, and that it alludes to the free decision that the slave takes to have his ear bored and be the lifetime possession of his master (Deut. 15:16-17). This argument, however, fails to resolve the problem. First, it moves between Hellenistic or classical concepts and the Semitic concept without any indication as to which practice is being followed in which part of the illustration. Also, the basic meaning of *doulos* is that of one born into slavery. Under the controlled form of 'slavery', which the Old Testament permitted for those having to sell themselves into temporary service to recover from debt, children were not born into permanent slavery. In such a case the 'slave' was released, along with all that was his, in the year of jubilee (Lev. 25:39-43). Finally, at the close of the chapter, Paul states, 'The wages of sin is death, but the gift of God is eternal life through Christ Jesus our Lord' (v. 23). It is unlikely that Paul would speak of a wage being paid in a slave relationship.

New Testament terms

Before we attempt to unravel the information available to us, it will be helpful if we clarify the terms found in the New Testament which speak of Christian service, setting them alongside their corresponding Greek terms and assessing their relevance for our present enquiry.

The first term to note is the verbal form of *doulos*: *douleuō*. What becomes apparent from an examination of the use of this verb throughout the New Testament is that it is never used of unwilling service. It always describes service, regardless of the motive, which may be either moral or immoral, as willingly rendered. The elder son in the parable of the prodigal son says, 'All these years I've been slaving (*douleuō*) for you and never disobeyed your orders' (Luke 15:29). The translators of the NIV may feel justified in rendering *douleuō* as slaving in order to emphasise the bitter feeling of the son at what his unworthy brother is receiving, but he is arguing that it was rightfully his property because the younger son had already taken his portion. In addition he had worked for his father, and what was now being 'misused' he had earned by his devoted work. Paul testifies to the Ephesian elders: 'I served (*douleuō*) the Lord with great humility and with tears' (Acts 20:18). He exhorts the Romans: 'Never be lacking in zeal, but keep your spiritual fervour, serving (*douleuō*) the Lord' (Rom. 12:11).

The use of the verbal form of *doulos* therefore suggests a situation quite different from a bondslave concept. There are other terms which Paul employs in regard to serving, but these relate to tasks to which one is appointed within the Christian community: i.e. *latreuō*, a task done solely for God; *diakonia*, spiritual ministry; and *diakonos*, the position the servant has in relation to those to whom he ministers. The final term is *diakoneō*. It is the verbal form used for the outworking of the position that the *diakonos* holds. So Matthew 20:28: 'The Son of Man did not come to be served, but to serve, and to give his life a ransom for many.'[6]

All these references to the deacon or minister (*diakonos*) pinpoint his position and the work he does. However, they fail to make specific reference to the relationship that existed between him and the Lord he served. These terms have nothing to say on this. In the LXX *doulos* can have a whole range of meanings, from a slave made so

[6]See Matthew 8:15; 27:55; Mark 1:13, 31; 10:45; 15:41; Luke 4:39; Acts 19:22; 2 Corinthians 3:3; 2 Timothy 1:18; Philemon 5; Hebrews 6:10; 1 Peter 1:12; 4:10,11.

by being taken as a prisoner of war, to one who serves Yahweh in the context of the covenant. We have also seen that in the New Testament *doulos* suggests willing service, and that there are also statements made by Paul that seem to conflict with a slave situation.[7]

How then did Paul understand the title *doulos*? Did he see it in some 'adjusted' classical sense, as Barrett suggests, or was there some other perspective from which he viewed it? Paul's claim to be a Hebrew of the Hebrews points not only to competence in the Hebrew language, but also a zeal for the Hebrew culture. What did he intend to convey to those who could not share directly in his training, but had to be taught through the medium of a common language?

For Paul's biographer, so deeply influenced by Paul himself, Paul was not in a classical mould (which would have been the most natural for Luke as a Greek), but a Hebrew theological one.[8] Luke saw Paul's calling to be the shadow of his Master, who so clearly fulfilled Old Testament expectation of the ideal servant. In Acts Paul is constantly robed in the mantle of Christ. Paul is separated to do the messianic covenant work spoken of by Isaiah, to be a light to the nations (Acts 9:15; 13:47). He is rejected, especially by his own countrymen, as was Christ (Acts 9:29; 13:50; 14:19; 17:13; 22:17-21). There is a parallel in the offence of their work. Christ was rejected because he sought to win sinners, Paul because he sought to win Gentiles, who to the Jews were sinners. The preaching of Christ and of Paul produce the same effects on those who did not believe, blindness and hardening, and both outcomes are based on the predicted results of Isaiah's ministry in Isaiah 6:9-10. Paul's vision in the Temple (Acts 22:17,18) is acknowledged by some to be based on Isaiah's own vision. Paul's journey to Jerusalem is certainly paralleled by that which Luke had already recorded of one who set his face like a flint to go up and be betrayed (Luke 9:51; 13:22; 18:31). Both are subjected to similar exhortations to consider the unreasonableness of their

[7]Brown, 'USE', 732-3 acknowledges the difficulty of Paul seeing himself as an abject slave but seeks to resolve the problem by saying that he compared himself to the imperial slaves who represented the interests of the Emperor. 'A slave of the emperor garnered power in a way that almost no other type of slave could.' Brown's argument is that the imperial slave spoke for the Son of God, i.e. the emperor.

[8]Hays, *Echoes*, 14 says: 'To read Paul against this background of inner-biblical exegesis is to understand his place in the stream of tradition in a new way. He saw himself as a prophetic figure, carrying forward the proclamation of God's word as Israel's prophets and sages had always done, in a way that reactivated past revelation under new conditions.'

missions (Luke 13:31; Acts 21:10-14). And finally, like Christ, Paul is misrepresented by the leaders, hounded by the mob and tried by the governor of Jerusalem (Luke 23:1; Acts 25:1, 2). Here the parallel ends, for Christ's death at Jerusalem was foreordained, Paul's was not to die there. What was predetermined for Paul was that he would eventually stand before kings and rulers (Acts 9:15). This he did when finally he arrived in Rome.

This picture of Paul as the servant, in the Hebraic theological sense, is no coincidence. It is supported by Paul's own description of his ministry. He considered his call, described in Galatians 1:15, as being set apart from birth, a call which parallels the Old Testament prophets. In 2 Corinthians Paul was forced to defend his calling as an apostle. In chapters 3–7 he compares the Old and New Covenants and their ministries. In 3:6 Paul states that God 'has enabled us to be ministers of the New Covenant'. In 4:1 he says, 'Since through God's mercy we have this ministry, we do not lose heart.' Paul then proceeds to develop his comparison between the two covenants with reference to the motive of his ministry. He says, 'Christ's love compels us, because we are convinced that one died for all, and therefore all died. And he died for all, that those who live should no longer live to themselves but for him who died for them and was raised again' (2 Cor.5:14-15). This reference to the death of 'once for all' echoes Romans 5:12-19, a passage accepted by some scholars as referring to Isaiah 53. That this Corinthian passage also reflects that same prophetic passage is borne out in that Paul proceeds to speak of the new creation (5:17), which is brought about by this representative death (5:21). This is the very theme of Isaiah, for he too goes on to speak of all things being made new in the context of the New Covenant that the Servant's death establishes (Isa. 65:17). Thus Paul sees his ministry as being to proclaim the fulfilment of all that Isaiah had predicted. He is elevated above the evangelical prophet in that he proclaims the fulfilment, and not just the expectation.

Perhaps the most significant passage of 2 Corinthians is chapter 6. Paul starts the section, which describes the sufferings into which his work brings him, by quoting from the Servant Songs, and concludes it with a further quotation from the Songs (Isa. 49:8; 52:11).

As God's fellow workers we urge you not to receive God's grace in vain
– for he says, 'At the time of my favour I heard you and on the day of

salvation I helped you.' I tell you, now is the time of God's favour, now is the day of salvation (2 Cor. 6:1-2).

As God has said: 'I will live with them and walk among them, and I will be their God, and they will be my people.' 'Therefore come out from them and be separate, says the Lord. Touch no unclean thing, and I will receive you.' 'I will be a Father to you, and you will be my sons and daughters, says the Lord Almighty' (2 Cor. 6:16-18).

It is evident that Paul saw his own ministry as a servant of the New Covenant, as Moses, Isaiah and Israel herself were the servants of the Old Covenant. As the prophets addressed Israel and appealed for fidelity, so Paul appeals to the church at Corinth. The credentials of Paul's ministry is that he is fulfilling all that the suffering servant(s) suffered in their ministry to Israel.

The question is, does Paul see himself in line as a suffering servant because he is an apostle, or because he is a Christian? The importance of this question is this: if it is because he is an apostle, then it follows that his experience of suffering is part of the apostolic office and need not apply to Christians in general. If it is because he is a Christian, then all Christians are called to this same realm of suffering, and so if *doulos* is applied to Christians, as in Romans 6, it is not to be equated with slavery, but with the covenant figure of the Servant mentioned in the Old Testament.

Paul never saw his sufferings as being unique, this is beyond doubt. They were part of the sufferings to which the corporate servant, i.e. the Church, was called:

For you, brothers, became imitators of God's churches in Judea, which are in Christ Jesus. You suffered from your own countrymen the same things those churches suffered from the Jews, who killed the Lord Jesus and the prophets and also drove us out (1 Thess. 2:14-15).

Paul warned those whom he visited during his tour of encouraging the churches that they must through much suffering enter the kingdom of God (Acts 14:22). Clearly he presupposed the inevitability, if not the necessity, of suffering.

This suffering was not something to be merely endured, for it actually formed part of the will of God (2 Thess. 1:4-5). This suffering is in no way vicarious, as was Christ's passion, but it is essentially the same as the sufferings Christ experienced during his ministry of proclamation. Because of this, Paul frequently links his own suffering, and that of other believers, with Christ's. To be God's servants means being rejected by those who insist on walking in darkness.

> Now I rejoice in what was suffered for you, and I fill up in my flesh what is still lacking in regard to Christ's afflictions, for the sake of his body, which is the church. I have become its servant by the commission God gave me to present to you the word of God in its fullness – the mystery that has been kept hidden for ages and generations, but is now disclosed to the saints. To them God has chosen to make known among the Gentiles the glorious riches of the mystery, which is Christ in you, the hope of glory (Col. 1:24-27).

Such suffering is not endured in isolation, for the believer is part of Christ's body, and Christ is the head. 'I am Jesus whom you are persecuting' (Acts 9:5). Again Paul says: 'Its parts should have equal concern for each other. If one part suffers, every part suffers with it; if one part is honoured, every part rejoices with it' (1 Cor. 12:25-26).

For Paul, suffering is not merely a sign of being part of the kingdom of God. It is a means of spiritual maturing and preparation for the glory and splendour of Christ's appearing. This parallels the theme of Isaiah who saw Israel's suffering as necessary for the bringing in of the Messianic Kingdom (Isa. 40:1-10; 54:11-14).

> Not only so, but we also rejoice in our sufferings, because we know that suffering produces perseverance, perseverance character, and character hope. And hope does not disappoint us, because God has poured out his love into our hearts by the Holy Ghost, whom he has given us (Rom. 5:3-5).

> Now if we are children, then we are heirs – heirs of God and co-heirs with Christ if indeed we share in his sufferings in order that we may also share in his glory. I consider that our present sufferings are not worth comparing with the glory that will be revealed in us (Rom. 8:17-18).

There is deep significance in these passages that speak of the suffering of believers. The theme of suffering for the believer in Romans goes back to 5:3-5. Not that that is the first reference to suffering in Romans. In 4:25 Paul has affirmed that Christ 'was delivered over to death for our sins and was raised to life for our justification'.

Some see both 4:25 and 5:15-17 to be reflecting Isaiah 53. Now, if this is so, and Paul links all believers (as he does in 5:12ff.) with the suffering of their Representative, they will not only be his servants (6:13), but will also share his rejection and suffering. This is the theme of 5:3-5 and also of Romans 8. In chapter 8 Paul emphasises the relationship and its blessings. Believers are in Christ; they have no condemnation, but they do share in his sufferings as the suffering servant.

We may also note how Paul links his own suffering with those of other believers: 'I consider that our present sufferings' (8:18); 'the Spirit helps us in our weakness' (8:26); 'if God is for us, who can be against us' (8:31); 'we are more than conquerors' (8:37). This is an attitude quite different from that which Paul adopts towards the Corinthians and Galatians who had moved from the truth of the gospel because of its intellectual or religious offence. There he set his sufferings against their allegedly superior position (2 Cor. 10-11; Gal. 2:17-3:5). He relates to the Thessalonians and the Philippians as he does to the Romans, because they are partakers of the sufferings of the gospel (Rom. 8:22-38; 1 Thess. 2:14f; Phil. 1:29-30).

Furthermore, Paul in this section (8:36) quotes from Psalm 44:22.[9] Examination of this Psalm shows that it summarises the message of Isaiah 40–66, its message being to those suffering in exile. The same historical background is alluded to, and even the same language is used, not in relation to an individual, as in Isaiah 53, but in relation to the nation. Paul seems deliberately to be linking the experience of the Church awaiting the consummation of its salvation with the faithful Jews awaiting their deliverance from exile to return to the place of promise.

That it is no coincidence that Paul selects Psalm 44 is shown by the fact that in Romans 10, where he goes on to describe the work of the Church in proclaiming its message, he quotes from Isaiah 52:7, a passage which presents a similar picture to that painted by Psalm 44,

[9]There is considerable difference of opinion as to the historical setting of the Psalm. The early church fathers of the Antioch school saw it as originating in the Maccabean period, a date also accepted by Calvin. The uncertainty of the date of the Psalm does not affect our thesis, for Dodd, *According*, 133, has shown the method of exegesis followed by the early church was not based on a strictly historical parallel, but on expansion, development and application of the original principle. In this case, the Psalm speaks of God's faithfulness to his people in the midst of judgment, which is a timeless principle spanning both covenants.

but which tells of the work of the faithful remnant, who have waited for God's redemptive act. They are God's servants, chosen to proclaim the message of deliverance and renewal.

> How, then, can they call on the one they have not believed in? And how can they believe in the one whom they have not heard? And how can they hear without someone preaching to them? And how can they preach unless they are sent? As it is written, 'How beautiful are the feet of those who bring good news!' (Rom. 10:14-15).

Bornkamm sets the original passage in Isaiah in its context when he says:

> In its original context the quotation describes the situation of the few who at the time of the exile stayed on in Jerusalem after it was laid waste and eagerly awaited the return of the exiles from Babylon. Watchmen were posted on the heights surrounding the city and looked forward to seeing the forerunners of the return. At long last the first messenger appeared afar off on the mountains. There upon the watchtower the watcher broke into shouts of rejoicing. These passed from mouth to mouth. The forsaken city resounded with jubilation. Their tidings of joy were the dawn of Jerusalem's salvation. This, as Paul sees it, is the condition of the whole world; the message about Christ which sets men free is to sound to the ends of the earth (Rom 10:18) with its citation of Ps 19:5 [EV, 6].[10]

Thus Paul is not only quoting from but actually drawing his theology from the prophecy of Isaiah. As Jerusalem was under judgment for its sin, so is the world. As Yahweh reserved to himself a remnant, so he has done so now. As the task of the remnant, isolated by Isaiah from the nation in its faithlessness and given the title servant, was to announce the restoration, so it is the Church's task to prepare men for that Day. God has put all men, Jew and Gentile alike, under judgment. The true remnant is made up of all who have saving faith, which is what distinguishes the true Jew from the mere physical descendant of Abraham (Rom. 4:12). This argument becomes even clearer when one appreciates Paul's dependence on Isaiah throughout his letter. This is illustrated by the constant use he makes of the prophet to support his argument and of how he uses the quotations as the scaffolding of his letter.

[10]Bornkamm, *Paul*, 165.

If he is so anxious to use the writings of Isaiah in such a credible manner, being so faithful to the original message of the prophet that he merely adjusts the chronological perspective as to the timing of fulfilment, then we ought to expect him also to have remained faithful to Isaiah's concept of servanthood, and that is what we have found. The threefold use of the 'servant' in the Old Testament, found with particular clarity in Isaiah, is in Paul's mind when he uses *doulos*. Paul sees Christ, the Apostles, and the Church to be cast in the same mould as Isaiah saw the Messiah, the prophets and Israel.[11]

The Servant and Jesus

It has long been recognised that Isaiah 53 is a key text for Evangelical theology. It has been seen to be the controlling Old Testament text for interpreting Jesus' death as a vicarious atonement. The main problem with this argument has been that Isaiah 53 has been so sparsely used in the New Testament. A text of such importance quoted so little is rejected as being foundational for the early church's theology.

I want to suggest that there was a deliberate avoidance of this text by the New Testament writers. This was not because they did not view Jesus' death as a vicarious atonement, for they certainly did. Despite this they avoided using this key text for interpreting the death of Jesus. This was not because they had not noticed its rich suggestiveness, nor because they were not interested in the subject. The reason they avoided its use is clear once the doctrine of the servant has been understood. As we have just seen, the servant role

---

[11]The dependence of the New Testament writers upon the Old Testament for their interpretation of history is summed up by Dodd, *According*, 109 and 128: 'It must be conceded that we have before us a considerable intellectual feat. The various scriptures are actually interpreted along lines already discernible within the Old Testament Canon itself in pre-Christian Judaism – in many cases, I believe, lines which start from their first historical intention – and these are carried forward to fresh results. They interpret and apply the Old Testament upon the basis of a certain understanding of history, which is substantially that of the prophets themselves. Though not stated explicitly in the New Testament, it is everywhere presupposed. History, upon this view, or at any rate the history of the people of God, is built upon a certain pattern corresponding to God's design for man, His creature. It is a pattern, not in the sense of a kind of master-plan imposed upon the order of human life in this world by the Creator Himself, a plan which man is not at liberty to alter, but within which his freedom works. It is a pattern, disclosed 'in divers parts and divers manners' in the past history of Israel, that the New Testament writers conceive to have been brought into full light in the events of the gospel story, which they interpret accordingly.

was not limited to Jesus, but was shared by the whole people of God. It was this fact that made the text impossible to use for the early church. The apostles knew that if they used it to interpret the significance of the death of Jesus the Servant, then it would inevitably be used to interpret the significance of the sufferings of the church, the corporate servant of the Lord. If the Servant's sufferings were vicarious, then so were the church's, for she also was a servant. This was far too great a price for the early church to pay for using a text that would have naturally spoken to them, as it has to countless millions throughout the church's history, of the suffering of the Servant.

In saying the above I am not suggesting that either Jesus or the apostles had no theology of vicarious atonement, only that they purposely avoided using this most suggestive text for their model. In fact, they did not need to use it, for as we will soon see, they had a much more powerful and totally uncomplicated model to use: the Passover. We shall see as this work proceeds that in this model, neglected so long by New Testament scholars, lies the paradigm, used by both Jesus and the apostles, to interpret his death.

Conclusion

Thus I conclude that our study has identified a fundamental error in the understanding of scholars regarding the use and meaning of *doulos* in the New Testament. The traditional Hellenistic setting in which *doulos* is set has been seen to be inadequate to explain the theological implications which surround its use. A Semitic setting, however, proves itself authentic for interpreting many of the concepts where Paul has allegedly been lacking in clarity. Paul, nor indeed any Christian, is not a slave of Christ, but is a servant with all of the dignity and privileges that such a calling carries.

In this study we have so far observed how Paul read and used the Old Testament Scriptures. In this chapter we have seen that, having been conditioned by a basically Hellenistic humanistic worldview, we must make every effort to free ourselves from unrecognised presuppositions that have enslaved Paul in a Greek prison. This is not a challenge for only one school of theology, but for all. Even those who have sought to acknowledge Paul's dependence on the Old Testament have often failed to realise the extent to which they have been influenced by this Greek view of Paul's thinking.

Section Two

Passover and Community

Chapter Five

The Paschal Community and the Body of Sin

The Exodus was not of an individual Jew, but of the Jewish people as a community. Obviously it was individual Jews who benefited, but it was essentially a corporate event. Likewise, although each individual Christian has shared individually in the redemptive benefits of Christ's death, it is not historically an individual experience. The description of salvation that Paul and, I would argue, the rest of the New Testament writers give is about the salvation of God's people, corporately. It is this corporate salvation that I want to explore in the next two chapters.

The focus of Romans 6 is not individualistic, as is so often claimed, but corporate. I will argue in chapter seven that baptism in this context does not refer to individual initiation, but rather to the creation of the believing community as the body of Christ. If this interpretation is accepted, then it will lead to reappraising the meaning of what Paul meant when he said, 'that the body of Sin might be destroyed' (6:6). The corporate introduction to this statement, if baptism is corporate, requires that we revisit the statement of verse 6. The Jews died to the reign of Pharaoh through their deliverance during the night of the Passover. Is there any dependence on this model when Paul speaks of Christians having died to Sin?

In his *New Testament Theology*, Rudolf Bultmann argued against the then prevailing consensus that Paul's view of man was Greek, and claimed that it was in fact Hebraic. As a result of this reappraisal he claimed that when Paul spoke of 'the body', in the majority of cases the reference to the term should be extended to include the whole personality of man. This was a distinct advance in understanding, for Bultmann argued that Greek thinking limited the term *sōma* (body) to the corpse of man. Bultmann had argued that Jewish thinking was not analytical, and examination of the use of *sōma* in Jewish literature showed that it was used in speaking of the whole of man, including his personality or self. Bultmann's argument was presented to the wider English-speaking world by Robinson in his work, *The Body, a Study in Pauline Anthropology*. Bultmann's argument was

85

convincing enough to enable Best to say that it is now generally
recognised that in his anthropology Paul is a Jew rather than a Greek.[1]

Detailed discussion

The following section will probably only interest those who are
acquainted with the literature covering the topic. It is provided for
those who want to follow this discussion and have a response to the
prevailing position. For those not interested in following this argument
you may reasonably leave the text at this point and rejoin it at the
heading 'corporate solidarities' a few pages on.

Robinson was able to make use of Bultmann's work to support a
sacramental concept of the body of Christ. Robinson pursued what
seemed to be the inevitable logic of the principle of Semitic
completeness in the expression 'body'. He argued that the
ecclesiastical body of Christ *is* the whole Christ. Indeed, for Robinson
the body of Christ (the church) *is* Christ. However, Gundry discounted
the evidence presented by Robinson as being both inadequate and
badly evaluated.[2] He claimed that there was no holistic meaning behind
the biblical usage of *sōma* in either the Old Testament or the New
Testament. By his counter-argument Gundry attempted to block
Robinson's road to a sacramental ecclesiology.

It is not the purpose of this chapter to make a detailed comparison
between the two positions outlined above, other than where they have
a bearing on the theme being considered. The aspect to which we
shall therefore pay attention is the use of 'body' in a corporate context.

Robinson argued that when Paul wrote of the body of Christ, as in
Ephesians 5:30, he was not intending that 'body' should be understood
as a mere simile.[3] It speaks of organic unity, not only of the body, but
of the body with its head. Robinson claimed that the concept is
fundamental to the understanding of Paul's theology of the church.
The church is not merely a body of people in subjection to Christ, but
is actually *the* body of Christ. This is shown to be Paul's thinking in
the accounts of his conversion.[4] Jesus' question, 'Why do you
persecute me?,' demonstrates for Robinson the existence of an organic
unity. In persecuting Christ's people Paul was literally persecuting
Christ himself.

[1]Best, *Body, passim.*
[2]Gundry, *Soma in Biblical Theology.*
[3]Robinson, *Body*, 66-7.   [4]*op. cit.* 58.

Gundry discounted this argument. He identified Acts 9:4-5; 22:7-8 and 26:14-15 as the fountainhead of Robinson's argument and said:

> it is a long step from persecuting Christ in Christians to a sacramental literalism in which Christians are the physical body of Christ.... If the dominical saying 'He who receives you receives me' (Matt. 10:40; cf.18:5; Mark 9:37; Luke 9:48; 10:16; John 13:20) does not imply fusion with Christ's physical body – and who would dare to say that the parallel clause 'He who receives me receives him who sent me' (cf. also John 5:23; 12:44-5; 14:9-11) implies a physical fusion between Christ and the Father? – then neither do the words to Paul on the Damascus road need to imply the kind of sacramental literalism which is drawn out of them.[5]

Gundry noted how Robinson's sacramental view had forced him to equate physical resurrection to baptism, something which Gundry described as un-Pauline. It led, he claimed, to the contradiction of the same physical body both dying and rising concurrently. Gundry saw Robinson as trying to escape the scandal of the physical resurrection, but 'by a tour de force of literalizing the corporate body of Christ and limiting the resurrection to the formation, growth, and final revelation of the body'.[6]

The main weakness of Robinson's argument, which Gundry does not explore, is that to achieve his sacramental literalism, which he then used as a basis to establish his universalism, he has to do a complete reversal on the very foundation upon which he had built. Robinson says:

> The fundamental idea for which Paul is arguing may be viewed as a reversal of the principle familiar to the Old Testament, that the remnant, or ultimately the one, can represent many. This principle Paul sees was central to the divine operation under the old covenant, according to which a vicarious minority, progressively reduced by sin, carried God's purpose for the whole world.... Rather, it is the many who represent the one. 'For as many of you as were baptised into Christ have put on Christ...Ye are all one man in Christ Jesus. And if ye are Christ's, then ye are Abraham's seed, heirs according to promise' (Gal. 3:27-29). The many, to whom no limit can be put either to race or class (Gal. 3:28), now constitute the one (Gal. 3:16); but it is a unity which is inclusive rather than exclusive, representative, not simply vicarious.[7]

[5]Gundry, *Soma,* 240
[6]*op. cit.* 241
[7]Robinson, *Body,* 61.

In claiming that universalism was a part of Paul's thinking Robinson was following Dodd in his reasoning.[8] By claiming that the emphasis is now inclusive rather than selective, as was the Old Testament principle, these two scholars were being unfaithful to Paul. They were claiming that Paul was able to make fundamental changes to the outlook in which he had been nurtured and trained. Such a change will have to be demonstrated, for many recognise Paul's debt to the Old Testament. The fact that Paul so clearly follows the Old Testament concept of representation in Romans 5, which speaks not only of the old order, but also of the new, ought to suggest caution in accepting Robinson's interpretation. The point of the passages that he quotes from Galatians is not that there is no distinction within mankind between regenerate and unregenerate, but that within the family of God, no distinction can be drawn between man or woman, Jew or Greek, for *they* are all one in Christ Jesus.

The tears Paul shed for those he saw as lost (Acts 20:19; Col. 1:28-29) and his belief that Christ at his appearing would take vengeance upon those who did not repent (2 Thess. 1:8, 9) indicate that Paul continued to see a deep division through the human race. There is no reversal of the Old Testament principle, as Robinson argues, but a visible expansion of it. The remnant are collected from beyond Israel and these make up the true people of God who become one new man (Eph. 2:15-16; Col. 3:9-10). Paul taught that both unbelieving Jew and unbelieving Gentile stand under judgement together, as believing Jew and believing Gentile stand in grace together (Gal. 3:22-29). If Robinson wanted to hold to a complete reversal of Hebraic concepts, how could he so fervently assert that Paul can only be understood from the viewpoint of those concepts he himself later rejects to make way for universalism? This same criticism is supported from another perspective by Gundry:

> However much we might wish for universalism, it is another weight too heavy for *sōma* to bear. *Sōma* does not necessarily represent the physical oneness of all men and the entire creation in a salvific destiny. It may rather represent an individuation which at the judgement will separate between those who have done good and those who have done evil (II Cor. 5:10). The corporate use is limited to believers. Whether or not all will become members of that body through faith depends on factors other than the use of *sōma*.[9]

[8]Dodd, *Studies*, 83-128.   [9]*Soma*, 243.

Also, it must be pointed out that Robinson's suggestion, that Paul left the Old Testament pattern of the one representing the many so that the many represented the one, is not accurate, for both concepts are inherent in the Old Testament and live comfortably side by side. The concept of corporate solidarity allowed the Jews to see Abraham as representing Israel while at the same time Israel represents Abraham. This is true of other representative figures such as Moses, David and the Servant. Thus there is no departure or development in Paul's theological thinking, as suggested by Robinson, but the clear consistent use of his Old Testament theological background using concepts which are naturally at home in Jewish thought.

Corporate solidarities

Despite these reservations expressed about Robinson's work, there has been a development which has been neither adequately appreciated nor discussed. The work of Bultmann and Robinson has caused many scholars to reinterpret Paul's statement in Romans 6:6 where he says: 'For we know that our old self was crucified with him so that the body of sin might be rendered powerless, that we should no longer be slaves to Sin.' Traditionally the term 'body of Sin' has been understood as sin that indwells man. Robinson argued that the Semitic use of 'body' points to an important principle of human existence that directs us back to man's interdependence. He claimed that many of the problems of Western society were caused by ignoring this principle of solidarity and interdependence. Neglecting the concept of solidarity has resulted in the break-up of traditional social structures, leaving modern Western man severed from his roots. Robinson argued that the biblical concept of the solidarity of man as expressed in the understanding of 'body' helps man to identify his significance and role in society. He reasoned that the multinational corporations, which impersonally determine the existence of hundreds of millions of people throughout the world, are an expression of this all-embracing solidarity: 'This is the "body of sin and death", in which he is involved at every level of his being, physical, political and even cosmic. The great corporations of modern society are expressions of this all embracing solidarity.'[10]

Robinson warned that Western man was tempted to seek salvation by exalting the individual against the collective or by attempting to

[10]Robinson, *Body*, 8-9.

withdraw from the body of socio-historical structures. Paul's answer to this dilemma, says Robinson, was to argue that solidarity is the divinely ordained structure in which personal life is to be lived. This God-appointed corporate structure is the church, which is the product of the redemptive work of Christ.

Robinson was not consistent in his understanding of the term 'body of Sin', because he later abandoned equating it with the solidarity of fallen man, and returned to the traditional individual interpretation when he wrote: 'The body of sin and humiliation must be done away (Rom. 6:6).'[11] The context of the statement leaves no doubt that Robinson was speaking of the individual's body.

The earlier corporate interpretation of Bultmann and Robinson has been followed (not necessarily in its sacramental application) by a number of scholars. I give their references in their appropriate contexts to assist in a fuller understanding of how they have arrived at their interpretation. First, we note the exposition of Herman Ridderbos:

> the concrete mode of existence of sinful man, can sometimes be identified with sin as the 'body of sin' (Rom. 6:6.), the 'body of flesh' (Col. 2:11), the 'body of death' (Rom. 7:24). Accordingly, the life from Christ by the Holy Spirit can be typified as a 'doing away with the body of sin', 'putting off of the body of the flesh', 'putting to death the earthly members', 'deliverance from the body of this death' (Rom. 6:6; Col. 2:11; 3:5; Rom. 7:24).... All these expressions are obviously not intended of the body itself, but of the sinful mode of existence of man.[12]

> What is intended by this body of sin is, as we have already been able to determine in another context, the present human mode of existence ruled by sin. Of this bondage to sin the cross and the death of Christ have made an end.[13]

> That sin, as it were, lays hold of the body 'from without' and thus subjects the entire man to itself as a slave.... All sorts of expressions and pronouncements in Paul's epistles give evidence of this 'direct' connection: 'Sin-body' that must be done away with, so that 'we' no longer serve sin. **Here the** body, in its being ruled by sin.[14]

[11]*op. cit.* 32.
[12]Ridderbos, *Outline*, 229f.
[13]*op. cit.* 208.
[14]*op. cit.* 194.

Torrance is even more explicit in his understanding of 'the body of Sin'. He says:

> in his death, the many who inhered in him died too, and indeed the whole body of sin, the whole company of sinners into which he incorporated himself to make their guilt and their judgement his own, that through his death he might destroy the body of sin, redeem them from the power of guilt and death, and through his resurrection raise them up as the new Israel.[15]

This corporate view of 'the body of Sin' is also shared by Bruce who writes:

> This 'body of sin' is more than an individual affair, it is rather that old solidarity of sin and death which all share 'in Adam', but which has been broken by the death of Christ with a view to the creation of the new solidarity of righteousness and life of which believers are made part 'in Christ'.[16]

It is perhaps T.W. Manson who came closest to the thesis being worked out here. He questioned the traditional assumption that in the phrase 'body of Sin' the term 'of Sin' is a genitive of quality; he argued that it 'does not yield a very good sense'. He took it to be a possessive genitive, and said, 'It is perhaps better to regard "the body of sin" as the opposite of "the body of Christ". It is the mass of unredeemed humanity in bondage to the evil power. Every conversion means that the body of sin loses a member and the body of Christ gains one.'[17]

Manson is supported by Nygren who, because he saw the earlier part of Romans 6 to refer to water baptism, was not able to go beyond the conclusions of others. He says of Romans 6:6: 'There is another body that must die. Paul speaks of it expressively as the "body of sin".... it is this body to which man formerly belonged when he was

---

[15]Torrance, *Reconstruction*, 203, see also 198. However, Torrance contradicts this statement elsewhere saying that it is the church that is the body of sin. He says: 'After baptism we see the church as the Body of sin or sinners, into which Jesus Christ incorporated Himself to be the Saviour of the Body. After the Lord's Supper where that union is confirmed, He immersed Himself in sacrificial death for Sin, that the Body of sin being destroyed He might raise it again, a glorious Body in His resurrection' ('Atonement', 249).

[16]Bruce, *Romans*, 38.

[17]Manson, 'Romans,' 945.

under the dominion of sin and death.'[18]

Nygren, commenting on Romans 5, says, 'If we begin with such sociological alternatives as "individual or collectivity", we shall not arrive at what Paul has in mind. The only way to understand him is to take him seriously, on the one hand, the idea of the body of sin and of death of which we are by nature ("in Adam") members, and on the other hand, the body of Christ into which we are incorporated by faith and baptism.'[19]

Although not emphasising the corporate, Keck's remarks fit the picture that we are noting:

> The Adamic situation is deeper than being wrongly related to God and so needs more than a rectified relationship. Sin entails also participation in a domain marked by Sin's enslaving power, whose consequence is death. Thus, the exposition of Adam in 5:12-21 prepares for 6:1–7:6, where Paul argues that freedom from this yoked tyranny of sin and death is through participation in an alternative domain – Christ's death and resurrection.[20]

Gundry dissents from the consensus indicated above regarding the corporate meaning of 'body' in Romans 6.6: 'The body of sin is not equivalent to "flesh", it is the body which sin, or the flesh, dominates, as in Romans 8:12-13.'[21] He then goes on to compare it with Romans 7:24: 'The body of death is not "flesh" in the sense of sin itself; it is the physical body destined to die because within its members dwells the law of sin and death.'[22] And again: 'Just as Christ's mortal body had to give way to an immortal one, so also the believer's "body of sin". *to sōma tēs hamartias* therefore does not refer to an abstract mass of sin, to the system of sinful desires, to sin personified as a sphere of power in the old Aeon, or to the sinful personality, but concretely to the physical body which has been dominated by sin, is doomed to destruction, and will receive resurrection.'[23]

Gundry is somewhat reluctantly supported by Moo, who, commenting on the proposal of others that the term body of Sin should be seen as corporate, stated that:

---

[18]Nygren, *Romans*, 234.
[19]*op. cit.* 306.
[20]Keck,'Romans', 25.
[21]*Soma*, 39. See also Mauro, *Wretched*, 74.
[22]*op. cit.* 39.
[23]*op. cit.* 58.

This view should not be dismissed as quickly as it sometimes is because it does explain several things. The lack of the possessive pronoun in the clause ("our old man was crucified...so that the body of sin...with the purpose that we should not serve sin"), the singular *sōma* and the fact that this *sōma* is the subject of the passive verb 'be destroyed' or 'rendered impotent'. Nevertheless, this view suffers from the fatal defect of insufficient lexical support. The text would have to offer more reasons than these to substantiate so rare (for the NT) a use of the word.[24]

In reality Moo's concerns are not well founded. There is no lexical support for the popular view of 'the body of Sin' either, so that also would have to be rejected. Furthermore, the context, if my exegesis is accepted, is corporate, flowing from the clearly corporate imagery in chapter 5. The corporate interpretation does have far more to offer than the individual understanding which is in fact the understanding that needs to be demonstrated, for the traditional understanding depends on the meaning *given* to this one verse and it has no support from the overall argument that Paul is making.

Gundry's rejection of the corporate meaning of 'body of Sin' was the result of an error in his methodology. Having argued that *sōma is not holistic*, he used the evidence he collated to show that 'body of Sin' *is not corporate*. The two meanings are, however, quite unrelated. Evidence for rejecting the holistic interpretation cannot be transferred to a corporate meaning. The two domains and meanings are quite distinct. In fact Gundry acknowledged this when he considered the use of *sōma* in 1 Corinthians 6:19-20. There he dismissed a corporate understanding for *sōma* because he claimed that the Corinthians would not have understood Paul, for he does not introduce the topic of the church being the body of Christ until chapter 12. He did, however, acknowledge that if it could be shown that *sōma* was corporate, that is, refers to the church rather than the individual body, then his argument for rejecting a holistic interpretation for *sōma* would no longer be relevant: 'An ecclesiastical use of *sōma* in these verses would of course eliminate them from the debate over the anthropological meaning of *sōma*.'[25]

In rejecting the holistic anthropological meaning of *sōma*, Gundry thought that he had given sufficient evidence for rejecting a sacramental meaning for 'the body of Christ'. This mistake arose

[24]Moo, *Romans*, 1: 392.
[25]Gundry,, *Soma*, 60.

because he failed to appreciate that he was confusing the corporate usage, which has a federal origin in that Christ is the head/lord of his body, the church, and the holistic understanding, which has nothing to do with federalism. Gundry also confused the imagery of 1 Corinthians 6, which we shall shortly see is also corporate. This error was not introduced by Gundry, but by Bultmann, and not identified by succeeding scholars. Bultmann confused the holistic meaning which he wanted to establish in the use of the language of 'body' and assumed that the same holistic meaning occurred when the term was used to describe the church as the body of Christ. Failure to recognise that the terms had distinctively different usages meant that when the holistic meaning was rejected it was thought that the issue of the sacramental use, and therefore of its corporate meaning in such passages as Romans 6:6, was settled. In fact, no such case had been made, for it would have required a totally different argument to achieve this.

Gundry confused definitions; Robinson, however, overlooked the consequences of his own sacramental interpretation of the body of Christ. If his claim that the body of Christ *is* Christ, then it follows that the body of Sin *is* Sin – not just its realm of rule and power, but one with Satan, and to be identified as Sin, or Satan incarnate in unredeemed human life. It may be this that Gundry sees when he says: **'does not** refer.....to sin personified as a sphere of power in the old Aeon.'[26]

It is crucially important to realise that it is one thing to reject a holistic/sacramental interpretation, either of the body of Sin or of the body of Christ, and quite another thing to reject concepts of solidarity that are widely accepted as a part of Semitic thought. Such a position, of fully understanding the concept of solidarity, will leave us with all the benefits of both extremes. In this concept there is no confusion of identity, but neither is there any loss of unity.

In fact, Gundry's study has been challenged by Ziesler.[27] He has shown that there are clear cases in the LXX of *sōma* being used to describe the total person rather than merely the corpse. This adds weight to the case I am making but my case does not depend on it.

Robinson, Ridderbos, Bruce, Manson and Nygren came to accept various degrees of solidarity inherent in the term *the body of Sin*.

---

[26]*op. cit.* 58.
[27]Ziesler, 'Septuagint',133-45.

These conclusions came from their reading of Bultmann's work, and their own independent studies of the Pauline letters. Unfortunately, the corporate meaning of 'body of Sin' has become entangled in a debate over the claim that 'body' was used holistically, while the two issues are quite separate. But even if the corporate meaning of 'body of Sin' is accepted as valid, it is still questionable whether the concept can be transferred from one section of the Pauline corpus to another, for, some argue, Paul's concepts developed and even changed. The important question therefore is whether it can be shown from the context of Romans 6 that Paul himself had this corporate concept in mind.

A corporate perspective makes better sense of the ongoing argument that Paul is advancing in his letter to the Romans. It is the inevitable consequence of an argument that begins in chapter 5 in which the central theme is the solidarity of man with his head, whether Adam or Christ. This corporate thinking is evident in the corporate baptism into Christ in 6:1ff. The corporate understanding of 'the body of Sin' is the necessary link preparing for the corporate understanding of chapter 7, which has in recent years become a widely accepted principle for interpreting the chapter.[28]

There is other evidence that is relevant beside the exegesis that has been offered. The reference in Romans 6:19 to the members being yielded to unrighteousness makes better sense when it is seen as a reference to corporate membership, i.e. relating to the discipline of those who are failing to make a break with the service of Sin. It is therefore not about the individual controlling his members but an appeal to the church to discipline its members.

Also, in 6:6 Paul refers to 'putting off the old man'. Once again this has traditionally been seen as a reference to the sinful self that dominated the life of the believer in the pre-converted state. However, the same terminology is used in Ephesians 2:15 where Paul says 'to create in himself one new man out of the two, thus making peace'. He then goes on to say in 4:22-23, 'put off your old self (*anthrōpos* – man), which is corrupted by its deceitful desires; to be made new in the attitude of your minds, and put on the new self (*anthrōpos* – man), created to be like God in true righteousness and holiness.'

The exhortation is parallel to that in Romans 6:6ff. Thus, the new

---

[28]See Wright, *Messiah*, 146; Moo, 'Israel', 122-35; Westerholm, *Law*, 181-89; and Trudinger, 'Autobiographical,' 173ff.

man, which Paul exhorts the Romans to put on, is corporate, for 'the new man' in Ephesians is the church, and the two who have been united to form this new man are the believing Jews and the believing Gentiles.

This corporate understanding is further supported by Colossians 3:9-15:

> Do not lie to each other, since you have taken off your old self (*anthrōpos* – man) with its practices and have put on the new self (*ton neon* – the new), which is being renewed in knowledge in the image of its Creator. Here there is no Greek or Jew, circumcised or uncircumcised, Barbarian, Scythian, slave or free, but Christ is all, and is in all. Therefore, as God's chosen people, holy and dearly loved, clothe yourselves with compassion, kindness, humility, gentleness and patience. Bear with each other and forgive whatever grievances you may have against one another. Forgive as the Lord forgave you. And over all these virtues put on love, which binds them all together in perfect unity. Let the peace of Christ rule in your hearts, since as members of one body you were called to peace.

The realm where distinctions are abolished (here there is no Greek or Jew, v. 11) is clearly corporate. This is indicated by two considerations. First, 'here' is clearly the realm where all distinctions are abolished, and this is the new man. Second, the meaning of the one body into which they were called (v. 15) is obviously corporate. These descriptions of corporateness are in the context of the description of the old and new self (vv. 9, 10). The rendering of *anthrōpos* as *self* by the NIV and *sarx* as *flesh* in the AV has inevitably promoted the individualistic understanding and confused the mind of the English reader. Furthermore, that Paul's exhortation is corporate is shown in that he appeals to them, 'as God's chosen people clothe yourselves' (v. 12).

Thus, identifying the imagery of the old and new man as being corporate, and appreciating that it is part of the description of the 'body of Sin' in Romans 6:6, along with the other considerations we have presented, establishes a corporate meaning for the term the 'body of Sin'.

Romans 7

The correctness of this corporate interpretation is borne out in the seventh chapter of Romans. Traditionally the passage about Paul's struggle with Sin has been interpreted in an understandably individualistic way. However, in recent years there has been a growing awareness that Paul is either acting out the role of mankind in its bondage to Sin, or representing the Jewish nation as it grapples with the consequences of the giving of the law (Rom. 5:20). Either way, the perspective moves away from an individualistic understanding to that of a corporate one. Paul, if our argument so far is valid, is showing that the Exodus Israel experienced under Moses never brought her into the freedom from Sin that she professed to have received. The law was given to make this clear. All the expectations of the redemption from Egypt turned to horror as the sincere Jew realised that the deliverance had been nothing more than political. The covenant people still share in the existence of Sin and Death, as do all other people. That Paul is playing out the experience of Israel is suggested by the reference that 'I was alive without the law'. Few would dispute that Paul was brought up under the law as a devout Jew, so this would not fit in with his own experience. It does, however, fit the experience of Israel, released from slavery in Egypt, coming to Sinai and receiving not the crowning experience of her freedom, but the sentence of a condemning law. However it is also true that Adam once lived without the law and when it was given he experienced death as a result of disobedience. The fact that the argument is rooted in chapter 5 with its Adamic basis ought to warn us of the danger of restricting the story to Israel.

This corporate dimension is encountered in the illustration found in 7:1-6. The passage has perplexed most commentators. The main problem has been to discover what the law of the husband referred to. The fact is that the context of the illustration has not been appreciated. If Paul is using the Exodus as the model for explaining Christian salvation, then we can begin to break into what the illustration is saying. In the original Exodus the husband was Yahweh who redeemed Israel from Egypt to be his bride. In the New Exodus setting, the new husband is Christ. In the Exodus from Egypt the deliverance was from the power of Pharaoh, in the New Exodus it is from the power of a former husband. Clearly the former husband is symbolised by what Pharaoh and Egypt represent, which has to be Sin, as is made clear in 6:14. The old husband is Sin, i.e. Satan. Thus the law of Sin and Death is the law of the old husband whose power, i.e. that of the covenant, has been broken through Christ's representative death. When it is appreciated that there is a New Exodus motif, we can see that Paul is working out how Yahweh can take the church as his bride, as he had taken Israel. It can happen only if man's covenant with Sin can be broken, and this can only be done by death. Of course the illustration is not about the experience of the individual Christian but about the Christian community. The Old Testament salvation from Egypt was not about individuals but about a community, which of course was made up of individuals. The corporate view is further upheld in that the individual is never spoken of as being the bride of Christ: it is always the church (2 Cor. 11:2; Eph. 5:25-33; Rev. 19:7). To try to fit the argument into an individual perspective is to take it out of its original context, a procedure that is bound to produce exegetical problems.

The deliverance from Egypt had not been a deliverance from Sin. Paul is insisting that the Jews are but 'a subclass of man in Adam'.[29] The old relationship established in Adam's disobedience had not been cancelled by the Exodus. Their privileged status had not brought them out of the kingdom of darkness. A greater Exodus must take place to bring about freedom from the tyranny of Sin. Thus in the illustration the old husband is Sin (Satan) and the new husband is Christ. This interpretation gains support from the text. Paul's statement that he is sold under Sin (7:14) is not referring to the purchase of a slave, but to wife purchase, commonly practised in the ancient world.[30]

It might be argued that the reference to 'a law at work within my members' in 7:23 overturns the argument previously made until it is appreciated that the reference to members has a corporate dimension. It does not denote a highly dualistic understanding in Paul's thinking, but a corporate one, so basic to Semitic thinking. Paul speaks not only as the representative of the Jewish people, but also as of mankind. He knows that they, as individuals, are members of the body of Sin, and are bound under the covenant of Sin. He speaks as one who reviews the history of Adam, whose sin has brought all of his offspring into membership of the kingdom of darkness, the body of Sin. It is similar to the use of 'members' in 6:12. There the appeal is not to the individual not to use parts of his body for the service of sin, even though it would be a natural further application, but to the congregation not to allow any member to serve Sin. It is therefore corporate and about the purity of the community.

[29]Wright, *Messiah*, 141.
[30]For bride purchase in the ancient world, see Balsdon, *Women*, 179-80.

There is no way out of this bondage to Satan, which the law of Sin secures unless death cancels the relationship. Paul cries in desperation, acting out the despair of Adam and his descendants, as well as his own, for a deliverer who will break this solidarity with Sin and Death (7:24). It is a cry that all seekers, both Jews and Gentiles, will make. It comes as the result of seeing that they are in need of the same mercy as the rest of humanity who are also under judgement because of their oneness with Adam.

When one links Romans 7:25a with Colossians 1:12, these passages establish that Paul is not primarily talking of his own *sōma*, but the *sōma* of Sin as identified in Romans 6:6. He is reasoning in terms of the Second Exodus from the kingdom of darkness which he calls 'the body of Sin' or 'the body of this death'.

Romans 8

It is the relief of acquittal that marks the opening of the eighth chapter. Paul states that the longed-for salvation has been realised, and this is not on the grounds of what man must do but on what God has done.

This deliverance is not according to the flesh, but according to the Spirit (8:1). This freedom is not through the keeping of the law, but is based on a perfect sacrifice for sin (8:3). This statement clearly picks up all the other cultic statements made earlier in the letter, and emphasises that the sacrifice was the Son of God, given freely by the Father. It is Christ's death that liberates and brings the children of God out of their bondage. Thus, by entering the very realm of Sin's domain the Son challenged Sin at the point where its (his) power was strongest. Subjecting himself to the full force of Sin's attack, in the realm of human likeness and weakness, but without sin in his own person, he entered into conflict to deliver his own people (8:3). This fulfilled the righteous requirements of the law, for it was to this event that the law and the prophets had pointed (1:2; 3:21). The Exodus under Moses had not been deliverance of the spirit, but of the flesh, of human existence apart from God. No eschatologically profound deliverance had been secured in the Exodus. It pointed to the greater reality that Christ would establish.

When Paul speaks about walking after the flesh, this could mean living in flagrant opposition to the law (Gal. 5:19ff.), but it could equally involve seeking righteousness by a meticulous performance of the law's demands (Phil. 3:3). Such legal righteousness rejected the

divinely appointed way (Rom. 10:1-4). The unbelieving Jew put his
confidence in Moses and the sacrifices of the temple, not in God
(who had set the temple sacrifices aside) and the sacrifice of his Son.
Now the true salvation, from Sin and Death, has been achieved, and
it is through Christ our Passover. Paul insists that there can be no
neutral zone in man's relationship with God (Rom. 8:6). To be at enmity
with God is to reject his purposes. This does not necessarily mean a
deliberate rejection of the law's requirements, but of the law's purposes,
the goal to which it pointed. This is where Paul and his fellow
countrymen stumbled so often. Rather than being guided by the law,
they had made it the goal in itself. It had actually become the barrier
to doing the will of God, for they made its keeping, which they gloried
in, the grounds of their hope of participating in the eschatological
salvation.

The logical conclusion of accepting the above argument is that
Paul sees the relationship between Satan and the members of his
community, the body of Sin, as parallel to that existing between Christ
and his people. This ought not to be too difficult to accept in that the
New Testament is constantly making comparisons between the
members of these two communities that show corresponding
relationships. Believers are citizens of the kingdom of light, unbelievers
of the kingdom of darkness. Believers are the children of God,
unbelievers are the children of the devil. Believers are the servants of
God, unbelievers are the servants of the devil. These parallels ought
to suggest that Paul would not find any difficulty in taking these
comparisons to their ultimate conclusion. Believers are members of
the body of Christ, unbelievers are members of the body of Sin.

But how did Paul, or possibly more accurately, the early church,
since Paul received his gospel, come to such an understanding? To
answer this we must again remind ourselves of the extent of the
influence of the prophet Isaiah on the early church, exemplified in his
being the major propounder of the New Exodus motif.

Apostolic use of the Old Testament

Dodd has identified how the early church made use of blocks of
testimonia.[31] Two references we can easily identify as forming such
a block are Isaiah 28:11 and 16. Clearly as part of a block the verses
circumscribed by these two verses would have been well known by

---

[31]Dodd, *According*, 28-60.

the early church. Indeed, these 'stones passages' are used more than any other Old Testament passage by the New Testament writers to speak about the covenant Yahweh would establish through his Servant (Matt. 21:42-44; Mark 12:10; Luke 20:17; Acts 4:11; Rom. 9:32; 1 Pet. 2:4-6). The verses between these texts tell of the very opposite, the covenant Israel bound herself in as she ran from the claims of Yahweh, a covenant that was made with death. Isaiah said:

> You boast, 'We have entered into a covenant with death, with the graves we have made an agreement. When an overwhelming scourge sweeps by, it cannot touch us, for we have made lies our refuge and falsehood our hiding place.' So this is what the Sovereign Lord says: 'See I lay a stone in Zion, a tested stone, a precious corner stone for a sure foundation; the one who trusts will never be dismayed. I will make justice the measuring-line and righteousness the plumb-line; hail will sweep away your refuge, the lie, and water will overflow your hiding place. Your covenant with death will be annulled; your agreement with the grave will not stand.'

Whitehouse comments that 'The expressions "covenant with death" and "agreement with Hades" are obscure, and various explanations have been offered. On the whole it seems most probable that those are references to the arts of sorcery and necromancy which were largely practised at this time.'[32]

Snodgrass supports this understanding: 'It is likely that Isa xxviii.16 was not always connected with the correction of temple malpractice. In the original context the priests, and the prophets (v.7) and the rulers of the people of Jerusalem who had made a covenant with sheol (vv. 14-15) were the ones to whom the oracles were given.'[33]

Bright is even more specific and sees the passage as addressed to the nobles of Judah who have scorned Isaiah's advice and made a treaty with Egypt, invoking the names of the pagan gods and looking to them for protection.[34] Bright points out that death – *sheol* (*moth*) in verse 15 is also the name of the Canaanite god of the underworld and fertility. He thinks that, since the pact was with Egypt, the reference is probably to Egyptian deities of similar character, such as Osiris or Seth in whose names the pact was sealed. If Bright is right, and this is the background of Paul's thinking in interpreting the passage,

[32]Whitehouse, *Isaiah*, 297.
[33]Snodgrass, '1 Peter', 104.
[34]Bright, *PBC*, 509.

i.e. it refers originally to returning to 'Egyptian' bondage, it is easy to see how natural it would be for it to be utilised to describe the condition unbelievers are in when they have rejected the mercy of Yahweh.

This concept of a covenant with other gods is not unique to Isaiah. Exodus 23:32 warned the Jews not to make covenants with other gods. In this one verse there is enough evidence to establish that the Old Testament saw the possibility of a covenant with other gods than Yahweh. Again this injunction, just like the Isaiah passage, is in an Exodus context.

Furthermore, Snodgrass claims that Isaiah's covenant with death would have been widely understood in Rome.[35] This position is further supported by the observation of Grech that 'Paul's world-picture was not so different from that of Isaiah as to render a hermeneutical translation necessary'.[36]

The covenant referred to by Isaiah is manifestly the very opposite of the covenant of Yahweh. At the time of Isaiah no developed doctrine of Satan existed. Death was the great enemy. It cut man off from the covenant community and from his God. It was therefore natural for Paul to see that he could legitimately expand its reference point to Satan, for he is in reality the enemy man has bound himself to in a covenant relationship. If Rowley is right in his interpretation of the Isaiah 28 passage, then the step from seeing Death as the great enemy to a personal, evil opponent of Yahweh had already been taken by Isaiah himself. The unbelieving Jews had placed themselves in covenant with this sworn enemy of Yahweh, and Paul is merely adapting the theology of this passage, taking it beyond the unbelieving Jews of Isaiah's day and applying it to the whole of mankind. This link, of equating death with Sin, both being personified as Satan, is further supported in that when Paul speaks of the law of the husband in Romans 7:2-3, he then goes on to apply it in Romans 8:1 with the words: 'Therefore, there is no condemnation to those who are in Christ Jesus, because through Christ Jesus the law of the Spirit of life has set me free from the law of sin and death.' This expression, 'the law of Sin and death', parallels sin and death in the manner used in Isaiah's warning. Strictly speaking death should be given a capital, Death.

Can it be shown that Death, like Sin, is a personification of Satan? The Targum certainly makes the equation, identifying the angel of

[35]Snodgrass, '1 Peter', 104.
[36]Grech, 'Testimonia', 322.

death in Exodus 12 with Satan. Also, there are p
Corinthians 15:45-55 and Revelation 20:14 (both argu
passages!), in which Death is personified as the l
destroyed by Christ. Kennedy in presenting the Old '
of Death says:

> They that go down to Sheol cannot praise God. All bonds of intercourse
> with the most high are snapped. Sometimes the dead are described as if
> existing in the under-world almost beneath the sway of another tyrannical
> power. There is a kind of personification of Death, resembling that of the
> Greek Hades, when it is said in Ps. 40:14 "Like sheep they are laid in
> Sheol; death shepherds them."[37]

In a note on the above quotation Kennedy further says:

> In ancient literature it is hard to distinguish between a person and a
> personification. Animistic ideas lie deep in the naive, popular
> consciousness. Bousset, grouping together such passages as Isa. xxv:7f;
> 4 Ezra viii:53; Apoc. Bar. xxi:23; Test. Levi 18; 1 Cor. xv:26, 55, all of which
> treat of the destruction of death at the end, would relate the figures of
> thanatos, Hades (*cf.* Rev. xx:13) and the angel of Hades closely to that of
> the devil, finding in them personal opponents of God. (*Religion d.
> Judenthums*) p.241 note 3). So also Kibisch on 1 Cor. xv:20 (Esch d.p.,
> p.162) and Titus p.200 (on sin and death in Paul). We need hardly refer to
> the frequency of such personifications in Greek literature.[38]

Thus there is justification in linking *Sin and death* in Romans 7–8
with the law of the husband, Satan. The law of the husband is the law
of Sin, and is the law of Sin and Death. These are all expressions that
cover Satan's covenantal authority over man who is his bride.

Is there any more evidence to show that there was a similar concept
or experience of solidarity and covenant in pagan religious thought
paralleling that which existed between Israel and Yahweh? If this
understanding can be established, then it would be a natural transition
for Paul to make from seeing the New Israel in eternal covenant with
Yahweh, to seeing the unbelieving community in a similar covenant
with 'the god of this age' (2 Cor. 4:4). It would merely be a refocusing
of Old Testament theology where Israel was in covenant with Yahweh
and the nations were in covenant with their gods.

---

[37]Kennedy, *Conception* 108, note 2.
[38]*op. cit.* 108.

is this concept that has been established by Smith. Writing of the condition of solidarity in the non-Jewish world he says:

> The circle into which a man was born was not simply a group of kinsfolk and fellow citizens, but embraced also certain divine beings, the gods of the family and of the state, which in the ancient mind stood connected as the human members of the social circle. The relations between the gods of antiquity and their worshippers were expressed in the language of human relationship and this language was not taken in a figurative sense but with strict literality. If a god was spoken of as a father and his worshippers as his offspring the meaning was that the worshippers were literally of his stock, that he and they made up one natural family with reciprocal family duties to one another.[39]

This relationship between the pagans and their gods differed from Israel's relationship with Yahweh. Israel's relationship rested on Yahweh's free choice of them as his people, whereas the pagan relationship was by birth. As Oesterley and Robinson have written:

> The early Israelite may have thought of Yahweh much as the Moabite thought of Chemosh but the relationship rested on a different basis. Chemosh always had been a Moabite and never could be anything else; Yahweh had existed as a God independently of Israel, and, if need be, could so exist again, or could, on the other hand, extend His interests and His influence to others than to the original Israel. The connection between God and people was not 'natural' but...artificial.[40]

This solidarity of the heathen, naturally, with their gods, and that of Israel, by election, with her God, is paralleled in the New Testament. John emphasises the necessity of personal salvation in order to become a member of the covenant community (John 1:12,13). This is because even the Jews, on account of their unbelief, are not children of God but children of the devil (John 8:42-47). This exclusion from the New Covenant, because of unbelief, can only be reversed by faith in the grace of God displayed in the giving of his Son as the Paschal victim of the New Exodus (John 2:25–3:16). This Johannine picture is also confirmed by Paul. The Ephesian Christians had been 'like the rest – by nature children of wrath' (Eph. 2:3), and this was not only true of Gentiles but also of unbelieving Jews (1 Thess. 2:14-16). The early

[39]Smith, *Religion*, 29f.
[40]Oesterley and Robinson, *Religion*, 140.

church would find no difficulty in transferring these concepts to herself and unbelieving mankind once they had realised that they were the true Israel and inheritors of the promises of the covenant.

The body of Adam

There is one further problem that needs to be resolved to complete the argument for a corporate interpretation of the term 'the body of Sin'. It is to explain why it is, if the evidence so far presented is correct, that Paul speaks of 'the body of Sin'. It should be obvious that if Adam and Christ are the respective representatives, then the counterpart of 'the body of Christ' ought to be 'the body of Adam'.

Scroggs has shown that the Jews of Paul's day were familiar with a concept known as 'the body of Adam', which was part of Philo's philosophy.[41] Scroggs argues that to avoid confusing his own ideas with those of Philo, who had already claimed the expression and used it in quite another way, Paul uses the term 'body of Sin' as a synonym for a term that had become adulterated. Scroggs is supported by Davies:

> Paul accepts the traditional Rabbinic doctrine of the unity of mankind in Adam. The doctrine implied that the very constitution of the physical body of Adam and the method of formation was symbolic of the real oneness of mankind. In that one body of Adam east and west, north and south, were brought together, male and female, as we have seen. The 'body' of Adam included all mankind. Was it not natural, then, that Paul, when he thought of the new humanity being incorporated 'in Christ' should have conceived of it as the 'body' of the second Adam, where there was neither Jew nor Greek, male nor female, bond nor free.[42]

Best, however, rejected Davies' conclusions:

> We have no direct evidence that the phrase 'The body of Adam' was ever used to designate mankind. Paul does not use it, nor is it to be found among the Rabbis. Paul does speak of mankind as 'in Adam', and with that he contrasts redeemed humanity as 'in Christ', but that is hardly relevant here. Indeed the very fact of this comparison in 1 Cor. 15:22 might suggest that Paul has no idea of the phrase 'the body of Adam', for that phrase would have suited the argument of the passage just as well, if not better. The vital connecting phrase, 'the body of Christ,' is nowhere

[41]Scroggs, *Adam*, 15.
[42]Davies, *Rabbinic*, 57.

directly related to speculation about the First and Second Adam, and it occurs much more widely in the Pauline Epistles than that speculation. In view of this we cannot accept the suggestion of Davies.[43]

In addition to Best's argument I would add two further points. Firstly, there is absolutely no suggestion that Paul is avoiding the use of 'the body of Adam'. Elsewhere, when Paul sees a word or concept being misused he strips it of its pretence and then puts forward the truth, as he sees it in Christ. This is so whether it is the Colossian heresy he is exposing or the misuse of the law that is leading the Galatians back into bondage. There is no hint whatever in his argument that Paul means anything other than 'the body of Sin'.

Secondly, the insistence Paul lays upon the significance of death to Sin (Rom. 6:2, 6, 10) makes it difficult to substitute 'Adam' for 'Sin'. It becomes even more difficult to maintain this hypothesis when 6:10 is reinterpreted from 'the death he died he died to sin once for all; but the life he lives, he lives unto God' to 'the death he died he died to Adam once for all'. Clearly such a reinterpretation suggests concepts that will be difficult to accommodate consistently in any system of interpretation. Furthermore, Paul never attempts to introduce Adam into his argument once his representative role in the Fall is dealt with in chapter 5. He is thoroughly consistent in speaking of Sin as the enemy, personifying Sin in chapter 6 so that it opposes not Christ, but God himself (Rom. 6:11,13,14, 23).

How, then, can the relationship be with Sin? Can Paul's rationale be discovered, or is there no overall system of theology that Paul draws on? For example, Munck argues that Paul never had a systematised theology, but says that he developed his theology in an *ad hoc* manner in the context of his evangelistic and pastoral work, writing both for advice and for teaching as the need arose.[44] For Munck it is foolish to systematise Paul's reasoning. It can only be understood in the context of the situation in which it was written and as an example of the further development of Paul's thought.

In response to Munck I would suggest that it is only reasonable to assume that Paul is inconsistent in his theology if clear examples can be given to substantiate such a position. I am aware of those who have made such claims and must limit myself to replying briefly to this position. I believe such conclusions are questionable because they

[43]Best, *Body*, 92.
[44]Munck, *Paul*, 67.

have almost invariably begun from the perspective of Paul adapting his message to the Gentiles. They are also the product of highly individualistic interpretations. I consider that it has been demonstrated that such a reconstruction never took place and that the corporate perspectives have at least to be considered. Finally, I have sought to show that the New Exodus model existed and that it was from this Old Testament type that the theology of Paul, and indeed of Jesus and the whole church, came.

Also, it seems quite inconceivable that a man of Paul's intellectual calibre should be so haphazard as to be indifferent to these alleged inconsistencies. At Paul's instruction, his letters were being passed around the churches (Col. 4:16). Was he not concerned for consistency? Surely he would know that self-contradictory statements would damage his message and authority. The readers of the first century were no less intelligent than those of the twenty-first century and would have had no less concern for self-evident contradictions. The arguments of his letter to the Romans show Paul to be a man of extremely disciplined thought. His insight into the dangers of introducing alien philosophies, his insistence upon the principles of the gospel being maintained, even against cherished Jewish ideas, all serve to show that we are dealing with the writings of a man possessing an outstanding intellect who also had a burning zeal for the gospel he preached. Is it reasonable to suggest that Paul was cavalier about the message he preached and how it held together?

To return to our investigation, why does Paul speak of 'the body of Sin', and how does he understand this concept?

What has been lacking from the discussion on this topic so far is a realisation that Jesus Christ is only the mediator of the New Covenant, and not the benefactor himself (1 Tim. 2:5; 1 Cor. 15:24-28). In other words, the church's ultimate relationship is not with Christ, but with God himself through Christ. Paul expresses this fact when he writes:

> The end will come, when he hands over the kingdom to God the Father after he has destroyed all dominion, authority and power. For he must reign until he has put all his enemies under his feet. The last enemy to be destroyed is death. For he 'has put everything under his feet'. Now when it says that 'everything' has been put under him, it is clear that this does not include God himself, who put everything under Christ. When he has done this, then the Son himself will be made subject to him who put everything under him, so that God may be all in all (1 Cor. 15:24-28).

The Son here is spoken of as the Messianic figure who was promised to Israel and who would rule creation, as is shown by the quotation from Psalm 8. As the representative of God amongst men, Christ has secured for his brothers all that a redeemer in the Old Testament was responsible for ensuring. Christ has emancipated his people from Sin and its power and, having fulfilled all his various roles as the Redeemer, he completes his work by yielding the kingdom up to God the Father. From now on, Christ's position will no longer be Messiah/Mediator; instead he resumes his eternal position with the Father, and the mystery of the Godhead is then complete.[45] Beyond the statement of Paul we cannot go, for it would be speculation.

What bearing does this have on the concept of 'the body of Sin'? It is surely this: just as the ultimate relationship of the redeemed is not with Christ, but is with the Father himself, so the ultimate relationship of unredeemed humanity is not with Adam, the mediator, but with Sin. The reason Paul contrasts 'the body of Christ' with 'the body of Sin' is because Adam's work is completed and Sin, at present, has all things subjected to himself. Thus Satan could tempt Christ, offering him the kingdoms of this world. Christ's work is not yet completed. He has yet to subject all things to the Father. 'The body of Christ' will cease when the Kingdom of Christ is incorporated into the Kingdom of God. The body of Adam has ceased; indeed it did so even before the human family began to multiply, because that kingdom was already the kingdom of darkness (Col. 1:13) under Satan's rule. It is 'the body of Sin'.

Conclusion

I have sought to understand what Paul meant by the term 'the body of Sin'. The concept is not individualistic, as is so often held, but is corporate, speaking of the state of unredeemed humanity in its relationship to Satan (Sin). This conclusion is supported by the context of the argument in Romans 6 as it develops from the description of two communities described earlier in the letter. It also finds support from those who have concluded that Pauline anthropology is Hebraic rather than Hellenistic as well as by a consideration of the way the accompanying expression 'our old man' is used elsewhere. This latter expression is always used with a corporate meaning as a contrast to the expression 'the new man', which is a description of the church,

---

[45]See comments by Dodd, *Studies*, 54, and Bruce, *Corinthians*, 147.

made up of both Jews and Gentiles. Furthermore, the likely origin of this concept is Isaiah 28. This was a chapter widely cited in the New Testament, a fact which suggests that its fuller significance for the doctrine of salvation was widely known.

Once again we have found that the model that Paul has been following is that of Israel's deliverance from Egypt. In that historical deliverance Israel was redeemed through the death of a representative, her firstborn. By their death, admittedly avoided by the substitution of a lamb, her covenant with Egypt and her gods was terminated and a new life under the headship of Moses began.

The covenantal bondage in which man exists through his union with Adam demonstrates the need for the death of one who can act on his behalf, for it is only through death that such relationships can be severed. Thus, in Christ's death, there is not only a dealing with the guilt of sin and its consequences, but also the severing of the relationship with Sin, in which unregenerate mankind is involved. It is an experience that encompasses the individual, but is much more than solitary salvation. It is the deliverance of the community by the covenantal annulling effect of death, the death of the last Adam. Having been delivered from membership of 'the body of Sin', the church has been brought into union with a new head and made to be the members of a new body, 'the body of Christ'.

Once again, we have seen Paul's thinking, in this case, on the subject of the church, to be completely Semitic. He has not Hellenised his message but clearly expected the Gentile seekers after God to become acquainted with biblical redemptive history. We have further demonstrated that the Hellenised Paul is not the Paul of the New Testament. Thus, the Paul of the New Testament continued to think and live in the theological expectations of Old Testament redemptive history and thinks in the same framework as did his Lord and Saviour.

Consequences

The rediscovery of the corporate thinking of Paul has a number of important consequences for theological study. They are as follows:

1. It establishes the essential Jewishness of Paul's thought and the error of interpreting him from a Hellenistic framework.

2. It follows that the body is not in some way the bearer of sin nor is sin a deformation that is biologically inherited as some have suggested. Being in Sin is nothing less than being in Adam. It is

relational rather than legal, even though ultimately it has to have some sort of legal framework when it is being described. Whether a man or a woman is righteous or a sinner in the biblical pattern of thinking depends upon the community to which they belong.

3. It demonstrates that Paul begins his theology with the community and not the individual. There has been a fundamental error in traditional methods of exegesis in which the New Testament text especially has been interpreted as though it spoke of the experience of the individual believer. We have found that this is a mistake of massive proportions, which has left Christianity with a enormous emphasis on the individual with hardly any texts to support its doctrine of the church. In the reading of the text that I am proposing, we find that Paul began with the church and then provided a few texts to direct us as to how the teaching applied to the individual. This reverses the whole perspective and by this method we have a strong doctrine of the church, which becomes the basis of understanding the doctrine of individual application.

4. Appreciating that the body is not the seat of sin as the traditional interpretation of the 'body of sin' suggests, allows us to realise that our humanity is God-given, even in its fallen condition. There ought not to be any shame in being human, nor in what such reality implies. It should help us to recognise that there are many natural emotions and desires that in themselves are not sinful and need no repentance; it is only their misuse that requires such a response.

5. It helps us to realise the solidarity man has with God's creation and that the remnant community is not to reject the world as being somehow evil. Rather, this world is still God's world, and he continues to value it and care for it. Christ died not only for man but for the whole cosmic order, to redeem it and restore it to its former glory.

6. It demonstrates the nature of Paul's doctrine of Sin. Paul sees that behind the conflict and alienation that man experiences is a whole universal order of rebellion. Man is at the centre of this struggle as a result of being made in God's image. Satan, the one who has sought the establishment of a different kingdom from that which God rules, has taken man, and all that he was made responsible for through creation, into bondage in the kingdom of darkness. The redemption of Christ is about the deliverance of man and 'nature' from this alienation and death.

Chapter Six

The Paschal Community
and the Eschatological Marriage

In chapter 4 we argued that Paul did not generally describe Christians as slaves of Christ in a classical sense and in chapter 5 we argued that Paul had a corporate dimension in mind when he used the term 'body of Sin'. There are, however, several texts that could undermine these conclusions. Paul refers to himself as 'unspiritual, sold as a slave (*doulos*) to sin' (Rom. 7:14), and in 1 Corinthians 6:19-20 he writes, 'You are not your own; you were bought at a price.' Such statements are a clear challenge to the covenantal corporate claims that have been made, for these descriptions of slavery suggest both slave purchase and individualism.

To answer the difficulties that purchase language throws up it will be necessary to clarify the biblical understanding of two related themes. The first is the ultimate purpose that lay behind the covenants, both old and new, and the second, since it leads from the first theme as we shall see, is the Hebraic pattern of establishing a marriage. To deal, then, with the first of our questions: What was the ultimate purpose of the old and new covenants?

It is widely accepted that Paul shared the Old Testament perspective that the ultimate relationship between God and his people was like the marriage relationship. When Israel betrayed Yahweh, it was promised that following her exile the establishing of the New Covenant would secure this relationship between God and his people (Isa. 62:5; Jer. 31:3, 31-34; Ezek. 36:24-30; Hos. 2:19-20). It was Hosea, who through the tragic failure of his marriage, grasped the depth of the sinfulness of Israel's rejection of Yahweh's love. As his own heart broke through the faithlessness of Gomer he learnt the depth of Yahweh's grief caused by Israel, his faithless spouse. It was not just the rejection of a moral or a religious code, but of love itself – God's love. Robinson claimed that Hosea came to see Israel's faithlessness in a totally different way from any other of the prophets, it was 'not any accident that the most common metaphor for apostasy in this book is fornication'.[1]

It is because the image of marriage carried two deep but opposing lessons that it became so widely used. It expressed something of the depth of the relationship Yahweh sought to establish with his people, but it also revealed the evil of rejecting the love that Yahweh sought to give them. Robinson again expressed this succinctly when he said: 'Hosea has, after all, through his own bitter agony, reached deeper than any other prophet into the secrets of religion.'[2]

Both in the Old and New Testaments the marriage relationship between God and his people is seen as something that is yet to be consummated, it is always treated as an eschatological goal. Two reasons can be given for this.

The first is that if such a relationship actually existed in this age it would introduce concepts that could so easily slide into the practices condemned in both the Old and New Testaments, i.e. those of the fertility religions, which resulted in sacred prostitution. Such practices would have totally undermined fidelity to the covenant.

The second reason is that the concept of sonship better served the principle of obtaining an inheritance. Under Hebrew law, as it was later to be under Roman law, it was the son who received the inheritance from the father, and not the wife. This concept, of the church in this age being the son, and in the next age being the bride, not only avoided the danger of distorting biblical morality, but provides for a concept of salvation which is yet to be, and at the same time already is.

The second biblical practice that needs exploring is how a marriage was arranged. How did a man 'obtain' his wife? It is a matter of controversy amongst scholars as to how a wife was secured in ancient Israel. Some biblical texts appear to suggest that wife purchase was practised. Jacob worked seven years for Rachel (Gen. 29:18, 20, 30). David paid one hundred foreskins to Saul for his daughter Michal (1 Sam. 18:22-27). Not all scholars agree that wife purchase is meant in these instances. De Vaux, for example, acknowledged that, in the tenth commandment, a man's wife was put amongst his possessions such as cattle, servants and house. He argued that, despite this evidence, the nobility of womanhood in ancient Israel would not permit such a degrading practice. He claimed that the money or payment made to the woman's father – which clearly cannot be regarded as a

---

[1]Robinson, *Prophecy*, 81.
[2]*op. cit.* 78.

dowry, as it is not handed over to the daughter, but retained by the father – was not a purchase price but a payment for loss of service that the father incurred in giving his daughter in marriage.[3]

Yet it would appear from de Vaux's definition that purchase never takes place in any business transactions; it is only the compensation owed because the previous owner no longer possesses what was once available to him, whether it be a car, house, or anything else! It is extremely difficult to see how de Vaux could maintain his position, even if one has sympathy with his concern to uphold the ideal of womanhood in ancient Israel.

But would the dignity of womanhood be jeopardised if payment were established? It is all too easy to read values of the twenty-first century back into history. At the beginning of our era the Roman woman had a degree of freedom for which modern women's liberation movements are still striving, and yet they never objected to the (admittedly only token) practice of bride purchase.[4] We shall see that there are theological considerations that will lead us to conclude that bride purchase was practised in the Ancient Near East and that this model was used by Paul.

Just as the meaning of *doulos* has been settled by its context and theological associations, so the concept of bride purchase can be examined from a perspective wider than its immediate sociological setting, for it too can be examined from theological considerations.

Paul's classical treatment of the marriage relationship is found in Ephesians 5:22-27:

> Wives, submit to your own husbands in the Lord. For the husband is the head of the wife as Christ is the head of the church, his body, of which he is the Saviour. Now as the church submits to Christ, so also wives should submit to their husbands in everything. Husbands love your wives, just as Christ loved the church and gave himself for her, to make her holy, cleansing her by the washing with water through the word, and to present to himself as a radiant church, without taint or wrinkle or any other blemish, but holy and blameless.

Clearly Paul exhorts Christian husbands to have a high regard for their wives that is based on their worth. The regard Christ had for the church was such that he paid for her with his own life: he 'gave himself for her'. This is enforced still further in Paul's address to the

[3] de Vaux, *Israel*, 27.
[4] Balsdon, *Women*, 179-80.

Ephesian elders at Miletus where, exhorting them to be faithful to their calling, he said, 'Be shepherds of the church of God which he bought with his own blood' (Acts 20:28).

It was obviously a purchase price that Jesus paid to secure the church as his bride. Because of this, the Epistle to the Ephesians takes on a wider perspective. When Paul talks of them having been redeemed (Eph. 1:7) he echoes the redemption of Israel from Egypt. The church's destiny is, like Israel's was, to become the bride of the Lord (Eph. 5:22-27).

The concept of bride purchase is upheld in 1 Corinthians 6:13-20:

> The body is not meant for sexual immorality, but for the Lord, and the Lord for the body. By his power God raised the Lord from the dead, and he will raise us also. Do you not know that your bodies are members of Christ himself? Shall I then take the members of Christ and unite them with a prostitute? Never! Do you not know that he who unites himself with a prostitute is one with her in body? For it is said 'the two will become one flesh'. But he who unites with the Lord is one with him in the Spirit.
>
> Flee from sexual immorality. All other sins a man commits are outside of his body, but he who sins sexually sins against his own body. Do you not know that your body is a temple of the Holy Spirit, who is in you, whom you have received from God? You are not your own; you were bought at a price. Therefore honour God with your body.

Traditionally the meaning of this passage is interpreted as referring to having been freed from slavery to sin by the payment of a price. Before examining the validity of this view, we must carefully note the context of the passage. Paul is dealing with sexual immorality, and the immediate problem is the case of incest referred to in 5:2. Paul follows his statement of being bought with a price (6:20) by dealing with pastoral problems relating to marriage (7:1ff). To introduce a slave purchase concept here is to insert something that is not directly relevant. In addition, the immediate passage is full of marriage language. 'The Lord for the body...One flesh... he who unites himself to the Lord.' Paul is not appealing to readers who are owned as slaves, but to people who are related at a much deeper level, as those who belong as a marriage partner. A few months later he wrote to them, 'I have promised you to one husband, to Christ, so that I might present you as a pure virgin to him' (2 Cor. 11:2).

Examination of the accepted view of sacral manumission, as

advocated by Deissmann,[5] and generally followed by most commentators, reveals exegetical difficulties. Deissmann's argument is that in 1 Corinthians 6:20 Paul focused on the process adopted for the release of a person from slavery. He points out that in the Ancient Near East a slave could pay a sum of money into the treasury of the local temple and through this means the god of that temple technically purchased him. The slave was freed from his old master because he had become the property of the god. This sort of practice had its parallel in Israel. Jesus criticised those who avoided their family responsibilities because they had dedicated their property to Yahweh. Through this dedication of their wealth to the temple they officially owned nothing, and therefore had no means, it was claimed, to fulfil their normal family duties to relatives who needed their financial help.[6] The reality was that the one who had made such a dedication continued to enjoy the property to the full; it passed into the temple treasury only at death. Christ saw the practice as reprehensible and denounced it.

There are a number of difficulties in Deissmann's case for slave purchase. First, is it conceivable that Paul would have used such a morally confused argument? The liberated slave, now the property of a new master, had, in fact, no more moral or religious responsibilities once the transaction had been completed than he had previously. He lived as other men lived, in practice no more devoted to the god whose property he now was, than one who was born free. The new ownership was merely technical. If Paul had argued from such a practice he would have introduced into the Corinthians' minds the very concepts he desired to remove. They would have concluded that redemption was only technical ownership. It would encourage, not discourage, the Corinthians to live lives that had no relation to the price paid. If Paul had been using sacral manumission as his model, he would have been endorsing the Corinthians' attitude to libertarianism.

The second difficulty for the sacral manumission model is that it would lead to theological confusion. To say that Paul used the temple practice of redemption as his illustration is to reverse the entire emphasis of Pauline theology. For Paul, man has absolutely no part in his redemption; it is entirely a gift given by a sovereign, electing God. An illustration in which the whole drift is of man paying for his own release, which is then attributed to his god, is totally contrary to Paul's theology

[5]Deissmann, *Light*, 324.
[6]Edersheim, *Life*, 2:18f. see Mark 7:11.

of redemption. The illustration takes the initiative completely out of God's hands and puts it entirely into man's, and this cannot be attributed to Paul.

The argument of Deissmann has also been rejected by Ridderbos:

> It is highly doubtful, however, whether such a connection may be made. Irrespective even of the material differences (with regard to price etc.) there is no formal similarity here. For in Paul's representation God does not appear as the purchaser, nor does the priest standing in his service, but Christ, who through his death redeems his own. The price is not paid by God but rather to God. And with that the real point of resemblance has fallen away.[7]

He goes on to note the problem presented to theologians over the centuries by the concept of ransom or payment, but insists that whilst there is no business transaction between Christ and God, yet 'one should take no less care to see that the objective character of what is here called "to redeem", "ransom", etc. is not compromised'.[8] The 'objective' character of these concepts is perfectly preserved, without compromise, when the concept of the annulling of the covenant through Christ's representative death is incorporated into the work of redemption (see chapter 8).

The idea of the Corinthians, or a Corinthian, being united with a harlot (1 Cor. 6:19-20), which has normally been seen to be a reference to a temple prostitute, has been disputed by the foregoing exegesis because it has questioned the temple links by challenging the meaning of 'bought with a price'. Is there an alternative setting for this statement that will make better sense of the surrounding text and that will be in harmony with bride purchase?

A few scholars have tentatively suggested a corporate setting for this passage. For example, Kempthorne has queried the traditional understanding of *body* in verse 18 and has suggested that it refers not to the body of the offending man, but rather to the church, the body of Christ. Kempthorne thus argues that sinning against the body is sinning against the church.[9]

However, Gundry, in assessing the view of Kempthorne that *sōma* in 1 Corinthians 6:18 refers to the church as the body of Christ, comments:

---

[7]Ridderbos, *Outline*, 193.
[8]*op. cit.* 193-94.
[9]Kempthorne, 'Incest', 568-74.

But we may suspect over-interpretation in the proposal of a double meaning. And the precipitous importation of the Church as The Body of Christ, a theme wholly undiscussed so far in the epistle and presumably unknown to the Corinthians, once again proves problematic. Moreover, the association of 6:12-30 with chapter 5, by which an individual reference is supplied, raises a doubt. Although *porneia* occurs in both passages, in 6:12-20 the female partner in immorality is *porne*, a prostitute, but in chapter 5 the female partner is the wife of the man's father. An equation between the two, therefore, seems doubtful, especially if the *porne* is a temple prostitute, as the figure of the temple in verses 19-20 and the local color of the Temple of Aphrodite near Corinth both suggest.[10]

On these grounds Gundry rejects Kempthorne's view, and having already reviewed the various expositions put forth, decides upon the view of Alford, quoting from him as follows:

The assertion (that every sin is outside the body), which has surprised many of the commentators, is nevertheless strictly true. Drunkenness and gluttony, e.g., are sins done in and by the body, and are sins by abuse of the body, – but they are still *ektos tou sōmatos* – introduced from without, sinful not in their act, but in their effect, which effect it is each man's duty to foresee and avoid. But fornication is the alienating of that body which is the Lord's, and making it a harlot's body – it is sin against a man's own body, in its very nature, against the verity and nature of his body; not an effect on the body from participation of things without, but a contradiction of the truth of the body, wrought within itself.[11]

The difficulty of this interpretation, which Gundry favours, is that it introduces a way of thinking that is nowhere else evident in Paul's letters. Indeed, it gives a distinct impression of a pattern of thought that derives from a Western analytical mind with a background of psychological research rather than the biblically based reasoning of Paul. Further, it is totally against the New Testament understanding given by Jesus of the true origin of defilement: 'All that causes defilement comes from within a man' (Matt. 15:16-20). And it is clear elsewhere that Paul saw a far wider category of sins as being relevant to the argument than those advanced by Alford:

[10]Gundry, *Soma*, 75.
[11]*op. cit.* 72.

> Do you not know that the wicked will not inherit the kingdom of God? Do
> not be deceived: Neither the sexually immoral nor idolaters nor adulterers
> nor male prostitutes nor homosexual offenders nor thieves nor the greedy
> nor drunkards nor slanderers nor swindlers will inherit the kingdom of
> God (1 Cor. 6:9-10; see Eph. 5:5-7).

But what of Kempthorne's argument? Is Gundry's criticism valid?
I would suggest that it is not reasonable of Gundry to argue that the
body concept was unknown to the Corinthians at this point. The book
of Acts shows that Paul realised from the outset the existence of
solidarity between Christ and his people. He was arrested by the
very statement, 'Why do you persecute me?' (Acts 9:4) One can
only assume that an explanation of this phrase would have been sought
by an inquirer at an early stage to understand the significance of the
statement for Paul's message. It surely cannot be maintained that
this concept had developed no further in his thinking until it emerged
in 1 Corinthians 12–14. The bride/bridegroom analogy, from which
some believe the body of Christ concept came, had existed for centuries
within Judaism, and Paul's statement in 2 Corinthians 11:2 that he had
espoused the Corinthians to Christ certainly does not suggest that the
Corinthians lacked understanding concerning the imagery, for Paul
does not bother to explain himself beyond the statement.

Furthermore, Paul uses 'body' language when he instructs on the
eucharist in 1 Corinthians 11:29 and clearly expects his readers to
understand his meaning. If it is argued that the term is used to speak
of the sacrament, it has to be explained why the section returns to the
behaviour of the Corinthians and their lack of respect for those who
should be cared for (11:33-34). This suggests the sinning against the
body is ecclesiastical rather than eucharistic, and that the language
was not introduced in chapter 12 (as Gundry argues). But even if this
point is not accepted, there is an earlier text that is indisputable. In
10:17 Paul writes, 'Because there is one loaf, we, who are many, are
one body, for we all partake of the one loaf.' This use of *sōma* is
undeniably ecclesiastical in its meaning, although it is within a
eucharistic context. This adds support to the meaning argued for 11:33-
34, because both are in the same context, that of the eucharist and
the well-being of the body. Thus Gundry's rejection of Kempthorne's
reading of 1 Corinthians 6:18 on the grounds that the Corinthians could
not understand a corporate use of *sōma* is not valid.

But above all these considerations is the fact that Paul speaks of the Corinthians as being 'members' of Christ in 6:15. Gundry observes this terminology and concedes it to be 'body language', but dismisses the problem by saying it anticipates the introduction of the body concept later in the epistle.[12] But Gundry is missing the true significance and importance of the passage. To say that Paul introduces this concept of the Corinthians being members of Christ into his argument – a concept which has not yet been explained – is to ask us to believe that Paul would leave his readers to guess at the meaning of an expression which is at the centre of his argument, viz. their relationship with Christ and the possibility of it somehow being severed. This is made even more difficult to accept when one realises that this warning is one of the main reasons for the writing of the letter. Paul was anxious to warn them of the consequence of fornication. To accept Gundry's interpretation and criticism of Kempthorne's exposition one has to accept the failure of Paul to present his argument, for he has been unable to explain himself in commonly held concepts. It would seem to me that this is not compatible with one whose discipline in logic has been widely acclaimed. I suggest, therefore, that the body concept was already known to the Corinthians and that Gundry is wrong in saying that it emerged for the first time in 1 Corinthians 12.

In addition to these comments on Gundry's position I must also restate our earlier conclusions. We have seen the allusion in 1 Corinthians 6:19-20 regarding slave purchase, and that the Greek background in which the passage is normally set (and this is followed by Gundry) refers not to slave purchase but to bride purchase. The reference to the temple is not in a Greek context but in an Hebraic one, and interestingly the temple is coupled throughout the New Testament with a bride figure.[13] In other words, the church's true worship will be attained when her full relationship is realised. Then the temple, which is a type of true worship and an expression of man's relationship with God, will have no further place. Thus the context which Gundry has assumed and in which he has set his exegesis is highly questionable, and with it so is Gundry's exegesis.

That this relationship between the temple and the bride is part of the apostle's thinking is supported by the Hebrew word for bride, *kallah*, meaning 'the complete' or 'perfect one'. This is probably the thinking behind Paul's statement in 1 Corinthians 13:9-12:

[12]*Soma*, 72
[13]John 2; 1 Corinthians 6:15-20; Ephesians 2:19-20; cf. 5:25-33; Revelation 19:8; cf. 21:22.

For we know in part and we prophecy in part, but when perfection comes, the imperfect disappears. When I was a child, I thought as a child, I reasoned like a child. When I became a man I put childish ways behind me. Now we see but a poor reflection; then we shall see face to face. Now I know in part; then I shall know fully, even as I am fully known.

This suggestion is also supported by his reference to *knowing*, a term constantly used throughout Scripture of the marriage relationship. The theme of this passage, which seems to speak of completion in the context of the marriage relationship, is worship (1 Corinthians 12 and 14), thus supporting this overall observation regarding the relationship between the temple and the bride.

The framework for all of this, as in Romans 7:1-4, is the New Exodus. Indeed, Taylor has suggested that the statement in 1 Corinthians 6:20 concerning being bought with a price probably reflects Jesus' statement in Mark 10:45, 'to give his life a ransom for many'.[14] Now it is this very statement that Hooker has claimed refers to the redemption of the firstborn by the Levites following the Passover.[15] She points out that the only place in Scripture where one human life was substituted for another human life was in the case of the Levites who were substituted for the firstborn following the Passover. Thus there is a hermeneutical model functioning in which the 'ransom for many' operates within the Passover scheme, a paradigm already used by Paul to explain the significance of Christ's death (1 Cor. 5:7). If these observations are correct, then they link 1 Corinthians 6:20 with the Passover. The divine marriage between Yahweh and Israel was understood to have taken place at that time. This then supports the claims that have been made earlier that 1 Corinthians 6:16 reflects the matrimonial language that is part of the Passover.

This divine marriage is the eschatological goal of the redemption that is in Christ. It is not only mentioned here in the Corinthian correspondence. An echo of it surfaces in 2 Corinthians 5:5 where Paul speaks about the church being prepared for the coming change when she will not be found naked. Clearly New Exodus imagery is present in chapter 5.[16] It would make sense to expect to find a reference to the eschatological marriage in a passage so heavily dependent on the New Exodus theme.

A further factor that has probably hindered the identification of

---

[14]Taylor, *Atonement*, 23.

[15]Hooker, *Servant*, 73.

[16]i.e. the quote from Isaiah 52:11 in 2 Corinthians 5:17, which refers to the anticipated new creation following the second exodus.

the wedding theme is the tendency to interpret the passage from an individual perspective. This is not because the grammar demands it, but because tradition has dictated it. As we have seen, the believer is never called the bride of Christ, but the church is. If this is a corporate argument, then the reference to a wedding garment is consistent and makes sense of the flow of the argument. The passage closes with the statement that God would dwell with them (2 Cor. 6:14-18), temple imagery, which is always, as we have seen, closely connected to the theme of the church being the bride of Christ.

The traditional interpretation of one flesh in 1 Corinthians 6:16 has constantly thrown up problems in exegesis. Moffat explains one of them without seeking any other solutions when he says: 'So strong does Paul feel on this point that he actually applies to illicit passion, or cohabitation, what was originally used of married love.'[17] The problem produced in understanding the one flesh concept in the traditional framework causes Conzelmann to say, '*mia sarx* is accordingly for Paul not an essential mark of Christian marriage, but simply, describes sexual union in general. I Corinthians is not to be understood simply as an interpretation of Genesis 2:24.'[18] Conzelmann says this in spite of the clear allusion to Genesis 2:24 in verse 16. Another problem is noted by Simon: 'the apostle seems to suggest that once a man's body has been used for fornication; it is no longer his to offer to God. We may not be able to follow him in the most rigorist interpretation of this line of thought, but we are hardly likely to find a more "positive" approach to the sins of the flesh than put before us here.'[19]

These problems, together with those which we have previously noted, cannot be explained adequately while it is held that Paul is dealing 'merely' with the problem of a man having a sexual relationship with a temple prostitute. While we have sympathy with the application of this passage to sexual relationships, restricting it to this setting will never resolve the problems that have been raised.

The prevailing understanding of Paul's argument in 1 Corinthians 6 is due in large measure to the fact that the conclusion of the argument has been 'obvious', as has its setting. The meaning of the conclusion has been read back into the discussion and this has in turn controlled the exegesis of the marriage immagery in the text. It is assumed that *sōma* in verse 19 refers to the individual believer, and it clearly does not. It is assumed that the purchase in verse 20 reflects sacral

[17]Moffat, *Corinthians*, 125.
[18]Conzelmann, *Corinthians*, 111.
[19]Simon, *Corinthians*, 85.

manumission, but it does not, for if it did, Paul by his own argument would have done more serious damage to his gospel than any of his opponents were ever able to do. And further, it assumes the practice of sacred prostitution in Corinth, and we now know that it did not happen.[20]

The prevailing understanding also assumes that the practice of reading the epistles on an individual level is the only way to read the texts, because no alternative has ever been raised. We have seen from our consideration of Romans 6:6, 'the body (*sōma*) of sin,' that there is a corporate way of reading the passage that cuts across Hellenistic presuppositions. And that method at the very least must be considered. Also, there has been a serious failure to take the apocalyptic nature of the argument in chapter 6 seriously. That this is the dimension of the argument ought to be clear in that Paul begins the section with a clear statement concerning the Corinthian believers role in the coming eschaton as judges (1 Cor 6:2). This propels the following argument away from the moral lapses of the Corinthians to the implications that such behaviour has for the eschatological community. It is this context that I am arguing that chapter 6 should be read in.

Added to all this is the failure to realise that the arguments are about salvation history, about God's dealing with the church. The neglect of the clear marital imagery, that so obviously speaks of covenant and community, has, with the other above listed points, been the reason for a total misreading of the text that drives through all the exegetical clues because they cannot possibly fit into the individualistic reading that has been followed for most of the church's history.

A proposed corporate interpretation

Are there any factors that, if introduced, would help to complete the picture which was in Paul's mind? I believe that there are.

First, it needs to be seen that the relationship Paul is so alarmed about in 1 Corinthians 5:1ff is not a case of a lapse into immorality, but

---

[20]'Stabbo's comments about 1,000 religious prostitutes of Aphrodite, and those of Athenaeus, are unmistakably about Greek and not Roman Corinth. As temple prostitution was not a Greek phenomenon, the veracity of his comments on this point have been rightly questioned. The size of the Roman temple of Aphrodite on the Acrocorinth ruled out such temple prostitution; and by that time she had become Venus – the venerated mother of the imperial family and the highly respected patroness of Corinth – and was no longer a sex symbol' (Winter, *Corinth*, 87-88). See also Baugh, 'Cultic Prostitution,' 443-60, who argues for its absence in Ephesus and then extends his argument to cover the whole Roman empire.

[21]Bruce, *Corinthians*, 53.

a permanent relationship between a man (the professing believer) and his father's wife. Bruce translates Paul's complaint as 'and of a kind that is not found even among pagans; for a man is living with his father's wife'.[21] Bruce prefers this more precise rendering because the word 'immorality' is a weak rendering for *porneia*, which means fornication. In fact, *porneia* is occasionally attested for *erwah* in Rabbinic Hebrew, and for *zenut* in the Zadokite Document, of cohabitation within forbidden degrees. Paul could easily have quoted from the law (Lev. 18:8; Deut. 22:30; 27:20.), the Jerusalem decree (Acts 15:20, 29; 21:25), and even pagan authors.[22] It was against every known form of morality, and the pagans themselves denounced its practice in their own societies.

Now it is this relationship, of a son and a stepmother, living together as man and wife, that caused Paul such deep concern. They have entered into a permanent relationship. The question that requires an answer before we can go any further in unravelling Paul's thinking is whether he could ever acknowledge such a relationship as being *one flesh*. Would he give it the same status and dignity as a marriage that is according to the law of God?

Throughout chapters 5 and 6 Paul is concerned only with the man; he does not comment on what should be done to the woman, who is, presumably, an unbeliever. Paul, in fact, explains that it is not the duty of the church to discipline the unbeliever in this tragic affair, only the believer: 'What business is it of mine to judge those outside of the church? Are you not to judge those inside? God will judge those outside. Expel the wicked man from among you' (1 Cor. 5:12-13). Paul lays down principles for dealing with improprieties within the church. They are told not to take their problems before the secular court, for this will bring disgrace to the church's testimony as a whole. They themselves are to deal with the matter, and are qualified to do so in that they have been appointed ultimately to judge both men and angels (1 Cor. 6:2).

Paul proceeds to explain that the body has legitimate pleasures, but only within the limits prescribed by the law of God. Once food is misused, it leads to gluttony and becomes master of the eater. Equally, once sexual experience is indulged in outside of God's prescribed limits, it also ceases to be the source of marital blessing that it is intended to be. The difference between food and sexual experience, however, is very distinct. Sexual union, engaged in its appointed way, seals relationships with people. Such relationships are part of the much

---

[22]E.g. Euripides' *Hippolytus*, representing the Greeks, and Cicero's *Pro Cluentio* 14, representing the Romans.

larger community of the church, they are the living units that make it. It is this inter-relatedness that clearly causes Paul profound concern. He sees that corruption of this type in the body of Christ threatens the purity of the whole body (and note the Paschal/Exodus content of the appeal):

> Your boasting is not good. Don't you know that a little yeast works through the whole batch of dough? Get rid of the old yeast that you may be a new batch without yeast – as you really are. For Christ, our Passover lamb, has been sacrificed. Therefore let us keep the festival, not with the old yeast, the yeast of malice and wickedness, but with bread without yeast, the bread of sincerity and truth (1 Cor. 5:6-8).

Now we come to that passage that is the cause of so much difficulty, 1 Corinthians 6:15-20. It is claimed that Paul is saying that a man becomes one flesh with a prostitute through coitus, and so the immoral Christian has a oneness with both Christ and a prostitute. Having already discounted the claim that Paul has a Greek temple/slave-market in mind, is there any other evidence that can be brought to bear to unravel this passage?

Kempthorne's view is that the prostitute figure of chapter 6 is linked with the woman in the case of incest in 5:1ff. I do not make a link that equates the two as being one and the same person, but I do see that the problem of chapter 6 is coming out of the incest of chapter 5. Also, with Kempthorne, I see that the sin against the body probably includes a reference to the corporate body, the church. For as we have seen, Paul is concerned over the influence of the leaven of sin. Paul is disquieted (back in 5:6-8) not only about the offender, but also for the body of which the offender is part, in case it is putrefied by the presence of such sin in the body. It is obviously true that the offender does sin against his own body, but both the preceding and (as we shall see) the subsequent arguments have a wider framework than the individual.

Another point that suggests a corporate understanding is Paul's use of *melē* (a member), a term that is never used in Scripture to express a marriage relationship, rather the concept is always used of a corporate relatedness. It never speaks of a man being a member of a woman or vice versa. It is used by Paul to denote the relationship of the individual believer with the body of Christ (Eph. 5:30). This passage, if the language of Paul is to be allowed any reasonable degree of consistency, does not refer to an individual prostitute figure, but to *a society* called the harlot. This is supported in that to take away a member of Christ is to take away from the Christian community. To add that member to an individual, so that they become one flesh, would lead to an imbalance. This exegesis is confronted by Moule, but because of the individualistic/Hellenistic setting he followed he discounted his own insight. He said, commenting on 1 Corinthians 6:15:

> If whole individual bodies belong to Christ as his limbs, then he must be more than an individual body. It is true that in the very same verse, Paul asks the indignant question: 'Shall I then take the limbs of Christ and make them limbs of a harlot?' Which, if we pressed the analogy would have to imply that a harlot, too, had more than an individual body made up of a plurality of persons.... Paul only used the outrageous phrase 'a harlot's limbs', by a kind of false analogy, and simply to emphasise the scandal of intimate union of the same person with both Christ and a harlot.[23]

But Moule's explanation must be challenged. Admittedly the language of making members of the Corinthian congregation into members of the harlot is unique to this passage, but the idea behind it surely is not. In 1 Corinthians 5:5 Paul told the congregation to deliver the offender unto Satan. In 1 Timothy 1:20 he says that he has handed Hymenaeus and Alexander 'over to Satan to be taught not to blaspheme'. Similar imagery is found in Revelation 2:22 where Jesus says, 'So I will cast her on a bed of suffering, and I will make those who commit adultery with her suffer intensely, unless they repent of her ways.' The background is that Jesus is warning the church at Thyatira that if her members continue to tolerate Jezebel and practise all manner of sexually immoral acts with her, and if they continue to eat food sacrificed to idols (the very issues Paul is dealing with in 1 Corinthians), then he (Jesus) will throw them into a bed of suffering with her. In other words, the concept of handing over to Satan is very clearly taught elsewhere in both Paul and the rest of the New Testament. The language of taking members of Christ and making them the members of a harlot is nothing more than a different way of saying the same thing. Paul is not using a false analogy to emphasise the scandal of a Christian being in sexual union with a harlot, but he is describing a spiritual reality of discipline that others had or were to experience.

[23]Moule, *Origins*, 73.

The identification of the prostitute as a community explains how Paul can use the same language to describe her relationship with her members as he uses to describe the body of Christ's relationship with its members. So in 1 Corinthians 6:16: 'Do you not know that he who unites himself with a (*tē*) prostitute is one with her in body? For it is said, "The two will become one flesh." But he who unites himself to the Lord is one with him in spirit.' And in Ephesians 5.30 he says: 'For we are members of his body. "For this reason a man will leave his father and mother and be united to his wife, and the two will become one flesh." This is a profound mystery – but I am talking about Christ and the church.'

In both passages we have parallel expressions that clearly relate to one another. The language of marriage is used in both passages to indicate the corporate relationship that exists, one that is obviously based on covenant.

It might be reasoned, however, that Paul speaks about the immoral believer being 'one with her in body' (1 Cor. 6:15-16), which must surely be evidence of a physical union, and that he is therefore speaking of a prostitute. My answer is, 'Yes, it is a physical union, but no, it does not necessarily mean an individual prostitute.' Paul's doctrine of the church is more than 'spiritual', it is also physical: 'Your bodies are members of Christ himself' (1 Cor. 6:15).' Because Paul, as a Hebrew, cannot separate people from their bodies, he sees the church as possessing a physical dimension. There is a physical dimension to the relationship between Christ and his people; if there were not, the relationship that existed would be incomplete. Indeed, Paul is perfectly consistent in explaining that the final act of redemption is to change the believer's body.[24] He never abandons the essentially Hebraic nature of his thinking and therefore sees an importance in the body that a Greek mind could never accept. It is this relationship which Paul admits is a profound mystery, and which allows him to describe the church and Christ as being one flesh and to make full use of the marriage analogy (Eph. 5:31-32). Also, it is because this is the church's relationship with Christ – physical, one body – that he can use the same language to describe the relationship between the immoral Corinthian and the harlot, for as we have seen, she is the church's counterpart.

[24]Romans 8:11, 18-25; 1 Corinthians 15:35-49; Philippians 3:20-21; 1 Thessalonians 4:13-18.

I would continue to argue for a corporate setting for the passage by considering Paul's statement in verse 19: 'do you not know that your body is a temple of the Holy Spirit?' This is normally interpreted as a reference to the believer's body being the dwelling place of the Holy Spirit. But that interpretation overlooks the fact that *sōma* (body) is singular, whereas *humon* (your) is plural. It is their corporate body, themselves as a church, and not their individual bodies, that Paul is referring to as the temple of the Holy Spirit. Indeed, the traditional individualistic interpretation is contrary to all other usages of the concept of the living temple by New Testament writers. Elsewhere this concept is always applied to the church,[25] never to the individual. The only occasion that it is used of the individual is when it refers to Christ's own body (John 2:19). All of this is supported by the use Paul makes of the definite article coupled with the singular for temple. Their 'body' is *the* temple of the Holy Spirit.[26]

Finally, in support of a corporate setting, we can also note that in his closing statement, 'you were bought with a price' (v. 20), Paul uses the collective plural pronoun, not the singular. This marries with the rest of Paul's statement regarding redemption, where the price paid is always for the church and never for the individual.[27]

I conclude that the traditional interpretation has been contrary to all grammatical considerations, and has prevailed solely because the passage has constantly been placed within a Greek framework and interpreted from a Greek individualistic perspective. Once the Hebraic eschatological setting has been identified, with its New Exodus framework, and the letter is interpreted as addressed to the church, speaking of her corporate experience, then the passage takes on a new meaning, which, unlike its alternative, is consistent with logical, theological and grammatical considerations.

The picture that has emerged is that Paul threatens the offending members of the Corinthian church with being delivered unto Satan. It is parallel to Israel who failed to maintain her purity and was ultimately

[25] 1 Corinthians 3:16; 6:19; 2 Corinthians 6:16; Revelation 21:3.

[26] This corporate exegesis is supported by Grosheide: 'Your body: Paul's words regard the body of every believer; but also the bodies of all the believers together. In vss 15 your bodies implies the individual bodies are members of Christ, but your body implies that the whole of the bodies is a temple of the Holy Spirit. The singular noun "temple" goes with the singular noun "body" ' (*Corinthians*, 151-2).

[27] Acts 20:28; Romans 3:24ff.; Galatians 3:13; Ephesians 1:7; 5:24; Colossians 1:13-14; see also Mark 10:45.

delivered over to her enemies in exile. This fits with Witherington's suggestion that in 1 Corinthians 5:2 it is the spirit of the congregation and not the individual that is the focus of salvation and that the model is Israel's historic experience of judgement.[28]

Old Testament imagery and the language of Paul

We have seen earlier that there are strong Old Testament themes operating throughout the passage. In 5:7 there is the explicit statement that Christ's death is a Paschal sacrifice – the very event when Yahweh redeemed Israel to be his bride. 6:11 is seen by many to be baptism language and if so then it anticipates 10:2, the Exodus, when Israel became Yahweh's bride. There is clear martial language in 6:16, and the purchase of the Corinthian church in 6:20 is, once the unacceptablity of sacral manumission is appreciated, echoing Israel's purchase by Yahweh to be his bride. Added to all of this is the realisation by some scholars that lurking behind the imagery that Paul uses is the story of Hosea, with Gomer going after other gods and playing the harlot. The tragedy of Hosea was greatly compounded for it spoke of *corporate* Israel's infidelity to Yahweh. It is this corporate concern that is at the heart of Paul's discussion and it is natural to see how Israel's history becomes the canvas on which Paul expresses his concern for the faltering people of God at Corinth.

The Old Testament marriage language and imagery continues in 7:4, and the language of children being sanctified in 7:14 makes no sense outside of the covenantal imagery of the Old Testament. In 8:1-13 Paul covers the serious issue of eating food sacrificed to idols, the very thing Israel did in Exodus 32:6 when she committed idolatry and came under the covenant curse for her unfaithfulness. This is picked up in 10:1-22, with members of the Corinthian congregation dying for the sins of the community. The whole backcloth to this unfolding argument is made apparent when the scriptures Paul quotes or alludes to are examined. They are woven into Paul's appeal to the Corinthians not to be like Israel in the Exodus. The texts gathered from the Pentateuch[29] follow Israel's redemption and then her fall

[28]Witherington, *Quest*, 216-17.

[29]1 Corinthians 5:7 alludes to Exodus 12. 1 Corinthians 5:12 alludes to Deuteronomy 17:7; 19:19; 21:21, 24; 24:7. 1 Corinthians 6:16 cites Genesis 2:24. 1 Corinthians 6:20 alludes to Exodus 12 and Isaiah 52: 3-4 and 9-10. 1 Corinthians 8:4 alludes to Deuteronomy 6:4. 1 Corinthians 9:9 cites Deuteronomy 25:4. 1 Corinthians 10:2 alludes to Exodus 14:21-22. 1 Corinthians 10:3 alludes to Exodus 16:13-16. 1

from grace. Paul's focus is therefore much wider than an individual's behaviour, important as that is; rather Paul's concern is how this behaviour, i.e. that of the son with his father's wife, putrefies the community and brings her into judgment.

The harlot, her identity

The question that is posed by the above interpretation is, what or who is this *porne*? She is corporate, she has members, but is there anything else we can discover about her? I believe that there is, and this will become apparent from identifying who she is. She is that same community that has already been identified as the body of Sin, and it is precisely because she is the church's counterpart that Paul can use ecclesiastical language concerning her. She is that same *porne* that John speaks of in Revelation 17:

> This title was written on her forehead
> Mystery
> Babylon the Great
> The Mother of Prostitutes
> And of the Abomination of The Earth.

John had already described her activities in Revelation 17:1-2: 'Come, I will show you the punishment of the great prostitute, who sits on so many waters. With her the kings of the earth committed adultery, and the inhabitants of the earth were intoxicated with the wine of her adulteries.'

That John follows what is being argued by Paul, of two covenant communities, is evident by the fact that he proceeds, after describing the judgement of the prostitute (ch.18), to present the true bride, adorned for her husband.

> 'Then I heard what sounded like a great multitude, like the roar of rushing waters, and like loud peals of thunder, shouting:
>
> 'Hallelujah!
> For our Lord God Almighty reigns.
> Let us rejoice and be glad
> and give him glory!

Corinthians 10:4 alludes to Exodus 17:6. 1 Corinthians 10:5 alludes to Numbers 14:29. Note the clear statement that 'these things occurred as examples to keep us from setting our hearts on evil things as they did' (1 Cor. 10:6).

For the wedding of the Lamb has come,
and his bride has made herself ready' (Rev. 19:6-7).

The question that must be answered is whether scholarship will support these conclusions regarding the identification made, and the principles employed to reach it. The identification of the harlot of Revelation 17 gives rise to five distinct lines of interpretation.

The historic interpretation makes a straight equation between Babylon and the Roman Empire. Turner, an exponent of this view, points out the problem it has to face in the following extract:

> One would think this (great harlot) more appropriate of Jerusalem than of Rome. The Hebrew prophets constantly accused the holy city of the spiritual sin of fornication, namely religious syncretism and imprudent association with foreign kings; in v.2 this city, whatever it is, is accused of just that kind of association with the kings of the earth. It is difficult to resist the conclusion that all this is very fittingly applied to Jerusalem. Such a conclusion is strengthened by the observation that the last words of chapter 18 ('in her was found the blood of prophets and of saints, and of all who have been slain on the earth') remind us vividly of words which Jesus used of Jerusalem in Mt. 23:25 ('that upon you may come all the righteous blood shed on the earth from the blood of innocent Abel to the blood of Zechariah.... O Jerusalem, Jerusalem; Killing the prophets...'). So once more the question arises whether Revelation is not directed against militant and persecuting non-Christian Judaism, which arrested the spread of the Gospel in its earliest days, rather than secular Rome. On the other hand there are considerable difficulties in the acceptance of such a view and the rejection of the more usual identification with Rome. V.12, for instance (the ten kings), would most naturally be a reference to the Roman emperors, and the seven hills of v.9 look like those on which Rome is built.[30]

The second interpretation applies the image to Rome specifically, but also with a wider application to godless society. This interpretation overcomes the problem Turner has noted for the historical interpretation, but it would require us to accept that John sees beyond the historical situation to the universally historic manifestation of Babylon. While this is more attractive in that it overcomes the problems the historical interpretation faces, it is difficult to understand why, if John could see beyond the Roman Empire to succeeding, or even

---

[30]Turner, 'Revelation,' *PBC*, 149.

previous, empires, he should make Babylon apply particularly to Rome and to the principle of rebellion exhibited elsewhere. If he had the breadth of vision that enabled him to see beyond his own immediate situation, he would better have first established the general principle and then applied it to the particular situation he was in. This, as we shall see, is in fact the position of another interpretation.

The third interpretation, supported by the Reformers and many of their followers, sees Babylon as representing the Papacy which links religious and secular authority, as it did in the Middle Ages. While it would solve the problems Turner has noted, it has been challenged by the Reformed scholar Hendriksen.[31] He has pointed out that the description used by John is not *an adulteress* – as the Reformers' interpretation of the Roman Church having forsaken the covenant would require – but a harlot having no covenant with Yahweh.

The fourth interpretation is an updated presentation of the Reformers' view. It sees Babylon as the Roman Catholic Church, and many of the images used are seen as describing her influence in the emergence of a new Europe that will become a second Holy Roman Empire. Such views were popular while the European Common Market was made up of seven states, symbolising, in this view, the seven hills of Rome. But the view has serious problems, one of which is that the European Community has outgrown that number. The position clearly lacks credibility.

The fifth interpretation, which we will call the eschatological interpretation, sees the harlot as unredeemed human society. Ladd, a representative of this point of view, writes:

> The great harlot is seated upon many waters. This is a very important statement and provides us with one of the clues in the identification of the harlot. This description does not fit historical Rome, for while the Tiber flows through the city Rome was not built on many waters. The phrase does describe the historical Babylon because the city was built upon a network of canals. Jeremiah spoke of Babylon as the city which dwells on many waters (Jer. 51:13). John himself interprets the meaning of this phrase, 'The waters you saw, where the harlot is seated, are peoples and multitudes and nations and tongues' (v.15). Babylon became the personification of wickedness, and John has taken over the Old Testament symbolism and used Babylon to represent the final manifestation of the total history of godless nations. The city had a historical manifestation in first-century Rome, but the full significance of the wicked city is

[31]Hendriksen, *Conquerors*, 274.

eschatological. Rome could be seated on many waters in the sense that she drew her strength and sovereignty from her conquest of many nations, but it will be even more true of eschatological Babylon who will seduce all the world to worship that which is not God.[32]

This eschatological setting for Babylon, with its existence rooted in pre-eschatological history, supports the exegesis I have given on 1 Corinthians 6:19-20. But I have in fact gone beyond Ladd to see in the harlot a deeper significance for the history of salvation. Babylon is the body of Sin, with all the covenantal implications we have discussed. This wider covenantal interpretation has the support of Olshausen who, seemingly without appreciating its significance, not only identifies the whore of Revelation with the harlot of 1 Corinthians 6, as argued here, but supports seeing her as the counterpart of the church. Commenting on 1 Corinthians 6:15-16 he says:

> The whole passage is evidently grounded upon the comparison which is instituted between Christ and His Church (Eph. 5:23 ff), and it is not improbable that, when the apostle said that he that is joined to an harlot is one body with her, he had in view the great whore that sits upon many waters (Rev. 17:1).[33]

Torrance's remarks on Babylon also support the connection between the harlot and unredeemed man. Although he identifies the immediate representation of Babylon with the Roman Empire, he goes on to say:

> Babylon is, in fact, an imitation Kingdom of God; based on the demonic trinity. Ostensibly Babylon is a world-wide civilisation and culture, magnificent in her science and arts and commerce, but it is drugged with pride and intoxicated with its enormous success – Babylon is the worship of this world, the deification of economic power and worldly security. There is no doubt but that our world is in the grip of this wicked Babylon today – Babylon represents human collectivity.[34]

Therefore Paul's comments in 1 Corinthians 6 and the identification of the harlot as godless human society have been established. It was a theme that was not confined to Paul, but shared by the writer of the Apocalypse, and by implication, the whole church, otherwise the

---

[32]Ladd, *Revelation*, 221-2.
[33]Olshausen, *Revelation*, 110.
[34]Torrance, *Apocalypse*, 140.

Corinthians would have missed its significance.

Furthermore, in 2 Corinthians 6:14ff. we find the same eschatological themes as is found following Revelation 17: the call to come out from among them (2 Cor. 6:17; cf. Rev. 18:4); the promise that God would be their God (2 Cor. 6:18; cf. Rev. 21:7); and God's promise to live with them (2 Cor. 6:16; cf. Rev. 21:3). This shows clearly Paul's familiarity with and use of the same terms found in Revelation and which I have argued are the correct sphere for interpreting the meaning of the harlot in 1 Corinthians 6.

There is yet another section of Paul's writings that might be related to John's vision of the eschatological harlot. In 2 Thessalonians 2 Paul, writing about the ultimate manifestation of evil before Christ's return, says:

> Concerning the coming of our Lord Jesus Christ and our being gathered to him, we ask you, brothers, not to become easily unsettled or alarmed by some prophecy, report or letter supposed to have come from us, saying that the day of the Lord has already come. Don't let anyone deceive you in any way, for that day will not come until the rebellion occurs and the man of lawlessness is revealed, the man doomed to destruction. He opposes and exalts himself over everything that is called God or is worshipped, and even sets himself up in God's temple, proclaiming himself to be God. Don't you remember that when I was with you I used to tell you these things? And now you know what is holding him back, so that he may be revealed at the proper time. For the secret power of lawlessness is already at work; but the one who now holds it back will continue to do so till he is taken out of the way. And then the lawless one will be revealed, whom the Lord Jesus will overthrow with the breath of his mouth and destroy by the splendour of his coming. The coming of the lawless one will be in accordance with the work of Satan displayed in all kinds of counterfeit miracles, signs and wonders, and in every sort of evil that deceives those who are perishing. They perish because they refused to love the truth and to be saved. For this reason God sends them a powerful delusion so that they will believe the lie and so that all will be condemned who have not believed the truth but have delighted in wickedness (2 Thess. 2:1-12).

In verse 7 Paul mentions 'the secret power of lawlessness'. It is this term, used in such an unusual way, that may be further evidence that we are rightly discerning Paul's mind. What is this mystery of iniquity? It would seem to be linked with the title in Revelation 17:5, 'Mystery, Babylon the Great', and if it is, it would be a reference to the manifestation of the secret principle of evil. But can this be upheld?

Coppen outlined the use Paul makes of the term 'mystery'. He noted that Paul's use of the terms 'revelation', 'mystery', 'knowledge' and 'perfection' are linked very closely together to form 'a network of theological concepts'. Coppen observes that in Paul's earlier letters the calling of the Gentiles is a special aspect of the mystery, but in later letters, 'The mystery becomes principally the mysterious being of Christ, the universal significance of his being, and the mystical participation in this being, the fullness of divine grace.' In the Captivity Epistles, 'The mystery is no longer primarily the ultimate salvation of the Jews, nor the calling of the Gentiles, nor the miracle of the parousia, nor the glory of the final beatification in God; rather all of that is recapitulated in Christ.'[35]

Such an observation ought not to surprise us. It is, in fact, the inevitable result of the logic on which Paul has been basing his message. If (as from the very beginning he has in fact done) Paul has built his understanding on the concept of solidarity and representation, and if he has argued that God has put forth Christ as the last Adam to regain all that was lost by the first, then the final goal can be nothing less than the recapitulation of all creation. The relevance of this recapitulation for the church is that she will be the bride of Christ. Coppen says of that final state: 'Christ then is the mystery of God made visible, as the church in its turn will render the mystery of Christ visible.'[36]

Commenting on 2 Thessalonians 2:3 Coppen says: 'It remains that the Qumran literature offers numerous partial parallels to our text.... But we must not lose sight of the differences; the texts do not speak, as does St. Paul, of a personage who will be the ultimate incarnation of impiety, nor do they evoke the Messiah as the adversary and the conqueror of the man of sin.'[37]

It is this basic difference that we must note, for Paul speaks of the mystery of iniquity being related to the appearance of the man of sin. How are we to understand Paul's concept of mystery here? There is, in fact, only one key. As explained by Coppen, the mystery of Christ is to do with redemption, and finally, with the total recapitulation, when Christ shall be all in all. If Paul is consistent in his use of this technical expression we can only conclude that it is the opposite which is here

---

[35]Coppen, 'Parallels', 133.
[36]*op. cit.* 14.   [37]*op. cit.* 104.

taking place – the full display of man's alienation from God. The mystery of iniquity is the full revelation of unredeemed man's relationship with Sin itself as he yields himself to be its servant. Surely it is this concept of unrestrained evil and willing service of the anti-Christ that binds Paul's statement in 2 Thessalonians 2:3 to John's statement in Revelation 17:5. In both, the idea of mystery is tied in with the eschatological goal of the unredeemed in their relationship to Sin.

As a result of identifying the harlot figure of 1 Corinthians 6 we can turn to other passages in Paul's letters to see if her exposure throws any new light on Paul's statements. The first such passage is 1 Corinthians 10:15-33, in which Paul warns the Corinthians concerning attending meals which were held in honour of pagan deities. Paul's concern was, as Bruce expresses it, that 'those who shared such a feast under the patronage, for example, of Serapis, whether in his temple or in his private house, were considered to have perfect communion with him.'[38]

Paul warns them:

> Therefore, my dear friends, flee from idolatry. I speak to sensible people; judge for yourself what I say. Is not the cup of thanksgiving for which we give thanks a participation in the blood of Christ? And is not the bread that we break a participation in the body of Christ? Because there is one loaf, we, who are many, are one body, for we all partake of the one loaf. Consider the people of Israel; Do not those who eat the sacrifices participate in the altar? Do I mean then that a sacrifice offered to an idol is anything? No, but the sacrifices of pagans are offered to demons, not to God, and I do not want you to be participants with demons. You cannot drink the cup of the Lord and the cup of demons too; you cannot have a part in both the Lord's table and the table of demons (1 Cor. 10:14-20).

The nature of the two feasts is clearly equated. The table of demons speaks of the relationship that the participant has with them, just as the table of the Lord speaks of the relationship the believer has with him. The Lord's Supper is a covenant meal, and the warnings and appeals made to the Corinthians in chapters 10 and 11 follow the ancient pattern, exhibited in the Old Testament, which were given to the covenant community before they were called upon to proclaim

---

[38]Bruce, *Corinthians*, 96.

their relationship with Yahweh by partaking in the covenant renewal feasts. The direct comparison Paul gives between the two tables clearly implies that what one meant for one community, the other also meant for its counterpart. They both proclaim the existence of a covenant relationship with their respective patron. Now it is patently obvious that Paul does not believe in the existence of such deities, but he does see them as a cloak used by Satan to have control over their devotees. In other words, their relationship, their covenant, is with Satan.

This interpretation, of involvement in evil, is supported by Moffat who says concerning the passage being considered:

> He is thinking as a Jew who believed not so much in monotheism as in what was henotheism. The one God is superior to all other beings of the celestial realm, and yet the latter exists; good angels and spirits are media of his supreme power, while the evil (2:8) are already maimed and in the end to be disarmed, though at present they may, and do, exert an evil influence over any of the Lord's loyalists who are not careful to avoid their sway, particularly when that sway operates through their rites of sacrificial worship.[39]

Deluz holds the same position: 'Neither pagan feast nor the Lord's Supper offers purely bodily nourishment; they go beyond that. But pagan rites do not put the worshipper in communion with Jupiter, Minerva or Venus, for these have no existence. They are merely disguises worn by Satan to entice men to join his unholy carnival.'[40]

The seriousness of attending the table of demons is such that it is to be compared with the consequences of fornication, which Paul has dealt with earlier. Both bring the believer into a dangerous relationship with Satan, and both expose the lapsed believer to the Lord's discipline. This relationship of these two areas of Satanic influence is supported by Hèring:

> It is not only treachery to take part in pagan religious banquets, but there is also the risk of defiling the body of Christ to which the Christian belongs and of being cut off from it like a gangrenous limb. So we have here an exact parallel with the warning of chapter 5 according to which debauchery risks bringing expulsion from the body of Christ; even more strongly would it apply to idolaters.[41]

---

[39]Moffat, *Corinthians*, passim.
[40]Deluz, *Corinthians*, 130.
[41]Hèring, *Corinthians*, 96-7.

Thus Hèring not only supports our interpretation of the significance of the table of demons, but also our support for Kempthorne's view that sin against the body in 1 Corinthians 6 is with reference to the body of Christ.

Conclusions

To summarise the conclusions of this chapter. The 'body of Sin' in Romans 6.6 is the very opposite of 'the body of Christ'. This community is in covenant relationship with Satan, and it is also known as 'the harlot'. When this concept is introduced into both Romans 6 and 1 Corinthians 6 we find that it resolves theological and grammatical difficulties previously unresolved. Also, 'the harlot' has been seen to be the same community spoken of by John in Revelation and is linked with the eschatological mystery of iniquity in 2 Thessalonians 2:5-12. This suggests, as I have earlier claimed, that the New Exodus theme was fundamental to the entire church's understanding and therefore it is not appropriate to claim that there is not a New Testament theology but many theologies. This does not deny the fact that each author might bring his own insights to the theme, but they were insights that were under the control of the Old Testament model and not the result of flights of fantasy. All this shows that there was a very clear distinction in the early church between the church and the world, a distinction that was not merely one of belief, but of covenant relationships. The corporate setting for the reading and understanding of the epistles is also sustained, and New Testament theology is seen to be nothing less than an extension of Old Testament Paschal theology.

Implications

The above study, along with that of chapter 5, 'The Paschal Community and the body of Sin,' has alerted us to a corporate dimension in the thinking of Paul that is not normally appreciated. Indeed, we will soon see in chapter 7 that Paul teaches a corporate baptism of believers and in chapters 9 and 10 we will see that he taught a corporate act of justification. While there are sections of his letters that have always been seen to need a corporate reading, not least of all Romans 5, few have appreciated that this was typical of Paul's thought patterns. Almost without exception, Western commentators have tended to under-appreciate the corporate dimension of New Testament understanding. Hence their otherwise correct interpretation of Paul in individualistic terms is presented as an overemphasis of his teaching.

But what significance does the corporate identification of the 'body of sin' and the 'harlot' have for Christian understanding? First, it recognises that Paul was as far away from Hellenism with its dualistic understanding of man as it is possible to be. The Hellenistic 'body of sin', with its understanding of the body being in some way sinful, or even the place where sin resides, is from a different world than that inhabited by the apostle. He saw man as the chief of God's creative activity. Certainly he is a prisoner of Sin, bound in the kingdom of darkness, but that does not require that we bring into his doctrine of sin notions that are Hellenistic. This allows us to view man and his creative ability positively. His sinfulness does not lie in some sort of defilement that has taken him over and marred him, so making his physical state itself sinful, but in that he is the subject, tragically the willing subject, of the kingdom of darkness. In this condition he is at enmity with God and under his judgment. This is more terrible than we can begin to understand, but we are not to add notions that are not part of the biblical text. Sin does not dwell in man, but it does control him because of his membership of its kingdom.

Secondly, by seeing Paul's corporate perspective we are allowed to see that Paul begins with the community and not the individual. This clarifies not only Paul's anthropology, but that of the whole Bible. Man cannot be man other than in relationship to others. This is one reason that there can be no solitary Christians by choice. Man is made in the image of God, and the God of the Bible is a God who is himself a community. By beginning with individual experience, traditional exegesis stripped texts out of their corporate context and built a flawed account of Christian experience. It has left a few texts out of which a doctrine of the church could be built, and what has been built has been woefully inadequate to represent the wonder of God's new creation. By coming to the text corporately, we begin with the doctrine of the church, and the texts that are left over are those from which we construct individual experience. This does not deny the importance of individual experience, it simply locates Christian experience where God intended it to be, i.e. 'in Christ', which inevitably also means 'in his body'. By this Pauline method, we make much of the people of God, the church, and less of the individual. We also make better sense, I would argue, of the whole of Scripture.

Finally, by appreciating that the biblical doctrine of sin is different from the Hellenistic view that has dominated since Augustine brought his Hellenistic searchings into his reading of Paul, we are given a biblical doctrine of sin that allows us to see more clearly the glory of God's creation. We see that sin is relational more than it is legal. In claiming this we are staying faithful to the prophetic vision of sin, appreciated supremely by Hosea who saw that sin was the abandoning of God. This creation is fallen, marred, not what it was in its original conception, but it is not defiled in the sense that Sin has invaded it and made it dirty. There is no place for dualism in biblical thought, at least certainly not the dualism that, like a parasite, has fed off the biblical account of the fall of man, resulting in a view of man that denies the ongoing glory of man in creation. Man is defiled by Sin (Satan) and his own sins, but that must be understood in terms of Old Testament categories and not through alien concepts imported from outside of the biblical tradition. Also, we see creation for what it is, and man especially, a creation that God loves and has redeemed. We are thereby able to glory in the immensity of its wonder and beauty, and in the case of man, his creativity and potential, even as a fallen being. This is not to deny the awfulness of the condition of sin that man in Adam is in, but neither is it to allow Satan to have more than God has allowed him to have. This doctrine of sin is none other than Old Testament teaching, which demonstrates that Paul stayed true to his Jewish heritage.

Chapter Seven

The Paschal Community and Baptism

We have seen that Paul's understanding of servanthood is derived from his Old Testament roots where Israel was called into a covenant relationship with Yahweh and appointed to be his servant. Unless Yahweh had redeemed Israel she could never have become the covenant community and so could never have become his representative to the nations. Israel became the covenant people of God as a result of Yahweh's saving activity in the Exodus. I am now going to examine how the Lord God brought into existence the new covenant community, a people who, as we saw in chapter 4, have been appointed to be his servant to the world.

The background of all that Paul says in Romans 6 is found in Romans 5. In that passage Paul discussed two communities, one in Christ, the other in Adam. The apostle described how the members of these communities shared in either the transgression or the obedience of their representative head. Between this statement of two communities and the statement regarding 'the body of Sin',[1] Paul speaks of the baptism that the Romans have experienced (6:1-4). I have argued in previous chapters that the expression 'the body of Sin' is corporate, being an alternative image for the kingdom of darkness. It would appear, however, that the opening verses of Romans 6, if interpreted from an individual perspective, interrupt the flow of the solidarity concept essential for the argument in chapter 5 and so prevent it being a link with 6:6 that would identify 'the body of Sin' with the unredeemed community that has Adam as its head. If, however, the baptism spoken of in 6:1ff. is found to have a corporate dimension it would form a bridge between chapter 5 and 6:6 that continues the corporate theme and so supports my interpretation of 'the body of Sin'.

Baptism has divided the church for many centuries. To this day opinions differ as to the significance of the ordinance and what text speaks of what reality. While support for the view that baptism was

[1]Romans 6:6. I shall use upper case for Sin as it has been argued that Sin is a pseudonym for Satan.

derived from the mystery religions has declined, nevertheless there is still no clear consensus as to the origin and significance of the rite.

What is generally agreed is that baptism is closely associated with the death of Christ. Also, there is wide agreement that Paul used the Exodus of the Jews from Egypt as a type in his exposition of the significance of baptism. In addition there is some agreement that texts exist in which the emphasis is not so much on the believer's individual baptism in water, but on the believer's inclusion into Christ's baptism into suffering, i.e. his crucifixion. Furthermore there is widespread agreement that the passage we are considering is a key part of the argument of Paul and not only reflects the theology of the rest of the letter but actually pulls the various themes together.

The range of interpretations of Romans 6:1-4 encompasses those who see the passage referring to baptismal regeneration,[2] the reception of the Spirit in baptism,[3] water baptism as a symbol of regeneration,[4] the Spirit's baptism of the believer into the body of Christ at conversion,[5] and water baptism which witnesses to having shared with Christ in his death on Golgotha.[6]

Those who hold this latter view are divided into two groups; those who see water baptism as the occasion when the Spirit is given and what was done on Calvary is imparted to the believer,[7] and those who see the Spirit being given before baptism, with baptism being no more than the means of confession and not the occasion of regeneration.[8]

What is common to all these views is that they see the passage as referring to the experience of the individual believer, either as being regenerated by the Spirit through baptism or making confession in baptism of what the Spirit has already done for the one being baptised. A third understanding has no link with water but sees baptism to refer solely to the Spirit's baptism of the individual into the body of Christ. However, there is another possibility that the biblical evidence allows. This alternative view is based on the type used by Paul in 1 Corinthians

---

[2]Robinson, *Wrestling*, 70 says, 'Without baptism nothing that has been done for us would have any effect in our lives, for it is only here that it is done in us.'

[3]Turner, *Spiritual*, 105.

[4]Best, *Body*, 47; Murray, *Romans*, 1:214 and Marshall, 'Meaning', 138-9.

[5]Lloyd Jones, *Romans*, 35-36.

[6]Wright, 'Romans', 197.

[7]Best, *Body*, 73; Beasley-Murray, *Baptism*, 140.

[8]Stott, *Romans*, 173.

10:1ff., that of Israel's baptism into Moses, in which the whole community shared at the same decisive moment. It is not about water baptism, although that bears witness to it, nor is it about the individual being united with Christ at conversion. What I suggest is that this baptism refers to the major redemptive event that happened historically long before the work of regeneration in the individual took place and is the ground upon which the Spirit does his work in the church or in the individual believer. I shall explain this further as I proceed with the exegesis of key texts.

These observations point again in a New Exodus direction for understanding Paul's understanding of baptism, for his viewing the death of Christ in the context of the Passover event, with all of its associations with the Exodus, cannot be missed. The fact that the Exodus was seen in the Old Testament to be the event when the glory and power of Yahweh were publicly displayed, and the Second Exodus, i.e. that from Babylon, was seen as bringing the son of God (Israel) from the dead, naturally links the Exodus with the death and resurrection of the Son of God when the power and glory of God would be supremely displayed.

Difficult texts and corporate baptism

Romans 6:1-4
Romans 6.1-4 contains a problem that all views find difficult to resolve. Paul speaks in verse 3 of being buried by baptism into death. The difficulty here is that Paul reverses the order of things in a serious way. If baptism is a symbol of burial, then Paul is saying that believers are buried with Christ to produce or achieve death. This is an abhorrent picture, for burial comes after death and not before it. What the traditional interpretation understands is that Paul is teaching that believers are baptised into death rather than, as I am claiming he is saying, believers are buried with Christ as the result of a baptism that has united them with him as he was dying. Thus it was a baptism into his death. The burial is quite distinct from the baptism; it takes place as a consequence of the union created through baptism.

There is something else happening in the argument of Romans 6:1ff which is not usually identified. It is indicated by the way that Paul uses the plural and the aorist: you, together, were baptised. To this can be added the fact that Paul uses the anarthrous form to underline the uniqueness of this baptism, so he speaks in verse 4 of '*the* baptism into *the* death'.[9] Such evidence might be dismissed as inadequate if presented on its own, but when put into the context of the observations about to be made, especially Schnackenberg's observations on the construction of Galatians 3:24ff., which is widely recognised as a parallel passage to Romans 6, then the construction does begin to carry weight.

1 Corinthians 12:13

Another grammatical oddity occurs in 1 Corinthians 12:13 where Paul speaks of being baptised by one Spirit into one body. The most natural rendering of *eis* with the accusative is 'to form one body'. This is understandably dropped for the weaker 'into one body', for it would mean that the church would never exist until the last member had been incorporated into it to make the body complete.[10] Obviously this would be absurd, for the church is not only seen to exist, but is declared to exist, in the Scriptures.[11]

The mention of the baptism of the Spirit, a baptism that is *to form one body*, is the outcome of an argument in which Paul has likened the Corinthian church to the old covenant community. The sins of the Corinthians parallel the sins into which Israel had fallen. The baptism into Moses is the type of the Spirit's baptism to form the one body in Christ. In other words, chapter 12 is intrinsically linked to 1 Corinthians 10 with its assertion that the members of the old covenant were baptised corporately into Moses. It is the historical corporate baptism that is clearly to the fore in 1 Corinthians 10. It relates to Israel, not as individuals, but as the designated covenant community. In that historic moment of salvation the nation received Moses as its representative head, and so were baptised into him. Every succeeding generation of Jews, and each individual within those generations, saw themselves as actually involved in that act of salvation, and could therefore speak of it as their baptism into Moses. It is the antitype of this corporate-historical baptism of the people of God that has taken place to bring the Christian community into existence, and it is to this that Paul is referring when he says: 'The body is a unit, though it is made up of

---

[9]Kasemann, *Romans*, 166, says, 'It is hard to see why the article should be repeated before εἰς or αὐτοῦ added to θάνατου.'

[10]Best, *Body*, 69; Moule, *Origins*, 71; Schnackenberg, *Baptism*, 26.

[11]cf Acts 20:28; 1 Corinthians 1:2; 1 Thessalonians 1:1; 2 Thessalonians 1:1; Revelation 2:1, 8, 12, 18; 3:1, 7, 14.

many parts; and though all its parts are many they form one body. So it is with Christ. For we were all baptised by one Spirit into one body – whether Jews or Greeks, slave or free – and we were all given the one Spirit to drink' (1 Cor. 12:13).

Thus as in the type the Jews were baptised into Moses and drank of the water from the rock, so Paul goes on to explain that in the antitype the baptism is into Christ, and the Christian Church partakes of the Spirit (represented by the water), who comes from Christ (represented by the smitten rock).[12]

Thus, after a section that has followed typological exegesis of the experience of the old order, Paul describes how the new order has come into existence. The birth of the old order involved the giving of gifts to the Jews (Exod. 12:36; 35:30-35), gifts that were essential for the building of the tabernacle and for the worship of Yahweh. But Paul then shows that the gifts of the new order are spiritual, and they are given by the Spirit in order that the temple of the living God might be brought to its full purpose, to be the place where the Lord is found and worshipped (1 Cor. 14:24-25).

That there is a continuing comparison between type and antitype in the mind of Paul can be shown by an examination of the whole section of 1 Corinthians 10–15. Paul has compared the two patterns of salvation in chapter 10, showing one to be type and the other antitype. In chapters 11–14 he establishes the order expected by the Lord in the lives and worship of his people. The whole section is clearly modelled closely on the Pentateuch. As the Exodus displayed God's power and established a community through whom the Gentiles could find God, so Paul says in 14:25 that a Gentile 'will fall down and worship God, exclaiming "God is really among you!"' As the Pentateuch establishes the divinely ordered role of the sexes (Gen. 2:20-24; Lev. 20:7-14), so Paul gives an outline of this in 11:1-16, applying its principle to the church's ordinances and discipline. In 11:17-33 Paul gives instructions for the celebration of the covenant meal of the New Testament, as the Jews had been previously instructed in their covenant meal (Exod. 12:24-28.). Just as the Jews were given gifts both by the Egyptians and by the Lord, so the church has been given spiritual gifts; and as the gifts of the Exodus were used by the

[12]Ellis, 'A Note', 53ff, sees the reference to the rock to be an allusion to Isaiah, thus reinforcing New Exodus imagery, i.e what happened under Moses will happen in the Davidic Exodus.

community for worship, so these spiritual gifts are to facilitate the church in her worship and service (Eph. 4:9-13). Chapter 13 shows that the controlling principle is not to be the law (the type), but love (the antitype), which is the fulfilment of the law (Rom. 13:10). Paul continues in chapter 14 to speak of the need for orderly conduct in worship (14:26-39); so the antitype is to reflect the principle of orderliness contained in the type set up under Moses.

This section is brought to its conclusion in chapter 15, where Paul explains the significance of Christ's death and resurrection. This, taken with 11:23-26, shows Paul, the spiritual father of the Corinthians, instructing his children of the significance, not of the Jewish Passover, but the Christian Passover. 15:3 says that Christ was raised from the dead on the third day; 15:20 says that Christ's resurrection was the firstfruits of those who are raised from the dead; in the Old Testament the firstfruits were offered three days after the Paschal sacrifice (Lev. 23:11), so suggesting that the reference to the third day has a Paschal significance.

In addition, the conclusion of the chapter has Paul exulting over death and the grave. The Old Testament passage quoted (Hos. 13:14) is one where the prophet, after speaking of the Jewish exile, which he likens unto death, acclaims that even death itself (exile) will not hold God's people; but that they will return in glorious victory. As this referred to the Second Exodus, it is easy to see how Paul incorporates it into the overall type of the original Exodus. Paul sees the church militant journeying to the promised land, with the wanderings in the wilderness applying to the actual experience of the church now. Nothing, not even the greatest enemy, can stop her entering the Kingdom of God. Thus it is appropriate for Paul to make use of the promised eschatological New Exodus material of Hosea 13:14 when speaking of the resurrection of the church, for it is the type of her entering into her inheritance after redemption and pilgrimage.

The continuing development of this theme throughout 1 Corinthians 10–15 vindicates applying typological principles to understand Paul. This in turn supports my claim that 1 Corinthians 12:13 refers to a corporate baptism of all believers.

Galatians 3:26-29

Galatians 3:26ff. also has a significance not generally recognised. The construction Paul uses suggests that he sees all of the Galatians being baptised at exactly the same moment. This point is brought home clearly in the comments of Schnackenberg when he says:

> It would be possible to interpret the whole baptismal event as a unity in which the baptised are plunged; it represents Christ as a Pneuma-sphere into which they are removed. All (παντες v 26, ὅσοι v 27a, παντες v 28b) are immersed into Jesus Christ, without respect to national, social and sexual distinctions. But this exposition causes misgivings. The imagery would attain its complete effect only under the presupposition that all were immersed unitedly into the baptismal water, but that is hardly possible.[13]

Schnackenburg's Roman Catholic theology hindered him seeing anything else but water baptism in a passage, or indeed a letter, that makes no mention of water whatsoever.

What is also significant is that the passage clearly parallels Romans 6:1-4 and 1 Corinthians 12:13, for it is the Spirit who is the agent of all three baptisms and the outcome of union is the gift of the same Spirit and sonship which his presence establishes. This corresponds to Israel's experience where she became the son of God as a result of her deliverance under Moses' leadership and was given the Spirit to guide her through her wanderings.

I am going to argue (see page 208) later that this same corporate dimension lies behind 1 Corinthians 6:11. There is no mention of the word 'baptism' in that text, but there is reference to washing, sanctification and justification. We will eventually see that these terms are found in 1 Corinthians 1:30 and that they form part of the vocabulary that the Old Testament prophets used to describe the New Exodus.

Ephesians 5:27

Ephesians 5:27 is a corporate baptism, for it is the cleansing of the church as the bride in readiness for her presentation before the Father. The reference to water in the passage seems to be based on Ezekiel 16:9, a passage in which Yahweh describes the defiled condition of Israel when he took her for his own and washed her to purify her to be his bride. The mention of cleansing by the word probably reflects Ezekiel 37:4 where Israel in her exile is described as being a pile of dry bones. It was the word of the Lord that was proclaimed to her that brought her to life, and by implication cleansed her from the defilement of death to become the resurrected community. Paul in

---

[13]Schnackenburg, *Baptism*, 24. Earlier Schnackenburg had spoken of Galatians 3:27b as 'describing a profound ontological event,' *op. cit.* 21.

Ephesians 2:2 has already explained the natural condition of the church before her regeneration as being dead, and here in chapter 5 he explains the means by which the defilement is removed and the bride is cleansed for her presentation. Paul describes her glorious future and how it has been secured. The New Exodus pattern is supported by other sections of the letter, but I must resist going beyond our immediate study of baptism in Paul and restrict my comments to those passages that deal specifically with baptism.

Ephesians 4:6
The proposed corporate baptism explains the meaning of 'one Lord, one faith, one baptism' in 4:6. To put water baptism into a statement which is to do with the great foundational realities that the confession declares is obviously misplaced. It cannot be claimed to have the sort of significance possessed by the eternal truths Paul has listed. If, however, the one baptism is not a reference to water, but to the one great event in which the Spirit made the Lord one with his people in the event of his vicarious atoning death, then it fits logically and naturally. It is certainly in harmony with 5:27 where the cleansing is clearly the consequence of the death of Christ. That text refers to the baptism of the church, i.e. the bride, and 5:24ff. describes a corporate identity. This pattern is exactly that which we have observed in Romans 6:1ff., which must not be separated from the conclusion of the section in 7:1ff., which is about how a new marriage takes place as a result of dying to the old marriage relationship and therefore brings the significance of the death of Christ for his bride together.

If it is argued that the point of reference for the Ephesian baptism is marriage, but that of Romans, Corinthians and Galatians is sonship, then it must be pointed out that marriage is present in these letters (Rom. 7:1-6; 2 Cor. 11:2; Gal. 4:24-31), and that sonship is referred to in Ephesians (1:5). In other words, Israel was called the son of God, she was also described as the bride of Yahweh, a description that is decisively eschatological. Thus it would seem that sonship is reserved for the present state of being members of Christ's kingdom, and the bridal imagery is reserved for the eschatological fulfilment when the kingdom of God is finally consummated. This is not challenged by Romans 8:23, for adoption of sons refers to the completion of the 'adoption' process that ushers in the kingdom of God in which the church relates to Christ as his bride.

This corporate baptism fits the exposition that I have been arguing. It is most clearly seen in that Romans 6 has developed out of the argument expanded in chapter 5 of two communities bound in solidarity with their representative heads. To establish the freedom into which the people of God have been brought, Paul demonstrated that the believer is no longer part of the old solidarity of Sin and death and showed that a new solidarity exists. He has explained how this new freedom has been achieved. The whole of the argument of Romans is not related to the believer as an individual, but to the community of believers, the church. This perspective in no way alters the need for personal repentance and regeneration, but it puts the goal of the individual response to be entrance into the already formed and 'complete' covenant community, as it was in the Old Testament.

Pauline use of the preposition *sun*

Linguistic analysis has revealed a carefully followed pattern in the way Paul describes believers' relationship to one another and to Christ in the resurrection event. Best has noted that Paul used the preposition *sun* (with) to speak of the fellowship of believers.[14] He has also noted that there is a corporate dimension to the statement in Galatians 3:25-27.[15] This left his conclusions in a state of tension for he held that the baptism passages we have considered referred to water baptism. Best was not able to reconcile the fellowship allusions, which were clearly corporate, with the individualism that water baptism inevitably imposes.

Best noted that Paul deliberately designated select prepositions to convey the concepts of the state of the church at different moments of its inception and development. For the experience of the church sharing in Christ's death and resurrection Paul uses the phrase *with Christ (sun Christō)*,[16] whereas he speaks of the life lived in fellowship with Christ as being *in Christ (en Christō)*.[17] Best summed up the evidence of the use of these two prepositions: 'The formula "with Christ" has, thus, not the same social nature as the formula "in Christ". Christians are not brought so close together by it,

---

[14]Best, *Body*, 62.

[15]*op. cit.* 47/68.

[16]Romans 6:8; Ephesians 2:5; Colossians 2:20; 3:1; 3:3.

[17]Romans 3:24; 8:2, 39; 12:5; 1 Corinthians 1:2;15:22; 2 Corinthians 3:14; 5:15; 12:2; Galatians 1:22; 2:4; Ephesians 1:3; 2:6, 10, 13; Philippians 3:14; 4:21; Colossians 1:28; 1 Thessalonians 4:16; 2 Timothy 1:9,13; 3:12; Philemon 6, 23.

not given mutual duties by it; it emphasises the relationship of each believer to Christ rather than the relationship of each to the other.'[18]

Best's observations need further clarification. On closer examination of the texts we find that a pattern clearly emerges. There is no mention of being baptised together, but only of being raised together and seated together (Rom. 6:1-4; Eph. 2:4-7; Col. 2:12). The fulcrum for this change from an individualistic to a corporate dimension is clearly the event of the death of Christ. The believer is baptised into Christ's death, as an individual, and consequently raised, together with all other believers, to share in the blessings of the eschatological community. The question that must be posed is, when did this baptism take place and what was the nature of it?

It is very important to realise that if these texts refer to water baptism, then it means that before the believer's oneness with Christ was established, believers were seated in the heavenlies (Eph. 2:6). Hodge was aware of the need to emphasise that the raising up of the believer with Christ is an historic fact, that believers were actually raised with Christ when he came out of his grave.[19] What Hodge does not ask is how could this actual historical exaltation take place without any prior union. In other words, the logic of Paul's thinking requires that the unity is established long before water baptism is administered, even before the experience of conversion and the reception of the Spirit. Indeed, if the believer (or better the church, for the language Paul uses of being raised is corporate) was raised with him, then the unity had to be in existence even before Christ left the tomb.

Robinson has noted the believer's union with Christ in his death.[20] However, Robinson sees water baptism in texts that have no mention of water, and then inadmissibly uses the same texts to claim that the writer is referring to the one baptism of Christ into suffering in which all believers share by virtue of the union set up between them and Christ *in their baptism*. But this not only assumes the presence of water in passages that make no reference to water, but, more importantly, it does not adequately explain how the vital participation in the post-resurrection events can have been achieved if the union was to be forged centuries later. Also, Robinson's exegesis puts the emphasis on the 'one baptism *of* Christ', rather than on 'the one

[18]*op. cit.* 59.
[19]Hodge, *Ephesians*, 113.
[20]Robinson, 'Baptism', 257.

baptism *into* Christ'. Because of this he missed the corporate nature of the baptism.

This timescale problem is overcome once it is realised that alongside the baptism into Christ is the type of the baptism of the Israelites into Moses in their Exodus. All Jews, according to Gamaliel the second,[21] of all preceding and subsequent generations, were present in the coming out of Egypt, and shared in the baptism that made Moses their leader. It was then that Israel became the son of God and the Spirit was given to her to lead her through her wilderness journey.

This explains why Paul has been so decisive in his use of the preposition *sun*. There is no unity of believers, either with each other or with Christ, until they have been united together through baptism. Paul has been careful to define this baptism in terms of its occasion, for it was a baptism *into Christ's death*. As Moses, in the Exodus from Egypt, took out the people of God, for they were united with him through baptism, so Christ takes those who have been baptised into union with him from the realm of Sin and death. This baptism into Christ took place in his Exodus (Luke 9:31), in his coming out of the realm of Sin and death. It was a baptism into his death that all believers experienced, in the same historic moment.

There was no union, either with each other or with Christ, until it had been created by the Spirit. It was this baptism that brought the covenant community into existence. Therefore if one asks when did the church historically come into existence, the answer is at the moment of Christ's death, for it was then that the Spirit baptised all members[22] of the covenant community into union with their Lord and Saviour.[23] Once this union had been established, Paul was free to use the preposition *en* (in), which speaks of the fellowship of believers in Christ. From then on, in terms of ultimate reality, no believer could experience anything apart from all other believers, for their union with Christ is such that all other believers are also partakers in Christ's saving work.

What I am arguing for is that the baptism passages which we have considered are speaking neither about water baptism nor even

---

[21]Best, *Body*, 57, who quotes from Leenhardt, *Sacrement*, 18.

[22]Individually, yet because at the same moment they became Christ's body, corporately.

[23]This is not to deny the importance of Pentecost when the Church received the Spirit – the fulfilment of the promises of the Old Testament concerning the coming of the last days.

of Christ's baptism into his sufferings, even though these are important related themes, but about a baptism modelled on the baptism of Israel into Moses when Israel came into a covenant relationship with Yahweh through the representative he had appointed. In Romans 6 (and in 1 Corinthians 12:13, Galatians 3.:5ff, Ephesians 4:6 and 5:25-27) Paul is demonstrating how the old order has been brought to an end and how the new eschatological order has come into existence. It is because believers have shared in the death of Christ, with the consequence that they have died to all the covenantal demands of the old relationship that bound them mercilessly to Sin and Death (Satan), that they are now free to live lives unto God who has made them his own through Christ his Son.

Baptism and sonship

In Romans 6, 1 Corinthians 10:2; 12:13 and Galatians 3:27 there is a further link to establish common concepts of a corporate baptism apart from the grammar of the texts. In each passage sonship is part of the setting. Romans 6 links with sonship in chapter 8:14ff. In I Corinthians 10 the establishment of sonship is clearly part of the type. It was through the Exodus that Israel became Yahweh's son (Hos. 11:1). Being basic to the type, it must be a part of the antitype, and 1 Corinthians 6:1ff. supports this claim. There Paul urges the Corinthians to exercise their Messianic authority, i.e. their authority as sons of God. The Galatians passage (3:27-28) could not be any more explicit in expounding the relationship between baptism and sonship. In addition, in each of these three letters there is a claim that the distinction between Jew and Gentile has been ended. In Romans, it is expressed in 4:11-12 where Paul argues that all believers, both Jews and Gentiles, are children of Abraham; in 1 Corinthians 12:13 and Galatians 3:27 it is expressed even more explicitly: Paul says, 'There is neither Jew nor Greek, bond nor free, male nor female, for you are all one in Christ Jesus.' Just as the baptism into Moses at the Exodus established a covenant community in which all Jews had equal standing, so the baptism into Christ creates a community in which all distinctions are abolished, and in which all believing Jews and Greeks, males and females, have an equal standing before God.

The argument I have based on Romans 6 is fully supported in Colossians 2:11-13:

In him you were also circumcised, in the putting off of the sinful nature, not with a circumcision done by the hands of men but with the circumcision done by Christ, having been buried (*suntaphentes*) with him in baptism and raised (*sunēgerthēte*) with him through your faith in the power of God, who was raised from the dead. When you were dead in your sins and the uncircumcision of your sinful nature, God made you alive with Christ. He forgave all our sins.

Here is confirmed what has already been noted, the raising/ quickening is clearly corporate, the preposition *sun* being used to convey this. It might be thought that *suntaphentes auto en to baptismati* is an exception to what has been said regarding baptism not being of the body, but to form the body. However, Paul is not saying, as it is so often interpreted, that we have been buried with him in baptism, but that we have been buried with him, by, or because of, *the* baptism. Here again Paul has used the definite article with baptism (*to baptismati)* and for a correct understanding of *en* in this phrase I appeal to the immediate use of it by Paul in the passage we are considering. This shows that it can clearly have the meaning 'by' as well as 'in'. Thus, the passage is saying the same as Romans 6:3-4. By baptism (accomplished by the Spirit) we have been united with Christ in his death. Because this union existed we were buried together with Christ and with all other members of the eschatological community, and together we have been raised with him. This exegesis also points the way to understanding what the circumcision of Christ means. In the Old Testament, circumcision indicated entrance into the covenant that separated Israel from the nations. Here it is spiritual circumcision that has been done vicariously on the representative head. His suffering is applied to the church in her regeneration in which she and her members are given a circumcised heart.

Conclusion

Once again we have seen that Paul has stayed within the corporate categories of the Old Testament. He has modelled the creation of the New Testament community in the same terms as Israel's inauguration when she was brought out of Egypt. In reverting to the original Exodus Paul has not abandoned the New Exodus motif, he has simply merged the two exoduses of the Old Testament to form his model. This allowed him to use the Paschal sacrifice of the Egyptian Exodus to interpret the death of Jesus. The Babylonian Exodus was not based on a sacrificial rite and therefore needed augmentation. He joined the sacrificial element of the Egyptian Exodus with the promises of the prophets of a New Covenant to produce his New Exodus paradigm. It was this merger that was unique to the New Testament, for the Jewish material did not look for a suffering Messiah whose death would bring about the salvation of the new covenant community. Paul saw the death of Jesus to be his exodus and identified the moment of the birth of the community under its new representative to be in the moment of its Messiah's death. Thus all Christians have been baptised into his death. To be outside of that event is to be outside of Christ.

Again we see the clear use Paul made of the prophets' New Exodus model that had been enriched by the sacrificial threads of the original Exodus and fulfilled in the death and resurrection of Jesus. We will see in chapter 8 that the Passover is fundamental to Paul's understanding of the death of Jesus.

Section Three

Soteriology and Passover

Chapter Eight

The Paschal Community and Redemption

We have seen that Paul's use of the Old Testament is not arbitrary as many have thought. He had a profound respect for the original historical context of the passages that he quoted. In the original setting they almost invariably referred to the exile of Israel in Babylon and her subsequent salvation by Yahweh in bringing her back to her inheritance. These texts are skilfully transposed by Paul from the historical experience of Israel and used to describe what the condition of humanity is and how Yahweh has acted in salvation.

The precise language Paul used was also the result of devoted respect. Generally he did not force new meanings on to vocabulary but kept to their LXX meanings. In this there undoubtedly was a problem for the Gentiles. They had to learn this embedded theological content as against their own secular/religious meanings. Nevertheless, we saw how scholars have assumed that secular usage was uppermost in Paul's mind and how this has masked the theological richness of his meaning. Instead of appreciating that Paul used *doulos* with the same semantic range and theological constant as found in the LXX, they assumed that Paul used the term to speak of believers as slaves of Christ. I argued that Paul did not view himself as a slave; rather he saw himself as a servant, with all of the dignity that the prophets received as called by Yahweh into his service.

The same Hellenistic/Semitic confusion has dominated how other key salvation expressions have been understood. Until relatively recently the term 'righteousness of God' was understood to refer to God's moral perfection and excellence. This was seen to be expressed in his law and those who lived according to its precepts were deemed to be righteous. Without denying that these ideas exist in the expression, it must be appreciated that the term bears a much richer significance, one that is essential for understanding salvation history. The use that the Old Testament prophets made of this concept is a key to realising Paul's understanding of salvation.

We can understand the differences between the legal meaning, which is essentially Hellenistic, and the covenantal salvation history meaning, which is essentially Semitic, by considering the following example. A judge might be regarded as just or righteous in that he always upholds the law and applies it to those who come before his bench. However, what he is in his home might be totally different from what he is in his court. He might be cruel, unloving, sarcastic, jealous and many other things. In Old Testament terms such a judge could not be called righteous.

Similarly, the king was righteous if he worked for the good of his people and encouraged loyalty to Yahweh. Saul was regarded as unrighteous by the biblical author because he was not concerned about upholding righteousness but about his own reputation and position. David was perceived by the biblical author as righteous because, apart from his tragic episode with Bathsheba, he longed and strove for the reign of God among his people. In other words, he wanted truth and justice to characterise the lives of the Israelites.

God is not only righteous because he prefers good or even because he punishes evil. He is essentially righteous because he comes to the aid of those who are suffering, who have no hope if he does not deliver them. God's righteousness cannot be separated from his saving activity. Thus when Isaiah speaks of God's righteousness being revealed, he means that God is about to act to save his people.

This understanding of the righteousness of God is clearly intrinsic to Paul's meaning. When Paul speaks of God's righteousness he refers to God's saving activity in the death of his Son. When Paul writes about the righteousness of God appearing, he means the salvation of God coming through the death and resurrection of Jesus.

Yet it must be recognised that God's righteous activity can involve judgement as well as deliverance. God, because he is the God that he is, must judge those who reject his warnings and spurn his mercy. This is what happened to Israel when Babylon conquered her and took her into exile. Cut off from the Temple, exiled in Babylon where her broken relationship with her God was displayed to the nations, she was an object lesson to them concerning the righteousness of God. Yahweh had stayed true to the covenant stipulations and after many warnings had fulfilled the curses against those who had violated the covenant, even his own people. Only when Yahweh's judgement and righteousness had been carried out could he act to save Israel. Redemption is therefore indivisible from righteousness in the minds of the prophets and consequently in the mind of Paul. Indeed, redemption is the outworking of God's righteousness, his faithfulness to his covenantal promises, and cannot be understood properly outside of this Old Testament setting.

This is the reason why sacral manumission is utterly inadequate to describe the redemption that is in Christ. It not only lacks Old Testament theological foundations, but it fails to explain adequately the language and imagery that is used by Paul.

Romans 3:21-26

This passage has been extensively examined in attempts to find the paradigm used by Paul. The sacrificial language has been widely assumed to reflect the Day of Atonement because of the reference to the *hilasterion* in verse 25. The term was translated 'propitiation' until challenged by Dodd who claimed that it meant 'expiation'.[1] This in itself did not require a different setting from the Day of Atonement, but an adjustment in understanding what was taking place through the sacrifices made on that day. However Dodd was accused of not properly interpreting the evidence because he had ignored biblical texts that did not fit his theory and it was therefore argued that *hilasterion* should retain its propitiatory meaning.[2]

One response has been to say that *hilasterion* refers to the place of atonement, the lid of the ark of the covenant as used in Hebrews 9:4 and found in different places throughout Ezekiel.[3] Others questioned the Day of Atonement setting, arguing that if this was the model Paul followed, he would have used more imagery that reflected the festival. In support of this challenge it was pointed out that the public (*proetheto*) display of the sacrifice of Christ (v 25) is contrary to the privacy of the sacrifice of the Day of Atonement.[4]

Scholars unhappy with the Day of Atonement model have suggested that the reference to the *hilasterion* links the death of Jesus with the death of the Maccabean martyrs (4 Macc 17:22).[5] The Maccabean martyr prayed that his death would be an *hilasterion* (propitiation) for the nation's sins. The Jewish martyrs found in Isaac's willingness to die the inspiration they needed to be faithful to death.[6] Isaac

---

[1]Dodd, 'Cognates,' 325-60.

[2]Morris, 'Meaning,' 33ff.

[3]Schlatter, *Romans*, 98; H.C.G. Moule, *Romans*, 93; Olshausan, *Romans*, 152 and Black, *Romans*, 69.

[4]Buschel, *TDNT* 3:317.

[5]Barrett, *Romans*, 1:217-8; Wright, *Victory*, 607.

became the prototype of all martyrs and his willingness to die links into an extensive Rabbinic theological structure of atonement. This rabbinic teaching has been widely utilized in interpreting Paul despite the fact that there is an ongoing controversy as to the dating of the various rabbinic texts on which the structure is based. However, there are scholars who argue that, because there is no certainty that the rabbinic material existed before Paul, the material should not be used to interpret Paul's thinking.

While there is debate over the admissibility of rabbinic evidence concerning an early rabbinic martyrdom theology, most consider that the Maccabean material can stand in its own right, as they hold it to be pre-Pauline. But even this is far from certain. The dating of 4 Maccabees is put by some as late as AD 70. With this uncertainty it is wise not to place too much weight on its statements. But even if it is accepted as early enough to be contemporary with Paul, we do not know if the traditions of the Maccabean martyrs were known in Rome. This leaves some uncertainty as to whether Paul could expect his readers to follow allusions to the Maccabeans.

Despite widespread scholarly support for the Maccabean tradition we have motifs in this passage which cannot be contained in martyrdom theology. However, these terms – righteousness, justification and redemption – are naturally at home in the New Exodus model. Added to this is Paul's repeated claim that this redemption is borne witness to by the law and the prophets (1:3; 3:21). It would therefore be more natural to look to those writings to find Paul's model.

There is only one cultic event in which redemption is celebrated, and that is Passover. Passover/Exodus controlled Israel's self-consciousness, it controlled her existence. She could not define herself apart from the fact that Yahweh had redeemed her. Indeed, it was the one festival about which Jews and God-fearers had detailed knowledge, and her ethical system was founded on the fact of Yahweh's mercy toward her in redeeming her from slavery (Deut. 24:17). Now if Passover/Exodus is at the heart of Israel's self identification and understanding, and since most of the writers of the New Testament documents were Jews, then it should not be surprising to find that this same imagery is at the heart of the eschatological salvation to which Israel had been looking forward.

Consideration of this setting has probably been blocked due to the

[6]See 4 Maccabees 6.29. So Williams, *Death*, 230f.

description of the offering as an *hilasterion*. For most interpreters, there is no propitiatory value in the Passover. While an atoning content could be supported by appealing to a range of authorities, all that such an exercise would achieve is to illustrate the confusion that exists over the nature of the Passover. Even those who see propitiatory value in the Paschal offering, either originally in the Mosaic period or in the New Testament period, do not see a connection between the Passover and the passage we are considering. There is, however, evidence which has not been considered hitherto and which is vitally important to our study.

If Paul is following the theme of the New Exodus, his main source material would have been the law and the prophets (so stated by Paul himself in Romans 1.3; 3:21) i.e., the Exodus and the prophetic predictions of a Second Exodus following the exile. A crucial contributor to this expectation was Ezekiel, who, like Isaiah, saw the importance of the raising up of a Davidic prince (Ezek. 24:23-24; 37:24-25). Ezekiel saw the prince's main function was to build the eschatological temple and to provide sacrifices for the sins of the covenant community.

In Ezekiel 45:25 the prophet tells how the prince will offer an abundance of sacrifices for the sins of the people. What is significant is that these offerings are not made on the Day of Atonement. Indeed, Ezekiel never mentions the Day of Atonement in the context of the eschatological temple. What he does say is that these sacrifices will be offered *during the Passover*. This is of great importance. If Ezekiel, a priest who had preached against the sins of tampering with the laws of Yahweh (Ezek. 20:13-20; 23:30, 37-38), seeks to change the sacrificial system so dramatically, he can be doing only one thing: he is emphasising the importance of the Passover for dealing with the sins of the people. To make this point, he does the unthinkable and changes the law of Moses. The eschatological Passover will propitiate for the sins of the people. Indeed, Ezekiel anticipates what the Son of David himself will do, for he brought atonement right into the centre of the Passover celebration (Ezek. 45:21ff.).

It is also significant that Ezekiel has the Davidic prince making these Paschal atoning sacrifices. This imagery is similar to what the Gospels present, i.e. the dying King making the Paschal sacrifice. This is not limited to the Gospels' perspective, for Paul himself has introduced Jesus as the Davidic descendant in Romans 1:3, and, by the use of the cultic expression, 'the Spirit of holiness',[7] has indicated that it is Jesus, the Son of David, the Son of God, who achieves his people's redemption through his own death.

It seems to be the case that Paul draws extensively on the prophecy of Ezekiel. It has been recognised as the source of his ideas of the church being the temple of the living God,[8] brought about by the death of the Messiah. To see the Davidic leader making sacrifices for the temple and the people would naturally lead Paul's thinking in the inevitable direction of the cross. It was all part of the testimony of the law and the prophets.

This linking of the Day of Atonement and Passover has been previously noted, but the implications for understanding Paul's thinking concerning the sacrificial nature of the death of Jesus has not been appreciated. For example, Dunn has noted the introduction of atonement in Ezekiel 45 as grounds for seeing an atoning significance in the Passover in New Testament thought.[9] Howard also acknowledges that the sin offerings mentioned during the Passover of Ezekiel 45:25 lie behind the description of Jesus being the Lamb of God spoken of by John the Baptist in John 1:29.[10] He points out that the midrash on Exodus 12 describes the Passover as an atoning sacrifice. He claims that the link between the two feasts was so widely understood in Second Temple Judaism that the Baptist's hearers would have had no difficulty in understanding the statement that the Lamb of God takes away the sin of the world. If scholars are right in making a link between atonement and Passover on the basis of Ezekiel 45, then not only were readers of the Gospels expected to understand this fifth century BC association but so were the readers of Paul's letters. This means that there must have been a widespread appreciation of the significance of Ezekiel's description as a key to understanding the achievements of the death of Christ.

In addition to the significant fact that Ezekiel has linked atonement and redemption, there is also the use of the preposition *huper* (in place of) used throughout the Book of Ezekiel in the LXX, a usage that is particularly unique to Ezekiel. This is not only repeatedly used in the sacrificial imagery of the Hebrews letter, but throughout the Pauline cultic passages. It became the standard expression in the

---

[7]Kasemann, *Romans*, 11.

[8]Fee, *Corinthians*, 147; Fiorenza, 'Cultic,' 161; Swetnam, 'Revelation,' 229-30 and McKelvey, *Temple*, 96/104.

[9]Dunn, 'Understanding,' 132-3.

[10]Howard, 'Eucharist,' 331-2.

New Testament church for describing the substitutionary death of Christ. Such clear dependence, either directly or indirectly, underlines the importance of Ezekiel's modification of cultic arrangements and the use that the early church made of it.

The tabernacle imagery used in the letter to the Hebrews is not Platonic, as had earlier been thought, but is based on the eschatological temple described by Ezekiel. This explains how the writer could speak of Christ having obtained eternal redemption (Heb. 9:12), which is not part of Day of Atonement language, but it is of Passover. The writer used imagery from the Day of Atonement and merged it with the language of Passover, i.e. redemption. In other words, Hebrews follows the pattern of Ezekiel, putting the sacrifices of the Day of Atonement into the orbit of Passover celebration.[11] This suggests that this merger was basic to the early church's cultic thinking, for the material is handled, both in Paul and in Hebrews, in such a way that the convergence is taken as understood. Indeed a comparison of the themes in both Romans 3:24-26 and Hebrews 9:1-10 has shown them to be the same.[12] Some scholars have linked *hilasterion* in Romans 3:25 with its use in Hebrews 9:5 describing the altar where propitiation was made and its use in the LXX of Ezekiel 43:14, 17 and 20. If they are correct, then it further extends the link with Ezekiel in Romans.

The widespread influence of Ezekiel in the early church is further supported by the probability that his prophecy contributes to the description of the eschatological temple in Revelation. Interestingly, the cultic language of Revelation concentrates exclusively on the Passover (1:5-6; 5:6-9; 7:17).[13]

A further link between Ezekiel and Romans is the connection between Adamic Christology and Ezekiel's Son of Man.[14] Since Romans 3:21f. is describing a facet of the significance of the death of the last Adam, then if the Ezekiel/Adamic relationship is valid, it provides further evidence of Ezekiel's shadow over Romans 3:21ff. This suggests that the theme continues from the first chapters of Romans where the fall of man is very much in view. Thus the thrust

---

[11]Hebrews differs from Ezekiel in that whereas Ezekiel brought the Day of Atonement sacrifices into the Passover, Hebrews seems to take the language of the Passover (redemption) and inserts it into the Day of Atonement.

[12]Moo, *Romans*, 246. However Moo failed to see the absorption of Day of Atonement into the Passover.

[13]For Passover in the early church, see Shepherd, *Paschal*.

[14]Carson, 'Ambiguities,' 97ff.

of the argument is that Christ's death is the act of redemption that rescues man from the bondage and spiritual exile into which the fall has brought the children of Adam. In Romans 5 Paul continues to thread Adamic imagery into the plight of man and the role that Christ plays as the last Adam.

It is no accident that Neyrey has identified Lukan Christology as being Adamic based;[15] it is a reflection of the influence of Luke's travelling companion. It has been argued that while Son of Man imagery was applicable to the Jewish community, to have used it among the Gentiles would have appeared nationalistic and exclusively Jewish. In contrast, the last Adam imagery brought the theological content of the Son of Man into a figure that embraced both Jews and Gentiles. Luke's insistence in using the actual Son of Man sayings, despite the fact that he wrote for the Gentiles, indicates his concern to be faithful to the original sayings of Jesus.

Ezekiel's influence on Romans 5:1 can be seen in the statement *peace with God*, a link with Ezekiel 37:26, which says, 'I will make with them a covenant of peace.' It has also been demonstrated that Ezekiel 37 is present in 1 Corinthians 15,[16] and the argument of Romans 8 relating to the resurrection is a summary of that found in 1 Corinthians 15. Indeed, Ezekiel 37, the resurrection of the people of God, could well be an important influence on Paul's thinking in Romans 6:1-4 where he speaks of the resurrection of the church with Christ. It is, of course, well known that Ezekiel 37 was read at the Passover celebration. This would add to the naturalness of hearing the Ezekiel promises of atonement in the explanation that Paul gives.

Further, Ezekiel's influence on Paul has been detected in Luke's description of his conversion.[17] It can hardly be thought that Luke would have had a different view of this event from that of Paul himself. Indeed, if Kim is right that the seed of the gospel message is within

---

[15]Neyrey, *Passion*, 167.

[16]Schneider, 'Corporate,' 156-59, who claims that Ezekiel 37:1-14 provided Paul with a key type of the resurrection when Yahweh's Spirit breathed into an army of bones and gave them life. Schneider cites J. Grassi who points out that Rabbinic commentaries interpreted Ezekiel 37:1-14 as a prophecy of the final resurrection in the Messianic era, and that it was read in this sense during the Passover. Of course, Ezekiel 37 cannot but draw on the new covenant theme and its fulfilment in Ezekiel 36:22ff., which is certainly reflected in 1 Corinthians 11:25. Furthermore, we have already noted Passover influence in 1 Corinthians 15:3-20.

[17]Campbell, 'Contribution,' 238, who cites Segal's claim that Paul's conversion reflects Ezekiel's vision of God in Ezekiel 1.

the very call of Paul,[18] then it could be argued that Ezekiel's influence is even more pervasive than has ever been recognised.

In the light of the above links between the prophet and the letter of Romans it would seem reasonable to suggest that Ezekiel has had significant influence on the argument of Paul, and which his readers are expected to recognise. If this is so, then it is also reasonable to suggest that the significance of the Paschal offering of the Davidic king in Ezekiel 45:25 would have been appreciated.

The testimony of Jesus

There is, however, another possible source for interpreting the death of Christ as an atonement in the Passover setting and this comes from Jesus himself. It is clear that Jesus regarded his death as an atonement (Luke 22:19-20), and equally clear that the timing of his death was deeply significant both for himself and for the early church. The Paschal tradition and its reinterpretation did not need to wait for the emergence of a thinker of the calibre of Paul; it was evidently in place well before his conversion, as evidenced in the use he makes of traditional material. Thus there is no division between Jesus' understanding of the purpose of his death and the explanation found in Paul's letters.[19]

Other aspects of the Passover model

The Passover model is further supported by the reference to the *paresin* (the passing over) of sins previously committed (Rom. 3:25). Here there is a clear echo of the passing over of the angel of death on the night of the Passover. God no longer passes over, but has demanded the death of the firstborn son. There is not only an allusion to the Passover in the use of *paresin*, but to the way the same term is used by Isaiah, who, in a Second Exodus context, speaks of Yahweh keeping back (*paresin*) his anger (Isa. 64:10-12; 63:15; 42:14).

Another Paschal theme can be detected in the passage in the use of *proetheto* (v. 25) which speaks of *the public display*. This is a

[18]Kim, *Origin*, *passim*.

[19]There is a further link between Passover and *hilasterion*. It is found in the book of Numbers and is a consequence of the Passover. I will leave this passage until it is discussed in chapter 11, for it requires that certain theological concepts are established before we can appreciate the significance of the material. I believe that once the significance of the role of the Levite has been considered it will be seen that there were clear propitiatory elements within the Passover.

statement that has caused many scholars to reject the Day of Atonement as the cultic setting of the language. The presentation of the blood by the high priest on the Day of Atonement was in the solitude of the holy of holies. Some have sought to say that the presentation was before the angels. This, however, is to introduce something foreign to the natural reading of the text, for there is no hint of angelic witness or ministry in the letter.

There is only one sacrifice in the entire Old Testament that was given public display. It was the Paschal victim whose blood was daubed on the lintel and door posts of the homes it protected. It was the blood of this sacrifice that was the foundation of the act of the redemption of the Israelites. It is, I would suggest, the only sacrifice that fits this description given by Paul.

Further support can be given to the claim that 3:24-25 is based on the Passover by those scholars who have attempted to identify the form of the text. It is generally agreed that the passage reflects a liturgical formula used either as a baptismal or as a Eucharist confession. Whichever it may be, both themes are strongly linked with the death of Christ and its setting in the context of the Passover.

The claim that the passage has an Adamic content also fits the picture that is emerging. The redemption that Paul describes is that which reverses the catastrophic effects of the fall. This is evidence of the unity of the sacrificial language throughout Romans, which presupposed Adam's role in bringing man into sin (chap. 5). It is the death of Jesus, the last Adam, that reverses this tragedy. It is a redemption that brings man out of the spiritual bondage in which he has been incarcerated since he broke covenant with Yahweh. It is a salvation that comes through faith in Christ Jesus.

Paul concludes the section by insisting that the law is fulfilled in the redemption that is in Christ. The law and the prophets, i.e. the whole of scripture, had looked forward to this eschatological event of redemption. It is not a salvation that is for Jews alone, but for all who will have faith in the character and saving work of God. It is available to all who are willing to submit to God's Spirit and have their hearts circumcised so that they can share in the Lord's Pesach.

If we go beyond the passage immediately under consideration, we find further evidence as to the primacy of Paschal language and imagery influencing the understanding of Paul. Some studies have identified the Passover as formative in the composition of the imagery used in Romans 5:1 ff,[20] while others have identified the same imagery behind the dying and rising with Christ in Romans 6:1ff.[21] The following comments on 3:20-26 show how naturally the argument flows once the Passover setting has been identified.

3.20 Therefore no-one will be declared righteous in his sight by observing the law; rather, through the law we become conscious of sin. Being righteous before God is not just a matter of being declared innocent, which it certainly includes, as is so often understood. Righteousness is one of the key Old Testament concepts to do with Israel's return from exile. Isaiah said that Israel was declared righteous as a result of her return. The prophet's view of righteousness was not just forgiveness; it also meant that Israel was restored to her inheritance. The prophets saw that the giving of the law was the climax of this process. When Israel received the law at Sinai she was being given the great blessing of her inheritance, which would govern her life in the Promised Land. In reality, rather than the law blessing her, it did the very opposite. It showed Israel how awful her sin was and how far she was from God. Instead of being the guide for her life in the Promised Land, it became the evidence that she was still in bondage, in the kingdom of darkness. Israel, like all other people, was under Sin and the judgment of the law.

3.21 But now a righteousness from God, apart from the law, has been made known, to which the Law and the Prophets testify. This righteousness that has been secured through the death of Jesus is apart from the law. It cannot slight the law as though it did not matter, because God could never accept any arrangement that was unjust. This righteousness, while apart from the law in that it is not to do with how the law would normally operate, i.e. by the punishment of the guilty and the requirement of circumcision etc, has to satisfy the justice that the law demands. This is not a scheme that has been devised as a last attempt to solve the problem of sin, it is one 'to which the Law and the Prophets testify'.

3.22 This righteousness from God comes through faith in Jesus Christ to all who believe. There is no difference. This is a different righteousness from that known by the restored exiles. In

---

[20]Whitely, *Theology*, passim, also 'Atonement,' 250.

[21]See also Warnack, 'Hellsgeschehen,' 259ff. and 'Romerbriefs,' 274ff. Others who identify Passover as the background include Nixon, *Exodus*, 24, Knox, *Gentiles*, 91, and Cullmann, *Baptism*, 48

their case righteousness was based on their own sufferings. They had served the sentence that the law had demanded. The righteousness of God had been displayed in not sparing them suffering and in being faithful to the covenant by delivering them from exile. Yahweh's righteousness had been demonstrated in keeping to the threatened curses of the covenant when he gave Jerusalem into the hands of the Babylonians, letting them sack the city and take its citizens as prisoners. However it was an exile that was temporary and even their return was not the final salvation. The great act of salvation, which the prophets had foretold, was to deal with sin in a totally different way. Sin had to be dealt with once and for all. There was to be no more offering for sin. Indeed, this restoration was not to be to an earthly location. It was a restoration to the eternal presence of God himself where no sin could be tolerated and where no evil could gain entrance. To provide a lesser way of salvation would be a denial of God's own holiness. For this righteousness to be accepted, it had to put away sin and cleanse the people of God completely.

'There is no difference'. Paul stresses once again the culpability of both Jews and Gentiles as he has already asserted earlier. This salvation is not for a group that excludes others, either because they are too bad or too good. It includes the Jews, despite the privileges they had previously enjoyed. The term was probably used to reflect the conflict that existed between Jews and Gentiles, and it stressed the inclusivity of the gospel.

3.23 for all have sinned and fall short of the glory of God. The first-century Jew, reading this statement, knew it to be a part of the painful history of his people. Not only did it refer to the fact that the head of the human family had sinned and brought all his offspring into a state of alienation toward God, but it referred to Israel in her exile. God, through Isaiah, had said, 'I have created you for my glory' (Isa. 43:7). Israel's exilic condition was a denial of the glory of God. It was a picture of her shame and sinfulness. While Israel could acknowledge the sins of her ancestors, what Paul's contemporaries could not accept was that they were in fact in a state of exile that was far worse than the exile experienced by their ancestors in either Egypt or Babylon. The Jews who opposed Paul could not accept that they also were part of the kingdom of darkness (Acts 7:51-58).

3.24 and are justified freely by his grace through the redemption that came by Christ Jesus. This final act of justification that God offers is not the result of the community being punished for her own sin, but it is the result of one taking the guilt of man. Paul deliberately says that this is the achievement of Christ Jesus. In putting 'Christ' first in the term 'Christ Jesus', he emphasises that Jesus is the Messiah, the promised one who would be sent to deliver his people from their bondage. Because Jesus is the Son of David, who the scriptures had repeatedly promised would be raised up, then all that he does is according to the scriptures. Paul states that the church was justified freely by God's grace 'through the redemption that is in Christ Jesus'. The term 'justified' has New Exodus roots. The Jews had been justified when God delivered them from the control of their oppressors in exile. They had claimed to be the people of God, a claim that seemed ridiculous in the light of the reality of their condition. But it was a true claim, and God justified this claim when he delivered them from exile. Paul will later say that Jesus was delivered up for our offences and raised for our justification (Rom. 4:25), that is, God delivered, justified his people, when he raised up his Son, the promised seed of David from the dead.

This act of redemption is unique. The Egyptian deliverance centred on the death of a sacrifice that substituted for the firstborn on the night of the Passover. Each Jewish family slew a lamb and smeared its blood on the lintel and door post. When the angel of death came through the land, he saw the blood and passed over the home. Thus the Jews were redeemed by the blood of the Passover lamb. The deliverance of the Jews from Babylon was an act of redemption (Isa. 52:9; 54:5-6; 59:20; 62:12); but there was no vicarious sacrifice, the Jewish people themselves were punished for the sins that were the cause of their exile. Israel's deliverance was nevertheless an act of redemption, for Yahweh brought about her release from the bondage through a pagan king. He raised up the Persians who conquered the Babylonians and allowed the Jews to return. For this reason God said: 'I give Egypt for your ransom, Cush and Seba in your stead. Since you are precious and honoured in my sight, and because I love you, I will give men in exchange for you, and people in exchange for your life' (Isa. 43:3-4). The price of Israel's redemption was the overthrow of the Babylonians, those whom the sovereign Lord of history had used to fulfil his threat against his people.

But the redemption that has come through Jesus Christ is a totally different redemptive activity. It is one in which the covenant community is justified freely, not as the result of her own suffering, for this redemption is based on the shedding of the blood of Christ Jesus. The first point is important, because this redemption is as a result of the grace of God. We do not get what we deserve. The Jews when sent into exile received fully what they deserved. Once they suffered what God saw was appropriate (Isa. 51:17-32), then he delivered/redeemed them. But Paul is not talking about salvation at a temporary level where it was possible to be punished and the past put behind. Rather he means an eternal exile from the presence of God, a totally different exile from anything depicted in Israel's history. This exile in the kingdom of darkness has resulted in man being bound to Satan in covenant, a covenant that binds him in a hopeless and, humanly speaking, inescapable bondage. The nature of the exile caused by Adam is of a different dimension and order, and requires an act of cosmic redemption. The nature of this exile is of such significance that the offender cannot possibly make atonement.

This redemption that Paul writes about is through Christ Jesus. This in itself is not a startling statement, for the redemption of the Jews from Egypt was by Moses, and the redemption from Babylon was by a Persian king (Isa. 45:1-4). To say that this new act of redemption came by Christ is in itself not startling, that is, not until we read the clause that follows it.

3.25a God presented him as a sacrifice of atonement through faith in his blood. The redemption achieved by Christ is totally unique. It could not take place without the death of the Son of God. Here the emphasis is on removing man from the condemnation that Sin has brought about. Later, in Romans eight Paul explains the cosmic dimension of this redemption, something that he deals with elsewhere (Col. 1:15-19).

The word 'presented' *(proetheto)* means publicly displayed. Here we have another hint that Paul is describing Jesus as the Passover victim. Of all of the sacrifices that the Levitical law legislated for, there was only one that was displayed for all to see, and that was the Passover. The lamb's blood was daubed on the doorposts and the lintel, but all other sacrifices had their blood offered to God within the temple. The term 'sacrifice of atonement' is *hilasterion* and has already been examined. This term was traditionally translated as propitiation, and I have argued that this meaning should be retained. It has been largely rejected because the text does not support a Day of

Atonement setting, to which it was considered to belong. For the vast majority of scholars there was absolutely no propitiatory value in the blood of the Passover lamb and therefore it has not been given the consideration that it deserves. However, once it has been appreciated that there are very good reasons to say that the early church, through the influence of Ezekiel 45:25, saw the anticipated eschatological Passover to be a sacrifice of propitiation, then the natural setting for the passage becomes obvious.

Just as the Jews in Egypt on the Passover night had to put their faith in the efficacy of the blood of the Passover lamb, so the blood of Christ, the Christian Passover victim (1 Cor. 5:7), is where the faith of those who are threatened with judgment must be placed. The blood of Christ speaks of his death.

3.25b. He did this to demonstrate his justice, because in his forbearance he left the sins committed beforehand unpunished. The death of Jesus answers the dilemma as to how God who is holy could apparently deal so lightly with sin. There had been many times in human history when it seemed that God was not acting justly by ignoring sin. Paul is saying that this never was the case. God had withheld acting in judgment because he had a plan to rescue man from his condition of exile and judgment. In this saving act God demonstrated that he took sin seriously, indeed so seriously that he gave his beloved Son up to death. His justice and his love could not be demonstrated any clearer.

Paul says that God had in his forbearance (*paresin*) left the sins committed beforehand unpunished. *Paresin* means 'passing over'. Once again we find a distinct echo of the Passover in the passage. On the Passover night the angel of death passed over the homes of the Jewish people leaving them unpunished. Paul is saying that the reason God has dealt so patiently with sin throughout history was not that he was indifferent but because he had a plan to deal with sin that was far beyond what anyone could have dared to imagine. The plan was only possible because of a God of incredible love and mercy. The atonement, that is, the result of the death of Jesus, the Son of God, deals with all the sins of his people, past, present and future.

3.26 He did it to demonstrate his justice at the present time, so as to be just and the one who justifies those who have faith in Jesus. Paul again returns to the theme of the justice of God. There had been a question over this throughout the ages. Now, through the death of Jesus, this question has been forever settled. Now no one can ever question the commitment of God to justice. He has dealt with sin by the giving up of his beloved Son unto death in making him the Passover victim. He has demonstrated beyond any possible doubt both his love and his justice and in doing so silenced for ever any who would question his character.

By giving up Jesus to death God is just and the one who justifies those who have faith in Jesus. When God justified Israel she was in exile in Babylon, and he rescued her from her exile. In doing this he was justifying her claim to be the covenant people of God. Such a claim made by the Jews to their Babylonian captors would have been ridiculed. When God brought Israel back to her inheritance he was justifying the claims that she made, she was shown to the whole world to be the people of the covenant-keeping God.

Paul is here saying that God has now justified his people, those who have faith in Jesus. In the light of how the word 'justified' is continually used to speak of deliverance in the context of the return from exile in the Old Testament, it would seem that Paul is saying that God has now delivered his people from the exile to which Adam had delivered his offspring. A new covenant now exists which is the fulfilment of the promise Yahweh made to Abraham that through his seed all the nations of the earth would be blessed.

Supporting Paschal Texts

The Gospels

We know how Jesus interpreted his death in the light of the Passover. He deliberately took the symbols of the first Exodus and reinterpreted them so that they spoke of the deliverance that he was about to accomplish for his people. In chapter 1 we noted some of the material lying beneath the surface of the Gospels that strongly suggests that Jesus saw his death as bringing about the New Exodus that the prophets had promised.

A further text we need to consider is Mark 10:45: 'The Son of Man came not to be served but to serve, and to give his life a ransom for many.' It is the word 'ransom' (*lutron*) that has caused much debate as to where the seed of this statement lies. Many have been happy to see the allusion to the suffering servant of Isaiah 53 who gave his life a ransom for many. Hooker, however, has rejected this as the source because the term *lutron* is not found in the Greek text of Isaiah 53. Her observation is significant, even though she does not comment on how it points to Jesus interpreting his death as a Paschal offering. She notes that the only place where one human life is substituted for another human life is in the regulations following the Passover.[22] The Levites, man for man, were to be substituted for the firstborn of Israel who had been spared by the Lord. Because they had been spared, the Lord claimed them as his own. Strictly speaking, that meant as a sacrificial offering, but that would have defeated the purpose of the protection of the blood of the lamb. Instead, the Lord claimed them as living sacrifices, as priests, to serve him. But in order to allow them to remain with their families, the Lord arranged for the tribe of Levi to become priests in their place. They were the ransom. We see that Jesus uses language taken from the very heart of the Passover/Exodus event to explain the significance of his death. Indeed, the parallel Lucan text places the saying at the heart of the Last Supper with its immediate Paschal celebration.

The Epistles
The Corinthian letters give significant support for Paul's Paschal understanding of the death of Jesus. In 1 Corinthians 5:7 Paul speaks of Christ our Passover having been sacrificed. If we are to allow any basic consistency in the apostle's thought, then the second letter ought not to be separated from the first as a means of discerning his thinking about the cultus. In 2 Corinthians 5:21 the death of Christ is described in terms that at the very least suggest it is seen as a sin offering. This description should not be isolated from the passage in the earlier epistle as if it were a distinctively different strand of tradition, for the 5:21 statement follows on immediately from a statement which is clearly 'New Exodus'. The clause, 'If any man be in Christ he is a new creature' (2 Cor. 5:17), is a clear echo of the Isaianic promise of a new creation (Isa. 65:17), which was part of the New Exodus promise. Indeed, the earlier part of 2 Corinthians deals with the temporal nature of the believer's pilgrimage, a theme that depicts the church as the pilgrim New Exodus community. If there is any doubt about this, then the use Paul makes of the Isaianic servant material in the opening of chapter 6 ought to resolve the difficulty. The emergence of Israel from her shame in exile was the setting of the servant songs and the imagery is now transferred to describe Paul's ministry to a wayward section of the new Israel. Furthermore, in 11:2 Paul says that he has

[22]Hooker, *Servant*, 77.

betrothed them to Christ. Israel became Yahweh's bride through the Passover and Paul applied the same Paschal imagery to the church's relationship with her Redeemer – he is her Bridegroom. This shares the same conceptual background as Ephesians 5:25ff., which is about atonement as preparation for the divine marriage.

Further support is found for the link between atonement and Passover in Galatians 1:3, overtly New Exodus material, a fact recognised by most commentators. The cultic event, which describes the means of deliverance from God's wrath, is clearly presented in terms of a sin offering, which again is fused with the imagery of redemption and is in a New Exodus context. This is made clear in that 3:13 speaks of Christ having redeemed us from the curse of the law. This can be identified as having a New Exodus significance in that it goes on to link up with 3:24ff. which speaks of the community's baptism into Christ. Scott claims that the theme of adoption in this passage is based on Israel's redemption from Egypt when she became the son of God.[23] This is parallel to the description in Romans 6:1-4, 1 Corinthians 10:2 and 13:12, and Ephesians 5:25, which as we saw in chapter 7 forms a matrix of New Exodus texts.

The baptism of Ephesians 5:27 is corporate and is based, I would argue, on Ezekiel 16. In that passage Yahweh tells of how he chose Israel and redeemed her for his own. He washed her and made her clean through his word in order that she might be his bride. If this is the background of Ephesians 5, then it would be natural to see the sacrifice the bridegroom made in the setting of Passover, for that was the occasion of the original marriage between Yahweh and Israel. As in Romans, there is the bypassing of physical circumcision, for the reality has now been established, their hearts have been circumcised (Eph. 2:11). We have already noted that circumcision was required to celebrate the Passover. Indeed, in Ephesians 1:7 the sacrifice has already been described in Paschal terms, for it is redemption through his blood.

Colossians 1:12-14 speaks in New Exodus language for it is saturated with redemptive/Paschal imagery, while 1:20 describes the effect of the redemption (1:14) as the reconciliation of all things, which is again atoning imagery. (I shall argue in later chapters that the expression 'the firstborn of all creation' is not a hierarchial or ontological description but that it comes from the Passover where the firstborn

---

[23]Scott, 'Adoption,' 17.

was the designated victim bearing the judgment of the family's sin.) Paul is therefore saying that Christ's death is not only the means of the salvation of his family, but also of the whole of creation, hence he is 'the firstborn of all creation'.

Passover and New Testament theological motifs

Recognising that the linguistic and theological evidence all points to Paul developing the fulfilment of the New Exodus promises, a larger perspective for justification emerges. The eighth-century prophets spoke of the deliverance of Israel from her exile as her justification. We shall see in later chapters that this is the basis of Paul's doctrine of justification, the deliverance of God's people and their being brought into a new covenant relationship with their God. In other words, the Passover/ Exodus is part of the imagery of justification, for not only is it atoning, it also brings about the release and creation of the covenant community.

There is another link with the Passover that has to be given consideration. In Romans 2 and 4 Paul has dealt with the theme of circumcision. This is a theme which God-fearers would have been aware of before Paul's instruction, for Ezekiel 44:7 and 9, a passage dealing with the circumcised heart, was emphasised in the Hellenistic synagogues.[24]

One of the promises of the New Covenant was that the hearts, rather than the bodies, of the redeemed people would be circumcised. To celebrate the Passover the individual had to be circumcised. This was so whether the person was of Hebraic descent or a proselyte. Despite the insistence on physical circumcision it was stressed that what really mattered was what it represented – a circumcised heart. Paul, in Romans 2 and 4, states that the outward ritualistic requirement is of no value unless it truly represents what has happened to the heart. He argued that the outer without the inner is of no value, while the inner without the outer is no problem. These two discussions on circumcision must not be dislocated from their proximity to the description of Christ's death as a Passover offering which we have seen to be the setting of Romans 3:21ff. Only those with circumcised hearts can keep the Christian Passover and benefit from being in the covenant. It can hardly be coincidental that Paul's description of Jesus' death as a sacrifice of redemption (and therefore a Paschal offering) is always linked to the need of a circumcised heart.[25]

[24]Borgen, 'Early,' 64ff.

In Exodus 4:21-23 there is the difficult passage describing when Moses was attacked by the angel and his life was spared by his wife circumcising their son and throwing the foreskin at the feet of either the angel or of Moses. There are parallels between the occasion of the attack on Moses and the Passover: both events occur at night, the divine being has the intention of killing, and salvation occurs through a blood rite. The link between circumcision and Passover is made clear by Robinson when he says that 'Moses stands for Israel and is saved because of the smearing of the blood of Gershon and Moses as representative of the people as a whole is thus symbolically prepared for the imminent Passover celebration'.[26] Thus it could be argued that the circumcision of Moses' firstborn was the vicarious circumcision for the nation, and it was only because this representative act had been performed that the nation could celebrate Passover prior to their own circumcision.

There may be other undertones related to the rite of circumcision which Paul picks up from the theme of the circumcision of Moses. In Exodus 4:21-23 Moses is called a bridegroom of blood. This is seen by some to refer to an initiation rite which the male had to undergo before he could marry. If this is so, and is picked up in some way by Paul, then the reference to the circumcision of Christ in Colossians 2:11 may be interacting with this rite. Christ dies in order to secure for himself a bride (Eph. 5:26), and in his death his people underwent circumcision. As the Old Testament imagery is the circumcision of the groom, it would suggest, if we are correctly following the threads of Paul's thinking, that the 'circumcision' of the church is the result of the suffering which Christ, the groom, has undergone in the flesh.

The importance of circumcision as a qualification necessary to celebrate the Passover was taken up by the Rabbis. Indeed, so important did circumcision become in Rabbinic literature, it supplemented the blood of the lamb in order to achieve the efficacy required to protect the Jews as they sheltered in their homes. It was part of the redemptive blood: 'You shall mix the blood of the Passover sacrifice and of circumcision and make of it a sign to put on the houses where you live; and I will see the merit of the blood and will spare you.'[27]

---

[25]Romans 2: 28; 3:21ff; Galatians 3:13; 6:15; Ephesians 1:7; 2:11-18; 5:25; Colossians 1:13-15; 2:11.

[26]Robinson, 'Rescue,' 547

A development of the same theme is found in the targum on the Canticles which was read and commented on at the Passover:

> At the time when the glory of Yahweh was manifested in Egypt on the night of the Passover in order to kill the firstborn – he protected the houses where they were, lay in wait by the window, watched in wait by the trellis, and saw the blood of the Passover lamb sacrifice and the blood of circumcision stamped on the doors – He looked down from the height of the heavens and saw the people eating the sacrifice of the feast and he spared them and he did not give power to the destroying angel.[28]

The use of the Canticles during the Passover might at first seem odd, until it is remembered that the Passover celebrated the original deliverance from Egypt when Yahweh took Israel to be his bride. The targum on Ezekiel 16:6 has the same understanding.

The targum on Leviticus says: 'Life is in the blood of the Passover; life is in the blood of circumcision.'[29] Again Ex Rabba 15:13 (on Exodus 12:10) says: 'I pronounce sentences of death; but I declare unto you how in my mercy I will spare you because of the blood of the Paschal lamb and of the circumcision, and how I shall make atonement for you.'[30] Another targum says: 'And he desisted from him. There she said, But for the blood of this circumcision, my husband had merited death.'[31] Vermes says that the passage may be safely presumed to be prior to 200 BC. Another Rabbinic text says: 'It is written that the first Passover after the Exodus was celebrated by the mixing of the blood of both.'[32] A further Rabbinic text has, 'Because the memorial of the covenant with your fathers is before me, I revealed myself to deliver you, for it is known before me that you are oppressed in your

---

[27]TJ 1 Exodus 12.13 cf. also Exodus Rabbah 12:10 and 12:50 in connection with Ezekiel 16, cited in Daly, *Sacrifice*, 191. The thorny problem of the dating of the Rabbinic material is discussed in chapter 9. In the Rabbinic Passover tradition the blood of the lamb and the blood of circumcision are merged to effect deliverance. For Paul, there can be no vicarious significance in the circumcision of the believer's heart because there is no shedding of blood.

[28]Cited by Daly, *Sacrifice*, 192.

[29]Vermes, 'Circumcision', 191, cited by Daly, op cit. 191.

[30]Cited by Lyonnet and Sabourin, *Sin*, 133.

[31]Cited by Vermes, 'Baptism,' 311.

[32]Cited by Vermes, 'Circumcision,' 191 who goes on to say in note 2, of Ex R.XIX.7: 'It is important to remark that the pre-Christian tradition preserved here and in the Targum was interpreted in the sense of an atoning observance of the commandments of circumcision and Passover.'

captivity. I said to you: Because of the blood of the circumcision I will take care of you. I said to you again: Because of the blood of Passover I will redeem you.'[33]

In the account of the attack by the destroyer on Moses when he was on his way to Egypt and Zipporah warded off the danger through circumcising the eldest son, we are told:

> And she circumcised the foreskin of her son, and brought him before the feet of the destroyer, and said, 'The husband would have circumcised, but the father-in-law did not permit him; but now, let the blood of this circumcision atone for the fault of this husband.' And when the Destroyer had ceased from him, Zipporah gave thanks and said, 'How lovely is the blood of circumcision which hath saved my husband from the hand of the angel of death.'[34]

The last citation, whilst not mentioning the Passover directly, has clear links with it, shown in that it was the circumcision of the firstborn that spared the life of Moses.

Despite the link of circumcision with Passover, Abraham's circumcision is said to have taken place on the Day of Atonement: 'Abraham was circumcised on the Day of Atonement; year after year God looks upon the covenant blood of the circumcision of our father (Abraham) and creates atonement for our sins – He said because of your blood you shall live.'[35]

Another Rabbinic quote says: 'With two bloods were the Israelites delivered from Egypt, with the blood of the Paschal lamb and with the blood of circumcision.'[36] Vermes says that the blood of circumcision mingled with the Paschal blood showed that there was atonement significance in the Passover.

This connection between the Paschal lamb and circumcision ought not to surprise us when we reflect on the need of Moses' circumcision as a preparation for the Redemption from Egypt (Exod. 4:22-26). Despite these Rabbinic developments, it must be remembered that the Old Testament makes no suggestion that circumcision blood was regarded as sacrificial blood.[37] Nevertheless, as we have earlier noted, there is a possibility that Paul linked circumcision with the Passover

---

[33]Cited by Vermes, 'Circumcision,' 191.
[34]Cited by Schreiner, *Circumcision*, 104.
[35]Pesiq R 47 (19[1a-b],18).
[36]Cited by Vermes, 'Circumcision,' 191, note 2.
[37]Daly, *Sacrifice*, 188.

sacrifice as found in the Old Testament. Where Paul refers to the circumcision of the heart it is always within the immediate context of discussing the death of Christ. We have seen that these references to the sacrificial nature of the death of Jesus see him as the Passover sacrifice.

Priesthood

There is one final strand of evidence to consider that points to Paul's understanding of the death of Jesus as being Paschal. Paul not only sees believers as servants, he also sees them as priests. They share the priestly calling of Jesus and are called to offer worship to God. In Romans 12:1-2 he urges the Romans to offer themselves as living sacrifices and in Romans 15:16 he speaks of his own ministry as being a priestly service. The link of this theme with the Passover is that it was as a consequence of the Passover, where Israel's firstborn were spared, that Yahweh claimed the Israelites for himself as priests (Exod. 13:1-16). They were exempted from this service by the substitution of the tribe of Levi in their place. This is clearly the model that is the basis of Pauline understanding. The members of the covenant community are called to priestly service because they have have been spared as a result of another taking their place in the judgement of the Lord's Passover. We have already noted the link between Mark 10:45 and the Passover. In that arrangement the Levites were substituted to allow those who were spared through the death of the lamb not to have to live in priestly service. Here the suggestion is that having been spared through the eschatological Passover sacrifice, the people of God as a whole are called to, and not excused from, priestly service.

Martyrdom theology

We have found there are clear indications that Romans 3:21ff. is modelled on the Passover. This is a conclusion that is in conflict with the growing consensus which is shared across the theological spectrum, that both Jesus[38] and Paul[39] used the martyr model to explain the meaning of the cross.

The reason that Maccabees is considered to be the source of Paul's imagery is because it is thought that no other satisfactory way

---

[38]Wright, *Victory*, 582.
[39]Wright, 'Romans,' 45.

of interpreting *hilasterion* (propitiation/expiation) exists. Those who adopt this outlook are not convinced that the term is linked to its use in Ezekiel to describe the lid of the Ark of the Covenant (as in Hebrews 9:5) because they suspect that Paul would not have used an inanimate object to describe the significance of Jesus. Also, the imagery of Romans 3:21ff suggests a public sacrifice rather than the privacy of the conditions of the Day of Atonement, which is the second alternative. Having rejected the Day of Atonement they are forced to look for another source.

But there is a home for *hilasterion* which is within the canon of scripture. i.e. within the law and the prophets, *which Paul has specifically identified as the witness to this redemption.* As we have seen, all of the linguistic and theological indicators of the passage point in one direction, to the Passover. It fits what Paul has said about Jesus' death. Its purpose has been witnessed to by the law and the prophets. The reason why Passover has been discounted without any meaningful inquiry is that it is considered to be about redemption and not about atonement.

If it is true that Paul's understanding of the death of Jesus is that he is the great example of the Jewish martyr, then it means that his death is of no more ultimate significance than the death of any innocent sufferer. The death of Jesus adds to this store of merit in measure beyond what any other person's death could ever do, but he is still adding to something that exists. Not only have the righteous of the Old Testament contributed to the store of merit that Jesus adds to, but under this model all the sufferings of those who have suffered for their faith in Jesus are also contributing to this store of merit. In other words, martyrdom theology is a surrender of the great evangelical doctrine of the unique substitutionary sufferings of Christ. Without realising what has been surrendered, evangelical scholars have abandoned the historical doctrine of the uniqueness of Christ's atoning suffering and have replaced it with a doctrine that has no distinct Christian content. It fails to uphold the uniqueness of the sufferings of Jesus. This outcome is the result of embracing psuedepigraphal writings as the key to New Testament interpretation rather than taking seriously the statement of Paul that the redemption Christ has achieved was witnessed to by the Law and the Prophets.

Another reason for questioning martyrdom theology is the observation we noted in chapter 4 where we saw how the early church avoided using Isaiah 53 in the way that we might have expected. Our conclusion was that they were anxious not to attribute the significance of the suffering of the ideal servant to the church, i.e., that her suffering was also of propitiatory significance. To have closed the door on such confusion over Isaiah 53 and then open it by going to non-canonical writings such as Maccabees would be ridiculous in the extreme.

Furthermore, a major objection to the claims that this is a true reflection of Paul's understanding is that he never speaks about Christ our martyr, but he does say, 'Christ our Passover has been sacrificed for us.' The Old Testament is constantly quoted by the apostle, yet there is not one clear allusion, never mind citation, of the books of the Maccabees. Modern scholarship has pressed this model on to the New Testament text in a way that can only be described in scholarly terms as irresponsible, and has then developed doctrines from the supposed evidence that turns Jesus into a well-meaning religious leader who is confused over the purpose of his death and who got it totally wrong as to what it was to achieve.[40] The reason for this misplaced confidence in the Maccabean martyr model is the failure to appreciate the significance of the Passover for New Testament soteriology and, because of this, a misguided search for a model that includes the term *hilasterion* that had something to do with salvation.

These problems do not exist in the model I have proposed. In the Passover there is only one beloved Son. There is no confusion between his unique sufferings and those of others, no matter how noble and exemplary their death might have been. The Passover model not only avoids this serious surrender of the uniqueness of Christ's sufferings, but it fits all the grammatical and theological details of the passage, especially that of describing Jesus death as an *hilasterion*.

Conclusion

We have examined Paul's cultic language and the theological themes associated with it and have concluded that there is only one sacrifice that holds all of these strands together, and that is the Passover. This does not deny the importance of the Day of Atonement as an atoning event, but it was set up following the Passover. It would seem that

[40]Wright, *Victory*, passim, who says that Jesus believed that he was taking unto himself the full anger of Rome and that through this substitutionary death judgment was being taken away from Israel. Obviously judgment did fall on Israel in the fall of Jerusalem in AD 70. The only conclusion that can be drawn from such a theory is that Jesus got it totally wrong.

both Old and New Testament writers understand the original Passover to have been of propitiatory significance, but that all subsequent celebrations of the Passover were not, for they only celebrationed redemption. Alongside these celebrations was the Day of Atonement in which Israel's sin annually was atoned for. The prophet Ezekiel looked towards a final Passover offered by the Son of David that would be similar in achievement to the original Passover made by Moses, i.e, that it will be propitiatory. The New Testament writers together inherit and develop this understanding. Once again we have found that Paul has not departed from what Jesus taught. He shared the same perspective that Jesus had as to what his death achieved. Identification of this model opens the door to understand other aspects of Paul's theology and it is to these that we now turn.

Chapter Nine

Justification and the New Perspective

In recent years there has been an ongoing debate over what Paul meant by his use of the term 'justified'. It has been claimed that the Reformers read their own debate with Rome into Paul's debate with Judaism. Some Biblical theologians are now claiming that Paul's understanding of justification was not about being acquitted from sin, as understood by the Reformers. Rather, the term is claimed to be about being part of the covenant community. It is my intention to show that justification in the New Testament does have the forensic meaning that the Reformers understood, but at the same time a much wider content that relates to how God brings people into a covenant relationship with himself.

The nature of this topic is such that it inevitably faces methodological problems. To survey the recently propounded views and evaluate them is a task for a book in itself. To attempt to provide an alternative model and solution is another task. To keep the two chapters to a manageable size it will be necessary to limit the amount of detailed exegesis.

Since E.P. Sanders published his work, *Paul and Palestinian Judaism*, Pauline studies have been radically reshaped. Previously it had been assumed that Paul attacked Judaism for its legalism. The Reformers understood Judaism to have taught that salvation was achieved through keeping the law. Paul, it was thought, attacked this legalist position arguing that salvation was not achieved by keeping the law but that it was a gift given by God.

Sanders challenged this legalistic understanding of Second Temple Judaism. He claimed that the Second Temple texts show that Judaism never saw itself to be a religion of works. Indeed, it was the very opposite – it was a religion of grace. Sanders argued that Second Temple Judaism saw itself to be in a covenant relationship with God. Israel had been elected by God who had brought her into his covenant. Sanders argued that the law was not given as a means of achieving acceptance, but it was given because Israel had been already accepted.

It was because she had this unique covenantal relationship with God that the law had been given. Rather than the law being a crippling obligation, it was a joyous gift and privilege. It provided for the maintenance of the covenant through sin offerings, which dealt with the transgressions of both the individual and the nation.

This position, in which the law was seen as a gift from Israel's loving God, Sanders called 'covenantal nomism', covenant law. This identification dramatically altered the way statements of Paul concerning Judaism and the law were to be read. Paul's criticism of Judaism was no longer to be understood as targeted against her legalism but against her national pride. The Jews considered themselves superior to the rest of the nations because of their unique relationship with God. This pride in the covenant led Israel to insist that if Gentiles wanted to be accepted by God, they had to accept circumcision and become part of the Jewish community. Only those circumcised could know this unique relationship.

This description of covenantal nomism that Sanders has painted was not new. G. F. Moore had argued a similar case back in 1927.[1] Indeed, many Old Testament scholars commented that it was no different from the picture they found in the Old Testament. Israel was shown to have been confident of her calling by Yahweh to be his special people. What seemed to have been established by Sanders was that Second Temple Judaism had continued in this same covenantal context that her ancestors had enjoyed. Now if this was so, then it inevitably suggested that the mindset of Jesus and of Paul was that of covenantal nomism. It followed that their teachings had to be reinterpreted in the light of this new realisation. This meant that Paul (and indeed Jesus) could not have been attacking the Jews for their attempts to earn God's favour through their own achievements. Consequently, the Protestant doctrine of justification had to be examined afresh.

But what exactly is it that scholars are saying Sanders' work has challenged?[2] The rallying cry of the Reformation was that man is justified by faith without works. The arguments of Paul were the foundation upon which this doctrine was built. *The Apology of the Augsburg Confession* (1531) 4:2 says:

[1]Moore, *Judaism*, passim. In fact earlier than Moore, the English scholar Monifiore had argued similarly in the late 1800s.

[2]Wright, 'History,' 77f., points out that Sanders never understood the implications of his study for the doctrine of justification.

That man enjoys that acceptance with God called 'justification', the beginning and end of salvation, not through his own moral effort even in the smallest and slightest degree but entirely and only through the loving mercy of God made available in the merits of Christ and of his saving death on the Cross. This was not a process of gradual ethical improvement but an instantaneous transaction, something like a marriage, in which Christ the bridegroom takes to himself an impoverished and wretched harlot and confers upon her all the riches which are his. The key to this transaction was faith, defined as a total and trustful commitment of the self to God, and is itself not a human achievement but the pure gift of God.

Another important Reformed confession is the Westminster Confession, which defines justification as follows:

1. Those whom God effectually calleth, he also freely justifieth: not by infusing righteousness into them, but by pardoning their sins, and by accounting and accepting their persons as righteous; not for anything wrought in them, or done by them, but for Christ's sake alone; not by imputing faith itself, the act of believing, or any other evangelical obedience to them, as their righteousness; but by imputing the obedience and satisfaction of Christ unto them, they receiving and resting on him and his righteousness by faith; which faith they have not of themselves, it is the gift of God.

2. Faith, thus receiving and resting on Christ and his righteousness, is the alone instrument of justification; yet is it not alone in the person justified, but is ever accompanied with all other saving graces, and is no dead faith, but worketh by love.

3. Christ, by his obedience and death, did fully discharge the debt of all those that are thus justified, and did make a proper, real, and full satisfaction to his Father's justice in their behalf. Yet inasmuch as he was given by the Father for them, and his obedience and satisfaction accepted in their stead, and both freely, not for anything in them, their justification is only of free grace, that both the exact justice and rich grace of God might be glorified in the justification of sinners.

4. God did, from all eternity, decree to justify the elect; and Christ did, in the fullness of time, die for their sins and rise again for their justification; nevertheless they are not justified until the Holy Spirit doth, in due time, actually apply Christ unto them.

5. God doth continue to forgive the sins of those that are justified; and although they can never fall from the state of justification, yet they may by their sins fall under God's Fatherly displeasure, and not have the light of his countenance restored unto them, until they humble themselves, confess their sins, beg pardon, and renew their faith and repentance.

6. The justification of believers under the Old Testament was, in all these respects, one and the same with the justification of believers under the New Testament.

It is important to notice how the Westminster and the Augsburg Confessions differ. They are both speaking about the same doctrine, but the Westminster statement is set out in a far more systematic manner than is the Augsburg Confession. The Augsburg Confession is written in a distinctively biblical theological style. We will see that some of the problems that exist in the modern debate are possibly due to the emphasis of the Westminster Confession in which aspects of justification are carefully drawn out and defined in legal terms. The Augsburg Confession describes the doctrine in covenantal terms. There is no doubt that the framers of the Westminster Confession shared the same covenantal perspective expressed in the Augsburg Confession even though they produced a more systematic and forensic presentation.

Before we consider modern interpretations of justification, we must ensure that we are considering the right Paul. Sanders himself did not consider Paul to have stayed within the heritage he had received from Judaism. Rather Paul, following his conversion, moved away from this exclusively Jewish understanding and his resulting Christian convictions were an amalgamation of Jewish and Hellenistic thinking.[3] To interpret Paul as though he stayed firmly in the flow of Second Temple expectation is not to read him in the way Sanders reads him. If Paul has moved from his narrow Jewish position and has imbibed Hellenistic influence, then his critique of Judaism will be different from one who has remained strictly within the Jewish tradition. The point is that the method that has identified covenantal nomism to be the common pattern in Second Temple literature has denied its presence in the Pauline literature. If the reading, and by implication the method used in constructing that reading of Second Temple sources, is correct, then surely it would be expected that the same method of reading applied to the writings of another Jew of that same period ought accurately to identify it if he wrote from within the same nomistic tradition, even though he was criticising it.

---

[3]Sanders, *Palestinian*, 555, says, 'Paul does not have simply a "Jewish" or a "Hellenistic" or a Hellenistic Jewish conception of man's plight. It appears that Paul's thought was not simply taken over from any one scheme pre-existing in the ancient world.'

Scholars such as James Dunn and N.T. Wright argue that Paul stayed essentially within Palestinian Judaism, even though he now belonged to the 'Christian flock', and it was from there that he launched his critique of covenantal nomism. Sanders, however, argues that Paul left Palestinian Judaism and his convictions have become a hybrid of Jewish and Hellenistic beliefs. Sanders therefore effectively defends the traditional view of Paul the internationalist, the Jewish convert to a new religion. It follows that the constructions and critiques of covenantal nomism will be quite different depending on which Paul one is reading.

To accept Sanders' reading of Second Temple sources and yet to reject his reading of the Pauline letters (which is what Dunn and Wright do[4]), at the very least needs to be justified. Personally I think that Dunn and Wright are much closer to the Paul found in the pages of his letters than is the Paul that Sanders describes, but to fail to discuss or explain why Sanders' reading of one set of texts is correct and yet his reading of another set of supposedly similar texts is incorrect needs to be explained. It is not good enough just to say that Sanders is wrong in his reading of Paul when he uses the same method that has opened up the rest of the sources of Second Temple Judaism.

A possible, and to my mind the most likely, solution to this difficulty is that there is no such dominant common pattern. This obviously means that Sanders has been selective in choosing his evidence so as to create a pattern. But if this is correct, then the whole enterprise of seeking to create this newly discovered Paul, who has walked out of the pages of Second Temple literature, needs to be questioned. This is not to deny that there were strong elements of covenantal nomism in Second Temple Judaism, but to say that it was common to all forms of Judaism is going beyond what the evidence will allow.

---

[4]Of course, neither Dunn nor Wright unconditionally accept Sanders' conclusions. Dunn, for example, says, 'The most surprising feature of Sanders' writing, however, is that he himself has failed to take the opportunity his own mould-breaking work offered. Instead of trying to explore how far Paul's theology could be explicated in relation to Judaism's "covenantal nomism", he remained more impressed by the *difference* between Paul's pattern of religious thought and that of first-century Judaism. He quickly – too quickly in my view – concluded that Paul's religion could be understood only as a basically different system from that of his fellow Jews' (*Jesus, Paul, and the Law*, 186). The question that must be asked is, if Sanders can read Paul so badly, why should his reading of other texts be so heavily relied upon?

James Dunn and Justification

In constructing Paul's pre-converted mindset Dunn claimed that he was a Zealot. To achieve this setting for Paul, Dunn argued that because he was zealous concerning keeping the law, he could not tolerate the Hellenist 'Christians'. They were welcoming Gentiles into the covenant without circumcision. This was totally unacceptable; it ignored the demands of the law and was selling Judaism short. Paul's journey to Damascus was an attempt to block off unconverted, or rather uncircumcised, Gentiles from coming into the covenant community. But when Paul became a disciple of Jesus, his understanding of justification changed. His perspective was no longer nationalistic and exclusive. His 'conversion' made him see that God accepted the Gentiles as well as the Jews. He saw that believing Gentiles were in the covenant without having to submit to the demands of Judaism typified by its boundary markers of dietary laws, Sabbath observance and circumcision.

Dunn developed his argument of Paul's changed mindset by linking his confession that he had been zealous for the law with the example of Phinehas in Numbers 25:1-15:

> Paul evidently thought of himself as a 'zealot' in the same tradition (Galatians 1:13-14; Acts 22:3). He too had been willing to take up the sword in expression of such zeal. That can only mean that he had regarded the followers of Jesus as posing a serious threat to Israel's covenant status and distinctiveness. He must have seen the openness of these first Christians to receive Gentiles into their gatherings as something which broke down the protective barrier of the law and undermined Jewish set-apartness. For Jews who believed in a Jewish Messiah to fully accept Gentiles as of their own number, without requiring them to become Jews, was too much of a contradiction for the pre-Christian Paul. Such was his zeal for the Lord and zeal for the law that he was ready to persecute and 'destroy' the new movement.[5]

Because Dunn accepted Sanders' argument that Judaism was characterised by covenantal nomism, he concluded that Paul's negative references to 'the works of the law' were not to do with attaining righteousness by keeping the law. He claimed that they referred to Jewish insistence that believing Gentiles had to come under the 'boundary markers' of Israel. This meant that the Gentiles had to

---

[5]Dunn, *Old Doctrine*, 23. See also his *Theology*, 346ff. Wright, *What*, 26-29, also fits Saul of Tarsus into this same grouping.

practise the dietary laws, Sabbath observance, and the keeping of holy days. Above all, it meant that the Gentiles had to submit to circumcision. Gentiles who sought Yahweh were obliged to participate in these rituals if they were to be accepted by the Jews as part of the covenant community. Gentile converts who had submitted to circumcision began to make the same condition of covenant membership as had the Jews. For these enthusiasts for the law, without circumcision there was no membership, and therefore no salvation.

Dunn argued that the Scriptures taught that justification was about God's acceptance of Jews and then, in turn, Gentiles.[6] In other words, Dunn has a corporate perspective. It is the justification of ethnic groupings, i.e. Jews and Gentiles, that Dunn says was Paul's focus. Paul's argument was that all men are accepted by God through Jesus and all forms of national pride are denials of justification, i.e. of God's acceptance. Paul had to abandon an exclusive nationalist claim once he became a follower of Jesus and accept that Gentile believers, without circumcision, were now justified before God and had the same status as the Jews.

Paul, the disciple of Jesus, could no longer concur with circumcision as a condition of acceptance. As the apostle to the Gentiles, his concern was to be true to the Old Testament message that the Gentiles were to be brought into the covenant. Paul had discovered that the Jewish demands had nothing to do with the demands of God but were an expression of national pride or righteousness. The 'works of the law' in Paul's writings were not, according to Dunn, about works that earned salvation, but referred to the law's instructions to Israel to make her identity known through the boundary markers that the law dictated. When Paul asserts that 'no one is saved by the works of the law' he means that no one is saved by becoming a Jew. The works of the law were right for the Jewish people, they testified to their history and heritage from God, but they had nothing to do with salvation. For Paul, when a Gentile believed, he became part of the covenant community by virtue of being a spiritual descendant of Abraham.

In recent years Dunn has modified his opinion.[7] He is no longer so opposed to the traditional Protestant doctrine of justification, once the wider picture has been appreciated. In fact, commenting on Romans 4:4-5, he says that 'it is certainly correct to draw the great Reformation

[6]Dunn, *Old Doctrine, passim.*
[7]See Dunn's earlier position in *Galatians*, 161-2, and *Romans*, 1:204.

principle of justification directly from Romans 4:4-5'.[8] Indeed, Dunn acknowledges that Ephesians 2:10 is a clear expression of the Protestant doctrine of justification. However, because he holds Ephesains is non-Pauline, he sees the text not to support Paul's own view but that of the Pauline school.[9]

A preliminary assessment of Dunn's claims
We need to ask if Dunn's reconstruction is correct. Was Paul a Zealot in the way that Dunn has described? This has to be clarified because it assumes that Paul's earlier view was exclusively nationalistic. If he was a Zealot, then inevitably he would have held the Gentiles in contempt. A massive shift in his thinking and attitude would have been needed to accept the Gentiles as equals. A shift in thinking of such magnitude is rarely achieved without trauma. Yet there is not a shred of evidence that Paul had anything but the most natural of changes to his new role as an evangelist of the Gentiles following his encounter with the risen Christ. The naturalness of this transition, if Dunn's analysis is correct, has to be explained.

There is an alternative understanding of 'zealot', which retains the 'natural' change Paul experienced – Paul's activity as a zealot was not directed toward Gentiles, but towards fellow Jews. It was not nationalism in the sense of keeping Gentiles in their place; rather it was about keeping Jews in their rightful place, of being true to the law. This, it can argued, was behind Jesus' cleansing of the temple when he used force, even if limited and largely symbolic, and based on Old Testament examples. He was demonstrating God's judgment on the covenant community for not fulfilling their part of the covenantal requirements. There is no evidence that either Paul or Jesus would have participated in attempts to overthrow the rule of Gentiles who tried to stop Jews practising their religion.

Two important details for assessing the background of Paul and his meaning of 'zealous' have been overlooked. Both of these facts are serious challenges to Dunn's understanding of Paul as a Zealot. First, could a Zealot retain his Roman citizenship, as Paul did? It is inconceivable that a person with the feelings of resentment possessed by Zealots to Roman occupation could embrace such a privilege. In response, it could be argued that it was after his conversion that Paul

---

[8] Dunn, *Theology*, 367.
[9] Dunn, *Theology*, 371.

embraced his family's heritage. The second problem, however, is not so easily resolved. How could this young man, with such burning passion, choose to be a disciple of the liberally-minded Gamaliel? All that we know of this Jewish teacher suggests that he was fair and impartial (Acts 5:34-40). Such a choice by a Zealot is inconceivable. Paul had not chosen to be taught by someone who would merely sharpen his mind and convictions. Rather, he was Gamaliel's disciple and Paul was trying to model himself on his teacher's example and instruction.[10]

Hengel raises other issues that warrant caution in placing Paul among the Zealots. He points out that Paul uses the same word (*zēlōtēs* – a zealot) to describe both himself (Acts 22:3) and the zeal of his fellow countrymen in following the law (Rom. 10:2). Paul is clearly speaking of mainstream Judaism. Hengel points out that few leaders admired Phinehas in the first century. His example had been used to support the actions of the extremists which had brought much suffering to the Jewish people. But perhaps Hengel's strongest argument against Paul being a political Zealot is the fact that the Jewish High Priest had given him authority to make arrests in Damascus. Would a Jewish leader so sensitive to Roman concerns endow such a loose cannon with his authority?[11]

To identify Saul with the zealot movement is in fact to remove the crucial evidence of history. The pre-70 AD rabbis never were part of such a movement. They had refused to be drawn into the apocalyptic vision that was at the root of zealot motivation and expectation. It was because the rabbis had stood off from this movement that Rome came to consider them to be the safest grouping in Judaism and bestowed on them the status of official representatives of the nation following AD 120. This recognition gave Rabbinic Judaism a prominence that it never enjoyed pre AD 70. Now obviously if Rabbinic

[10]Wright, *Testament*, 194, acknowledges the liberal-mindedness of Gamaliel. Wright mentions that it was not unknown for a student to differ from his teacher and cites Nehunya who disagreed with the non-political activism of his teacher Akiba (198). The problem with this example is that Nehunya was one of a number of disciples of Akiba who became frustrated with their teacher's pacifist views and who turned from his teaching because of the increasing oppression of Rome. In other words, he shared Akiba's views when he became his student but later left them. This is not an example that matches Paul, for Wright is arguing that he became a disciple of Gamaliel when he disagreed with him. See Frinkelstein, *Akita*, passim.

[11]Hengel, *Zealots*, 177. For a contrasting viewpoint, see Farmer, *Maccabees*, 204.

Judaism had never identified with the zealot movement it is difficult to make a case that Saul as a student rabbi was ever part of such a movement. As noted earlier, disciples of Akiba turned from his pacifist position, but this was post AD 120 and reflected the growing frustration that, despite compliance, Rome continued to abuse the dignity and requirements of Israel's faith.[12]

Can Dunn's reading of Paul's development be sustained? A careful reading of Acts suggests not. There is no evidence that the Hellenists, represented by Stephen, were overriding the covenant and its requirement regarding circumcision. They were certainly concerned with the corruption that motivated much of the activity in the temple. Stephen, like Jesus before him, rejected the Temple as essential to the worship of God (John 4:21-24). Few would call Jesus a 'Hellenist'! Worship without the temple was possible but worship with a corrupt heart was blasphemous. There is not the slightest suggestion that these 'Hellenists' had forsaken the requirement of circumcision as a condition of entry into the covenant community. This has been assumed without any evidence to support it.

Early missions to the Gentiles by the New Testament church
Dunn's reconstruction has argued for a very early mission to the Gentiles which deeply offended Paul because the Hellenists did not demand circumcision of their converts. I want to challenge this claim and argue that Dunn has misread the evidence and has then in turn interpreted Paul's position in the light of this defective understanding.

The first evidence that Dunn gives is the evangelism of the Ethiopian

[12]Dr. David Instone Brewer, the Rabbinics specialist at Tyndale Library, Cambridge, commented on the above statement thus: 'It is *very* difficult to discover from rabbinic material whether or not they supported the zealots, because they never talk about it. Partly this is because the early rabbinic material was concerned with other matters (how to live out the Torah) and partly perhaps due to self-preserving censorship. Some good piece of evidence that they wanted to stand back from the Zealots is found in Ben Sira (not a rabbinic work, but it stands in the same kind of social group). In Heb. Ben Sira 45.23-25 Phineas is praised for his zeal (i.e. when he assassinated someone who wasn't keeping the Torah), but in the Greek version, written two generations later, this is totally changed, and there is no reference to Phineas. The most likely reason is that by this time the Zealots had taken Phineas as their role model, and the proto-rabbis wanted to disassociate themselves from this. This change is discussed by Hayward in his recent book on the Jewish Temple, but he doesn't link it to the rabbinic dissociation from the Zealots.' Cited with permission.

eunuch. Of course, it is true that shortly after Stephen's death Philip baptised the Ethiopian eunuch (Acts 8:38). But note that no suggestion is given of any enquiry being made as to whether he had been circumcised or not. All we know is that he was a God-fearer who had made the long journey from Ethiopia to Jerusalem to worship Israel's God. Was he a Jewish convert? That he was an actual Gentile convert to Judaism cannot be ruled out. All we know is that Philip baptized him at his own request. It would be unwise to hang claims of a Gentile mission on this one case, particularly one that leaves several important questions unanswered. What the account does reveal is that the Spirit who was about to direct Peter to the household of Cornelius was the same Spirit who had guided Philip into the path of the Ethiopian eunuch. Surely this is an indication that the acceptance of the Gentiles was in the hands of God rather than the church.

Dunn has assumed that Philip the 'Hellenist' accepted uncircumcised Gentiles into the church in Samaria. If Philip had done this, why was it not referred back to the Jerusalem church as Peter was later obliged to do after he had accepted the house of Cornelius? Neither is there any suggestion of a similar discussion following the acceptance of the Samaritans, such as happened when the household of Cornelius was baptised. In other words, though the Jews viewed the worship of the Samaritans as seriously deficient, they were still not classified as Gentiles. There seems to be no abnormality in the Samaritans becoming believers. There is no suggestion that the Jerusalem church leaders doubted the conversion of the Samaritans: what they wanted to know was whether the Samaritans had received the gift of the Spirit as the Jerusalem church had on the Day of Pentecost. It is possible that the reference to 'Simon the sorcerer' has caused Dunn to assume that he was a Gentile, but Israel of course had her own fair share of such in her ranks.

In fact, the first definite contact with Gentiles that could be called a Gentile mission was not from the 'Hellenist' side of the church. It was from the avowedly Jewish side. It was Peter himself, the apostle of the Jews, who was responsible. The vision of the sheet which Peter saw was the beginning of Gentile acceptance (Acts 10:9-48). Cornelius was a God-fearer, but there is no suggestion that he was circumcised. If he had been, Peter would not have needed the reassurance of the vision nor would he have had to defend his action in Jerusalem. The vision persuaded him that he would not be made unclean through contact with Gentiles. All of this was happening, according to Acts 9 and 10, with Paul out of the way in Damascus, pursuing believers who had no knowledge of this development.

Thus, it was the Jerusalem church that had taken the step of admitting into its ranks uncircumcised Gentiles. There is no suggestion that 'Hellenists' were involved. While Acts 13:1-3 records Paul's separation to the work of Gentile mission, the Gentile mission was not instigated by Hellenists as Dunn has argued, but by the strict Jerusalem church. It was joined naturally by Paul once his commission had been given. In other words, the Gentile mission was recognised and accepted by the church without any 'Hellenist' participation.[13]

Throughout this record, the process of accepting the Gentiles is seen as a natural progression. It was what the Scriptures had predicted. It was the taking of the light to the Gentiles that had been predicted by the prophets (Acts 9:15-16, 13:48; 26:15-18), it was the raising of the tent of David (Acts 15:14-19). The key matter that settled the acceptability of Peter baptizing the household of Cornelius was the pouring out of the Spirit. He had come upon the Gentile household as he had come on the Jerusalem church. This is fundamental for understanding the early church's attitude to the Gentiles. The apostles were not taken totally by surprise by this development. The prophets had said that the Gentiles would become members of the covenant community when the New Exodus had taken place.[14] In the early church's mind this was probably reserved for the future. But here God was clearly accepting them, and without

---

[13]The word 'Hellenist' is far too easily substituted as a short-hand version of 'liberal Jew'. Just because these Jews spoke Greek rather than Hebrew did not make them any less fervent for the law. There are many second-generation Muslims in England who cannot speak Arabic, whose first language is English, but who are more fanatical for their orthodox Muslim beliefs than are millions of Arabic-speaking Muslims.

It was the Hellenists who in Acts 9:28 sought to kill Paul. Now if they are the liberal section of the Jewish and Christian community, why have they turned on one who has supposedly accepted the Hellenist argument, i.e. that Gentiles are unconditionally accepted? The fact is that the weight that is put on the term Hellenists is too arbitrary to stand examination. These Hellenists did not seek to kill Paul because he preached acceptance of the Gentiles, but because he 'he preached boldly in the name of Jesus' (Acts 9:27). This can mean nothing less than that he was preaching that Jesus is the crucified and risen Messiah. In other words, Hellenists could be just as fanatical as any Hebrew-speaking Jew and it is folly to assume that the term automatically means that those called by the term have been accurately classified.

[14]Isaiah 2:1-5; 9:1-5; 19:23-25; 49:6-7, 22-23; 56:3ff; 60:3,10; 65:17.

their having been circumcised. He had given them his Spirit. The apostles could not deny that Gentiles were in the covenant community. God had caused the future to rush into the present. The day of the Lord, when the Gentiles would seek the Lord, had come. What right did anyone have to deny baptism or demand circumcision?

Dunn is therefore wrong to say that the Gentile mission was the reason for Saul's persecution. The Gentile mission had not begun. The 'Hellenists' were doing nothing new, nor anything that was unacceptable. They were simply members of Judaism who taught in the synagogues that Jesus was the Messiah. Others had done similar things before them and had urged other Jews to follow their Messiahs. The followers of these other Messiahs had not been treated in this way, although admittedly in these earlier cases there had been no accusation of opening the door to uncircumcised Gentiles.

There is no evidence that the early dispersed believers had embarked on a Gentile mission as Dunn has claimed. So why did Saul of Tarsus turn on the 'Hellenist' believers in Jesus? This question is in fact misleading. His outrage was not against the Hellenists *per se*, but against the church itself. Of course the priests did not like Stephen's attack on the temple; it was an attack on their power base. But this criticism was not a new departure. As we have already noted, both the prophets and Jesus had spoken against the corruption that its activities covered. In fact, it is more than conceivable that some of the Jews would have secretly approved Stephen's attack on the temple. Few saw it to be the eschatological temple that had been promised – after all, it had been built by a scheming Gentile! For many its destruction would bring the longed-for reality closer! It was standing on the very site of the eschatological temple that the Davidic prince would build. That was not Hellenism, it was more like nationalism!

Is Paul's pre-conversion attitude an important issue? Dunn certainly thinks so, as evidenced by his careful reconstruction. The picture we have of Paul's starting-point will almost certainly decide where we perceive him to have finally finished in his theological understanding. By putting the circumcision issue into Paul's mind from the beginning, Dunn determined the reconstruction of Paul's expectations and the course of his spiritual journey.

So, why did Paul persecute the church? He gives us his own answer to this important question. He later described why the Christian message offended the Jews. It was not the conversion of the Gentiles;

this was expected once the Messiah had come, even though most of the Jews would have expected the Gentiles to be circumcised to enter the covenant. The offence was that the 'Christians' proclaimed *a crucified Messiah*. This struck at the heart of national pride. The implication was clear to any Jew. If Jesus was the Messiah, he had not only been the victim of the Roman judicial system, but had himself come under the curse of Israel's law (Gal. 3:13; Deut. 21:23). To accept that their Messiah had been crucified by the Romans was to accept that they had no national hope. There could no longer be such a thing as special privileged status for Israel. To accept that the Messiah had been crucified meant that they would not triumph over their enemies. Israel could only serve God's purposes by accepting her original calling to be the suffering servant. She was to be the light to the nations. In fact, while Dunn has emphasised the attack in Stephen's speech on the temple, claiming that it proved that he was a Hellenist, it was not at the point where he spoke against the temple that the rulers attempted to silence him. The leaders had heard this sort of thing many times, not least from their own prophets. It was the statement that they had killed the Righteous One that infuriated them. 'When they heard this, they were furious and gnashed their teeth at him' (Acts 7:54). It was the claim that they had killed the Messiah that turned them into Stephen's killers.

Indeed, following on from what has been argued earlier, if the argument of Dunn is to stand, he has to explain why there was not an explosion of persecution against the Jerusalem church following the baptism of Cornelius. Here was the very thing that is supposed to have driven the persecution of the Hellenists. The official acceptance of Gentiles by the mother church was without so much as a whisper of any irregularity as far as the Jews were concerned. It is hardly possible that this decision would have been kept private. So receiving Gentiles without circumcision was not the issue that it was later to become within the church. The issue of circumcision almost destroyed the church and possibly emerged as a result of the Jews realising that the Gentile converts were soon going to outnumber them. The Judaizers were concerned not only about the covenant, but also about losing numerical strength and no longer being the controlling party. Circumcision was the solution to avoid this unacceptable situation.

There is thus no evidence to support the claim of Dunn that Paul persecuted the Hellenists for preaching to the Gentiles, let alone for accepting them without circumcision. What they were doing was preaching a crucified Messiah *to the Jewish people*. Once Paul had been confronted by the risen Jesus on the Damascus road, he was forced to accept the truth of what had so deeply offended him – that Israel's Messiah had been crucified. Not only had the Messiah been crucified, but he was risen. Added to these incredible facts was that the Spirit had been poured out on the followers of Jesus. Almost immediately his theological understanding was reconstructed, not with new teachings but with the very expectations he had always held to as a faithful Jew. The Messianic age had been brought in by the resurrection. But it was not the resurrection of the nation as generally expected, but of her Messiah. The Spirit had come, the promised gift that would be poured out in the coming age. What now had to be fulfilled was the ingathering of the nations (Isa. 2:1-5; 55:3ff.). Thus, Paul had not persecuted the believing Jews because they had preached to the Gentiles, but because they were disgracing Israel and her God by preaching *to the Jews* a crucified Messiah. Dunn has read the later Gentile circumcision controversy that caused Paul so much distress back into his early life. The controversy of circumcision was not an issue for Paul in his early years.

Was Paul a Zealot? Not in the way that Dunn has described. By identifying Paul as a Zealot Dunn has determined where his exegesis will eventually lead. I would not deny that Paul was concerned with issues that impinged on the political concerns of Judaism, but to suggest that he was part of a popular Zealot movement that inevitably had Rome as its number one enemy is not warranted by the evidence.

N. T. Wright and justification

Wright shares all that has been said of Dunn's understanding of Paul's pre-conversion position. He has identified Paul with the political protest movement and the Maccabean tradition that inspired it. The criticism I have given of Dunn's position also applies to Wright's as far as identifying the pre-conversion mindset of Paul and the reasons for his persecution of the infant church are concerned.

Both scholars are also deeply influenced by Sanders' view of covenantal nomism. In fact, Wright has claimed that he himself was the first to recognise the logical consequence of covenantal nomism. It requires, he argues, that the rediscovery of the characteristics of Second Temple Judaism means that the doctrine of justification has to be re-examined.[15] Wright claims that justification is not about entry into the covenant, as traditionally understood as far back as the Reformation at least, for according to covenantal nomism, the Jews were already in this relationship with Yahweh. Wright is aware that the prophets had said that Yahweh would justify Israel. Justification therefore, Wright argues, is about being declared to be *within* the covenant, a status which was the work of God's grace. When Yahweh declared Israel to be justified, he was declaring her to be his people.

Wright claims that Paul had the same covenantal nomistic perspective. The believer is not justified when he believes. Rather, justification is used by Paul in the context of covenantal nomism. It is about being declared to be in the covenant. Rather than creating the relationship, it affirms the past inclusion into the covenant community. It is a declaration that the status exists, rather than speaking of the creation of a new status. Thus, in Wright's mind, he has resolved the tension of covenantal nomism and justification: they are not in conflict but are part of the same picture. In making this claim, Wright has challenged the Reformers' understanding of justification. They had argued that it was about being accepted by God.[16] Wright criticised the traditional Reformed doctrine of justification as follows:

> it tends to merge justification with the events that it presupposes, thus virtually making faith appear to be a luxury which follows the justification which occurs in the cross and resurrection.... Justification does not cover everything from atonement to final redemption.[17]

Wright claims that the biblical doctrine of justification was distorted as a result of Augustine's use of the concept to answer Pelagius. Augustine had used it to demonstrate that good works could never earn salvation. This, claimed Wright, set the course by which the expression has since been understood. It has become the mould into which all other statements about justification in the Bible have been poured. From this revised mind-set the texts have been used to construct the widely accepted doctrine of 'justification by faith'. Wright's argument is that the doctrine of justification, as expressed by the Reformers, has distorted the biblical understanding. Paul did

[15]Wright, 'History,' 77ff.

[16]For a discussion of the Reformers' views, see Bray, 'Reformers,' 102ff., and Eveson, *Exchange*, passim. See also Appendix 3 at the end of this volume.

[17]Wright, 'Acquittal,' 30.

not use the concept to teach that man cannot make himself right with God. Wright says:

> Paul may or may not agree with Augustine, Luther or anyone else about how people come to a personal knowledge of God in Christ; but *he does not use the language of justification to denote this event or process.* Instead, he speaks of the proclamation of the gospel of Jesus, the work of the spirit and the entry into the common life of the people of God.[18]

According to Wright, justification, which for him is about being declared to be in the covenant, encompasses both the present and the future:

> This justification would thus be *eschatological*: it would be the final fulfillment of Israel's long cherished hope. But more importantly, this event could be *anticipated* under certain circumstances, so that particular Jews and/or groups of Jews could see themselves as the true Israel in advance of the day when everyone else would see them thus as well.[19]

Wright (following Dunn), correctly in my view, points out that Galatians is not about how a person is made right with God, but whether Gentile converts should be circumcised or not. Wright says that the issue is how you define the people of God.[20] The argument that Galatians 2–4 is dealing with 'is not how people came to a relationship with God, but who one is allowed to eat with. Who is a member of the people of God? Are ex-pagan converts full members or not? It is not: how individuals, Abraham then and the Galatians now, come to faith (as we say), but rather the question of who belongs to Abraham's family'.[21]

Wright concludes his construction of justification in Galatians by saying: 'What Paul means by justification in Galatians in this context, should therefore be clear. It is not "how you become a Christian", so much as "how you can tell who is a member of the covenant family".'[22]

Concerning 1 Corinthians 1:30, where Paul says, 'it is because of him that you are in Christ Jesus, who has become for us wisdom from God – that is, our righteousness, holiness and redemption,' Wright comments:

[18]Wright, *What*, 117, emphasis Wright's.
[19]Ibid, 118-19, emphasis Wright's.
[20]Ibid, 120.
[21]Ibid, 121.
[22]Ibid, 122.

It is difficult to squeeze any precise doctrine of justification out of this shorthand summary. It is the only passage I know where something called 'the imputed righteousness of Christ', a phrase more often found in post-reformation theology and piety than in the New Testament, finds any basis in the text. But if we are to claim it as such, we must also be prepared to talk of the imputed wisdom of Christ; the imputed sanctification of Christ; and that though no doubt they are true in some overall general sense, will certainly make nonesense of the very specialised and technical sense so frequently given to the phrase 'the righteousness of Christ' in the history of theology.[23]

Wright argues that the statement in 2 Corinthians 5:21, 'in him we might become the righteousness of God,' is not concerned with judicial acquittal but instead refers to believers being the instruments to establish God's righteousness. He points out that the servant theme is very much woven into the context of this statement, as is shown in chapters 3–4 and 6 of the letter, which speak of God's servants. Wright's argument is that as a result of God's salvation through Christ's death, believers are now his servants called to serve God's purposes in overcoming evil.[24]

Philippians 3:2-11 is about national, not personal, righteousness, says Wright.[25] Paul is stating that he was prepared to abandon all of his covenantal privileges as a descendant of Abraham in order to gain Christ. He is effectively saying that he has followed the example of Christ which he has described in the hymn in Philippians 2:6-11.

Wright deals with Romans 4:3, 'Abraham believed God and it was counted to him as righteousness', by first considering the context. He reminds us that the statement is the extension of the discussion on Israel's boasting in 2:1–3:31. Paul is seeking to show that the privileges that Israel has enjoyed do not give her an alternative way of acceptance by God. Her claim to have a special status that gives her salvation is not true.

Wright comes into Romans 4 aware of the insight of Hays that 4:1 reads as: 'What then shall we say? Have we found Abraham to be our forefather according to the flesh?' The answer to this is implied; it is: No. Hays suggests that the 'we' refers to Jews, so making the passage read as: 'Do you think that we Jews have considered Abraham our forefather only according to the flesh?'[26] Wright challenges this

[23]Ibid, 123.
[24]Wright, *What*, *op. cit.*; also Wright, 'Becoming,' 200-08.
[25]Wright, 'Romans,' 40.

identification of 'we' and says it refers to Christians, Jews and Gentiles alike. In other words, argues Wright, Paul is blocking the way for anyone to argue that becoming a spiritual child of Abraham meant following Abraham's example of being circumcised. Some Gentiles had possibly gone on to become 'members of the fleshly family of Abraham' through circumcision. If they had, it would suggest to others that converted Gentiles were to come under the same boundary markers.

Wright argues from this understanding that the statement of 4:3-4, 'Abraham believed God, and it was credited to him as righteousness', is not about good works:

> the discussion of 'works', 'reward', 'debt', and so forth in vv 3-4 functions as a metaphor within the wider categories of 'works of Torah' (i.e., badges of Jewish ethnic covenant membership).

Wright continues his argument thus:

> The 'justification by works' of which v.2 speaks is clearly an explanation of something in v.1; and v.1, as we saw, raised the question not whether or not Abraham was a good moralist but whether those who are in Christ have become Abraham's family according to the flesh. I suggest, therefore, that the metaphor of 'earning' by 'working', which Paul exploits in vv. 3-8, is secondary, occurring to Paul's mind not because he has been speaking of works in connection with 'works of Torah' in the sense already outlined, and now sees a way of ramming home the point.[27]

A preliminary assessment of Wright's claims

Is Wright correct in saying that justification is not about being made righteous but being declared to be in the covenant? To understand why Wright arrives at this position we must appreciate that Wright's

---

[26]Hays, 'Found,' 54ff.

[27]Wright, 'Romans,' 41. Cranford, 'Abraham,' 80-81, puts it more clearly than Wright. He says: 'The key issue is not faith versus works, but reckoning according to obligation versus reckoning according to favour. While to some this speaks of human effort versus reliance on God, this antithesis need not be assumed. This is made even clearer by the fact that Paul's argument in vv. 4-5 fails as a contrast between faith and human effort. Verse 4 suggests a works analogy well enough, but we would expect v.5 to balance the analogy by stating something like, "but to the one who does not work yet receives a payment, his reward is according to grace and not because of his own efforts." This parallelism never occurs, however, though traditional commentators assume that it was clearly expressed.'

method is inductive. If the Jews were covenantal nomists, then justification cannot be about coming into the covenant, for they were already in it. Wright assumes that Sanders is basically right in describing Judaism as covenantal nomism. In exegeting Scripture he allows this model to control his argument. If the Jews are in the covenant, then justification cannot be about being acquitted of sin.

Wright's assumption that Sanders' picture of covenantal nomism was Paul's position has already been examined by others. Fossum, for example, has argued that Rabbinic Judaism was the step-child of biblical Judaism.[28] Being the triumphant party following the fall of Jerusalem it left little trace of the parties which had opposing views in the period prior to the destruction of the city. These opposing parties were far from being peripheral groups. They probably had greater numerical support than the Rabbinics themselves had. To say that the Rabbinic texts represent Judaism is not only presuming that they accurately and faithfully recorded the rabbinical oral tradition; it also ignores the facts of history. Triumphant parties, whether political or religious, do not promote or even preserve the teachings of those whom they have conquered. It is a massive presumption to assume that pre-AD 70 Judaism is substantially mirrored in the Rabbinic texts. At most these texts mirror a part of, and certainly not most of, Second Temple Judaism. In other words, it is always the triumphant who write the official account of history, and it is their account. As it would be foolish to say that Lutheranism represented pre-Reformation Christianity, so it would be well off the mark to claim that Rabbinic Judaism represented Second Temple Judaism.

This then is the crux of Wright's case. If Sanders' case can be

---

[28]Fossum, 'Question,' 643, says: 'Since the Pharisees made up only one of many parties or sects which existed within the spectrum of Israelite religion when the temple was still standing, it is actually unfortunate to refer to Israelite religion in that period as "Judaism". This usage inevitably creates the impression that the religion which was shaped by Pharisaic Rabbinism and is commonly called by the same name is the natural and legitimate outgrowth of the religion of Israel, whereas Christianity and other children of Rebecca's are hybrids or bastards.' In fact Fossum points out how unsustainable is the argument that Rabbinic Judaism represents Second Temple Judaism by pointing out that it would mean that the Jewish state was headed by someone from an opposing minority party – the High Priest. Carson, *Responsibility*, 69 and 106, criticises Sanders for failing to come to grips with the diluted value of such words as 'grace' and 'merit' in inter-testamental literature. In the literature of the Rabbis there is an increasing dependence on personal merit as an approach to God. Abraham is singled out as one whose merits are especially powerful.

shown to be faulty, then Wright's exegesis inherits the same errors in method as Sanders'. There is no serious argument that the Rabbinic texts have covenantal nomism as their outlook, but there is serious questioning whether these are a faithful representative of *mainstream Second Temple Judaism*. We will see in the following chapter that there are certainly Pauline texts which, with the best will in the world, cannot fit into the picture that Sanders has constructed. It is only by careful selection of the biblical evidence, and by ignoring the fact that Rabbinic Judaism did not emerge as representing Judaism until after AD 70, that Sanders' argument can hold any water. These fault lines are inherent in both Wright's and Dunn's arguments.

Furthermore, we noted that Sanders saw Paul to be outside of mainstream Judaism. To immerse Paul back into covenantal nomism without first establishing his natural 'Christian' home is bound to be questionable. Wright clearly locates Paul within mainstream Judaism, but since he disagrees with Sanders on this crucial point, then he ought at least to discuss the tension that exists between his own view and that of Sanders. They are both going in opposite directions as far as the relevance of the literature of Second Temple Judaism is concerned for interpreting Paul's thinking.

A further concern has been raised by Talbert. Like others, he challenges the selective process employed by Sanders; but he also questions the claims that have been deducted from covenantal nomism, namely, that if Israel is in the covenant, then keeping the law is not about earning salvation. Talbert argues that if works are the grounds of the final eschatological justification, then works are a part of the salvation process:

> The ancient Judaism surveyed by Sanders cannot be described merely as covenantal nomism. Rather, once a covenantal, nomistic Judaism is set within an eschatological context, obedience to the law is no longer just a matter of 'staying in' God's people but much more of 'getting into' the Ages to Come. Once this is so, Judaism becomes a legalistic, covenantal nomism whose soteriology is that of synergism, and this legalistic, covenantal nomism is what Paul opposes. If that is so, an explanation of what is wrong with works that is very similar to the explanation given by the Reformers and their heirs comes again into play.... The heirs of the Reformers correctly see that some ancient Jews were legalists. The interpreters who have succeeded those with the new perspective rightly recognize the soteriological synergism of much of the Reformers and the

post-new-perspective interpreters correctly see that the heart of Paul's
theological struggle is between divine grace and human self-sufficiency,
whatever the particular circumstances evoking his letters may be.[29]

N.T. Wright is correct in my opinion to say that while the language
of justification is from the law court, the setting was not the law court
but the covenant. The Old Testament certainly uses legal language in
a covenantal setting. However, Wright is in danger of taking the Roman
law court into an Old Testament paradigm. The law that has to be
answered to is covenantal law, and when the secular forensic model
is introduced it becomes like the camel's nose, it demands all of the
tent and eventually takes control. Seifrid says, 'N. T. Wright, despite
his appeal to the "Hebrew law court" and its two-party form,
effectively turns it into the image of the modern courtroom.'[30]
Wherever Wright intends the law court room scene to be located,
what he has missed is the fact that justification is used in the context
of God accepting Israel *into* the covenant, i.e. it is the language of the
New Exodus. Wright acknowledges a New Exodus link but does not
develop it beyond noting that the promise of return from exile is
fundamental to the covenant made with Abraham in Genesis 15.[31]
The fact is that there is far more than this promise in Genesis 15 for
Paul to draw on. Israel was justified when she was released from her
bondage and restored to her inheritance. Justification is foundational
for New Exodus language as proclaimed by the prophets. This closely
parallels the New Testament perspective that links justification with
entering the kingdom of God (Rom. 4:25; 5:1,18; 8:30). It is a corporate
picture of the saving activity of God toward his covenant people.
Dunn has also missed this dimension as a result of his faulty analysis
of Paul's pre-conversion mind-set.

It is surprising that Wright should miss the significance of what the
prophets say concerning this vitally important New Exodus setting
for justification.[32] Indeed, he has made much of Jesus' understanding
of the New Exodus promises, and has used this model – although to

---

[29]Talbert, 'Revisionists,' 14-15.

[30]Seifrid, 'Perspective, 15 note 40. Seifrid refers his readers to Wright's book,
What Saint Paul Really Said, 96-99. Wright denies this, saying that he refers to the
ancient Jewish law court, *NIB*, 495, fn 93.

[31]Wright, 'Exodus,' passim.

[32]Wright, 'Exodus,' identifies the New Exodus setting of Romans 3–8. The article
is an expansion of his earlier essay, 'Romans.' Although Wright acknowledges the

my mind not to its full potential – to interpret Paul. Wright uses the wrong paradigms for unravelling Paul's teaching. He uses covenantal nomism and martyrdom as his hermeneutical keys. But justification in the Old Testament spoke of Israel being released from exile and being brought to her inheritance. In this redemptive historical setting there is certainly a legal dimension to justification in that it is Israel's sin that has caused her exile and this has to be dealt with. The cultic event of the original Exodus was the Passover. We have seen in chapter 8 that it was a propitiatory sacrifice. It is possible that the death of the servant figure in Isaiah 53 has this same significance. It is through his death that the deliverance of the Babylonian covenant community is achieved. It is because he suffers that many are justified and made righteous, i.e. delivered from captivity and returned to their inheritance. In the light of our earlier discussions this means that God has saved Israel and brought her back to the promised land. It was the remnant who returned to their inheritance. If justification is not considered within the context of this redemptive model, then it is bound to distort what Paul is saying and we will be left with a deviation from his thought rather than with its essence. I have no doubt that Wright wholeheartedly agrees with the importance of the covenant, but he has inadvertently deflected the argument by inserting it uncritically into Sanders' covenantal nomism.

promise of the Exodus in the covenant made with Abraham in Genesis 15, he does not make the same argument that I make. In my judgment he misses the point that the essential nature of justification is about *being brought into a covenant relationship with God* in which the righteousness of God is directed to the church and its individual members, a righteousness that makes the members of the covenant community to be the focus of God's saving concern and action.

Chapter Ten

The Paschal Community and Justification

The prophets have spoken about the exile as being a 'putting away' (Hos. 9:17), as being 'cut off' (Jer. 44:11). Justification in this context is about being brought back into a new relationship. This new relationship began with the return from exile and the creation of a new covenant (Isa. 55:3ff; Jer. 31:31-33; 33:15; Ezek. 36:22-32). This was Israel's justification. Because Paul followed the New Exodus paradigm he could adopt the prophets' perspective of justification, which is the restoration of Israel to fellowship with God. Thus justification for Isaiah was a blanket description that covered redemption, atonement and all of the blessings that Israel received as she returned to her inheritance. It was taken over by the early church to describe the activity of God in electing, redeeming and making atonement for the church. In other words, justification is the technical description of the whole of the salvation experience. In this sense the prophets speak of Israel's justification.

In the Old Testament justification is expressed by the verbal form of the noun *tsedeq,* righteousness (Job 11:2; 25:4, Pss. 51:4; 143:2; Isa. 43:26; 45:25). In the New Testament the noun righteousness is *dikaiosunē,* which means 'upright', 'righteousness' (Matt. 9:13; 10:41; Luke 18:9; Rom. 3:10; 5:19). The verbal form of righteous is *dikaioō,* 'to justify' (Matt. 12:37; Luke 10:29; Acts 13:39; Rom. 2:13; 3:20, 24; 4:2; 5:1, 9; 8:30; Gal. 2:16). It is used to describe the divine action in saving the elect community and, in so doing, bringing them into a right relationship with God (Isa. 51:5). Everywhere this verb is used by Paul it denotes God's action, which is the outworking of his grace.

Yahweh acted in righteousness toward Israel. Both words, 'justify' and 'righteous', share the same semantic domain in Hebrew. They are saying the same thing. So when Yahweh says that he will make Israel righteous, it means that he will justify her. This is not the declaration of inclusion but of being the object of Yahweh's righteous saving activity. It is because Yahweh kept covenant with his people that he acted in righteousness. But there is a negative side to God's righteousness. Because Yahweh is righteous, he punished Israel when she refused to repent. The positive side, of course, is that he saved her when she repented.

Isaiah described three aspects of this righteousness or justification. He said that Yahweh would deliver Israel (Isa. 42:6; 51:5), protect her on her pilgrimage as she returned to her inheritance (Isa. 58:8), and safely establish her in her inheritance (Isa. 32:1; 54:14; 62:1-2). These three themes are the outworking of Yahweh's righteousness, his saving activity, his justification of Israel. This has a clear echo in Paul when he said, 'He has delivered us from such deadly peril, and he will deliver us. On him we have set our hope that he will continue to deliver us' (2 Cor. 1:10). Romans 3:26 says concerning God's saving activity, 'so as to be just and the one who justifies those who have faith in Jesus.' This statement of Paul echoes the statements of Isaiah (43:26; 45:25), where Yahweh's salvation is about the return from exile in which both Yahweh and Israel are justified. This national or corporate justification raises the issue of the justification of the individual. We will deal with this later in the chapter.

As the New Exodus model is increasingly appreciated, we begin to see how justification fits into Paul's doctrine of corporate baptism. Paul's major discussions on baptism are not concerning water baptism. These key passages are about the covenant community sharing in the actual event of the death of Christ as a result of the Spirit uniting her with her head. All of the texts – i.e. Romans 6:1-4; 1 Corinthians 10:4; 12:13; Galatians 3:24ff. and Ephesians 4:6; 5:27 – have a New Exodus context. They do not describe the experience of the individual's baptism, but the community's corporate baptism accomplished by the Spirit – as 1 Corinthians 10:1-4 makes abundantly clear. Indeed, Paul links baptism and justification in 1 Corinthians 6:11 where he says, 'And that is what some of you were. But you were washed, you were sanctified, you were justified in the name of the Lord Jesus Christ and by the Spirit of our God.' Sanctification is linked with justification and certainly there is no recognisable *ordo salutis* in the description. What must govern the interpretation of this statement is the introduction to the section which begins in 5:8. It states that 'Christ our Passover is sacrificed for us'. We have seen in a previous chapter that the end part of 1 Corinthians 6 is corporate, based on Israel's experience of salvation. The washing is not the rite of baptism, but the death of Christ. The setting of the passage is the same as that in

Ephesians 5:27. It speaks of the corporate washing of the bride, as the end of 1 Corinthians 6 confirms. The significance is that in this New Exodus cleansing, the justification of the covenant community took place. Like Israel, they were brought into a covenant relationship with God. This is evidenced by the use of marital language in 6:14f. As Israel was sanctified by her removal from the defilement of Babylon, so the church has been sanctified by her removal from the kingdom of darkness, the body of Sin. The mention of justification in Corinthians is significant because there is no evidence that this church was confronting Judaism. It shows that justification was not just a polemic doctrine, but part of Paul's understanding of the whole process of redemptive history. However, as we have seen, his focus was the community rather than the individual, and the act is historical. It is speaking of the corporate salvation accomplished by Christ's death and resurrection.

The role of the law

I pointed out in the previous chapter that the understanding of both Wright and Dunn concerning the 'works of the law' as a reference to the boundary markers of Judaism is too simple a solution and fails to answer a number of problems. Why does Paul speak of Moses' ministry being one of condemnation (2 Cor. 3:9)? Indeed, Paul contrasted his own ministry with the ministry of Moses. Moses' ministry brought condemnation whereas his own ministry brought righteousness. In Galatians 3:21-22 Paul says, 'If a law had been given that could impart life, then righteousness would certainly have come by the law. But the Scripture declares that the whole world is a prisoner of sin.' Whatever Rabbinic Judaism thought of Israel's status, Paul's position seems at this point diametrically opposed to it. The law is not evidence of acceptance, but of separation. Israel was a prisoner of Sin. Paul speaks in Romans 10 of Israel not knowing 'the righteousness that comes from God' and of having 'sought to establish their own', and therefore 'they did not submit to God's righteousness'. But 'Christ is the end of the law so that there may be a righteousness for everyone who believes'. Such a statement cannot be reflecting covenantal nomism of the kind that Sanders and his followers have accepted. Paul clearly describes an attempt to gain righteousness as a result of keeping the law.

Also, what did Peter mean when in the presence of Paul he urged the Jerusalem council not to impose the yoke of the law on the Gentiles

(Acts 15:6-11)? His argument was that the Jews themselves had not been able to bear it. It was, therefore, not right to demand that the Gentiles achieve what the Jews had failed to achieve. This reference to keeping the law cannot possibly be a reference to circumcision. It would have been inconceivable for a Jew not to be circumcised, so it would have been meaningless to say that the Jews had not been able to bear it. The same would be true of the other boundary markers, dietary laws and Sabbath keeping. There is no evidence of failure to fulfil these regulations. The yoke of the law in this context must be more than a reference to national boundaries or boundary markers. It surely refers to the moral obligations that the law made on those who were members of the old covenant community, obligations which they had failed to keep.

Peter's understanding is shared by Paul, as shown by his message in the synagogue at Pisidian Antioch. He told his hearers: 'Therefore, my brothers, I want you to know that through Jesus the forgiveness of sins is proclaimed to you. Through him everyone who believes is justified from everything that you could not be justified from by the law of Moses' (Acts 13:38-39). This statement can be interpreted in no other way than what traditional Reformation exegesis has claimed it to say. It is not about being declared to be in the covenant but about entry into the covenant.

The identification of the works of the law as a boundary marker is a helpful insight, but it must not be imposed on texts that cannot bear that meaning. Some of those texts clearly state that the law condemns. Justification must have some bearing on how people are delivered from this condemnation.

Wright's claim that Paul lived a comfortable life with the law when he was a Pharisee is not a problem as far as I am concerned. The argument that Paul was crushed by the requirements of the law to the point of desperation depends on one's interpretation of Romans 7. This has been discussed elsewhere, with some arguing it has a corporate perspective. But even in this historical storytelling, there is something of Paul. Paul can represent mankind because he is a part of its problems. At some point the comfortable Jew, basking in the gift of covenant law, begins to sense that this is not the end of the story. At this point he enters the story existentially.

There are certainly biblical texts that suggest delight in the law (Pss. 1:2; 119:14, 20, 24, 30; Rom. 7:22) and others that speak of fear of the law (Rom. 2:12; 3:19; Gal. 3:10, 22). How can these two attitudes be reconciled? I would suggest that they are harmonised only within the New Exodus model. Israel's deliverance was a picture of the coming eschatological salvation. Israel's experience was real and historical. It gave her privileges above all other nations, but it was only temporary; it was only the type and not the reality. The Jews later came to consider that their marriage to Yahweh took place at Sinai. Here Israel came under the law of her husband. This was the foundation of all her privileges and boastings. She had the gift of covenant law. In fact, the apparent conflict of delight and fear of the law are seen in the Old Testament accounts of the Exodus. In Exodus 20 the giving of the law caused great fear. Israel was given the law of her Saviour God. The Exodus account makes it clear that it was an altogether awesome and frightening experience. However Ezekiel 16 reflects on this same event and sees Sinai as the occasion of the divine marriage. In this revision the law is given not by Israel's judge, but by her lover, her husband. The law in this thinking is a token of God's love for his people. It is this latter tradition that is repeatedly referred to in the writings of Paul. We have already seen how fundamental the New Exodus was to Paul's thinking. Just as Israel was redeemed to be Yahweh's bride, so the church was redeemed to be Christ's bride. Just as this Old Testament New Exodus material described Israel's release from bondage and her return to her inheritance as her justification, so Paul reasons within the same theological framework. Justification of the people of God is inseparably linked to the death and resurrection of Christ. It is about being brought from the kingdom of darkness into the kingdom of God's Son.

But Paul insists that Israel's experience of Exodus whether from Egypt or Babylon was only a rehearsal of the forthcoming eschatological salvation. Israel is still but a part of mankind. In fact, she is also shut up under Sin (Gal. 3:23), separated in reality from God. She had been chosen to stand in as the bride in the historical rehearsal. Tragically, she refused to acknowledge the temporary nature of this covenant and has become blind and hardened to and by the message of the gospel. She will not acknowledge that she has only attended the rehearsal for the marriage, she insists it was the real thing. She is now behaving like Pharaoh; she opposes the Exodus of the people of God. Only if she will put away her pride and come to the new place of covenant-making, the cross, will she share the true salvation of which the prophets had spoken.

Thus the law served two functions. It was a gift to Israel to celebrate her 'acceptance' by Yahweh. But it was also her 'minder'. Paul says that the law was put in charge (*paidagōgos*) to lead us to Christ so that we might be justified by faith (Gal. 3:24). It is widely acknowledged that *paidagōgos* was not a schoolmaster but a person, often a slave, who accompanied the child to and from school. If this is Paul's argument, then he is saying that the Jews rejected the greater function of the law, which was to bring them to Christ so that they could be justified. Because they ascribed to the law a function that made it an end in itself, they were guilty of idolatry. They idolised the law itself because they gave it a place above the will of God. They followed the law's letter and not its spirit. The law became a curse to them. The law's ultimate purpose was to guide them to the One who alone could save them. If they rejected this purpose, it shut them up as prisoners under Sin.

Despite the widespread acceptance of understanding the *paidagōgos* as a guardian, elsewhere I have suggested that Paul here saw the *paidagōgos* (the law) function as a best man. Evidence exists that shows that the term *paidagōgos* was also applied to this role, and I would suggest that this meaning fits Paul's argument better. In this role the *paidagōgos* was responsible for securing a bride for the master's son. If this is the imagery that Paul is using, then the illustration and its teaching have to be adjusted. It is not about the law acting as a jailer, locking man up as a slave of Sin. Rather, Paul is speaking of the law's function in recognising the legal rights that Sin (Satan) has. Satan, in this understanding, has rights that the law of God has to recognise, for it recognises all covenant relationships. Man, who has played the spiritual harlot and turned to Satan for his favours, has become the possession of Satan. While the law can do nothing other than recognise that relationship, it is also able to recognise the validity of the representative death of Christ for his people. Through that covenant-annulling death, the law is able to function as an aid to deliverance. The law also alerts to the condition that man is in. It functions as the representative of the bridegroom in presenting the claims of the intending husband to the one he wishes to marry, as in the case of Isaac and his servant. In such ways the law functions as the *paidagōgos*, bringing the redeemed community to Christ to be his bride. Thus the church comes under the law of her husband, the law of Christ.

Circumcision and covenant membership

Circumcision was the vital prerequisite for covenant membership in the Old Testament. While Paul denies its requirement for the members of the New Covenant, he does not abandon the symbol completely. He argued that membership of the New Covenant community is conditional on the circumcision of the heart (Rom. 2: 25-29; 4:9-11; Gal. 6:15).

Again, in the Old Testament circumcision was essential for anyone who wanted to share in the Passover (Exod. 12:43-44; Josh. 5:8-11.). This event identified the members of the covenant community. In this celebration they bore witness to what Yahweh had done for them. Paul again developed this theme. It is only those whose hearts have been circumcised who can share in the Passover. The celebration of Passover is at the heart of the experience of the covenant community.

A final theme of Old Testament circumcision imagery that Paul has possibly adopted is to do with circumcision as a requirement for marriage. In the incident of the circumcision of Moses' son (Exod. 4:25), Moses is called by his wife a 'bridegroom of blood'. Some scholars say that this refers to the necessity of circumcision in primitive societies as a preparation for marriage. In other words, if these ideas from the Exodus account are in Paul's mind – and in Colossians 2:8, he speaks of being circumcised with the circumcision of Christ in his death – then the imagery possibly embraces marital concepts. Indeed, Ephesians 5:25 speaks of Christ's death as a washing, preparing the church for her nuptial encounter. The church is clearly sharing in the death of Christ in both passages, and, as both are very heavily dependent on the New Exodus, it is reasonable to suggest that the reference to the circumcision of Christ is recalling an ancient significance of circumcision as a preparation for marriage. The circumcision of the heart is the prerequisite for entry into the covenant community and it is equally a prerequisite for that to which the covenant brings the people of God. It is the required preparation for the eschatological marriage in which the covenant community becomes the bride of Christ. The heart of the believer can be circumcised because Christ has undergone a greater and far more significant circumcision that prepares his bride for her union with her Lord.

It is at this point that we can ask whether Wright is correct to say that faith is the badge of membership of the new covenant community.[1]

[1] Wright, *What*, 125.

I do not think it is what Paul would have said! For him it is no longer physical circumcision that matters but spiritual circumcision. The evidence of this is the life that is lived in obedience to Christ. The heart of such a person has been circumcised. Life that is clearly part of the new creation is the evidence of salvation; this is the badge of membership. It may be that Wright means a life lived in obedience, but the claim that 'faith' is the badge of membership does not make this clear.

Justification and Abraham

The key text in Paul concerning justification is Romans 4:3, which speaks of Abraham being declared righteous by Yahweh. Paul says: 'What does the Scripture say? "Abraham believed God, and it was credited to him as righteousness".' The background of the Genesis statement which Paul quotes was that God had promised Abraham, who was in extreme old age, that he would have a son, who would in turn father a great nation. Abraham's faith that God would make his offspring into a mighty nation was based on the conviction that God is not limited by the hopelessness of man's condition (Rom. 4:18-25; see also Heb. 11:11-12). Abraham and Sarah, his wife, as far as having a family were concerned, were well past their 'sell-by date'. Yet despite the impossibility of reversing this state of affairs in human terms, Abraham believed that God would be faithful to his promise and give him a son. Another key detail from the Genesis account is that Abraham was uncircumcised when the covenant was made with him. He was effectively a Gentile! For Paul, Abraham's faith and his uncircumcised state are the two key details of the covenant and it is these features that he argues must be to the fore in its New Testament application.

If Paul's understanding of justification and righteousness comes from the Law and the Prophets and not from the criminal law court, then it must affect how we understand Romans 4:3. The Law and the Prophets provide a distinctly covenantal framework for Paul's argument.[2] What Paul is saying is that Abraham believed that God would make his son his heir and that he would become the first of millions of offspring. He was effectively believing that God would be

---

[2] Note that Paul has said that this righteousness is borne witness to by the Law and the Prophets (Rom. 3:21). Schrenk, TDNT 2:195, notes the covenantal relationship with justification when he says that 'the righteousness of God is primarily His covenantal rule in relationship with His people'.

faithful to the promise he had made, and God responded by crediting to him righteousness, i.e., accrediting to him the status of what he was to become, the head of a redeemed covenant community. If this understanding is correct, then both Genesis and Paul see that the primary issue with which Genesis 15:6 is dealing is Yahweh's *acceptance* of Abraham. God committed himself to Abraham in covenant, saying that he would act righteously toward Abraham, always keeping faith with his promise. Abraham's faith was his response to the promise that Yahweh had given him; it was his 'Amen, I want to be part of your covenant'. The matter of Abraham's sin and its forgiveness is secondary, even though still very important. No covenant with Yahweh could be established without a proper dealing with sin. For the covenant to be established and ratified it is implied that the sin of Abraham has been dealt with. But again, to make that the primary issue of the passage is to miss the clear covenantal significance of what is happening.

The emphasis on the criminal legal setting that has dominated the traditional understanding of 'counted righteous' has left its own problems. Terms like sacrifice, redemption, inheritance, Spirit etc. have no part in such a model. The growing appreciation that Paul stayed within the framework of Old Testament covenant theology, developing it in the light of the Christ event that had brought to completion the covenant promises, suggests that this is the correct paradigm for understanding Paul's thinking. Within the covenant framework, of course, was the law, which made demands that had to be satisfied. When the terms of the covenant were broken, there was only one way back into fellowship with God, and that was on the basis of the law's demands being satisfied. Thus the law is covenant law. Justification is not modelled on criminal law, but covenantal law. This adjustment, which focuses on the Old Testament covenantal meaning of justification and righteousness, does not remove the necessity of God's free and gracious acquittal from the guilt of sin that has been at the heart of Protestant theology. It is giving justification its correct biblical home, within the setting of the covenant.

This covenantal and Paschal reading of justification is supported in Romans 5:9 where Paul says, 'Since we have been justified by his blood, how much more shall we be saved from God's wrath through him.' Whiteley has noted: 'The fact that in Rom. 5:9 the blood protects us from the future wrath of God again suggests a reference to the

original Passover.'[3] This link between justification and Passover is
made clear in Romans 3:24-5 where Paul writes: 'and are justified
freely by his grace, through the redemption that came by Christ Jesus,
whom God put forward as a propitiation by his blood, to be received
by faith.' Justification is therefore the outcome of redemption. In other
words, justification is the product of the Passover sacrifice and, as in
the Old Testament, it is about being delivered from God's wrath. This
has distinct echoes of the Jewish nation's deliverance from Egypt
when she was not only protected from judgment on the night of the
Passover but was also brought out from under her enemy's control.
To use Isaiah's language, she was justified, she was the object of
Yahweh's righteous activity. The merging of Paschal/Exodus language
in such a crucial section where Paul is discussing the role of the last
Adam in ending man's exile from God is clear proof that the New
Exodus is a dominant metaphor in Paul's doctrine of salvation.

Thus Romans 5 is a crucially important chapter that is often
overlooked in this debate. 5:12f. expands further on the theme of
justification. The section is about Christ, the last Adam who delivered
his people from the consequences of the fall. Few would dispute that
the backcloth to Paul's thinking is that the fall has brought mankind
under the domain of Sin (Satan). Indeed, justification is the essence
of the argument that is being made; as Ridderbos has said, the 'Adam-
Christ parallel is based on justification'.[4]

The above leads us to conclude that justification is more than a
declaration; it is the activity of God that is focused on the rescue of a
people from enmity with himself, achieved through the death of Jesus.

In other words, the heart of Paul's doctrine of justification is in
Romans 5:16-18:

> Again, the gift of God is not like the result of the one man's sin: the
> judgment followed one sin and brought condemnation, but the gift
> followed many trespasses, and brought justification. For if, by the
> trespass of the one man, death reigned through that one man, how much
> more will those who receive God's abundant provision of grace and of
> the gift of righteousness reign in life through the one man, Jesus Christ.
> Consequently, just as the result of one trespass was condemnation for all
> men, so also, the result of one act of righteousness was justification that
> brings life for all men.

[3]Whiteley, 'Atonement,' 250
[4]Ridderbos, 'Earliest,' 85.

The passage is unmistakably about deliverance and renewal. It is about being brought from Satan's control into the realm where Christ rules, for he is the new community's representative head. It is not about being declared to be in the community, but about the means by which the transfer was made possible. It needs to be noted, however, that the passage is not about the justification of the individual believer, but of the many who have been made righteous (v. 19). In other words, the argument being put forward in this crucial passage is essentially corporate.

Another dimension of justification is identified in Romans 5. The argument is about man becoming sinful because of the disobedience of Adam. Adam's guilt is imputed to his offspring. As the work of the last Adam is to undo this, he not only brings us out of captivity to sin, he has imputed to us his own righteousness. This is surely at the heart of the argument. Thus while there are texts that should not be used to speak of such imputation, e.g. Genesis 15:6, yet nevertheless this important doctrine of the Reformers cannot be so easily jettisoned as Wright has done. The correction that I would introduce to the Reformers' understanding is that this imputation is a corporate imputation, it is to the community that is in Christ, and individuals enter into this glorious state as they believe and avail themselves of the blessing of the gospel. Thus, while it is not individually given, it is individually availed.

To impose a forensic meaning on the statement of 'counted righteous' in Genesis 15, rather than letting the statement be understood in its own context, is not likely to uncover its original meaning. The chapter is about God entering into a covenant with Abraham. He promises him that his seed will be as numerous as the stars in the sky. The passage states that Abraham believed God and that it was credited to him as righteousness. Immediately Abraham was told that Yahweh was going to give him the land, and that he was going to take possession of it. Abraham's response was to question God: 'How can I know that I shall take possession of it?' Yahweh's response to this challenge was to inaugurate formally the covenant he had made with Abram, a covenant that Yahweh took responsibility for and that had been implicitly in existence since Abram had responded to Yahweh's call to leave Ur of the Chaldeans (Gen. 12:1-9). In the inaugural ceremony that Yahweh instituted with Abraham in Genesis 15:6-18, it is obvious that the initiative is entirely God's.[5] It is clear that the covenant is essentially about Yahweh's commitment to protect the promised seed from bondage and exile. This is at the heart of what the covenant promised and of how the crediting of righteousness should be understood. In other words, the justification cannot be separated from the Exodus.

Now while I have argued for the covenant setting of Genesis 15, what must not be missed is that this is also the setting of the argument of Romans 4. The chapter begins with, 'What shall we say that Abraham, our forefather, discovered in this matter?' The matter that is being referred to is the argument that has been thrashed out in 3:21-31, and at the heart of it is that 'a righteousness from God, apart from the law, has been made known, to which the Law and the Prophets testify'. This use of righteousness in 3:21 is inseparable from its use in 4:3. There would have to be very good reasons for severing the latter statement from the earlier use and the context that controls it. The context of 4:3, as we have seen, is saturated with covenant imagery, and that must control the meaning of righteousness in 3:21. The later part of chapter 3 has reasoned that the Mosaic covenant has not given the Jews any greater *ultimate* privilege over the Gentiles. The whole section leading into Paul's use of the story of Abraham's acceptance by God is to do with the covenant status of peoples.

[5]Abram believed God and he credited it to him as righteousness. He also said to him, 'I am the Lord who brought you out of Ur of the Chaldeans to give you this land to take possession of it.' But Abram said, 'O Sovereign Lord, how can I know that I shall gain possession of it?' So the Lord said to him, 'Bring me a heifer, a goat and a ram, each three years old, along with a dove and a young pigeon.'

Abram brought all these things to him, cut them in two and arranged the halves opposite each other; the birds, however, he did not cut in half. The birds of prey came down on the carcasses, but Abram drove them away. As the sun was setting, Abram fell into a deep sleep, and a thick and dreadful darkness came over him.

The Lord said to him, 'Know for certain that your descendants will be strangers in a country not their own, and they will be enslaved and ill-treated four hundred years. But I will punish the nation they serve as slaves, and afterwards they will come out with great possessions. You, however, will go to your fathers in peace and be buried at a good old age. In the fourth generation your descendants will come back here, for the sin of the Amorites has not yet reached its full measure.'

When the sun had set and darkness had fallen, a smoking fire pot with a blazing torch appeared and passed between the pieces. On that day the Lord made a covenant with Abram and said, 'To your descendants I give this land, from the river of Egypt to the great river, the Euphrates...'

Justification and the prophets

This theme of righteousness/justification is very much part of the prophets' understanding of Yahweh's dealings with Israel. 'Put away' in exile, Israel was promised that Yahweh had not forsaken her. He would redeem her from her enemies and bring her to her inheritance. He would create a new covenant with her and betroth her in righteousness (Isa. 62:5; Jer. 3:1-23; Hos. 2:14-20; Matt. 22:4, 25:10; Rev. 19:7). Into this new relationship the Gentiles would be incorporated (Isa. 2:2-4; 56:3-8; 66:18; Acts 15:14-19). While this is especially the language of Isaiah, it is not restricted to him. It is a common theme that links the classical prophets together (Hos. 2:16, 19; Isa. 54:1-8; 61:10; 62:4-5; Ezek. 16: 59-63). Israel's redemption is an aspect of God's justification of her. Her justification, however, will be completed only when all of the promises Yahweh has made to her are finally fulfilled. Justification, therefore, covers the whole scope of salvation history, from Israel's election to her being perfected as the bride of Yahweh.

It is in this New Covenant context that we need to read Romans 4. It is only by being focused on this context that we keep in mind that 'righteousness' has specific covenantal roots and associations. To dissociate what Paul says from this background will leave us bringing into the text ideas that might not have been part of Paul's thinking and might not be essential to the term 'justified' in the understanding of Paul.

The justification of the Gentiles

Is there any further evidence to support this interpretation that 'counted righteous' refers to Abraham being brought into covenant with Yahweh? I believe that there is. The only other Pauline text that refers to Genesis 15:6 is Galatians 3:6. Here Paul says: 'Consider Abraham: He believed God, and it was credited to him as righteousness.' The passage which precedes this statement speaks of how the Galatians were leaving the true gospel. Paul has demonstrated how easy it is to be inconsistent, and told how he had been forced to rebuke Peter publicly for withdrawing from table fellowship with the Gentiles because Judaisers had arrived in Antioch. In verses 15-16 Paul says that Jewish believers know that justification is only by faith in Jesus Christ. He then asks, if Jews discover the reality of sin through their faith in Christ, does this make Christ responsible for promoting sin?

His answer is an emphatic no, and states that the law's requirements have been satisfied. The argument Paul uses is a condensed version of the one used in Romans 6 and 7. Death has fully satisfied the demands of the law. When Paul speaks of death he refers to the death of Christ in which all believers have shared. This is not a mere theoretical concept. Its reality is such that it has brought Paul into a totally new relationship with God. What Paul argues is that the new covenant centres on the death of Jesus, which has brought believers into a relationship with God that the law was unable (because it was never intended) to secure. To drive this point home, Paul asks the Galatians in chapter 3 how they came into the covenant: was it by works or by faith? What is significant is that he is not asking if they were forgiven by keeping the law. Surprisingly, he asked if they received the Spirit by observing the law or by faith (Gal. 3:1-5). This is the very question that introduces the statement regarding Abraham being justified by faith. The statement is therefore nothing less than their being asked how they came into the covenant. It was the very point raised by Peter at the Council of Jerusalem in Acts 15:7-11:

> Brothers, you know that some time ago God made a choice among you that the Gentiles might hear from my lips the message of the gospel and believe. God, who knows the heart, showed that he accepted them by giving the Holy Spirit to them, just as he did to us. He made no distinction between us and them, for he purified their hearts by faith. Now then, why do you try to test God by putting on the necks of the disciples a yoke that neither we nor our fathers have been able to bear? No! We believe it is through the grace of our Lord Jesus that we are saved, just as they are.

It is clear that the issues that Peter raised are identical to those dealt with by Paul in Galatians. The evidence that the Gentiles have been accepted by God is that he has given them his Spirit, which is linked with their hearts being purified by faith. This is the thrust of both Peter's and Paul's arguments. It is abundantly clear that the debate in the Council of Jerusalem was not concerning the acceptability of an individual Gentile, but the believing Gentiles as an entirety. In other words, we are finding the same sort of corporate argument that we have found to be going on throughout the letters of Paul.

Certainly Schreiner would agree with this conclusion. He has claimed that *dikaiosunēn* in Romans 9:30 does not refer to maintenance of covenant status:

The obtaining of righteousness by the Gentiles in Rom 9:30 involves *entrance* into the covenant, since the Gentiles were previously outside of the circle of God's people. The close relationship between the calling of the Gentiles (Rom. 9:24-26) and their obtaining righteousness (Rom. 9:30) provides further evidence that righteousness here refers to entrance into the people of God.[6]

In other words, righteousness is essentially relational. It is covenantal, and to obtain righteousness means that God has brought the recipient into his covenant in which he acts in righteousness, i.e. in covenantal faithfulness.

Another passage that is related to the theme of justification is 2 Corinthians 5:19, in which Paul states that sin is not counted against men. 'God was reconciling the world to himself in Christ, not counting men's sins against them. And he has committed to us the message of reconciliation.' In saying that 'sin is not counted against them', Paul is focusing on the fact that sin excludes from the covenant. There is a solution to what would otherwise be an eternal exclusion. It is possible because of the redeeming grace of God in Christ Jesus. That the Corinthian passage is covenantal in its setting is borne out in that earlier, in 3:7f., there is a clear comparison between the covenant under Moses and that under Christ. Indeed the whole of 3:7–6:18 is based on the theme of the New Exodus.[7] Furthermore, the same passage is also based on Adamic Christology,[8] which, as we have earlier seen, is nothing if it is not covenantal. The Corinthian passage is saturated with the theological concepts of covenant which these two themes contain. The statement in 5:19 parallels Romans 4:3 where the focus was on how Abram was brought into the covenant. Here God provides a way by which man is able to enter the new covenant.

Another text in 2 Corinthians supports justification being the antithesis of judgment. In 3:9 Paul says, 'If the ministry that condemns men is glorious, how much more glorious is the ministry that brings righteousness.' Thus Paul sees the old covenant, i.e. its law, to be the instrument of judgment. Those within the covenant of the Old Testament were not justified in the sense of having received what the New Testament calls salvation, which is found only in Christ who has inaugurated the New Covenant. If the three detected themes –

[6]Schreiner, 'Attain,' 211, note 5, emphasis mine.

[7]Webb, *Home*, passim.

[8]Pate, *Adam*, passim.

justification, New Exodus and last Adam – are authentic to this 2 Corinthian passage, then justification is about the return of man from spiritual exile. This is supported by Paul's statement in the synagogue at Pisidian Antioch. At the end of a speech in which he has recalled redemptive history, stressing the promises made to Abraham and David, he says: 'Therefore I want you to know that through Jesus the forgiveness of sins is proclaimed to you. Through him everyone who believes is justified from everything you could not be justified from by the law of Moses' (Acts 13:38-39).

It is interesting to note that in Romans 4:7-9 Paul follows the same logic that Peter has used in his argument in Acts 15:7-11 as to why the Gentiles should not be required to submit to circumcision. We have already noted that Paul's use of Genesis 15 has continued in the context of the theme of covenant. What we do need to recognize, however, is that Paul's use of Psalm 32:1-2 is much more judicial. David there was speaking of Yahweh holding back his judgment. He recognised that he was guilty and deserved condemnation, but instead of judgment, he was given mercy. The use of this Psalm is clear evidence that the forensic aspect of justification was very clear in the apostle's thinking. It was of course within the context of the covenant that the statement was made.

The texts considered above show how Wright's and Dunn's understandings are inadequate to express Paul's doctrine of justification. These texts are avoided because they cannot be contained in covenantal nomism. We need to recognise that Sanders' evaluation of Judaism was mostly limited to post-AD 70 and is not significant for pre-AD 70 as it failed to recognise the diversity within Judaism. The evidence of the extent of this diversity has been destroyed, but few would question the incredible complexity of the Judaism*s* of this period. This diversity could quite easily contain the sort of positions that the Reformers assumed Paul to have been addressing, even if there is a need, as I am about to argue, to avoid some of the linguistic pitfalls that scholars from all theological positions have fallen into.

The evidence of this section strongly suggests that there is a forensic aspect to justification that the Reformers correctly identified. My argument is not with this important fact. My concern is to demonstrate that this forensic understanding is best understood as being the condition of entrance into the covenant and that this often overlooked covenantal aspect is a vital key for appreciating the fullness of the biblical doctrine of justification. My stress on the importance of the covenant does not favour Wright's understanding, for he says that justification is about being declared to be within the covenant. Rather the covenantal aspect of justification means that there are uses of the word 'justified' which are not forensic but are about the establishment of a covenant relationship between Yahweh and the one who is called to salvation.

But the strongest evidence that 'counted as righteous' means brought into the covenant is found in the Old Testament. Psalm 106 speaks of Phinehas who took action against the ungodliness of his fellow countrymen for indulging in sexual immorality. Verse 31 states that 'This was credited to him as righteousness for endless generations to come'. The original account in Numbers 25:10-13 makes it clear what being counted righteous means.

> The LORD said to Moses, 'Phinehas son of Eleazer, the son of Aaron, the priest, has turned my anger away from the Israelites; for he was as zealous as I am for my honour among them, so that in my zeal I did not put an end to them. Therefore tell him I am making my covenant of peace with him. He and his descendants will have a covenant of a lasting priesthood, because he was zealous for the honour of his God and made atonement for the Israelites.'

The meaning of 'counted as righteousness' could not be clearer. It means that Phinehas was brought into a covenant relationship with Yahweh.

This covenant-making significance for the term 'justified' or 'counted as righteous' is supported by the New Exodus motif itself. Israel's justification, her return from exile, was in fact the creation of the New Covenant. It was this, of course, that was ultimately the product of the death of Christ, which was his exodus and which has brought about the deliverance of the Christian community from the power of Satan.

But why has this covenantal dimension been overlooked? I believe that the covenant perspective was missed because of the emphasis put on *logizomai* being an accounting metaphor.[9] It certainly is, but

---

[9]Dunn, *Theology*, 377, comments, 'Reckoned, as Paul well knew, was an accounting metaphor.' This comment is not that significant, for Paul knew that the word also had other meanings. The context of the specific usage alone is of ultimate significance. Paul uses the forensic sense in Romans 2:13; 3:4, 20; 4:2, 5; 5:1, 9; 8:30, 33 and 1 Corinthians 4:4. The covenantal significance is found in Romans 3:24, 28, 30; 1

it is also other things in the Old Testament; it is also, for example, a legal metaphor. Whatever it means in the Genesis text, what is not permissible is to trawl the range of meanings from the biblical literature and amalgamate them into a new model or metaphor that is used as the key to a particular use of the word. Such a practice is a fundamental abuse of linguistics. It is the same type of misuse as saying that, because the word 'bat' can mean a flying mammal as well as a device used for playing ball games, we are entitled to say that some texts intend to suggest that the word speaks of the way that the ball 'flies' from the bat in a game of cricket! It is what Genesis 15 says about *logizomai* that matters, not what Proverbs or Leviticus say. What has happened in this linguistic confusion is the very thing that James Barr warned against.[10] The range of meanings of the term have been imported from other passages and an illegitimate hybrid meaning has been constructed. In doing this, basic linguistic rules have been ignored. It has been assumed that meaning(s) from various usages in different contexts can be merged to produce an amalgamation of the various meanings. This collective meaning is then applied to a particular use, namely, in this instant to Genesis 15:6, regardless of the specific context of the text. It is not the range of possible meanings that matters, but the meaning that the context gives in any particular usage.

Thus, going back to the New Exodus model, justification is repeatedly used to speak of Israel's release from captivity. As a result of her release from exile, she was shown to have been acquitted, declared righteous, for her sin had been atoned for. In Israel's case, being declared righteous was nothing to do with God overlooking her sins. She had paid double for her sins (Isa. 40:2). She had paid the price for breaking the conditions of the covenant and this meant that God could now justify her claim to be his covenant people. This was done as he led her back from exile to retake possession of her inheritance, in particular, the land and Jerusalem. Paul changes this rationale, for it is not the delivered people of God who have paid the price of covenant breaking, but the Son of God, the Paschal victim (1 Cor. 5:8).

It is most significant that in Romans 4:25 Paul says that Jesus

Corinthians 6:11; Galatians 2:16, 17; 3:8, 11, 24; 5:4; Titus 3:7. 1 Timothy 3:16 possibly speaks of Christ being justified by the Spirit in the sense that the Spirit was the one who equipped Jesus for his messianic (i.e. covenantal) mission. Thus Paul's individual use of 'justify' needs careful consideration.

[10]Barr, *Semantics, passim.*

'was delivered over to death for our sins and raised for our justification'. The death of Jesus was understood to be his Exodus (Luke 9:31). We have seen that Romans 3:21-25 is about Christ our Passover. It is through his death and resurrection that the covenant community has been delivered from the kingdom of darkness and brought into its inheritance, the kingdom of God (Gal. 1:4; Eph. 1:7; Col. 1:13-14). Thus justification is not only inseparable from the death of Christ, but it also took place for the people of God in the events of both his death and resurrection. It is the consequence of the baptism into Christ, as I have discussed earlier.

Test cases
In Romans 4 Paul is pressing the Jewish believers to recognise the grounds of their salvation. They never came into their covenant with Yahweh as a result of Abraham's works, even less their own. They became the covenant people solely because of the free grace of God. By arguing from the case of the Abrahamic covenant's inauguration, Paul demonstrates that the Jewish people, personified in Abraham their ancestor, were never accepted in the way that was being imposed on the Gentiles. The demands of the Judaizers were therefore not God's commands but man's demands. In this context Paul was not dealing with the justification of the individual by God, but of the Gentiles. His argument centres on how God had dealt with the Jews and what their condition was as far as the law was concerned when the covenant was made with them.

This is not denying that the individual has to respond in faith to share in this salvation. Faith and repentance are required before any one can become inheritors of the covenant's blessings, which include forgiveness, reconciliation etc. As the individual Jew had to be circumcised to belong to the covenant community, so in the New Testament the individual must be circumcised in heart to become a member of the Israel of God (Gal. 6:16), the new man. On this model, the individual believer, at conversion, enters into the experience of the justified community and so into an individual experience of justification. The imputation of righteousness has been understandably concluded to be demonstrated by Paul's statement that 'the man who does not work but trusts God who justifies the wicked, his faith is credited as righteousness' (Rom. 4:5). But such a reading has lost the plot of the discussion.

First, because the 'works' to which the passage clearly refers are
the works required for covenantal acceptance, i.e. circumcision. Once
the issue being discussed, i.e. of the status of the Gentiles corporately,
has been identified, there is no suggestion in this text that Paul is
talking about someone trying to gain acceptance through moral
achievement. Second, the accounting meaning has violated the
covenantal context of Genesis 15, Romans 3–4 and Galatians 3. I
would argue that covenant is the context of both Romans and Galatians.
And finally, the text is not speaking about gaining personal individual
salvation; rather, when read in a corporate context, it is seen to be
about how peoples are brought into covenant with Yahweh.

That justification is not just linked to the Exodus but specifically
with the Passover is evident in that it is the theme that both precedes
and follows Romans 3:21, which as we have seen in chapter eight is
Paschal. Also Galatians 3:13, which is accepted as a Paschal text,
follows the statement that no one is justified before God by the law in
3:11. The issue of justification again rises in verse 24, and immediately
following in verse 26 is the assertion that the Galatians have all been
baptised into Christ, an event which is intrinsically bound up with the
death of Christ in its Paschal context. We have already noted how
justification and Paschal blood are linked in Romans 5:9. But while
Passover, as traditionally understood, is vitally important, and even
more so if my arguments concerning its propitiatory content are valid,
it is only the beginning of the redemptive activity of God in which
Yahweh justified his people. Thus justification cannot exist without
propitiation, for propitiation makes justification (i.e. the making of the
covenant) possible. In chapter eleven I will argue that the first and
the eschatological Passovers are in fact propitiatory sacrifices.

Furthermore, when we recall that we have found that Paul's
doctrine of Sin is essentially relational, then we would expect that his
doctrine of justification is about the restoration of the relationship that
has been forfeited. Passover was seen by the prophets (Ezek. 16:1-
14 and Hos. 2:14-20) as the event when Yahweh took Israel as his
bride, and we have seen that Passover is imbibed with propitiatory
and justification language and imagery. It was because Passover was/
is seen to be the occasion of the divine marriage that the Song of
Songs has been sung as part of the Passover celebration by the Jewish
community. It celebrates, in their understanding, the marriage of
Yahweh to Israel. And the point is that all of these themes that we

have found in Paul are found in Old Testament redemptive history and they are focused in the Passover. It is therefore Passover that was at the heart of the Old Testament's understanding of covenant making[11] and therefore of justification and it is the same model that we find in Paul's thinking.

It is essential to understand that individual justification is not the focus of the argument being presented in Romans 4:3, for the letter is essentially corporate/covenantal, and so is the argument concerning justification. This passage is not dealing with the acquittal of the sinner from his guilt, but of the acceptance of the Gentiles into the covenant. From this acceptance by God flows all the blessings that election brings, and it is into these blessings that individuals enter experimentally when the same Spirit works in their hearts to produce faith in the God who justifies the ungodly. We found earlier that this is exactly the same way that Isaiah uses the term when speaking of Israel's justification as a result of Yahweh rescuing her from exile. It spoke not of individual Jews but of the remnant.

Also, while I have argued that Galatians 3:6 is based on a corporate argument, there is evidence that this is not the sole dimension of Pauline thought. The appeals in the letter to the Galatians are not so much to the community as to those members of it who are seceding to Judaism (4:8-9). In Galatians the argument about justification is certainly corporate, but the warnings to individuals emphasize that it has to be appropriated or applied personally by faith. If the Gentile believers accept circumcision they put themselves outside the covenant of grace. In the same letter Paul speaks of the personal outworking of this when he says, 'I have been crucified with Christ and I no longer live, but Christ lives in me. The life I live in the body, I live by faith in the Son of God, who loved me and gave himself for me' (Gal. 2:20). Also, Paul's testimony in Philippians 3, where he speaks of not desiring to have his own righteousness, i.e. covenantal privilege, but that which is of Christ, clearly shows the more individually appropriated righteousness, i.e. covenantal acceptance, that we are familiar with as part of Paul's understanding. To these considerations must be added the very illustrations that Paul uses. Abraham's and David's faith and their consequential justification are obviously cases of individuals being

---

[11]And so the covenant making ceremony at Siani recorded in Exodus 24 was the formalizing of what had taken place, i.e. that Yahweh had rescued Israel to be his bride.

justified, even though they are discussed as federal representatives of their people.

Tying up loose ends

The covenant-making dimension of justification resolves some long-standing problems that most have recognised. In Romans 6:7 Paul says, 'because anyone who has died has been freed (*dedikaiētai*, which strictly speaking is 'justified') from sin (*hamartias*)'. It is the way Paul uses *dedikaiētai* which is the cause of considerable difficulty for the traditional understanding. The problem is that Paul uses this technical term in the middle of an argument that many scholars regard as being about Christian experience, i.e. victory over sin. It is the introduction of justification into this context that is so difficult, for if it is translated strictly according to its forensic meaning, which most give to it, it means that Paul is arguing that justification is the outcome of dying to sin. This is clearly contrary to the whole tone of Paul's insistence on justification being a free gift of God's grace, as previously worked out in this epistle (chapter 4). It is because of this problem that the overwhelming consensus of translators and commentators alike accepts that Paul must be intending us to understand *dedikaiētai* as 'freed' and not 'justified'. It is reasoned that the argument means that the man who has died has been freed from any charge that the law could have had against him. It is argued that the statement is based on the legal precept that it is useless taking a dead man to court, since because he is dead he is effectively freed from the punishment of sin.

This explanation, so widely adopted, not only imposes upon Paul's vocabulary a meaning that is nowhere else ascribed to *dedikaiētai* in Paul's letters, but also ignores the meaning of *hamartias* (sin). It involves identifying sin with crime (*aitia*) and that is undisciplined thinking. Sin is offence against God; crime is offence against man. If Paul had said 'he that is dead is freed from crime', or even better 'is freed from law', then it would be plainly true, for human law cannot pursue a man beyond death. But when we talk of death freeing a man from sin, this is clearly not the meaning. 'Man is destined to die once, and after that to face judgement' (Heb. 9:27 cf. 2 Cor. 5:10). Furthermore, such reasoning has abandoned the concept of sin generally agreed to be in Romans 6, namely, the personification of Satan,[12] and has reverted to defining sin as transgression.

How then can these exegetical problems be resolved? Only, I would maintain, by placing them into a covenantal, i.e. New Exodus, context. Sin is the personification of evil, Satan, the husband of the body of Sin. Because this covenant relationship exists, man cannot enter into a relationship with Christ; instead, he belongs to Sin. Such a relationship with Christ, whilst the former union exists, is impossible. It would involve God himself in an act of spiritual adultery. However, if death were to annul the relationship – either the death of Sin, or the death of the unbelieving community – then the remaining partner would be 'justified' in remarrying. In other words, if it is possible for man really to share in the death of Christ to Sin, then in that representative death the covenant is annulled. Sin can then lay no charge at the church's door; she is justified from Sin, and free to marry Christ. Thus, to be justified from Sin fits naturally into the same model that I have argued for earlier. It is the release (*justified from*) from the covenant that man is in with Satan.

This very argument is what Paul illustrates in chapter 7:1-4. This perspective not only explains how Paul can use *dedikaiētai* and *hamartias*, but also identifies the former husband of the illustration in 7:1-4; he is Sin. In fact, the exposition goes even further than this, for it identifies the law of 7:4 to which the believer has died. It is not the law of commandments, but the law of the husband. It is the law of Sin, the authority Sin has over the sinner through the covenantal relationship. It is the law of Sin from which those who are in Christ, those who have shared in his death, are freed (Rom. 8:1-2).

This line of reasoning resolves the problem of the illustration in 7:1-4 which has caused so much difficulty to scholars over the years. The apparent fact that Paul casts the law in two roles, that of the former husband, and that of the law which gives the husband (the law!) control over the wife, is a problem only because the illustration is being pressed beyond its intended limit and is isolated from its original

[12]For synonyms of Satan, see Martin, *Colossians*, 51; Dunn, *Romans*, 1:360; MacGregor, 'Principalities,' 342, and Sanday and Headlam, *Romans*, 169. Ford, 'Euphemism,' 189ff., shows how euphemisms were used to avoid the use of an offensive or sacred original. Sin is personified in the Old Testament and Paul, so Wedderburn, 'Structure,' 342. See also chapters 5 and 6. Wright, 'Romans,' 39, says: 'In Paul's usage, "sin" refers not just to individual human acts of "sin", of missing the mark (the basic meaning of the word) as regards the divine intention for full human flourishing and fulfillment. "Sin" takes on a malevolent life of its own, exercising power over persons and communities. It is almost as though by "sin" Paul is referring to what some other parts of the Bible meant by "Satan".'

conceptual context. Such exposition causes the breakdown of the illustration because it is being interpreted outside its New Exodus setting. In the New Exodus it was promised that Yahweh would betroth Israel in righteousness (Isa. 46:13; 51:6, 8). Paul is explaining how Yahweh is able to stay righteous while accepting the church into a covenant relationship which is symbolised by marriage. Only because Christ has died as the church's head is the old relationship brought to an end. Now Yahweh can take 'Israel' to himself in righteousness.

Finally, it needs to be remembered that, as we saw earlier, Romans 6:7 is not talking about the death of the individual believer. The New Man that results from the death of Christ is the church; the Old Man is unredeemed humanity. The imagery is perfectly consistent with the Old Testament model that we have been following throughout this study. The model that controls Paul's thought is that of the Passover/ New Exodus, and, in this context, justification is not only about being free from accusation of an unlawful relationship, but also essentially about the creation of a covenant for which God himself takes total responsibility.

If what has been argued above is correct, then it opens the door to a fuller understanding of what is accomplished in the death of Christ. Traditionally, the emphasis is on the payment for sins that have been committed. I want to argue that this did happen, but that it is secondary to something far more amazing.

Because man is bound up in the relationship that has been created through Adam's disobedience, he is estranged from God. But he is more than that, for he is bound up in the same sort of relationship that he was called to have with God, but now it is with Satan. He is in a covenant relationship that God, who is a covenant God, has to recognise. For him to do other, and to rescue man without any regard to the relationship that man has freely entered into, would lay him open to the charge of adultery, taking another 'man's' wife. This is the point of Romans 7:1-6.

So how can this relationship be ended? How can Christ justly take the church as his bride? Only if death ends the former relationship. Romans 5 has made it clear that God has treated man with the very dignity that his decision necessitated. One man's disobedience made many people sinners. That relationship was acknowledged and respected. But now the last Adam has rendered obedience for his people. He has died in their place. His death has terminated the covenant and those who call on the name of the Lord can be saved. They are freely transferred from one ownership to another, and the former husband cannot make the charge of adultery, for death – Christ's death – has ended the covenant.

Now this is even more glorious than the payment of the price of wrongdoing. Indeed, I would suggest that this is the big picture that the New Testament presents regarding the significance of the death of Christ. It has freed his people from the control of Satan. I would argue that this is the perspective of the early church's preaching to the unconverted: they are locked up and separated from God, but by calling on the God of Abraham they will be delivered from the kingdom of darkness. The emphasis on personal sins which need to be forgiven is much more focused on the redeemed community, for sins will spoil their fellowship with God and dishonour his holy name.

The above argument is supported by Sanders. Although he fails to appreciate the corporate and covenantal dimension of Paul's thought, he identifies the larger picture of Paul's doctrine of Sin:

> Paul has a more radical conception of sin than that of transgression. Humans are not just sinners, they are enslaved by its power: Sin. Repentance and acquittal of individual transgressions do not fully meet the human problem. People are not just guilty, they are enslaved, and they need to escape. Paul thought that the power of Sin was so great that one must die to be set free of it, and accordingly he reinterpreted Christ's death. People who become one person with Christ share his death and thus escape bondage, and they then share his life, being free from the power of Sin. Herein lies Paul's distinctive contribution to thought about the death of Christ.[11]

This statement by Sanders becomes far more focused when one realises that the enemy is no less than the former husband and that the power he once had over believers was the covenantal authority that the law gave husbands over their wives. It was this abuse of the law and thus its turning into an instrument of Sin that Paul debates when he answers that question, 'Is the law sin?' The representative death of Christ has broken Sin's authority by ending the relationship and with it Sin's power.

---

[13]Sanders, *Paul*, 79.

Conclusion

I have agreed with Wright that it is correct to attempt to interpret the New Testament in the light of the New Exodus model. However, in my judgment this has not been done correctly because of his preference for Sanders' covenantal nomism and because of his use of the pseudepigraphal writings. This directed him into a Wisdom Christology that has in turn caused him to miss the strength of the Passover motif in the New Testament as a whole and in Paul in particular. Wright's use of intertestamental literature has not only caused him to use the Macabbean martyrdom model to interpret Jesus' own understanding of his death as that of a martyr, but also to locate Saul of Tarsus as a member of the Zealot Movement. This supposed connection with the Zealot Movement led Wright to conclude that Saul persecuted the Church because of its failure to demand the circumcision of the Gentiles as the starting point of their acceptance. Because Wright accepted much of Sanders' covenantal nomism, his methodology lacked the theological controls that would have guarded him from abandoning the Reformers' understanding of justification.

It has been shown that while Sanders may have established that post-AD 70 Judaism was covenantal nomistic in character, he has not been able to demonstrate that post-AD 70 Judaism was the same as Judaism before the fall of Jerusalem. Indeed, the issue is widely recognised as being so complex, made up of so many opposing theological groups, that it is better to speak of Judaism*s*. This is of vital relevance for interpreting Paul, and indeed for interpreting Jesus also. It is therefore unwise to assume that Paul was always addressing the features of covenantal nomism. Despite urging caution in adopting this reconstruction of Second Temple Judaism, I would nevertheless suggest that Sanders has served scholarship well in that we have been forced to examine our own presuppositions.

My conclusion is that Paul did critique Judaism regarding her self-righteousness, but it was not the only critique. He also warned her of the law's inability to achieve 'legal justification' because of her inability to keep its moral requirements. This at least suggests that not all of Paul's interlocutors were of the covenantal nomism type.

I have argued that there are a number of references in Paul and the Acts of the Apostles that can only be interpreted in the Reformers' sense of justification from guilt and judgment. However, I have also argued that there has been confusion over the use of the terminology of justification. It is a violation of linguistic principles to collect a range of texts that contain the same term and draw from each text the range of semantic possibilities that are then amalgamated into a concept to contain within itself the range of semantic meanings. It is even less acceptable then to use this hybrid model to unlock the meaning of every theological use of the term. The same linguistic rules apply to theology as to other areas of literary study. The context must determine which meaning within the semantic range is chosen. What most certainly must not happen is that the whole range of meanings is dumped into a particular use of the term. This has been the weakness of the Reformed method and its use prevented the Reformers seeing a wider theological meaning than the one generally focused on, i.e. that of acquittal. Our discussion has shown that there are uses of the term that are clearly relating to the establishing of a covenant.

I have argued that justification is not, as claimed by Wright, the declaration of being *in* the covenant. Rather, it refers to *the creation* of a covenant between Yahweh and his people. We have seen that an important strand of the Old Testament doctrine of justification is the restoration of Israel to fellowship with Yahweh. I have argued that at the very heart of this New Exodus theme is the Passover and this is the crucial event around which Paul's doctrine of justification is built. The New Testament certainly continues this strand of thought but widens it out to all mankind. All believers in Jesus as Messiah, of all ethnic groups, become part of the justified community. While the New Testament speaks of justification as a past achievement and centres in what God has done in the death of Jesus, it also has a future sense, yet to be completed, when the saints are finally brought into their inheritance at their resurrection. I would suggest that part of the problem behind Wright's interpretation of justification is that he has concentrated on the Westminster Confession definition that, as we saw earlier, is more systematic than other confessions. In selecting this and isolating it from the wider theology of the Reformers and indeed the writers of the Confession itself, he has presented a caricature while at the same time unwittingly highlighting the linguistic confusion in the method of the Reformers. Despite this widespread confusion in method, the Reformers, in my view, had the heart of the biblical understanding of justification.

We began this chapter noting the content of the Apology of the

Augsburg Confession. I want to reflect on it again, but this time in the light of the argument subsequently presented. I have argued that justification is about God's salvation, about the creation of the covenant. It is about God saving a people from their bondage to Sin, a bondage that we have discovered to be a covenant relationship through which Man has become the bride of Satan. This salvation is about God taking responsibility for his people and ultimately bringing them into the experience of eschatological salvation where the expression of his love is described as a marriage. It is these same elements, admittedly used to describe individual justification, that are found in the Apology of the Augsburg Confession (1531). Thus 4:2, says:

> That man enjoys that acceptance with God called 'justification', the beginning and end of salvation, not through his own moral effort even in the smallest and slightest degree but entirely and only through the loving mercy of God made available in the merits of Christ and of his saving death on the Cross. This was not a process of gradual ethical improvement but an instantaneous transaction, something like a marriage, in which Christ the bridegroom takes to himself an impoverished and wretched harlot and confers upon her all the riches that are his. The key to this transaction was faith, defined as a total and trustful commitment of the self to God, and is itself not a human achievement but the pure gift of God.[14]

---

[14]For further discussion on the Reformers and justification as covenant making, see appendix 3.

Section Four

Christology and Passover

Chapter Eleven

The Firstborn and the Jewish Cult

The study of Romans 3:21ff. has led to the conclusion that the Passover was the source of the language and imagery used by Paul to describe the death of Christ. After decades of research, there is a growing appreciation that the traditional titular method of approaching Christological study has failed to yield significant results. This growing recognition has caused some to question the very methods that have been employed in the reconstruction of the early church's thinking. For example, Osborn stated that a new approach to the Christological material is needed, and said: 'Christological theory is in the process of a paradigm shift in methodology. Where this process will take us is not at the moment apparent.'[1] Wright endorses this shift: 'Today there is tacit agreement that the study of titles is not the way to proceed – even to the extent of some leading Jesus-scholars relegating them to the margin of their enquiries.'[2]

Part of this methodological shift has been to recognise the antiquity of the Christological material. It is increasingly being realised that the liberal reconstruction that saw Christological development to have been driven by the Gentile mission does not fit the evidence. Holloway for example, has cautioned against such reconstruction: 'it is dubious to erect historical reconstructions without acknowledging and taking into account, the pre-history of such traditions.'[3]

It has also become clear that the New Testament church was interested in soteriology and not in ontology, and that in the New Testament, just as in the Old Testament, redemption and creation are inseparably linked. Moreover, it is increasingly being realised that much of Pauline Christological material does not result from interaction with Hellenistic philosophy, but is in fact heavily indebted to primitive Hebraic motifs. These observations give grounds for exploring the Passover as a setting for the development of New Testament Christological beliefs.

In the light of these observations, it would seem that an examination

[1]Osborn, 'Christology', 49.
[2]Wright, *Victory*, 614.
[3]Holloway, 'Christology', 280.

of Christology in a Paschal setting would be a valid line of enquiry. If, as I have argued, Passover has moulded Pauline cultic thinking, then it may also have moulded his Christological understanding. Such a suggestion becomes even more reasonable when it is realised that the cross, centred firmly in the Jewish Passover, defines the person of Christ. The central character in the Passover was the firstborn, and this is a description that is applied to Christ. We shall therefore examine the use of this term in Biblical literature to see if it has any soteriological/Christological significance.

The context of its usage is vital for an accurate understanding of the use of any term. This is where our study of the Old Testament material relating to the firstborn presents numerous difficulties. The contexts of passages outside of the Pentateuch in which references to the firstborn occur are difficult to establish. They are not normally ones where there are substantial pointers to a definite historical context. More often than not, the passage presupposes a common understanding, which two and a half thousand years or so of history have removed, so minimising any degree of certainty of what they originally meant.

For this reason, any study of Old Testament material on the subject of the firstborn must be undertaken with considerable caution. We will inevitably have to depend on cumulative argument rather than on 'hard evidence'. Justification for attempting such a task is the evidence for the presence of Paschal themes in Paul, the clear dependence of Paul on the Old Testament for the Second Exodus motif, and the growing awareness that the Christological terms have their roots in the Old Testament.

The firstborn as a representative

In the Passover narrative it was the firstborn son who was designated by Yahweh to represent the family. This was bound up with the family's deliverance from the angel of death. It is vital to note that it was not the family as a whole that the lamb represented, but only the firstborn. The firstborn's life was threatened because *he* represented the family. It is this representative role, I believe, which links the New Testament statements that Christ is the Lamb of God and that Christ is our Passover with the statement that he is the firstborn. To be more precise, Christ is the firstborn, the one who represents his family. Because no other could face the angel of death and so discharge

Christ of his representative role, he died as the paschal lamb had done. He was both the firstborn and the Passover offering, for in the Christian Passover they are one. This double designation firstborn/ Lamb of God is not an obstacle to my argument. In Christ many offices and titles converge. Prophet and priest converge with king, priest converges with victim, and Saviour converges with judge. The New Testament writers would have little difficulty in applying such a principle of converging diversity to yet another realm of Christ's offices and work. The firstborn and paschal lamb converge to become one and the same entity. The Exodus was the Old Testament's foreshadowing of the redemptive work of Christ and it is little short of astonishing that scholars have failed to look into the significance of the firstborn in that first act of redemption in seeking to interpret the application of the title to Christ by the New Testament writers.

The interpretation I am presenting takes the term *prōtotokos* and rejects the traditional ontological interpretation by placing it firmly in the context of redemptive history. The point is not that Christ is the firstborn, but that he acts as the firstborn. It is a description expressing the work he has done in his death. This is borne out even in the Old Testament usage of the expression in the Passover narrative, for the 'firstborn' could, in fact, be the second, fifth, or even tenth born in the family. If he was the first male to be born he was the firstborn.[4]

The significance of my explanation for the description in Colossians 1:15, 'the firstborn of all creation', ought to be obvious. For Paul, redemption, like the fall, has a cosmic dimension. Romans 8 shows the whole creation waiting for restoration. This will happen at the climax of Christ's redemptive work, when his people will be released from bondage and will be glorified. The firstborn's significance in the Exodus was only for his family. The significance of the death of Christ, the Christian Passover, goes beyond his own family to the universe that was caught up in the tragedy of the fall. So he is 'the firstborn of all creation'.

This is developed even further when we recognise that the firstborn

---

[4]This observation is supported by Michaelis who commented on the etymology of the Hebrew *bekor* (firstborn) that it 'neither connected with the Hebrew words for "to give birth" – it can be used for fruits etc. as well. Nor is it related to the words for "one", "first", nor the similar word for "head", "chief" – to the concept which it was designed to express there did not necessarily belong a comparison with other things of the same kind, since the first might also be the only one' (Michaelis, *TDNT* 5:873).

is synonymous with the Old Testament redeemer. They are one and the same person. This is never explicitly stated in Scripture, probably because the equation was obvious to any Jew.

The first responsibility that fell upon the shoulders of the redeemer was that of securing revenge for his family. When a member of the family was murdered, the redeemer's duty was to exact blood vengeance on the guilty party; the law of retribution meant that the responsibility rested upon his shoulders (Gen. 4:14-15, 23f.; Num. 35:22-29; Deut. 19:4-10). In the latter part of Isaiah, where Yahweh is often called the redeemer, Yahweh promised to act as the avenger of his people (Isa. 43:3-4, 14-15; 47:4; 49:25-26; 59:16-20). In the New Testament Christ himself is presented fulfilling this same role (Luke 1:68-79; 18:7; 2 Thess. 1:6-9; Rev. 6:9-11).

The next role of the firstborn/redeemer in the Old Testament was that of securing property that had been lost to the family through debt. In Ruth 4:4 Boaz requested Naomi's nearest kinsman to perform the responsibility of acting as the redeemer to secure the family field. In Leviticus 25:8-34 the principle of Jubilee is outlined. It fell to the 'nearest relative' (v. 25) to act as the redeemer, whenever possible, to recover the family's property. Once again, we find Yahweh promising to act as Israel's redeemer in securing what she had lost (Isa. 51:11; 52:8-10). Israel was promised the return of her own land to her possession. Again, in the New Testament, we find this role attributed to Christ as he recovers the Kingdom of Heaven for those who were deprived of it by sin (Col. 1:13-14; Heb. 9:15; Rev. 21:1-4).

The third role of the redeemer was to fulfil the law of the levirate. This law appointed the redeemer to act as the protector of the widow in the family. If a woman was widowed and childless it was the responsibility of the redeemer to take her as his wife and raise up a family on behalf of the deceased brother (Deut. 25:5-10; Ruth 3:13; 4:1-8). Once again, this aspect of the redeemer's role is used to illustrate the salvation Yahweh promised his people. 'He will save Jerusalem from her widowhood and raise up children for her' (Isa. 49:20-21; 50:1-2; 54:1-8; 62:4-5). This same role is applied to Christ, who takes the church to himself, and acts as her husband (John 3:28-29; Rom. 7:1-4; 1 Cor. 6:20; Eph. 5:25-32; Rev. 19:6-8).

The argument outlined above assumes three important points: That the firstborn's death was vicarious, that he represented his family, and that the title redeemer was dropped in favour of 'firstborn'. These details need to be examined further and established as valid if my claims are to be upheld. I shall therefore seek to answer the following questions.

a) What was the significance of the death of the firstborn? If we have established a representative role in which the firstborn died for the family we then need to ask:

b) Why was it that at the Passover it was the firstborn and not the father who represented the family?

c) Why do we have two titles, namely, firstborn and redeemer, when the title 'redeemer' would have adequately covered the roles that both titles suggest?

Passover and the death of the firstborn

Our first task then is to enquire into the significance of the death of the firstborn in the Passover. Yahuda saw no more significance in the death of the firstborn than that it represented a battle between Yahweh and the Egyptian gods. He pointed out that the firstborn son of Pharaoh had the same rank as his father, for he had the title 'Sa-Ra-en-Khetef' i.e. 'the son of Ra from his body', and was therefore a god. Yahuda argued from this that the significance of the death of the firstborn was 'to defy the mighty gods of Egypt, to expose their impotence to protect the offspring of the "Son of Ra".' Therefore the death of the firstborn of the nation was a means of convincing Pharaoh and his people that the death of the ruler's firstborn was no accident.[5]

Yahuda's explanation of the death of the firstborn is clearly inadequate. If the scope of the firstborn's death was only to support the claim that the death of Pharaoh's firstborn was no accident then there would have been no need for Moses to require the Hebrews to secure protection by the death of a lamb. The death of all of Egypt's firstborn would have sufficed.

Stalker noted that 'set apart' in Exodus 12:12, which literally means 'cause to pass over (*herebhir*)', is the word used for sacrificing children to Molech in 2 Kings 16:3 and Ezekiel 20:31. He does not posit direct borrowing: 'The usages of the two peoples are quite different. Though in Israel the firstborn were to be set apart to Yahweh as his, they were to be "ransomed" from him, a term which could suggest that they were sacrificed in theory, though not in actual fact.' Thus Stalker sees a sacrificial intent behind the purpose of the

---

[5] Yahuda, *Accuracy*, 85-6.

firstborn's death, although he does say that 'details of the motivation are somewhat confused. Exodus 12:11ff connects the Passover with the smiting of the firstborn of the Egyptians, while Exodus 12:27 connects it with the sparing of Israel.'[6]

It is argued by some that, by New Testament times, the Passover was regarded as having expiatory value. This view is supported by Brown who thinks this change came about because by that time lambs were sacrificed within the Temple area by the priests.[7] Against this view Dodd argued that though there was probably expiatory significance in the Passover ritual in its very earliest stages, which he sees to be pre-Mosaic, it had been dropped long before New Testament times.[8] From the evidence we have considered we would suggest that the original Passover was regarded as an expiatory sacrifice, and that all subsequent Passover celebrations were memorials of the original without any expiatory value. If this is so, then it would suggest that while the sin of the nation was dealt with in the original Passover, it was on the annual Day of Atonement that the ongoing sin of the nation was dealt with.

Passover and circumcision
In Exodus 4:22-26 the Lord speaks to Moses saying, 'Then say to Pharaoh, "This is what the LORD says, Israel is my firstborn son, and I told you, 'Let my people go, so that they may worship me.' But you refused to let him go, so I will kill your firstborn son".' At a lodging place on the way the LORD met Moses and was about to kill him, but Zipporah took a flint knife, cut off her son's foreskin and touched Moses' feet with it. 'Surely you are a bridegroom of blood to me,' she said, so the LORD let him alone' (at that time 'bridegroom of blood' refered to circumcision).

The full significance of this passage will only be appreciated when we see it as a statement about what God is to do in the coming Exodus event recorded in chapter 12.

Cole pinpoints the relationship between Israel and the Egyptians in this passage: 'Israel, considered collectively, is God's firstborn, presumably as being His chosen people and as "first-fruits" of all the peoples (Jer. 31:9). If Pharaoh will not give God's firstborn up to God, to whom all firstborn belong, then Pharaoh's own firstborn must die

[6]Stalker, *Ezekiel*, 221.
[7]Brown, *John*, 1:62.
[8]Dodd, *Interpretation*, 234.

instead. Since "Israel" is collective here, it is reasonable to suppose that "Pharaoh" is also a collective term; thus, "your firstborn" includes all the firstborn in the land. Otherwise we should have to assume that the original reference was to Pharaoh's son alone and no other.'[9]

Thus, Israel, the nation whom Yahweh elected to be in a special relationship to himself, is threatened by Pharaoh. Moses is sent as Yahweh's spokesman. The comparison is between Israel collectively and the firstborn sons of Egypt. Pharaoh had sought not only to control Yahweh's firstborn, but the policy of killing the male babies was a deliberate one that endangered Israel's very existence. Even though this policy was probably abandoned during Moses' own infancy, it still bore witness to the dispensability of Yahweh's firstborn. Yahweh will now demonstrate his own might on Egypt.

But the second part of this Exodus passage is just as significant for our understanding. It is a passage that has caused considerable difficulty for Old Testament scholarship. Why does Moses become the victim of a savage attack by Yahweh? Moses is on his way to Egypt. He is apparently acting in obedience to a call that few others would even contemplate; yet he falls foul of Yahweh's anger. Why?

There are many technical questions in the account of the circumcision of Moses' son that are all worthy of serious study but are not essential for our own enquiry. What is clear from the passage is that, whatever its purpose, and whatever its precise ritual structure, Zipporah performs a vicarious act upon her son for the sake of her husband.

It is this representative relationship between Moses and his son that links the preceding passage with the warning of Yahweh that was about to be given to Pharaoh. The judgment that was to fall on Pharaoh, the representative of the Egyptian people, was to fall on both his own firstborn and the firstborn sons of his people. The phrase, 'surely you are a bridegroom of blood to me,' is explained by the author as referring to circumcision. It has been suggested that this is a reference to a premarital circumcision ceremony that was commonly practised in some cultures. This seems to miss the point of the statement Zipporah makes. If it were this, it would have been something in the past, prior to their own marriage, whereas the force of the accusation clearly relates to the act she has just performed. It might, therefore, be better to see it as her exclaiming that her marriage to

[9]Cole, *Exodus*, 78.

Moses has brought her to face death in her husband's experience and that this has been averted only at the cost of blood, in the circumcision of their son.

The intention of Yahweh to strike the firstborn is repeated in Exodus 11:4-7. In this passage Yahweh impresses upon the Israelites their certain safety in the coming judgement. Not even a dog will bark against them. There will be absolutely no cause for alarm. Not so for the Egyptians. For them, every firstborn will be struck dead by the visiting angel of death. The fact that Pharaoh, who was a firstborn, survives the Passover suggests that the judgement was not inclusive of all firstborn, but only of the youngest generation of each family and species of animal.

It is not until chapter 12 that the protection of Israel's firstborn is explained. Their firstborn must be protected by the blood of an innocent victim. Every family must be safeguarded by the blood of a lamb. While the blood spares the firstborn, the whole family are to eat of the lamb. Sharing in the Passover is described as eating it. It is a clear sign of sharing in the deliverance in which the whole community participate through the death (though averted for the Jews) of the firstborn.

The importance of the Passover for the whole nation of Israel through all generations is not just an afterthought to the Exodus event. Far more space is given to explaining the significance of the Passover and how future generations are to celebrate the event than to the actual account of the critical night itself. All that is said of the inauguration is contained in two brief verses (Exod. 12:29-30). The event was not only to be celebrated annually by every succeeding generation of Jews, but it was to confront them at critical points in their lives. The birth of their firstborn son, the most treasured moment in the lives of any Jewish couple, was to be overshadowed by the reminder that he did not belong to them, for he was the Lord's. This was also true of animals. The donkey, an unclean animal, was to be destroyed, but because it had such a practical value to the Israelite, it could be redeemed by the death of a lamb. At lambing time the air must have carried the stench of burning flesh throughout the land. It would have been a constant reminder that the firstborn belonged to the Lord. There was to be no child sacrifice. 'Redeem every firstborn among your sons' (Exod. 13:13). The vicarious nature of the firstborn's role was clearly to be taught to succeeding generations:

In the days to come when your son asks you, 'What does this mean?' say to him, 'With a mighty hand the LORD brought us out of Egypt, out of the land of slavery. When Pharaoh stubbornly refused to let us go, the LORD killed every firstborn in Egypt, both man and animal. This is why I sacrifice to the LORD the first male offspring of every womb and redeem each of my firstborn sons.' And it will be like a sign on your hand and a symbol on your forehead that the LORD brought us out of Egypt with his mighty hand (Exod. 13:14-16).

The Passover and its significance was to be at the forefront of Israelite thought and theology. Their experience was to determine their treatment of aliens (Lev. 19:33-34). Indeed it moulded their whole ethical framework, for it was to be the response of gratitude from those who had been redeemed. Furthermore, the practice of the use of phylacteries in prayer and the placing of the law at their doors was a consequence of this injunction. The Passover and its implications confronted the Jews daily.

The vicarious nature of the death of the firstborn seems to be reflected in the Levite representation described in Numbers 8:19. In the earlier verses we find instructions concerning how the Levites were to be prepared for their service in the tabernacle. They had been taken by Yahweh in place of Israel's firstborn, who belong to him, because they had been spared. Yahweh then gave the Levites to Aaron's sons, the priests, to serve in the tabernacle. In other words, the Levites are substitutes for the firstborn. We find this unusual explanation of the role of the Levites: 'Of all the Israelites, I have given the Levites as gifts to Aaron and his sons to do the work at the Tent of Meeting on behalf of the Israelites and to make atonement for them so that no plague will strike the Israelites when they go near the sanctuary.'

This passage not only once again reveals the solidarity aspect with the Levites representing both the firstborn and Israel, but it contains the unexpected statement 'to make atonement'. This cannot be a reference to sacrifices which the Levites will offer for they were excluded from such service. Only the Aaronic priests were allowed to offer sacrifices. The passage therefore suggests that, in some way, the very presence of the Levites performed a propitiatory act by turning the wrath of Yahweh from the people.

This protective concept is found earlier in the book of Numbers when instructions are given as to where the different tribes are to camp in relation to the tabernacle. Numbers 1:53 says: 'The Levites, however, are to set up their tents around the tabernacle of the Testimony so that wrath will not fall on the Israelite community.' Thus, the Levites, substituted for the firstborn, continue the propitiatory function. This takes place outside of the tabernacle, so endorsing our earlier suggestion that it had nothing to do with offering sacrifices for the nation. As the lambs had performed this role of saving the firstborn from wrath on the night of the Passover, so now, the firstborn substitutes, the Levites, continue to perform this same function of keeping wrath away from the congregation.

Obviously it could be claimed that the Levites avoided wrath coming upon the nation by fulfilling the cultic requirements. If they failed to fulfil the functions allotted to them, then wrath would come upon the people. But this interpretation does not do justice to the strong statement that they 'make atonement for the Israelites'. If the passage said that they were to serve so that wrath did not come upon the people, that would be valid. But the text does not say that. The statement is emphatic, they are there 'to make atonement' so that the plague does not come upon the people when they come to the tent of meeting. The statement is therefore not about averting wrath by fulfilling the cultic regulations; rather it is speaking of their ministry in the place of the firstborn as being an atonement.

This interpretation finds support in the way the passage was interpreted rabbinically: 'This prerogative was then conferred upon the tribe of Levi who, moreover, dedicating themselves, man for man, to the service of the Lord, served as an atonement for the firstborn, that they might not be destroyed as they deserved.'[10]

The realisation that the wrath is directed against the firstborn and not the family causes us to ask why it was against the firstborn and not against the father, who was the head of the family?

I have earlier proposed that the firstborn represented the family on the night of the Passover. Is there any evidence to support this? I would suggest that there is. The vicarious suffering of descendants is suggested in the Decalogue. The warning in the second commandment that Yahweh visits the sins of the fathers unto the third and fourth generation has caused Sanders to note that it implies vicarious substitution in which the children bear the sins of their forefathers.[11]

---

[10]Ginzberg, *Legends*, 3:226.

[11]Sanders, *Palestinian*, 194 says, 'If the sons are punished for the transgressions of

The warning is in the context of the Exodus, the commandments being given as the climax of the redemptive event. If its historical setting is kept in mind, then there is an inevitable link with the immediately preceding event, the Passover.

There is therefore a propitiatory role that the death of the lamb and the presence of the Levites play. They are not separate roles, for they are linked in that they both represent the firstborn. The lamb died in the place of the firstborn, and the Levites were functioning in the place of the firstborn. The firstborn, it would seem, were threatened because they fulfilled a representative role for the family, and if they had no provision made for them, then they died bearing the wrath of God.

The link between the firstborn and atonement is illustrated in Psalm 78. In verse 38 the waywardness of Israel in the wilderness is referred to. She constantly provoked Yahweh to anger. The Psalmist praises Yahweh for his mercy saying: 'Yet he was merciful, he atoned for their iniquities and did not destroy them. Time after time he restrained his anger and did not stir up his full wrath.'

The Psalmist further wrote about the Egyptians: 'He unleashed against them his hot anger; he did not spare them from death but gave them over to the plague. He struck down all the firstborn of Egypt, the firstfruits of manhood in the tents of Ham. But he brought his people out like a flock; he led them like sheep through the desert' (Ps. 78:49-52).

The thrust of the Psalm clearly shows how Yahweh's anger was only averted by atonement. On the night of the Passover his judgement was fully revealed. That judgement focused on the firstborn, the first fruit of Egyptian manhood. There can be only one explanation of how the judgement did not visit the Jewish homes – a vicarious atonement had been made.

It is true that the Hebrew text has $y^e kapp\bar{e}r$ '$\bar{a}w\bar{o}n$ 'forgive their iniquity', but this does not exclude the notion of atonement. The passage makes it clear that Yahweh's people were in danger of the same judgement that came upon the Egyptians. The forgiveness or mercy that the Jews received was through the provision of an alternative for

the father, themselves, then they are not punished for those same transgressions. The entire view that descendants suffer for their ancestors' sin is, as indicated, very rare in Tannaitic literature, but it is interesting, since it leads to something like a view of vicarious atonement.'

the firstborn, namely, the Paschal lamb. It was a provision made by Yahweh, therefore he forgave their iniquities.

Another passage that points to an atoning significance in the death of the firstborn is found in Micah (6:6-7). The prophet is asked by Israel what it should do to atone for its sin. The people are represented as saying, 'With what shall I come before the LORD and bow down before the exalted God? Shall I come before him with burnt offerings, with calves a year old? Will the LORD be pleased with thousands of rams, even ten thousand rivers of oil? Shall I offer my firstborn for my transgression, the fruit of my body for the sin of my soul?'

The reference to this offering of the firstborn as an atonement bears a number of possible interpretations. Henderson says: 'It was customary among the ancients, on calamities or dangerous emergencies, for the rulers of the state, to prevent destruction of all, to offer the most dearly beloved of their children as a ransom to divine vengeance.'[12]

Smith saw this passage as proof of the practice of human sacrifice in Micah's day, nevertheless he refused to accept it was for atonement, interpreting it rather as an attempt to please Yahweh, but going to extremes to achieve that goal.[13]

McKeating argues against using the passage to show that human sacrifice was widely practised. He claims that the question asked is rhetorical, expecting the answer, 'Of course not!' The argument is, 'If the costliest sacrifice cannot achieve such an end, what is the point of the ordinary sacrifices of rams, calves or oil?'[14]

Pusey sees the passage as a rebuke: 'They would not withhold their, their firstborn sons, from God, part as they were of themselves. They would offer everything (even what God forbade) excepting only what alone He asked for, their heart, its love and its obedience.'[15]

Von Orell regards the passage as definitely reflecting an attempt to expiate for sin by means of the firstborn's death: 'The climax grows in boldness; shall I give my firstborn for my sin, properly, as my sin, but with the sense of expiating for sin, having both significance.'[16]

The range of opinion shows the wide scope of interpretation

[12]Henderson, *Prophets*, 257.
[13]Smith,*Commentary*, 126-7.
[14]McKeating, *Amos*, 186-7.
[15]Pusey, *Prophets*, 237-8.
[16]Orell, *Minor*, 214.

regarding the reference to the sacrifice of the firstborn. It would seem to me that there is no forcing of the intended meaning of the passage in saying that it expresses belief, even if only popular belief, in the possibility of dealing with a crisis by the death of the firstborn. This is suggested by the attitudes of the surrounding nations who did follow such practices.

The redemptive significance of Micah 6:6-7 is further supported by Rabbinic authorities for in them the text is linked to Isaac in Genesis.[17] As we shall soon see, Isaac's willingness to die was claimed to have atoning significance by the Rabbis.

This reasoning supports those scholars who see here a suggestion that the sacrificial death of the firstborn might be offered as an appeasement to God's wrath, and an attempt to avert his judgment. If this is true, it links up with what I have claimed for the purpose of the firstborn's death in the Passover, and we do not need to look for any immediate external influence for Micah's understanding. The people felt that the conditions indicated that God's judgment would fall, and they ask, 'Will it be as when it fell in Egypt, and will it be averted in the same way?'

Zechariah also refers to the firstborn: 'And I will pour out on the house of David and the inhabitants of Jerusalem a spirit of grace and supplication. They will look on me, the one they have pierced, and mourn for him as one mourns for an only child, and grieve bitterly for him as one grieves for a firstborn son' (Zech. 12:10). The text of this passage poses a problem in that some manuscripts give 'look on him whom they have pierced', while others have 'look upon me whom they have pierced'. The majority of commentators accept that because the latter *look upon me*, with Yahweh speaking, is so difficult, it must be the original and the 'looking upon him' must have been introduced to overcome the problem of speaking of the piercing of Yahweh.

Mason argues that it is Jehovah who has been thrust through in the person of his representative. This view could, of course, fit either reading. Mason sees that the one pierced is probably a little-known figure belonging to the prophetic circle. He comes to this conclusion because the mourning over the treatment of the one who has been pierced follows, rather than precedes, repentance. Mason sees this as hardly suggesting the role of the 'Suffering Servant', still less a Messianic one.[18] In other words, it is not the cause of repentance, but

[17] *Vayera* Lv 4-6 [10] a

an effect of it. But this requires that we should expect repentance to be a natural consequence once the evil has been exposed. This, however, cuts across what Zechariah is actually saying. The repentance will be of divine, and not of human, origin. Once this has been given the protagonists will see their crime in a new light that will lead to bitter mourning.

Mitchell dismisses a Messianic identification for the one pierced by saying: 'Those who identify the one pierced as the Messiah overlook one point of great importance, namely, that while the effusion of the Spirit and the effect produced by it are evidently future, the act of piercing the nameless victim belongs to the past. This means that the one pierced was not the Messiah whose advent all will agree was still future when these words were written; but someone who had at that time already suffered martyrdom.'[19]

But this comment cannot be sustained. It requires that we take Zechariah to be speaking from the vantage point of his own historical situation, looking forward to what will happen, whereas examination of the passage shows he is speaking from the vantage point of the vision of the outpouring of the spirit of prayer and supplication, and from that point of view the piercing is a past event. In other words, it is past not from the point at which Zechariah lives, but from the event he is speaking about. When the outpouring of the spirit of prayer and supplication takes place the offence will already have been committed. Moore argues that the interpretation can only be that the Messiah is pierced and adds: 'This evasion is utterly inadmissible and the text still stands, asserting that the Jews would look at Jehovah whom they had slain, a prophecy which can only be interpreted in the light of the cross.'[20]

The passage clearly links a redemptive event with the death of one likened to a firstborn. Obviously the original purpose in referring to the firstborn is to emphasise that the grief will be intense. However, the mention of grief over the loss of the firstborn could not but recall the Passover event to any Jew. The passage's significance and meaning would go far beyond what a superficial reading of the text might convey. The passage would draw together the strands of Jewish redemptive history, and at the heart of that is the role of the firstborn.

[18]Mason, *Books*, 118-19.
[19]Mitchell, *Haggai*, 330.
[20]Moore, *Zechariah*, 200.

This understanding is supported by the context itself. The preceding verses speak of the nations judged by Yahweh as he defends Israel, a theme that obviously has its counterpart in the Exodus events. This understanding, even if we cannot say with certainty that this is what Zechariah thought, is how the New Testament writers understood it. This is supported by the way John uses the passage in the opening of Revelation, in a setting glorying in the redemptive work of Christ (Rev. 1:4-8). It is also used in John's Gospel, in the very context of Christ's death, which John links with the Passover event (John 19:36).

The Passover and the Day of Atonement
In the closing chapters of Ezekiel we are given the prophet's vision of a new temple. The eschatological temple will be the centre of Israel's worship of Yahweh. Ezekiel rearranges the celebration of the great feasts as described in the following:

> This is what the Sovereign LORD says: In the first month on the first day you are to take a young bull without defect and purify the sanctuary. The priest is to take some of the blood of the sin offering and put it on the doorpost of the temple, on the four corners of the upper ledge of the altar and on the gateposts of the inner court. You are to do the same on the seventh day of the month for anyone who sins unintentionally or through ignorance, so you are to make atonement for the temple. In the first month on the fourteenth day you are to observe the Passover, a feast lasting seven days, during which you shall eat bread made without yeast. On that day the prince is to provide a bull as a sin offering for himself and for all the people of the land. Every day during the seven days of the feast he is to provide seven bulls and seven rams without defect as a burnt offering to the LORD, and a male goat for a sin offering (Ezek. 45:18-23).

This account merges the Passover with the sacrifice of the Day of Atonement. 'This decree marks a notable break with tradition; the distinctive sacrifice to be provided is the sin-offering, and Passover thus becomes a propitiatory rite, the language of Lev. 16:8 which is concerned with the Day of Expiation. The paschal meal, an essential feature of all the codes, is not so much as mentioned; perhaps it is taken for granted.'[21]

Cody notes the merger of the two feasts with the emphasis being on the absorption of the sacrifice of atonement by the Passover and

---

[21]Cooke, *Ezekiel*, 504.

comments: 'The feast of the 10th of the seventh month in post-Exilic Judaism is the Day of Atonement, whose ritual, given in Lev. 16, has absorbed the expiatory rites of the 1st and 7th of the first month for which Ezek. 45:18-20 does provide.'[22] Cody seems to be confused in his understanding, for it is not the Day of Atonement that absorbs the expiatory rites of the Passover, but the Passover that absorbs the expiatory rights of the Day of Atonement.

Fairbairn also noted how the Day of Atonement sacrifices were assimilated into the Passover, and how the offering for the Passover is transferred to the feast of Tabernacles. However, he saw no other significance than that it illustrates how Ezekiel was able to make free use of Old Testament ritual and 'how he only employed it as a cover for the great spiritual truths he sought to unfold'. Fairbairn fails to say what these great spiritual truths were.[23]

Hengstenberg has noted that 'in this festival the enhancing of the offerings appears quite prominent, which is explained by this, that the grace of redemption sealed by this festival was to receive so rich an accession by the events of the future.'[24]

Stalker comments that 'Ezekiel's offerings are at variance with those recorded in Numbers and elsewhere, proving that the cultic practice of a dynamic faith changes with time.'[25]

Zimmerli thought the sacrifices of the Day of Atonement were moved to the beginning of the year to be included in the Passover: to show much more fully the cleansing of the sanctuary (and of the community) from the sin which has accumulated throughout the year.[26] He further notes that there is no mention of atonement in the ritual itself (although this surely would be implicitly understood to be in these very sacrifices, i.e. of the Day of Atonement). He noted how the application of the blood of the sacrifice was according to the Passover ritual, and comments that the blood clearly had the power to remove sins.[27] Zimmerli sees the restructuring of the feasts with sacrifices taken from other occasions of celebration to be an example of a process which is strongly at work in history: 'That of leveling out festivals which to begin with in their rituals are clearly distinct.' The sin offering

---

[22]Cody, *Ezekiel*, 240.
[23]Fairbairn, *Ezekiel*, 485.
[24]Hengstenberg, *Prophecies*, 459.
[25]Stalker, *PCB*, 304.
[26]Zimmerli, *Ezekiel,* 2:482.
[27]*op. cit.* 2: 484.

was brought into the Passover to correct 'their danger of religious white-washing with false, festal joy the intention of God that he means to remove sin. Before the burnt offerings in which man could easily see his pious activity and alongside these burnt offerings of every single feast day the sin offering is set.'[28] Finally, Zimmerli comments that 'the sin offering of a bull gives both feasts a strong character of atonement'.[29]

While this is a conclusion I would accept, I do need to ask if Zimmerli is right to see the alteration of the feasts as nothing more than an example of religious evolution. Could a priest such as Ezekiel, so conscious of how Israel had adapted her religion in the past at great moral and spiritual cost, so easily partake in the same exercise; or is he saying something vitally significant, so significant that he has to do the unthinkable for a priest: he rearranges the divinely commanded structure of the great feasts? It is difficult to accept that he is intending to add to the significance of the Passover; but is he by this reconstruction intending to remind his people of the original and final eschatological significance of the Passover, i.e. that it was a deliverance from judgment? This significance is not only emphasised in transferring the required offerings of the Day of Atonement to Passover, but in making them more copious than the law itself required.

This understanding of the Passover is not widely shared. Yet the range of evidence suggests that the death of the firstborn was in some way related to atonement for the sins of the people.

The firstborn and family representation

The next question that we have set ourselves to answer is: Why was it the firstborn, and not the father, who represented the family? As the Passover event took place after 400 years of exile in Egypt, it is reasonable to suppose we might find some significance in the role of the firstborn in that nation's understanding. This is, in fact, what Trumper claimed. He considered that the text of King Unas revealed the firstborn's special significance in Egypt. In that text, the dead King has succeeded in making his way into heaven. The passage describes the terror of the gods when they see him arriving, as they soon discover that he is mightier than they, and he starts to assert his authority over them. One of the lines describing the King says: 'He is

[28]_op. cit._ 2: 486.
[29]_op. cit._ 2: 486

God the firstborn of the firstborn.' Trumper went on to point out that from the writings of Herodotus we learn that it is probable that the sacred bull representing Apis, which was kept in the temple, was the first and only born. It is specifically stated that the cow who was his mother had no subsequent offspring.[30]

The influence of Egyptian religious belief is clearly seen in the episode of the golden calf Israel worshipped soon after leaving Egypt (Exod. 32:1-4). It could be argued from this that the significance of the firstborn also came from Egyptian religious belief. The dynasty depended upon the survival of the firstborn son of Pharaoh. If he did not in turn give birth to another son of Ra, his throne was directly threatened. It is obvious that with the birth of the firstborn his significance became even greater than his father's, for the future of the nation, the throne, and even Ra himself, was then focused upon the welfare of the new son of Ra. The father's death would be by no means as calamitous as the death of his firstborn. The firstborn's representative role was more crucial than that of his father, until such time as he himself had fathered a son.

The firstborn and Isaac

But there is yet another setting that could have given the death of the firstborn such central significance in representing the family. Its origin is in the willingness of Abraham to offer up Isaac (Gen. 22:10). Even though the sacrifice was not actually completed, Jewish understanding came to regard the offering as accepted by God as though it had actually been made. This became the basis of a developed doctrine of atonement through the sacrifice of Isaac. Jewish understanding, in keeping with the doctrine of solidarity in which the many share in the experience of their representative, came to see that Isaac had 'died' for his people and so through his death God had extended mercy to Israel. What is of significance for our study is that Isaac was the firstborn of the covenant people. In the offering of Israel's firstborn, the Jew saw himself offered up and so sacrificed to God. The evidence for the significance of the offering of Isaac has slowly emerged over the last century. The testing of Abraham to see if he would obey God and offer up Isaac is known in Rabbinic studies as the *Aqedah*, which means 'the binding'. This is also the term used for binding the sacrifice to the altar in preparation for its slaughter.

[30]Trumper, *Mirror*, 121-2.

According to Vermes there are two types of Targum tradition with regard to Genesis 22. There is the primitive kernel represented by the *Fragmentary Targum* and *Neofiti,* and the secondary version represented by *Pseudo-Jonathan* and a *Tosefta* fragment of the Jerusalem Targum. The distinctive features of the oldest targumic traditions are:

1. Abraham told Isaac that he was to be the sacrificial victim.
2. Isaac gave his consent.
3. Isaac asked to be bound so that his sacrifice might be perfect.
4. Isaac was favoured with a heavenly vision.
5. Abraham prayed that his own obedience and Isaac's willingness might be remembered by God on behalf of Isaac's children.
6. Abraham's prayer was answered.

Pseudo-Jonathan presents the whole episode as a test of Isaac's fidelity, as well as of Abraham's love of and faithfulness to God.

Vermes shows that the targumic tradition about Isaac's active role in the 'sacrifice' was already implicit in three works of the first century A.D., namely *The Jewish Antiquities* of Josephus, *4 Maccabees* and Pseudo-Philo's *Liber Antiquitatum.* Josephus wrote that the offering of Isaac was not only a test for Abraham, but also insisted on Isaac's merit and on his voluntary self-surrender. In *4 Maccabees* Isaac is presented as the proto-martyr, and in several other passages there is an allusion to the power of the blood of the martyrs, though with no explicit reference to Isaac. *Liber Antiquitatum* stresses the willingness, even the joy, of Isaac and relates Isaac's 'sacrifice' to other sacrifices offered to and accepted by God for the sins of men. Finally, *Liber Antiquitatum* presents Isaac as being hopeful for the beneficent effect of his self-offering upon future generations.

Vermes shows further that in *4 Maccabees* Isaac was implicitly the model of a martyr's death offered for the sins of Israel. He suggests that this is linked with Isaiah 53 where in verse 7 the servant is compared with a lamb brought to the slaughter, just as Isaac was. Moreover, Isaac's sacrifice was ordered by God, as was the servant's.

Vermes emphasises the sacrificial nature of Isaac's offering by linking Isaac's free consent with the tradition in later midrashic texts that Isaac's blood was shed. The *Fragmentary Targum* explicitly mentions a prayer by Abraham for the pardon of the transgressions of Isaac's descendants. Other Targums are not as explicit, but it seems that the 'sacrifice' was thought to have played a unique role in the salvation of Israel. Vermes concludes from the testimony in Rabbinic sources that the Temple sacrifices (which were offered on the supposed site of Isaac's binding) were intended to be memorials, reminding Yahweh of the one 'sacrifice' that was efficacious, i.e. that of Isaac. Vermes argues that this suggests that the atoning efficacy of the *tamid* offering and of all the sacrifices in which the lamb was immolated, and perhaps even of all expiatory sacrifices, depended on the power of the 'sacrifice' of Isaac.[31]

A second tradition

There is another interpretation of the significance of the *Aqedah*, identified by Vermes as the secondary version. It rejected the expiatory significance of the *Aqedah* because no blood was shed, and interpreted its significance as that of an example of faithfulness even unto death. Swetnam notes how the writer of the epistle to the Hebrews emphasised that without the shedding of blood there is no remission of sins, and thinks that this is to stress the obvious superiority of Christ's sacrifice, whose blood was actually shed. But there is further significance in the *Aqedah* for our study of the firstborn. Le Deaut's work supports Vermes' claim that a Rabbinic tradition saw a propitiatory significance in the offering of Isaac. Le Deaut noted from the study of the intertestamental *Poem of the Four Nights* found in the best text of the *Codex Neofiti 1* at Exodus 12:43, that there are four key events affecting Israel. These are creation, the birth and sacrifice of Isaac, the Passover in Egypt, and the end of the world. All are said to have taken place on the night of the Passover. Le Deaut also noted that *Jubilees* also linked the sacrifice of Isaac with the date of the Passover. This led him to conclude that in the events of the Passover there exists a vital significance for the Jewish interpretation of the *Aqedah*.[32] Swetnam supports this view, believing that if there was a connection between the Passover and the *Aqedah* it would probably have been based on the common factor of the redemption of the firstborn and would probably have preceded the Exile.[33]

There is a further link between the *Aqedah* and the theme of the firstborn. Not only was Isaac the firstborn of the Covenant people, but his binding was actually linked with the Passover itself. Indeed

[31]Vermes, 'Redemption', 195-203.
[32]Le Deaut, *Pascale*, 179-84.
[33]Swetnam, *Jesus*, 67.

the efficacy of the blood of the Passover lamb was not seen to reside in itself, but in it being a reminder of the sacrifice of Isaac. The *Mekilte de-Rabbi Ishmael* is a halakhic midrash which Swetnam thinks was edited no earlier than the end of the fourth century AD but dating in substance from the Tannaitic period.[34] The passage is concerned with selected sections of Exodus. The comment on the words 'And when I see the blood' from Exodus 12:13 demonstrates the Isaac/Passover relation: 'And when I see the blood I see the blood of the sacrifice of Isaac, for it is said, "And Abraham called the name of that place Adonai-Jireh" (The Lord will see) etc.'[35] In another passage it says: 'And as he was about to destroy the Lord beheld and He repented Him', etc. (1 Chr. 21:15). What did he behold? He beheld the blood of the sacrifice of Isaac, as it said, "God will Himself see the Lamb" etc. (Gen. 22:8).'[36]

With such a range of evidence, the *Aqedah* clearly seems relevant for understanding something of the significance of the role of the firstborn. Unfortunately the picture is nowhere that simple and requires further investigation.

Davies and Chilton have challenged the claim of Vermes that there is evidence of a developed *Aqedah* tradition in existence in the New Testament period.[37] They accept the existence of the *Aqedah* as a developed doctrine from the end of the second century A.D., i.e. from the time that the Targum traditions were recorded, but they do not accept any sayings prior to that date. These are rejected even though they are attributed to specific Rabbinic authorities which would take their origin back to the Apostolic period or even earlier.

While it is correct to say that Davies and Chilton's position is the only one that considers evidence whose dating is beyond dispute, nevertheless it imposes on the evidence restrictions that are totally contrary to the way that ideas emerge. Ideas are verbalised and debated before they ever come into existence in a written form, and this alone ought to permit us, without becoming involved in an argument over the dating of the material, to accept that the material would have had an existence – how long we would need to try to discover – prior to the date of it being committed to writing. The criteria that Davies and

---

[34]*op. cit.* 80 note 458.
[35]*op. cit.* 67.
[36]*op. cit.* 67.
[37]Chilton and Davies, 'Adeqah'.

Chilton have laid down have effectively done away with the existence
of oral tradition, the principles and reality of which are widely accepted.
The only materials they will accept as valid for determining the likelihood
of the *Aqedah* having an influence in the New Testament period are
the books of *4 Maccabees*, *Jubilees*, *Josephus* and Pseudo-Philo's
Liber Antiquitatum. They claim that these texts alone can be accepted
as relevent texts because their dating is beyond doubt, so making
their composition relevant to interpreting the New Testament. Having
accepted these as valid sources they then go on to dispute the evidence
deduced from them by Vermes in the following manner:

1. Philo refers to Isaac being dismembered, which rules out any
connection with the Passover because that sacrifice was not treated
in such a way.

2. Josephus presents Isaac's dedication as an example to those
who fought against Rome to encourage them to accept martyrdom.
Josephus makes no allusion to the theme of redemption. Also Josephus
makes little of Isaac's self-offering in comparison to the faith of
Abraham, which he emphasises.

3. Philo has Isaac saying, 'My blessing will be upon all men as
there will not be another.' This gives a universal significance to the
Aqedah which it was nowhere else given.

4. Davies and Chilton further reject the Passover Aqedah material
on the grounds that 'whereas there is no doubt that the Passover had
a redemptive significance, there is no evidence that it had an expiatory
significance. The unhappy confusion of distinct concepts is partly
responsible for the current prevalent view of the *Aqedah*.'[38]

Davies and Chilton conclude after examining the four works which
they have accepted as prior to the New Testament: 'Our discussion
of all the relevant passages in this source allows us the confident
assertion that there is no evidence of the *Aqedah* to be found.'[39]
They confidently assert that: 'The current consensus on the
development of the *Aqedah* is fundamentally misguided.'[40]

When they examine the New Testament they dismiss any reference
to the *Aqedah* in Romans 8:32 while accepting that there is a faint
possibility of an allusion in John 3:16; 1 John 4:9 and Mark 1:11.[41]

[38]Davies and Chilton, 'Aqedah', 546 note 81.
[39]*op. cit*. 528.
[40]*op. cit*. 546.
[41]I suggest that these texts are better interpreted in the light of the Passover model.

As to the assessment of Davies and Chilton of the New Testament evidence our argument has shown that not only is there possibly a far greater presence of this theme of the *Aqedah*/Passover than they have allowed, but that it goes far beyond what even Vermes has identified. It is surprising that studies concerned with the presence or influence of the *Aqedah*/Passover theme in the New Testament have consistently failed to give due weight to considering the context in which a possible allusion or quotation appears. The context extends the specific allusion or quotation and produces factors that alter the balance of evidence.

But what of Davies and Chilton's assessment of the evidence in *4 Maccabees, Jubilees, Josephus* and *Pseudo Philo*? Have they made a valid assessment of the evidence in this area where there is no serious debate over the dating of the material? I believe that they have not made a correct assessment and I will now respond to their arguments in the order given earlier.

1. Davies and Chilton's argument that Philo refers to Isaac being dismembered, whereas the Passover lamb was not, is not a valid argument for dismissing Philo's evidence. I have already shown that Ezekiel 45:21-25 has brought the sacrifices of the Day of Atonement under the structure of the Passover celebrations, and these sacrifices, which were absorbed into the redemptive theme of the Passover, were dismembered. I shall show that this merger of the sacrifices under the theme of Passover was clearly present in the writings of the early church fathers.[42]

2. There is no reason why Josephus should not apply the *Aqedah* to non-redemptive themes. This does not preclude the existence of a central redemptive motif. The New Testament writers constantly use Christ's redemptive sufferings as an example for believers to follow in the face of persecution. This use of the sufferings of Christ for encouragement was achieved without in any way weakening the theme of redemption (Heb. 12:1-2; 1 Pet. 2:20-21).

3. The *Aqedah* does not require exclusive attention to be placed on the role of Isaac for it to have theological significance for the New Testament writers. Dahl has pointed out the significance of Abraham's faith in these words: 'There existed a specifically Jewish-Christian "doctrine of the atonement", more explicit than has often been assumed on the basis of Acts. The death of Jesus upon the cross was

---

[42] See Appendix 2.

interpreted as fulfilling what God had promised to Abraham by oath. Abraham had not withheld his son, so God did not spare His own Son, but gave him up for Isaac's descendants. As the sacrifice provided by God, he expiated their former sins.'[43]

In other words, the faith of Abraham is an integral part of the *Aqedah* doctrine for later Jewish and Christian understanding. In addition, when we remember the total abhorrence the Jews had for human sacrifice, it is to be expected that in Jewish literature it is Abraham's faith rather than the self-sacrifice that is emphasised. Jewish leaders only came to terms with the self-sacrificing aspect of Isaac's surrender as they were forced to respond to the pressure of the gospel of Christ whose theme was that an act of self-sacrificing love had brought about the redemption of the people of God. What Judaism could cope with was a doctrine of martyrdom, and this was clearly developed in pre-Christian Judaism, and the *Aqedah* was used to promote it. In this case, however, even though it was seen to expiate sin, it was not the sacrifice of a child in a cultic setting.

There is another point that needs to be considered regarding this claim of Davies and Chilton: it is that the text concentrates on Abraham's and not Isaac's faith and obedience. Levi has pointed out that the texts (which Davies and Chilton reject as later adaptations) which speak of Abraham's faith rather than that of Isaac are more likely to be pre-Christian. This is because a feature of texts that are responding to the Christian doctrine of redemption in Christ would inevitably have been to emphasis Isaac's adequacy to secure redemption for Israel.[44] The fact that these texts do not do this suggests that they have a pre-Christian origin and this in turn points to the existence of the *Aqedah* doctrine at an earlier date than Davies and Chilton are willing to accept.

4. It would be strange indeed if Pseudo-Philo, whose concern to commend Judaism to the Greeks was so great that he followed a syncretistic approach to religious belief, did not overstep the boundaries of orthodoxy when dealing with the *Aqedah*. The fact that he writes that Isaac said, 'my blessing will be upon all men because there will not be another', is hardly a problem. Indeed, the problem would be if this sort of thing had not been said in a missionary situation.

5. In response to Davies and Chilton's claim that there is no evidence

---

[43]Dahl, 'Atonement,' 27.
[44]Levi, 'Le Sacrifice,' 179.

that the Passover had any expiatory significance, I believe that crucial evidence does exist to show that it did. The early church, through the influence of Ezekiel 45:21-25, did attach an expiatory value to the death of Christ who was the eschatological Paschal victim. The evidence suggests that this view was not the product of the early church, but rather that it was part of Judaism. John the Baptist referred to Jesus as the lamb of God who takes away the sin of the world (John 1:29). There is no suggestion that his hearers had to have this allusion explained, which strongly suggests that the atoning significance of the eschatological Passover was well established in the mind of Judaism. Thus it is incorrect to say that there was no expiatory significance in the Paschal offering.

Confining our attention to the material that Davies and Chilton have admitted as valid, what are the possibilities for the development of the *Aqedah*? They are as follows:

1. That there are no *Aqedah* references or allusions in the New Testament. The evidence we have considered suggests otherwise, especially when the texts are read in their context.

2. That there are a few allusions in the New Testament which reflect the emergence of an Isaac typology in the early Christian community that was based on a parallel between the sacrifice of Isaac and that of Christ. This view has the support of most scholars but it does not require that there was anything like the *Aqedah* tradition promoting it. It could have emerged merely as a result of early teachers realising that a type was present in Genesis 22.

3. That there is a unique independent doctrine of salvation in the New Testament which is the product of the creative genius of Jesus/ and/or the apostles. The Jewish apologists responded to this doctrinal model by developing the *Aqedah*. This position leaves the Targums free to respond to the Christian doctrine of redemption by identifying appropriate features in Isaac that allowed them to develop the significance of the *Aqedah* and so produce a more effective answer to the ever threatening Christian insistence that the Jewish community needed to experience the redemption that was in Christ. This is the view held by Levi, who argued that the sacrifice of Isaac was just a strand of the Jewish doctrine of the merits of the fathers. The early Christian writers identified the significance of this for their understanding of Christ and developed it themselves. This then made the Jewish apologists go back to the account of the *Aqedah* to try to

defend their own position that Judaism had already been provided with its own sufficient sacrifice.[45]

4. There is an *Aqedah* doctrine in the New Testament, either emerging or developed, which was the result of an ongoing debate with the Jewish community about the nature and means of redemption. This possibility would reflect an ongoing debate, which was spawning ideas that were then incorporated into the New Testament writings. The Christian community, clearly the party taking the initiative and in the early stages of formulating its ideas, was able to respond more readily and incorporated its developing understanding of the *Aqedah* into its writings. Such an immediate response is rarely possible for institutions such as Judaism was, and it would have been some time later that the fully formulated Jewish response would have emerged.

5. There was in existence a fully developed Jewish doctrine of the *Aqedah*, which the early church used as a model to interpret the significance of the death of Christ.

I believe that the true account of the origin and influence of the *Aqedah* lies somewhere between the possibilities of 3, 4 and 5. This does justice to the oral tradition stage of development as well as the Rabbinic evidence together with the evidence of those sources which Chilton and Davies have accepted as sufficiently early to be undisputed. However, the most dominant model for the New Testament writers was not the *Aqedah* itself, but the Passover with the death of the firstborn. This probably came to the fore naturally, not only because it had been the model that Jesus himself had used to teach the church, i.e. the eschatological Exodus, but also because it was seen to be totally in harmony with the prophetic tradition. Furthermore, it had none of the inherent problems that the *Aqedah* stream had in confusing the meaning and significance of Christ's death, for he certainly was not a martyr; he was the Saviour, and that understanding was set in the context of Old Testament concepts of redemptive history.

---

[45]Fisk's conclusion in 'Again,' 507, is : 'It may be impossible to determine whether early Jewish traditions about Isaac fueled the imaginations of early Christians seeking them to make sense of the crucifixion, but the testimony of Pseudo-Philo does lend plausibility to the idea that at least some traditions of the *Aqedah* were available to early Jewish Christians.' It is my contention of course that the New Testament writers were not specifically interacting with this tradition but were developing their own Paschal Theology.

The firstborn and the redeemer

The third question that needs answering is: Why do we have two titles, namely, firstborn and redeemer, when the title 'redeemer' would have satisfactorily covered all the roles these two titles suggest?

Although the firstborn was intended to be the redeemer, he was not always so in practice. The difference in the roles of the two is that the firstborn acted in respect of sacrificial representation, as previously outlined, and this could not be abdicated or handed on. That role was inextricably bound up with the person of the firstborn. There was only one way in which this role could be avoided, and that was by substitutionary sacrifice. The redeemer's role, however, was one that could, and often was, handed on to the next of kin, either because of death or by abdication. There was no vicarious role in the work of the redeemer. It was essentially concerned with the social welfare of near kinsmen.

The two titles, firstborn and redeemer, are never explicitly brought together in the Old Testament. This need not be a problem for my thesis, for to the Jew the identity of the one with the other was so obvious that it would be like saying rain is water. Even so, evidence does exist to show how natural the relationship was. Boaz had to approach the one who was next of kin to Ruth's former husband before he could take her in marriage (Ruth 4:4). Although Boaz was related to her, there was another who had the responsibility of redemption before himself. Obviously the responsibility would work down through the members of the family. The eldest, or firstborn, was the redeemer. If the eldest was dead, or refused to act, it went to the next eldest brother. If there were no brothers, or if they all refused to act, the role of the redeemer fell upon the nearest relative who would accept the duty. The process of elimination clearly had to be gone through before a relative could take the responsibility on himself, as established in Leviticus 25:25.

Coupled with this, Edersheim has pointed out that the practice of inheritance under Jewish law gave the eldest son, the firstborn, twice the inheritance of any other member of the family. Hence, if there were five brothers the inheritance was divided into six parts and the eldest received two parts so as to fulfil the responsibilities of the redeemer.[46] The eldest, i.e. the firstborn, was clearly in Jewish law intended to act as the redeemer.

[46]Edersheim, *Life*, 2: 243 note 1

There is another sphere in which the firstborn/redeemer roles can be seen to be interrelated, if not synonymous, namely, Jewish Messianism. We have already noted that the king (a role later to be applied by the Rabbis to the Messiah) was called the Lord's firstborn (Ps. 89:27). This originally had reference to the Jewish king's promised superiority over the kings of the earth. This title is also linked with that of the 'Son of God' (Ps. 2:7). This title was conferred because the king had the responsibility of representing Yahweh to his people. He was to uphold Yahweh's laws, protect his people and sustain the poor, especially the widow. He was, in other words, the redeemer. This designation was applied to Yahweh in the context of kingship when he was declared to be 'Israel's king and redeemer' (Isa. 44:6). Clearly there is a close association between the titles 'Son of God', 'redeemer' and 'firstborn'. In fact, when we examine Isaiah 44:6 we find further evidence that our train of thought is correct. Isaiah says, 'This is what the LORD says – Israel's King and Redeemer, the LORD Almighty: I am the first and I am the last; apart from me there is no God.'

These very titles were gathered up together by John and used to honour Christ. For example, John writes in Revelation 1:4-8:

> Grace and peace to you from him who is, and who was, and who is to come, and from the seven spirits before his throne, and from Jesus Christ who is the faithful witness, the firstborn from the dead, and the ruler of the kings of the earth. To him who has loved us and washed us from our sins by his blood, and has made us to be a kingdom and priests to serve his God and Father – to him be glory and power for ever and ever! Amen. Look, he is coming with the clouds, and every eye will see him, even those who pierced him; and all the peoples of the earth will mourn because of him. So shall it be! Amen. 'I am the Alpha and the Omega,' says the Lord God, 'who is, and who was, and who is to come, the Almighty.'

That the last part of the passage is to be applied to Christ is confirmed by the fact that verse 17 of the same chapter has Jesus calling himself 'the first and the last'. John is therefore bringing together the very titles that we are considering, those of 'firstborn', 'king' and 'first and the last', and in a context saturated with terms of salvation he ascribes them all to Jesus. The death of the firstborn draws both the Paschal imagery and Messianic imagery together. The firstborn who dies is the firstborn over the kings of the earth.

The role of the king, the Son of God, God's firstborn, has been recognised as crucial in Old Testament thinking. Engell described the connection between the king and the Passover: 'The king is important in the celebration of the Passover as Moses acted as central figure in the Passover – who is modelled after the figure of the sacred king throughout.'[47]

This introduces a much debated question as to the role Moses in fact played, but what is not in dispute is the fact that the kings of Israel played a central role in the celebration of the Passover.[48] This association is supported by the observation of Moule who thinks that the setting of the Servant title in the New Testament could be Paschal and that it does not refer to the suffering Servant but the royal Servant, the descendant of David.[49] This suggestion fits into the exposition being suggested. Christ is the Royal Paschal victim. This is endorsed by Perrin who observes that 'Palestinian Christianity arrived at its Christology via a Passover setting'.[50]

The only point of disagreement with Perrin would be the timing of the Christological understanding. Once the primitive nature of the New Testament Christological material has been appreciated, there is no reason why it should not be recognised as very early, not so much developed by Paul, but given to him in a highly developed form. Paul is therefore not the originator of New Testament Christology but the receiver of it. The primitive community had arrived at these insights as the Spirit enabled them to reflect on the significance of Christ being their Passover who had achieved the New Exodus for his people through his death. Through reflecting on the predications of the redemption of creation indicated in Isaiah they came to see that Jesus' death was unique and achieved things that no creature could ever achieve. Only the Creator himself could redeem creation.

Rabbinic support
What we are saying finds support in the rabbinic interpretation of Isaiah 59:20: 'The redeemer will come to Zion, to those in Jacob who repent of their sins, declares the Lord.' In periqta 166b the particular form of 'plene' in which the word *go'el* (redeemer) is written is taken to indicate the Messiah as the Redeemer in the full sense. Hence, the

[47]Engell, *Essays*, 1.
[48]Because the kings of Judah were priests after the order of Melchizedek, see Bruce, *Thoughts*, 89.
[49]Moule, 'Influence,' 252.
[50]Perrin, *Pilgrimage*, 76.

Messiah is called both the firstborn and the redeemer in rabbinic literature. In fact, these titles are linked elsewhere in the rabbinic writings. Edersheim wrote:

> Ps. 2:7 is quoted as Messianic in the Talmud, among a number of other Messianic quotations (Sukk.52a). There is a very remarkable passage in the Midrash on Ps. 2:7 (ed. Warsh.p.5a), in which the unity of Israel and the Messiah in prophetic vision seems clearly indicated. Tracing the 'decrees' through the law the Prophets and the Hagiographa. The first passage quoted is Ex. 4:22, 'Israel is My firstborn son;' the second, from the Hagiographa, Ps. 110:1 'The Lord said unto my Lord,' and again 'The Lord said unto Me, Thou art My Son,' and yet this other saying, 'Behold, one like the Son of Man came with the clouds of heaven'. Five lines further down, the same Midrash, in reference to the words 'Thou art my Son', observes that, when that hour comes, God speaks to Him to make a new covenant, and thus He speaks, 'This day have I begotten Thee' – this is the hour in which He becomes His Son.[51]

We have long recognised that the servant in the Servant Songs of Isaiah oscillates between the individual servant and the community, but here we see that this solidarity extends to other titles of the Messiah as well, including that of the firstborn. Not only this, but equally as important, we can see that there are in fact clear connections between the various titles themselves. They are interlinked so that firstborn is linked to the suffering servant title; they are both facets of the same description and as such they illuminate the significance of the other descriptions or titles.

The significance of what we have considered is obvious. This interrelationship between the various Messianic titles enriches the significance of each of them. Thus, firstborn is coloured by all the redemptive concepts inherent in the person of the suffering servant. The firstborn, the king, is the suffering servant, the redeemer.

Edersheim has also brought to our attention the fact that the Rabbis linked the firstborn and servant with the title 'Son of God' of Psalm 2:7. This points to a redemptive significance behind the heavenly declaration made at Jesus' baptism which proclaimed, 'This is my Son, whom I love; with him I am well pleased' (Matt. 3:17), which many see to be an amalgamation of Psalm 2:7 and Isaiah 42:1. There are others who see a reference to Isaac in the voice from heaven.

But the strongest strand of evidence that Christ is the firstborn/

---

[51]Edersheim, *Life*, 2:716.

redeemer comes from the New Testament itself. Examination reveals a startling omission. Christ is never called the Redeemer.[51] Christ's work is constantly described as a work of redemption, but never is he given the title 'the Redeemer'. What we do find, however, is that he is called the firstborn, and that title is always closely related to his work of redemption. This omission is even more significant in that Jewish literature of the New Testament period contains many references to the Messiah being the Redeemer.[52]

In view of the fact that the Messiah was regularly called the Redeemer in Rabbinic literature, there can be only one explanation for the absence of the title 'Redeemer' from New Testament Christology. It has been taken up in the minds of the New Testament writers into the more definitive title of 'firstborn'. This development is quite natural, as Christ's redemptive role has its origin in the vicarious sufferings he underwent. This was not the case in the Old Testament. Only the firstborn had a vicarious role. The redeemer's role was quite separate and did not involve suffering or death. The redeemer was concerned only with social emancipation which never cost the one acting as the redeemer his life. Thus, when we come to the New Testament, the writers see it as quite natural to designate Christ as the firstborn, since it is from his vicarious sufferings that his redemptive work flows.

The significance of other Messianic titles used both by Jesus and the New Testament writers is also important for our study. The doctrine of the *last Adam* suggests the representative role that the firstborn fulfilled. It is through this position that Christ is the federal head and redeemer of his brethren (Rom. 5:9). Jeremias has argued that Paul avoided the use of *bar nāshā*, Jesus' self-description, as it would have confused his Gentile readers. Instead he rendered the substance of *bar nāshā* by *ho anthrōpos* (Rom. 5:15; 1 Cor. 15:21f; cf. 1 Tim. 2:5). It is evident that Paul knew the self-description of Jesus as Son of Man because of the way he used it Messianically in 1 Corinthians 15:27. Jeremias wrote: 'With his Adam/Christ antithesis Paul expresses the same thought as underlines Jesus' self description as *bar nāshā*, namely, that Jesus is the firstborn of the new creation of God. As Adam he stands at the head of the *aiōn mellōn* as the

---

[51]Warfield, *Person*, 328, notes that it is Justin in his *Dialogue with Trypho* who first calls Jesus the Redeemer.

[52]See Procksch, *TDNT* 4:350, note 8.

initiator of the perfect redeemed creation of God.'[53]

Jeremias' conclusions have the support of Ridderbos who claimed that the title 'firstborn of every creature' was not only to be linked with Adamic concepts, but is the very cornerstone of Paul's Christology which he says was implicit at the resurrection of Christ. Ridderbos comments: 'In other words, from Christ's significance as the second Adam all the categories are derived which further defined his significance as the firstborn of every creature.'[54]

Not only is there a case for claiming that last Adam concepts are linked with the description of Christ being the firstborn in redemption, but there are grounds for seeing a link between the Son of Man material and the firstborn description. Walker has argued that the Son of Man sayings come from Zechariah 12:10-14, which has powerful paschal associations.[55] On the next page, in my comments on Matthew 1:25, I suggest that there are distinct priestly ideas behind the Lucan use of the description of Jesus as Mary's firstborn. As Adam was seen in rabbinic writings to be the High Priest,[56] and the Aaronic High Priest was the family's firstborn, and some have seen a priestly theme to be present in the Son of Man sayings,[57] so there is the distinct possibility that virtually all of the descriptions of Christology are interlinked in the most amazing way through the theme of Christ being the High Priest of the New Covenant. This ought not to cause surprise, for it had been anticipated by Ezekiel in his vision of the Davidic prince serving as priest in the eschatological temple.

So to all the material we have considered relating to the firstborn we can add all that Paul has to say about the last Adam and, indeed, all that Jesus had to say about the Son of Man. Both titles are inseparably linked with the concept of the redeemer/firstborn figure.

The conclusion of this section of our study is that far from the Passover event having little influence upon the writers of the New Testament, it did in fact form the very substructure upon which they built their concepts. Indeed, we can go even further than this. The doctrine of Christ's Person is illustrated and clarified by the doctrine of his work. Therefore, rather than the expression 'firstborn of every creature' being a problem for the doctrine of the divinity of Christ, it

[53]Jeremias, *TDNT* 1 :143.

[54]Ridderbos, *Outline*, 84.

[55]Walker, 'Developments,' 599-60 and 605.

[56]Scroggs, *Adam*, 39 and 43ff.

[57]Higgins, 'Priestly', 236, and Rowley, *Faith*, 199; Vermes, *Jesus*, 135.

turns out to be the very opposite: it, in fact, becomes a key statement about it. No creature, no matter how exalted, could be the means of the redemption of creation. Only God himself could be the firstborn/ redeemer of the whole of creation. Thus, as the early believers reflected on the Old Testament Scriptures, on how Yahweh had promised to redeem creation, and saw it to have been achieved in the death of Jesus, they could come to no other conclusion than that Jesus was God. Their Christology was not ontologically based, although this was its inevitable conclusion, but functionally based.

This assertion is evident in that Christ is shown throughout the New Testament to be fulfilling those very promises which Yahweh gave, to save his people. While it could be argued that this is accomplished through his personal representative, i.e., his Son, and need mean no more than Jesus is Yahweh's appointed agent, it fails to take in the whole of the New Testament evidence. New Testament Christology is clearly basically functional, and not only is Jesus seen to be fulfilling the Messianic promises, but into this fulfilment model are drawn statements that can mean nothing other than that Jesus is uniquely and ontologically identified with Yahweh. It is Yahweh's titles and unique claims that the Son is given. Thus, for example, Jesus is 'the resurrection and the life' (John 11:25) as well as the first and the last (Rev. 1:8), titles that are clearly linked to the firstborn description (cf. Rev. 1: 5-7; Col. 1:13-20 and Heb. 1:1-6).

The *prōtotokos* texts in the New Testament.

There are seven references to the firstborn in the New Testament. They are Matthew 1:25 (paralleled in Luke 2:7); Romans 8:29; Colossians 1:15 and 18; Hebrews 1:6; 12:23; and Revelation 1:5. Because the Colossian passage is such a key text I shall deal with it in the next chapter where I can address it more fully. Here I will consider the remaining references and their relationship to the theme that we have been considering.

Matthew 1:25

The significance of the statement that Mary brought forth her firstborn and laid him in a manger has perplexed translators for generations. They were not able to understand why Matthew should say such an obvious thing. The whole narrative has stressed that until then Mary had no other children, the statement was therefore redundant. Indeed, the presence of the statement in the text has finally been excluded from most modern translations. To justify this exclusion an odd text is appealed to, which under normal rules of textual criticism would not be given any authority, for not only does it have no other support but it is very late indeed. The textual critic's maxim is that material is added through the course of time to make the text easier, but not normally removed unless, as far as the offending copyist is concerned, there is a very good reason.

To go along with the modern translators we have to reason that the alleged original reading simply referred to Jesus as Mary's son. At a later date a copyist added 'firstborn son' to his text and so introduced a new variant. The immediate problem for this position is that the textual evidence is saying the very reverse, for there is simply no evidence that the firstborn reference was ever not part of the earliest texts.

What would the reason be for adding 'she brought forth her firstborn son'? It is claimed that the redactor wanted to buttress the teaching of the virgin birth. Now this is obviously a possibility, if only the textual evidence for Matthew supported it. But what effectively blows the argument clean out of the water is that the same phrase is found in Luke 2:7, and in that case there is absolutely not a shred of textual evidence for saying that it has been added by a copyist. No Lucan text misses the statement out. Because of this, the very translators who opt to leave it out of Matthew 1:25 are stuck with it in Luke 2:7.

If the text is left untampered, what is Matthew seeking to say through this 'unnecessary' statement? Being a very Jewish story for the Jewish church, it is clearly marking Jesus as the Lord's firstborn. Every Jewish listener of the story of Matthew would instinctively know that this is the Lord's redeemer, the one who will save his people from their sins. Jesus is being introduced as the child born to die, the king, the firstborn, whose destiny is suffering to bring salvation to his people.

This is certainly supported by the way Luke uses the same phrase. He also, using the logic of the modern translators, unnecessarily repeats himself, or does he? There are a number of strange things in the account of Luke that are not so strange once we have the reason for this statement sorted out. Why do Joseph and Mary take the baby Jesus to the temple? It was next to the palace of Herod, the very seat of his government, and they knew that he sought the life of the child.

It was not that they had to do it in order to fulfil the law. Simply paying the prescribed half shekel to a scribe could redeem the firstborn child. In fact, despite saying that everything was done according to the requirement of the law, it is clearly limited to the purification of Mary, for that is what the sacrifice of the doves was to achieve. What is not mentioned, and this is incredible considering it would be the most important thing that every Jewish couple had to do on the birth of their firstborn, is that they never redeemed the child.[58] The child was no longer Joseph and Mary's, for he was the Lord's firstborn, for they failed to redeem him. This makes sense of Mary singing Hannah's song (1 Sam. 2:1-10; Luke 1:46-55), for she too gave her son to the Lord. It also explains why Jesus was surprised that Joseph and Mary had not expected him to be in the temple when he was found to be missing from the returning pilgrim party (Luke 2:49). The reply, 'Did you not know that I must be about my Father's business?', and his presence in the temple was part of his preparation, and suggests that Jesus was conscious of a priestly calling from his youth.

Again, it explains why he should say that Mary was not his mother (Luke 8:19-21). The natural ties had been severed because they had not redeemed him.

Romans 8:29
The meaning of this verse is normally interpreted as Paul saying nothing more than that Christ is the elder brother in the family of God. This, however, misses the flow of the Roman letter. Once it has been accepted that 3:21ff. is Paschal, and that Christ is the Passover sacrifice, then the term 'firstborn' takes on a soteriological significance. We saw earlier that one of the roles of the redeemer, who ideally was the firstborn, was to restore to the family their lost inheritance. This is the theme of the preceding verses. The whole creation, in bondage through the fall, has been redeemed. It waits for the final display of the redemption of the sons of God. It groans, waiting for its own liberation. This will happen when man is re-established as Lord of creation. Christ is the firstborn of many brethren in that he has acted on their behalf, to restore them not only to fellowship with God, but also to the dignity for which they were created. This is possible only because in the context of the Passover sacrifice, 3:21ff., he has died as the 'firstborn of all creation'. Further evidence

---

[58]Noted by Wright, *Testament, passim*, and Platcher, 'Place,' 10.

that the above exegesis is correct is given in the passage itself. It is easy to forget that the statement about Christ being the firstborn of many brothers is the conclusion of an argument that began at the opening of the chapter, and is a further development, as already indicated, of the 3:21ff. passage. Lest it be thought that the sacrificial language of 3:21 is too far removed to control the meaning of this statement, 8:3 says exactly the same thing. Christ by his death as a sin offering has brought the power of Sin to an end. By the gift of his Spirit he has equipped his people for their pilgrimage and made them his sons. The passage is following the redemptive event of the Exodus too closely to be a coincidence. Therefore the description of Christ as the firstborn of many brothers must be understood in the light of redemptive history.

Hebrews 1:6

In this verse Christ is spoken of as God's firstborn whom he has brought into the world. He has earlier been described as the express image of the invisible God and the one who, after cleansing his people from their sins, has sat down on the right hand of the majesty on high (1:3). The passage goes on to speak of the transformation of creation when he will 'roll them up like a robe, like a garment they will be changed' (1:12). The second chapter goes on to emphasise the oneness of Christ with his people, using clear Adamic imagery (2:5-8). Once again, the same motifs found in the other occurrences of the firstborn title are found, i.e. those of redemption, kingship and creation.

In 12:23 the writer tells his readers that they have come to the church of the 'first-born'. It is the church which belongs to the firstborn, for it exists as a result of his redemptive activity when he gave himself for her as the Paschal victim (9:11-15, 24-28).[59]

Revelation 1:6

The passage speaks of Jesus being the firstborn from the dead and might at first sight seem to be limited to what it is generally seen to refer to, i.e. that Jesus is the Messianic conqueror of death. However,

---

[59]Note how Hebrews retains the Day of Atonement ritual and combines with it the Paschal theme (i.e. redemption, 9:12). No doubt this order is followed so as to show the inadequacy of the priestly ministry and to use the imagery to set Christ forth as the Great High Priest. If the author had gone straight to Ezekiel 45:22-26 he could not have made the point of Christ's priesthood having replaced that of Aaron so clearly. The end is the same – Passover and the Day of Atonement are merged.

the title is immediately followed with a hymn of praise to the all-conquering Messiah, in which he is worshipped as the one who has 'freed us from our sins by his own blood, and made us to be a kingdom of priests to serve his God and Father' (1:5). The appointment of priests was a direct consequence of the Passover where God claimed for himself all those whom he had spared from death. This is clearly New Exodus material. The Paschal significance of the passage is reinforced further when John quotes Zechariah: 'Look, he is coming with the clouds, and every eye will see him, even those who pierced him, and all the peoples of the earth will mourn because of him. So shall it be! Amen' (1:7). The ruler who has been slain returns to claim his own. The two themes of the firstborn Paschal victim and the firstborn Messiah are clearly merged.

The firstborn theme is much wider than the few references that actually contain *prōtotokos*. When it is appreciated that the firstborn was also the beloved or the only begotten son, then the firstborn Paschal theme spills over into a much wider range of texts. So, for example, the reference in John 3:16 makes much better sense when it is appreciated that the setting of the statement is entirely within the context of the Passover (2:25) and that the language of wind and water is very much the imagery borrowed from the crossing of the Red Sea. The fact that Nicodemus came to Jesus by night recalls the timing of the Passover and the allusion to the raising of the serpent in the wilderness is clearly part of the original Exodus history. Thus, in John 3:16 the only begotten Son is the beloved Son, the firstborn, whose death saves his people.

Conclusion

The above evidence suggests that the role of the firstborn in the Passover was vitally important to the early church who used its imagery to describe the work of Jesus.[60] While there are possible extra-biblical sources that can be suggested as providing the seedbed for New Testament theological development, it seems that the New Testament writers stayed within Old Testament paradigms.

---

[60]It also explains why many of the Patristic Fathers focused on Passover when writing of the death of Jesus.

Chapter Twelve

Firstborn and the Colossian Hymn

The purpose of this chapter is to argue that the letter to the Colossians provides evidence of a Paschal theology in the early church. This is a perspective that until now has gone unnoticed. This oversight is despite the growing appreciation of the presence of the New Exodus as a controlling paradigm in the thought pattern of the early Christian community. Regardless of the growing recognition of the influence of the Exodus motif, the Passover as the heart of the Exodus has not been explored. Of course, at the heart of the Passover is the death of the firstborn.

My intention in the first part of this chapter is to search for the possible origins of the hymn, which is the most important part of the theology of the letter. If there is evidence that the Passover/Exodus celebration is a valid possibility, then the relevance of the hymn to a Paschal theology will be explored. If this theme can be identified as being present, then the theology of the letter is integral with the theology of Romans, which we have seen to have distinct Paschal/Exodus strands. This in turn will demonstrate the error of assuming that Paul was the originator of a new theological understanding. It will rather establish that there is no reason why Paul could not have written Colossians and also that Paul is one with Jesus in centring his death in the event of the Passover. It will also, if found to be Paschal based, provide further evidence that Paul's thinking is Semitic and not Hellenistic.

The Colossian letter has been at the centre of an ongoing unresolved debate in Pauline studies. There are those who say that the theology of the letter is uncharacteristic of Paul. This is largely because of the presence of a highly developed cosmic Christology, which is considered to be too late to be genuine Pauline material. It is claimed that this is proof that the letter is the product of a second century imitator. The motives for this imitation are seen to range from a Paulinist who sought to promote what he thought would be his teacher's views in the developing challenges to the gospel, to an impostor of a less worthy sort. Either way, Pauline authorship is denied and the letter disqualified as a source in any inquiry into Paul's thought.

I would argue that Paschal theology challenges the viability of rejecting Pauline authorship on the basis of supposed theological incompatibility. Indeed, I would argue that the differences are not due to development but due to the use of wrong paradigms and methods to interpret Paul. There are others, however, who see no need to question the authenticity of the letter even without appealing to the Paschal theology that I am proposing. These scholars are equally convinced that there is no basic conflict with other undisputed Pauline letters. They claim that any apparent variations in thought are merely the inevitable developments to be expected as the apostle adjusted his language and arguments to the particular problems that prevailed at Colossae.

The authorship and theology of the hymn

The authorship of the hymn has likewise divided scholarship.[1] Those who accept that the letter is Pauline divide into three groups. There are those who say the passage is an independent composition of the early church as a hymn in praise of Christ. Ellingworth is a representative of this group and says that the ideas in the hymn are congenial to Paul but not identical with his theology.[2] Others think that Paul quoted the hymn as a confessional statement. His aim, they argue, was to secure common agreement in introducing the theme of his letter.[3] To do this he used in the opening of the letter a passage that many of his readers would recognise from their worship. A third group see no need to deny Pauline authorship of the hymn.[4] These claim that it is Paul's own composition in praise of the cosmic Christ. Most of this group see the hymn as having been influenced by the Jewish Wisdom tradition.

Those who claim Pauline authorship of the letter, but deny the Pauline authorship of the hymn, quite often share a similar view to

[1] I will not discuss the structure of the hymn nor which lines belong to it. The standard commentaries deal with these aspects.

[2] Ellingworth, 'Colossians,' 252-3.

[3] So Allmen, 'Reconciliation,' 38-9, and Murphy-O'Connor, *Paul,* 242, who argues that the hymn was brought from Colossae by Epaphras.

[4] Rollins, 'Tendenz,' 125, says, 'Paul responds as a Jew and thinks as a Christian about the cross and resurrection.' Those who deny the Pauline authorship of the letter normally see the hymn to have been quarried out of Gnostic Wisdom traditions and adapted as a hymn to praise Christ.

those who deny the authenticity of the letter itself. Both normally see the hymn as an adaptation of a Greek or a Jewish hymn in praise of Wisdom. By the adaptation of this hymn, Christ is proclaimed as the unifying principle of creation and, as such, without any rival. Because he is without equal, there is no creature that can be allowed to share in the worship or honour that is due to him alone. The hymn is important for it is the key to the theology of the letter; as Lohse says, 'Colossians unfolds its Christology on the basis of the Christ hymn cited at the beginning.'[5]

The debate concerning the theology of the hymn mostly centres on the meaning of the term *prōtotokos* (firstborn). Some see the 'title' as hierarchical, while others see it to be ontological. Dunn, however, is clear as to what he thinks the origin of the term 'firstborn' is: 'The antecedent for the use of the word πρωτοτοκος (firstborn) in relation to creation is most obviously Wisdom.'[6] Casey argues that the historical reason for its adaptation was that 'The inclusion of a larger number of educated men had also forced attention on philosophical problems with which Palestinian Judaism was not concerned ... introduced ways of thinking which were foreign to all but the Hellenistic Jewish mind.... Nobody seems to be in doubt that OT and later Jewish Wisdom speculation has provided a great number of the motifs and even vocabulary.'[7]

Some see that the source of the Wisdom of the hymn is Judaism itself.[8] Vawter, while agreeing that the vocabulary was from Old Testament Wisdom vocabulary, yet argues: 'But only in some artificial sort of way can personified-Wisdom ideas be seen as the model for the portrayal of a cosmic redeemer.'[9] Although acknowledging that there are several blocks of similar material in the New Testament, he yet says, 'We do not really know what function this distinctive form served in the ecclesial communities that made use of it.'[10] Burney suggested that the hymn was similar to a Rabbinic Midrash in which Proverbs 8 was used to interpret Genesis 1.[11] This has been followed by many scholars and is the majority view at the present time.

[5]Lohse, *Colossian*, 214, so also Weiss, 'Colossians,' 306
[6]Dunn, *Colossians* 90.
[7]Casey, 'Earliest,' 268. So also Vawter, 'Hymn,' 71.
[8]Schreiner, Apostle, 156.
[9]Vawter, 'Hymn,' 72
[10]*op. cit.* 69.
[11]Burney, 'ΑΡΧΗ' 174.

While the Wisdom motif is widely accepted, even those who see it as being the most plausible meaning have misgivings. The difficulties centre on the fact that there are a number of unresolved tensions within the idea of Wisdom Christology. One of the problems is that neither the Torah nor the Messiah were understood to be eternal in Judaism, yet this is an attribute essential for the orthodox understanding of Christology.[12] Furthermore, as Martin, who accepts a Wisdom Christology, acknowledges: 'Nothing in the teaching on Wisdom adumbrates the theme of redemption, whether cosmic or personal.'[13] O'Brien notes that there is no statement in Jewish Wisdom literature, nor in any other Jewish literature, which shows that Wisdom was seen to be the goal of creation.[14] Balchin notes that the gender of *sophia* is feminine and that the title would more naturally be related to the Holy Spirit than the incarnate Christ.[15] Balchin claims that this is evidence of the church's 'discriminating creativity', in that it could adapt such material. Others do not believe that gender would have had the same significance for the ancients as it does for modern people.

Another problem is raised by Witherington. Even though he supports the Wisdom interpretation of *prōtotokos*, he acknowledges that 'One cannot say of Sophia (personified Wisdom) that she is the head of the body'.[16] His solution is to assign this to the Pauline hand as a result of his editing of the original hymn in praise of Wisdom.

The danger of getting the context of the hymn wrong has been noted by a number of scholars. For example, de Lacy says that it is inadmissible to collect Wisdom material from a range of sources without any reference to how it was used in its original setting and then use the collected texts to construct a Biblically based Christology.[17] This unease is accentuated when it is appreciated that there is a weakness in the original premise on which much of the work has been built. Most modern discussion is based on Burney's argument, yet the Rabbinic source which Burney used as his model (acknowledged by Burney, yet not with any caution considering the weight given to it) is late third century AD. Such a late dating seriously

[12]so Delling, *TDNT* 5:478-89.
[13]Martin, *Colossians*, 48.
[14]O'Brien, *Colossians*, 40.
[15]Balchin, *Significance,* 212.
[16]Witherington, *Narrative*, 106.
[17]De Lacy, 'Mediator,' passim.

weakens its usefulness as evidence of what was in the mind of the writer of the Colossian Christ Hymn.

The widely accepted Jewish Wisdom content of the hymn does have in its favour the fact that it has returned to Judaism for its origin. This does justice to the Semitisms that are much in evidence in the material and which could hardly be expected if the hymn was originally a Hellenistic work. It is however the presence of such an array of Semitisms that has persuaded O'Neill to postulate that the hymn is nothing more than a collection of Old Testament motifs about the creativity of God, strung together as a confessional statement.[18] Hunter observes the early position of the verb and the parallelism, which he thinks reflects a Semitic origin.[19] Pannenberg, though supporting the personification of Wisdom as the meaning of *prōtotokos*, says that early Christology was Old Testament based but its origin was lost in the second century.[20] If these Semitic observations are correct, then the hymn has to be interpreted from the perspective of the Old Testament theology out of which it has come.

What is widely accepted by scholarship is that the introduction to the hymn (vs. 12-14) is based on the New Exodus promise. It speaks of being delivered from the kingdom of darkness and being brought into the kingdom of light. The theme of the introduction is so emphatic that it is one of the few uncontested aspects of the letter. Klijn sees the language of verses 12-14 to be reflecting the LXX description of the Exodus or Isaiah 63:15-19.[21] Martin comments: 'The church, like Israel before her, celebrated her Exodus, the New Exodus, and rehearsed and recalled by dynamic story re-telling – so Col. 1:15-29,

---

[18]O'Neill, 'Source,' 91, also noted the poor metrical form of the hymn. He claimed that Colossians 1:9-23 and 2:6-15 were taken directly from Jewish sources. He wrote, '[T]he Christology which these citations express was not the result of long Christian meditation on the death and resurrection of Christ; rather, the Christology was something that had grown up in Judaism long before'(p. 99). O'Neill, *op. cit.* 97, also noted that the passage contains ideas which are at home in the cosmological meditations of parts of Judaism and so the author of the letter was able to quote these passages without comment. It would be obvious to him and to his readers that this redemption had been fulfilled in the death of Jesus Christ on the cross. The author could safely leave the texts as they were to speak for themselves.

[19]Hunter, *Predecessors*, 125.

[20]Pannenberg, *Jesus,* 156-58.

[21]Klijn, 'Study,' 428.

Phil. 2:6-11, 1 Tim. 3:16.'[22] Martin also says that the Christian confessional hymns 'stayed in the liturgical tradition of the Old Testament in which Exile in Egypt/Promised land were the major theme'.[23] Wright notes that 'Col. 1.15-20 is reinforced by the echoes of Jewish redemption ideas. He sees that in vv. 12-14, which evoke in particular the imagery of the Exodus, the time when Israel's God showed himself to be God of the whole world by defeating both the Egyptians and the mighty waters of the sea. The New Exodus was the act of New Creation, bringing the chosen race to a new birth out of chaos and slavery. The same impression is given by the verses (21-3) which follow the poem, in which the God of all the earth (v. 23) has become responsible for the reconciliation of the Colossians and their grafting into his true people (v. 22).'[24] Shogren notes that 1:13 is not about individuals entering the Kingdom of God but about the church corporately.[25]

If the introduction is, as would normally be the case, the major determining factor in interpreting the material that follows, then it brings the hymn into the Paschal setting. This is the hymn's inevitable setting because redemption (v. 14), in the original Exodus, was the Passover sacrifice. *Consequently, the hymn must be read in a redemptive context.* This is recognised to varying degrees by some scholars. There are those who see the whole of the hymn as speaking of redemption while others think that it is verses 18ff. that alone relate to this theme. Surprisingly, few see that this is what the introduction itself has determined. In fact, it is not only the introduction that fixes the context for the interpretation of the main text, but the conclusion tells what should have been understood in the reading or hearing of the text.

The importance of the introduction and the conclusion is so obvious that it need not be argued. Despite this, scholarship has repeatedly failed to take note of these two key determinative factors for the interpretation of the hymn. Here in this piece of poetry the conclusion states: 'through him to reconcile to himself all things, whether things on earth or things in heaven, by making peace through his blood, shed on the cross.' The conclusion clearly speaks of an act of cosmic

[22]Martin, 'Reflections,' 44.
[23]*op. cit.* p39.
[24]Wright, 'Poetry,' 452-54.
[25]Shogren, Entering, 180.

reconciliation achieved through the shedding of blood. Whatever the passage is about, surely to force it into discussions of philosophical abstractions of any sort is to miss the mark by miles. It is a discussion/reflection on the redemption that has been achieved through the shedding of Christ's blood. The setting for interpreting the hymn must therefore be cultic.

The choice of the background is straightforward in terms of identifying possibilities. It comes from one of the following:

a. It was a Greek hymn in praise of Wisdom.

b. It was a Jewish hymn in praise of Wisdom.

c. It was a hymn celebrating the Day of Atonement.

d. It was a hymn celebrating the Passover.

e. It was a confessional statement of the creativity of Israel's God.

My judgment is that the strong emphasis on redemption in the introduction and conclusion of the hymn supports the celebration of the Passover. This brings the term *prōtotokos* into the realm of soteriology rather than ontology in which it is normally understood to be rooted. This in turn suggests that a previously unidentified Paschal theology exists in the writings of the New Testament. While the importance of 'd' is central, we must note that 'c' is present because we have found propitiation to be in the original Passover sacrifice, and 'e' is present because the New Exodus is about Yahweh's new creation.

Redemption and creation

As we have noted, scholarship is increasingly appreciating that the New Exodus motif was widely used by Paul. What has not been appreciated is that at the centre of that model was the death of the beloved Son. His death was the key to the redemption of his people. In calling Christ the *prōtotokos* of all creation Paul is attributing to the death of Christ, the only begotten or only beloved Son, something that no other firstborn's death ever achieved. His death has achieved the redemption of the whole of creation. Indeed, cosmic redemption is certainly not a peripheral theme, it is at the heart of the hymn. It would therefore seem that Christ's status is not limited merely to representing his family, considerable as that would be as the goal of redemption. He also represents the whole of creation. As the last Adam he is 'the firstborn of all creation'. Such an understanding has removed the title from the category of an ontological description and has placed it firmly in the realm of soteriology.

Isaiah and the new creation. One of the great themes of Isaiah's prophecy was that the redeemer would bring about the redemption not only of Israel from her distress, but of the whole creation from under the curse. This expectation, in the setting of first-century Judaism with its widely held expectation of a New Exodus, would have given the primitive Christian community the material to work with in the very earliest stages of its reflections. They did not need to wait for help from Hellenistic insights to reach a cosmic soteriology. Cosmic salvation had been long anticipated within Judaism itself. Isaiah had predicted that creation itself would be renewed when the children of God were delivered from their captivity (55:12-13; 65:17-25). This is of immense significance, for this section of Isaiah is dominated by the theme of Yahweh being Israel's redeemer who restores her to her inheritance, the land. Yahweh is Israel's redeemer who for her sake redeems creation from the curse of the fall.

Thus the New Testament is making use of the New Exodus theme, presented with particular clarity by Isaiah. The favourite title of Yahweh is the Redeemer of Israel, so it becomes especially significant, as noted in the previous chapter, that the title 'redeemer' is absent from the entire New Testament as a description of Jesus. I would suggest that there can only be one explanation for this startling omission: Paul, like the other New Testament writers, has gone beyond Isaiah back to the first Passover. From there, he has introduced into his theology the significance of the death of the firstborn. The New Exodus, which is cosmic, is brought about by the death of the 'firstborn of all creation'. Significantly, in all those places in the New Testament where the death of Jesus is described in redemptive language, he is not called the redeemer but the firstborn. This is understandable once it is realised that the redeemer role could be abdicated and in itself did not entail vicarious suffering. It was essentially a social function and did not require the laying down of life. The firstborn was in reality to be the redeemer, but as mentioned previously he could abdicate that particular role. He could not, however, avoid the vicarious role of coming under the judgment of the angel of death, unless there was a vicarious substitute for him. In the Old Testament this was the Passover lamb; in the New Testament there is no substitute. Yahweh's firstborn must die to save his people.

Paschal links. The language used to exalt Christ further strengthens the linking of the hymn with the Passover. He is ascribed with such titles, not to compete with the pagan deities to which the Colossians were in danger of turning, but to underline the fact that he is the only one who can act as redeemer. Bedale has noted that *kephalē* (head) does not mean the head of the community as in Classical Greek, but rather, as in the LXX, it has the same meaning as *prōtotokos*, that is, husband and king/leader.[26] This is a very significant observation, for these are the very titles that were explicitly associated with the Passover. Yahweh spared the firstborn and led the people out as their king for the purpose of them becoming his bride. In other words, the connection noted earlier between the Old Testament and the New Testament, that it is only the Creator who can redeem, is being followed here with precision.

Adamic imagery. Nor is the reference to Christ as the image of the invisible God ontological. It is Adamic language referring to the role of Christ as the representative of Yahweh. While it might appear at first that such an admission weakens Trinitarian orthodoxy, the reverse is in fact the case. No creature, no matter how great, could redeem creation. As the Old Testament and the New Testament alike make clear, it can only be the creator, the Lord, who can do this. As in the Old Testament, the redeemer (firstborn) is Yahweh himself. Christ dies as the firstborn, the promised King of Israel, the last Adam, the head of the new creation, to redeem his inheritance.

Furthermore, Passover language lurks at the back of verse 18. While the statement primarily refers to the Adamic figure, the Davidic king who is the firstborn of the rulers of the earth, here it is applied to Christ's Lordship over the ultimate enemy, death itself. He is thus the king (firstborn) over death.

Furthermore, in the Old Testament the great Passover events were celebrated by the Jewish kings.[27] Indeed, according to Ezekiel the king was to be the main figure in the eschatological celebration of the Passover.[28] This has been taken up by the Gospel writers in the way they emphasise that Jesus died in the context of the Passover as King of the Jews. In other words, the use of the title 'firstborn from the dead' is drawing these redemptive threads together. As Redeemer

[26]Bedale, 'Meaning,' 211-15.
[27]2 Chronicles 30:1-24 and 35:1-19. See also Ezekiel 45:22ff.
[28]Ezekiel 40ff., see especially 45:22ff.

Christ has conquered death and delivered his people from the realm of darkness in which they lived in fear. If Paul had wanted to say Christ was the first to rise from the dead, as is so often suggested he means, he could have, and would have, used the term 'firstfruits'. However, even with such a term there is a saturation of Paschal imagery.[29] The significance of the term 'firstborn from the dead' is that Christ is the promised Messianic king who through his death and resurrection has brought everything, including death itself, under his Lordship. It was during the original Passover that Pharaoh was humbled and made to recognise the supreme lordship of Yahweh.

This Old Testament setting is further supported when it is appreciated that the claim that 'in him all the fullness dwells' (1:19) is not an ontological statement. Once again it is based on Old Testament prophetic expectation. The fullness refers to the completion of the purposes of Yahweh. His covenantal promises are brought to their climax in the person of Christ who is the promised Redeemer.[30]

The redemption of creation by the firstborn is upheld in verse 20 when the writer speaks of all things being reconciled through his blood shed on the cross. This is expanding the significance of the death of the firstborn of all creation, i.e. it achieves the reconciliation of all things. This is the high point of the hymn and is the climax of the movement that culminates in the redemption of creation. The hymn throughout is in praise of the Creator Redeemer and has grown 'from the central statement about the cross, that is, it developed, so to speak, from the second strophe backwards, just as the Old Testament doctrine

---

[29] 1 Corinthians 15:3 is based on the presentation of the firstfruits which took place three days after Passover (Lev. 23:11). Paul went on to call Christ 'the first fruits of those who sleep' (1 Cor. 15:20). Thus the imagery is thoroughly Paschal. This passage is most significant because as Dodd, *Apostolic*, 13 says, 1 Corinthians 15:3-8 is the *locus classicus* for the reconstruction of the *kerygma*. 1 Corinthians 15:20 is an early expansion of this *kerygma* evidenced in that three days links both events of resurrection and presentation of the firstfruits.

[30] Speaking of the fulfilment of the covenantal promises, which shadow the expression 'the righteousness of God' in Romans and Galatians, Moule has said, 'To a unique degree, Jesus is seen as the goal, the convergence point, of God's plan for Israel, his covenantal promises ....The Passover gathers up into itself a large number of strands of covenant promise: to speak of "its full realisation" is to use the root we are considering in a highly significant manner' (Moule, 'Fulfillment,' 294, 301).

of creation was fashioned as a consequence of the credal confession of God's historical act of redemption'.[31]

Servant imagery is adopted in 1:24-25. The servant theme is closely related to the Second Exodus pattern and the proximity to material that we have suggested is at the heart of the New Exodus motif is significant for supporting the proposed exegesis. It is the last Adam who is the Servant, the king of creation, the only begotten Son of God, the firstborn of the new creation. It is his atoning death alone that has brought about the reconciliation of all things to its Creator.

The New Exodus and Christ's victory

The cross is at the centre of the victory that Christ has achieved over all of his opponents (2:10b). Their power was shown to be impotent in the face of his self-sacrifice. Here again are echoes of the Exodus when the power of Pharaoh was broken on the night of the Passover. Until that time Pharaoh had appeared to be invincible, he was well able to match the challenges put to him by Moses. However, the Passover broke that arrogance and brought the man, who was once the mightiest man the world had known, to plead for mercy. The death of the firstborn son was a judgment on his family. The message of the Colossian letter is that there is no other Lord. All other claims to this position are false.

Once again the imagery of circumcision occurs (2:11). The rite was the essential requirement for partaking in the Passover and through that experience of sharing in the Exodus event. Paul is asserting that that requirement has been perfectly fulfilled in the death of Christ. He speaks not of an act done on them, but for them, through the death of Christ himself. There is no danger of this circumcision ever becoming a work, for it was done to Christ on man's behalf. It is grace from beginning to end.

That the New Exodus material continues to be present is supported by the reference to the forgiveness of sins. Every opponent – the law, which excluded Gentiles from the covenants of promise (2:14), and all powers and authorities (2:15) – has been overcome to make the

---

[31]However, Gibbs, the author of the above comment, failed to see the connection he had made with the great redemptive event of the Old Testament, i.e. the Exodus, and the passage he was expounding. Consequently, he failed to see the significance of the title 'firstborn of all creation' (*Creation*, 101).

believers' freedom possible. As the triumph of Yahweh over Pharaoh took place on the night of the Passover when the firstborn of Egypt were slain, so Christ has triumphed 'by the cross' (2:15) when he, the firstborn, died.

Because of this eschatological victory, the Colossians are free from all of the ceremonial regulations that had governed them in the previous age. These regulations were merely the shadow of what has now come in Christ (2:17). The church's death with Christ (2:20) means that believers have died to the law as a way of achieving righteousness.

Because the Colossians have died with Christ, they have also been raised with him and share his eschatological victory (3:1). They are to live in the light of this fact. As the Jews were called to live a new lifestyle as a result of their deliverance from Egypt, so the Colossians are urged to live worthy of the Lord their Redeemer (3:2-10). The appeal is not essentially to individual believers, although they must personally respond to the responsibilities of being part of the covenant community, but to the Colossian church.

The corporate basis of the appeal is supported by the command to put on the 'new man' (v. 10). The new man is not an individual, he is the Christian community made in the image of its head. The regular application of the term to the individual believer has caused confusion and distress in sensitive souls who have been distraught that they have not attained such a goal. The believer will not attain it until the church has attained it fully on the day of Christ's return. That is not to nullify the quest for personal holiness, but to set it in its proper context.

The salutations in chapter 4 are general and appears to add nothing of a theological nature to the main section of the letter.

In this volume I have argued for the Paschal/New Exodus motif as fundamental to the theology and letters of Paul. In this chapter I have provided evidence that the letter to the Colossians has the same theological perspective. There is therefore no need to treat the letter as anything other than a Pauline letter.

Conclusion

And so our study, as far as Paul and his doctrine of salvation is concerned, is concluded. It has necessitated looking at his use of the Old Testament and seeing how he stayed faithful to its thought patterns and expectations. We have seen how he saw himself to be part of the Hebrew tradition of the prophets declaring the will of Yahweh to his people, and going beyond that, to declare the message of Abraham's God to the Gentiles. This was something that the prophets rarely did, and then usually under constraint. In this Paul was extending the inevitable logic that came from the prophecies that the Messiah's coming would bring the nations into the blessings of the covenant. Because Paul came to see that Jesus is the Messiah, it was essential that the Gentiles should be evangelised in order to fulfil the scriptures.

We have seen that the assumptions that are made in any study affect the outcome of the work. We have challenged those who have claimed that Paul Hellenised the Christian message, so transforming it into something very different from what Jesus had proclaimed. On the evidence that has increasingly won scholarly support, that the New Testament documents, and Paul's letters no less than others, are Jewish, we have constructed a picture of Paul that has disagreed with the findings of some others who accept their Jewish character.

First, we have challenged the understanding that many have embraced, that Paul was a member of the Zealot movement before his conversion to Christ. The foundation of this argument is that Paul admitted that he was zealous for the law. It is argued from this that Paul persecuted the believers for proclaiming a law-free gospel, i.e. that the Gentiles were accepted by God without circumcision. It is understood that Paul was distressed that the Jewish disciples of Jesus taught that Gentile converts did not need to be circumcised nor follow the Jewish dietary laws nor Sabbath observance. I have argued, however, that this was not the reason for Paul's behaviour because the Gentile issue did not arise until Peter had accepted the members of Cornelius' household as members of the covenant community and baptised them. Examination of the evidence has led me to conclude that the persecution was not against the Hellenists *per se*, but against the church as a whole, and that the reason for the persecution was that they preached a crucified Messiah, something no Jew could countenance without being confronted with the resurrection. Thus the issue of circumcision was a later problem and Paul walked right into the centre of it in order to defend the Gentiles from having to submit to the badges of membership of the Old Covenant because the Old Covenant did not save. We have concluded that the whole circumcision issue was probably a political tool for the Jewish sector of the church to regain control of the movement, a policy which if successful would have altered the whole direction of the church's development and its impact on the world.

Another assumption was examined, namely, the growing dependence on Intertestamental Literature as the key into the mind-set of Judaism and, by implication, of the early church. We saw that while this literature is of considerable value in helping us to identify the major common issues that were within Judaism, yet because of the complexity of first-century Judaism, the texts are of very limited use for interpreting the New Testament. The danger has been of reading meaning into these texts that could not possibly be proved because of knowing neither the theological position of the stable they come from nor of having enough samples to construct a theology for the group. It is much safer to recognise the unquestionable influence of the Old Testament on the New Testament and to appreciate that the New Testament church had been taught how to read these scriptures in the light of the Christ event. Thus New Testament exegesis of the Old Testament is quite distinct from any other reading of the many Jewish claims rightly to understand the Old Testament texts. There is therefore no need to justify a Christian reading by appealing to other readings, for it is more likely to detract from a correct understanding than to facilitate it.

We have also seen that Paul had a much more corporate view of man than is commonly appreciated. This is in keeping with his Old Testament roots. We have found that the term 'the body of sin' in Romans 6:6 is likely to have referred to humanity outside of Christ. It is thus the kingdom of darkness, rather than the highly individualistic meaning that most commentators follow. We also found that focusing on this corporate framework of thought allows us to recognise the corporate dimension of the argument in 1 Corinthians 6:12-20 and to see that the reference to the harlot in verses 15-16 is probably a term that was used to speak of unredeemed humanity in its relationship to

Satan. These two corporate readings alerted us to the fact that Western expositors focus on the experience of individual believers whereas basic common sense ought to tell us that because they were written to churches, and of necessity communicated to the gathered church, their theology addresses the church's corporate experience of her God. This realisation caused us to seek to read the text of Paul's letters in a more corporate context and to search for better understanding of the grammatical and theological difficulties that had always been recognised but could not be resolved in the individualistic framework.

This corporate perspective helped us to pick up a previously unrecognised dimension of Paul's teaching on baptism. We noted the grammatical and theological difficulties that are associated with reading Paul's teaching as though he was expounding the significance of baptismal initiation and discovered that the texts made much better sense if we see them modelled on the Exodus event when Israel nationally was baptised unto Moses. Closer examination of the texts in the light of this clearly Pauline model helped us to see that Paul was speaking of the formation of the eschatological community rather than about individual Christian experience. We came to see that the baptism of the Spirit related to this historical saving activity and that it centred on the very death of Jesus, actually occurring in the historic moment of his death.

This corporate reading was to be a factor in the attempt to understand Paul's doctrine of justification. We found that the discussion takes place in the context of the Abrahamic covenant and that its immediate focus is not on individual justification but the way Yahweh had delivered his people from Satan's bondage and established an eternal covenant with them. In this reading we have disagreed with those who have argued that justification is about being declared to be in the covenant. It is, in our understanding, about the creation of the covenant. This is not to deny the necessity of the work of God's Spirit to bring individuals to repentance and faith and so enter into the blessings of justification when they appropriate for themselves the blessings secured historically on the cross, but it does stress that the doctrine, in Paul's understanding, is corporate. We further found that Paul's doctrine of justification is rooted in the Passover/New Exodus event.

We also explored the way Paul understood the death of Christ.

We found that Paul interpreted Jesus' death, as Jesus himself had done, as the fulfilment of the Passover. In examining Paul from this perspective, we found that the Colossian hymn's description of Christ being the firstborn of all creation fitted into the cultic introduction and conclusion of the hymn. This explained the repeated Semitisms found in the hymn that had no logical connection with the theme of personified wisdom that has been imposed on the hymn by most modern scholars. We found[1] in exploring the theme of wisdom in Paul that, rather than it having ontological roots, it was repeatedly used in the context of redemptive history. It is often used by Paul in a setting where the prophets were quoted when referring to Yahweh showing his wisdom in redeeming Israel from her bondage. Isaiah had predicted that creation itself would share in this redemption. In this we have unearthed a confused methodology that has led to the misreading of Paul in a crucial area. Paul did not bring the church to a 'high Christology', rather the church had it from reading the prophets long before Paul's conversion. Once this Paschal setting for Paul's (or better, the church's) Christology has been appreciated, we can see that the One who redeems creation through his death is none other that its Creator. That only the Creator can redeem creation, a fact repeatedly asserted throughout the Old Testament, strongly implies that the Creator/Redeemer has died on the cross. In the light of this understanding it becomes clear why Paul has used the language of Colossians 1:16. He is setting out the credentials of Christ being the Redeemer of creation – it is because he is its Creator. This in turn leads us into a Biblical Trinitarianism that is not the result of philosophical speculation but the result of Salvation history.

This Paschal perspective was found to explain the rest of Paul's statements concerning the death of Jesus, not least Romans 3:21-25 which we saw was loaded with signals that directed us to the Passover. The same Paschal pattern was found to be throughout the New Testament and so we established that there was atonement/propitiation in both the original and the predicted eschatological Passovers. We have established that this understanding was shared by all of the New Testament writers who wrote on the subject of the death of Christ and its significance for salvation.

We also surveyed the biblical literature to understand the role of the firstborn and noted that ideally he was the Old Testament *go'el* or redeemer. This identification explained why the latter term is never

[1] See Appendix 4

used of Christ in the New Testament, whereas the actual imagery of the work of the redeemer is used to describe his work. 'Firstborn' takes the work of the redeemer into the heart of the Passover sacrifice, and in this sacrifice Christ buys back his people from slavery, takes them as his bride, and redeems creation to restore it to humanity so that he can continue his rule over his inheritance. Christ as the Firstborn/Redeemer also executes judgement on the slayer of his people.

The conclusion of this study is that two major lenses have been missing from virtually all New Testament exegesis and that their absence has had a detrimental effect on properly appreciating the message of Paul. The first is the lens of the Passover and the second is the lens of a corporate reading of the texts. The rediscovery of these two factors bring a far more coherent understanding to the teaching of the apostle in the areas of Christology, salvation and anthropology.

Appendix 1

Review of Exodus and Paschal Theology

The New Exodus in the Gospels

Study of the New Exodus has generally been limited to viewing the New Testament from the perspective of the Egyptian exodus. The scarcity of research into the New Exodus promised by the prophets covers the whole New Testament.

Balentine studied the New Exodus presence in the Gospels as far back as 1961.[1] Bowman identified the New Exodus theme in the Gospel of Mark. He recognised that the Rabbinic writings had equated the Davidic prince with the Servant figure of Isaiah and saw it as the basis for the amalgamation of Psalm 2:7 and Isaiah 42:1 in Mark 1:11.[2] Despite this, rather than exploring the significance of the New Exodus as predicted by the prophets, Bowman interacted almost exclusively with the type of the Exodus from Egypt. He built his argument around the fact there was a Midrash on Song of Solomon 2:10ff. in *Midrash Ex Rabba* which spoke of the New Exodus of the Messiah as being like the first.[3] Bowman recognised the influence of Isaiah on the mind of Jesus and of Pharisaism in forming their missionary zeal and concluded that it would, in the light of Isaiah's expectation, be 'strange if Jesus Himself did not envisage the kingdom of God embracing all mankind'.[4] But Bowman's exegesis, limited to the Egyptian Exodus, is so strained that he has to put the giving of the law before the Exodus in order to keep any semblance of a parallel.[5]

Piper saw a wider influence of the theme: 'Exodus did not only provide the ideas by which the Primitive Church interpreted its own existence, fate and destination, but also helped to shape the Gospel Story.'[6] He noted how both Jeremiah and Isaiah had used the Exodus to interpret their own situation. Also he demonstrated the deep

---

[1] Balentine, *Concept, passim* and 'Jesus.'
[2] Bowman, *Mark*, 106-8.
[3] op. cit. 116 cf 100.
[4] op. cit. 172.
[5] op. cit. 199-200.
[6] Piper, 'Unchanging,' 16.

impression the Exodus had left on the understanding and worship of the Jews. He suggested that the reason why Paul began his sermon in the synagogue at Antioch in Pisidia was that he saw it as the first instance in which the coming of Christ announced itself.[7] Piper demonstrated the extent of the New Exodus theme throughout the New Testament and saw it to have come from Jesus himself.[8] While Piper's article was an extensive survey of the New Exodus theme in the New Testament, there is no suggestion that he has seen the creativity of the early church in linking the New Exodus promises of the eighth-century prophets, with all their theological motifs, to the Mosaic exodus. By missing this he, like others, failed to explore the full significance of the theme.

Klijn argued that the Gospels were built around the type of the Exodus.[9] He noted that a prominent part of all the Gospels is the passion narrative[10] and there saw a structural correspondence between the Gospels and Exodus.[11] Klijn argued: 'The authoritative sayings of Jesus that are interspersed through the narratives of his saving acts are then clearly to be identified as the new covenant equivalents of the directives of Moses to Israel in Exodus and elsewhere in the Pentateuch.' He concluded: '...the New Testament gospels and the Book of Exodus are to be viewed as a single genre.'[12] Klijn further noted how Luke set Jesus' career in an Exodus setting from the very beginning of his Gospel, citing Luke 1:68 and 2:38 as evidence.[13] While Klijn identified the Isaianic Servant as a theme, he did not appreciate the major contribution of the prophet to the New Exodus and so, like many others, restricted his understanding largely to the Egyptian Exodus.

Daube saw that there was a widespread New Exodus pattern that he detected by making comparisons between sections of the Gospels and established *Haggadah*.[14] He demonstrated that much of the Gospel material was based on the Passover eve liturgy provided by contemporary Jewish patterns of celebration, but he failed to appreciate

---

[7] see Acts 13:14ff., and especially verses 16-23.

[8] *op. cit.* 19.

[9] Klijn, 'Origins,' 1-17.

[10] *op. cit.* 5.

[11] *op. cit.* 6

[12] *op. cit.* 7.

[13] *op. cit.* 11.

[14] Daube, 'Structures,' 174-87.

the scale of this influence on the New Testament writers.

Sahlin commented that 'The typological parallel between the historical Exodus and the Messianic deliverance, which was thus anticipated by Early Judaism, is also fundamental for the New Testament, and to a far greater extent than we generally realize.'[15]

Davies also identified the Exodus as a key to understanding the Jewish scriptures: 'To understand the Hebrew canon, then, well-defined, extra-ordinary, historical memories – of the exodus, Sinai and the exile – have to be recognised as formative.'[16]

Mànek produced a study of the New Exodus as found in Luke and claimed that the departure of Jesus from Jerusalem was like the departure of the Jews from Egypt, both bringing judgment on those who did not believe.[17] He argued that the forty days that Jesus spent with the disciples after his resurrection were parallel to the forty years spent in the wilderness by the Jews before entering into their inheritance. However, because Mànek identified Moses as the type of Jesus, he totally missed the Davidic emphasis at the beginning of the Gospel and consequently failed to see that Luke expanded the Exodus typology to include the Babylonian Exodus with its Davidic leader.

While Marshall did not see the New Exodus link, his study on the title 'Son of God' showed that in its primitive form it was a functional description and related to Jesus' role as the Messiah.[18] In establishing this he showed that the Davidic prince was latent in the title, and, without Marshall realising it, with all of the promises that the prince's ministry would bring in the eschatological age as a result of the New Exodus.

Garrett said that Luke viewed the resurrection and ascension of Jesus and the subsequent fall of Satan – which together constitute the antitype to the exodus from Egypt – to have in turn become a new typological model for divine intervention in human history. Garrett recognises the influence of Isaiah on Luke.[19]

Nixon produced a short study on the theme of the Exodus in the New Testament and demonstrated the presence of Exodus themes

[15]Sahlin, 'Exodus,' 82.
[16]Davies, 'Canon,' 30.
[17]Mànek, 'Luke,' 8ff.
[18]Marshall, 'Reconsideration,' 326ff.
[19]Garrett, 'Bondage,' 670.

throughout, but without suggesting that he appreciated the significance of the motif as a major key for interpreting the New Testament.[20] Smith saw the influence of the Egyptian Exodus on the Gospel of John, but failed to see how the eighth-century prophetic predictions had been merged into the original type.[21] Marsh noted the importance of the Exodus for interpreting the Jesus event but like so many others did not appreciate the synthesis of the two Exoduses and so was dominated by the Egyptian model.[22] McCasland noted how the signs and wonders of the Gospels were based on the signs and wonders performed in the Exodus from Egypt.[23] Beasley-Murray acknowledged the expectation of a New Exodus but showed no appreciation of the prophets' predictions for understanding the New Testament.[24]

Murray noted the power of the original Exodus in shaping Zechariah's prophecy in Luke 1:67ff.[25] Baily focused on the song of Mary and its relation to New Exodus expectations.[26] Goppelt, in a work that was a study of typology, gave an extensive note on the influence of the New Exodus motif.[27] Dennison gave an excellent brief summary of the influence of the Exodus on both Old Testament and New Testament thinking.[28]

In recent years the theme of the New Exodus as seen from the perspective of Isaiah has been more clearly identified as having a major influence on New Testament thinking. Watts' work on the presence of the Isaianic New Exodus theme in Mark shows that the introduction of the Gospel was programmatic for the understanding of the Gospel as a whole.[29] Watts' contribution was to appreciate that Bowman had not given attention to the contribution of Isaiah and the prophetic expectation of a New Exodus. Watts' own failure was not to pay sufficient attention to the Paschal theme itself, so missing the cultic interplay between the two Exoduses that the New Testament

[20] Nixon, *Exodus*, 1ff.

[21] Smith, 'Typology,' 329.

[22] Marsh, 'Christ,' 57.

[23] McCasland, 'Signs.'

[24] Beasley-Murray, 'Kingdom,' 28.

[25] Murray, *Covenant*, 25; also see *Pattern*, 4-5.

[26] Baily, 'Vision,' 27-41.

[27] Goppelt, *Typos*, 38, note 99.

[28] Dennison, 'Exodus,' 6-32.

[29] Watts, *Influence*, 113ff. Watts has also written an excellent article on the New Exodus in the Bible, see 'Exodus,' in NDBT, 478-87.

writers make. This led him to consider that Isaiah 53 was behind Mark 10:45. Strauss has more recently demonstrated the importance of the Davidic figure for Luke-Acts and has noticed that his ministry is concerned with the fulfilment of the New Exodus promises.[30] Neither scholar has appreciated the significance of the Passover and because of this they have failed to explore a wealth of theological thought that would have brought rich reward.

Swartley sees the Sinai tradition to have influenced the introductions to the Synoptic Gospels, that the pilgrimage section has influenced the journey narratives, and the Zion tradition (i.e. the prophets) has influenced the passion narratives.[31] This last tradition focuses on the Son of David cleansing and providing a temple for the nations to worship in. Swartley has noted the Exodus motif's influence on the earlier part of the Synoptics but argues that the eucharist focused not on the Passover but on the Messianic banquet of Isaiah 25:6.[32]

Longman and Reid have produced a study on the theme of God as the divine warrior. It shows clearly that this theme is a key feature of Isaiah's New Exodus motif and that it is found throughout the New Testament.[33] This theme has been studied in greater depth by Yoo who concentrates his study in Matthew paying special attention to the exorcism of the Gadarene in Matthew 8:28-34.[34] Neuffeld studied the theme with special reference to the armoury imagery in the letter to the Ephesians.[35]

New Exodus in the Epistles and Revelation

The study of the New Exodus in the Epistles is not as advanced as that done in the Gospels. However, observations have been made on the presence of the New Exodus without appreciating the significance of the texts for establishing a hermeneutic model.

Davies says that Paul 'obviously regards the great deliverance at the Exodus and its companiments as the prototype of the mighty acts of God in Christ', and cites 1 Corinthians 5:6-8; 10:1ff; 15:20 and 2 Corinthians 3:1-17 as evidence.[36]

---

[30] Strauss, *Davidic*, 341.

[31] Swartley, *Scriptures*, 105.

[32] Swartley, *Scriptures*, 309.

[33] Longman and Reid, *Warrior*, 1ff.

[34] Yoo, *War*.

[35] Neuffeld, *Armour*.

[36] Davies, *Rabbinic*, 105.

Kirby identified the contribution of Isaiah to the New Exodus when examining the Old Testament basis of the use of the theme of light in Ephesians,[37] and argued that the Corinthians must at least have been aware of the details of the Passover otherwise Paul could not have made 'throwaway' statements about various Passover details.[38] However, he missed the opportunity of developing this theme because he thought that the dominant festival in New Testament Jewish thinking was that of Pentecost. He concluded this because of the importance of the festival in the book of Jubilees and the Dead Sea Scrolls.[39] To claim such an exclusive concentration on Pentecost in Jubilees is strange since Jubilees interprets history from a Paschal perspective. Indeed, Kirby explicitly states that believers are not on a pilgrimage,[40] thus cutting himself off from the theme of the New Exodus pilgrim community.

While some have noted the presence of Exodus material in the epistles, until recently there have been only a few who have appreciated the significance of the eighth-century prophetic expectation as a vitally important determinative theme for interpreting the epistles.[41] Goldsworthy, for example, sees the prophetic New Exodus promises influencing the theology of the New Testament without appreciating the extent of the themes that develop from the motif.[42] Carrington says that Paul used an Exodus Midrash in composing 1 and 2 Corinthians.[43]

Webb has also made a substantial study of the New Exodus theme in 2 Corinthians 6:14–7:1.[44] To establish the claim that the passage contains New Covenant material from the prophets, he analysed the preceding passage from chapter 2:14 and demonstrated that there is

[37] Kirby, *Ephesians*, 72.

[38] *op. cit.* 77.

[39] *op. cit.* 66ff.

[40] *op. cit.* 74.

[41] Wright, 'Romans,' 'Exodus,' and *Colossians* has made extensive use of the Exodus theme to interpret Paul. He has been followed by his doctoral student Keesmaat ('Exodus' and *Tradition*) who has concentrated on parts of Romans and Galatians. Webb uses the theme to interpret 2 Corinthians 4–6 in his *Coming*, as does Beale, 'Background.'

[42] Goldsworthy, *According*, 247, sees the New Exodus in the New Testament but only to a limited extent.

[43] Carrington, *Primitive*, 66

[44] Webb, *Home*, 1ff.

a New Exodus motif based on the prophetic expectation guiding the argument being developed by Paul. Webb linked the Egyptian and Babylonian Exoduses together as he interacted with the prophetic material and suggested that there might be New Exodus material in Ephesians 2:17 and in Colossians 1:20. In spite of this he does not seem to appreciate the importance of the theme for other parts of the New Testament. This omission obscured the significance of circumcision for the celebration of the Passover and caused Webb to miss the theme of spiritual circumcision. This would have been a useful insight alongside his interaction with the New Covenant material.

Keesmaat, a doctoral student of N.T. Wright, after surveying the Old Testament and Qumran material, notes the extensive influence of the Exodus theme in these literary sources and equates this influence to Romans 8:14-30.[45] She does not however suggest that firstborn in 8:28 has a *go'el* background. She has also examined Galatians 3–6[46] and shown it to be based on the New Exodus theme.

Wilder has studied the role of the Spirit in New Exodus expectation.[47] Longenecker also pointed to the importance of the New Exodus promises as a perspective for understanding the New Testament.[48]

Such evidence is rather limited and may be part of the reason why Sanders concludes: 'The Exodus typology does not seem to have determined Paul's thinking.'[49]

Casey produced an extensive study of the presence of the Exodus theme in Revelation and summarised the conclusions by saying: 'For John the Exodus is the event which orders and gives shape to his hope. To understand the meaning of redemption, the consequences of oppressing God's people, and the context of Christian inheritance, John turns to the intentions and activity of God first revealed in the Exodus. These, he says, are, "what must soon take place" (Rev. 22:6).'[50] Casey also noted a limited presence of the theme in other parts of the New Testament. Other scholars have studied the use of the Exodus theme in Revelation.[51]

[45] Keesmaat, 'Exodus,' 40.

[46] Keesmaat, *Tradition, passim*.

[47] Wilder, *Freed*.

[48] Longenecker, *Christology*, 39-41

[49] Sanders, *Palestinian*, 513.

[50] Casey, 'Exodus,' 42.

[51] So Koi, *Symbol*; Juster, *Key*.

Most of the aforementioned scholars failed to demonstrate the extensive presence of the New Exodus theme in Jewish literature contemporary with or preceding the New Testament. Those who made some attempt tended to deal with secondary sources that did not themselves adequately demonstrate the existence of New Exodus material. The only exceptions to this failure are Wright, who has demonstrated the extensive presence of this material within Judaism,[52] along with his doctoral student Keesmaat.[53] Indeed the presence of this theme in the intertestamental literature has been challenged,[54] but Evans responded in favour of Wright and provided sources that go beyond those that Wright had provided.[55] For most New Testament scholars the extent of this expectation is no longer an issue. What is still being debated is its significance.

Outside of the New Testament itself, Stanton has pointed out that Justin in *Dialogue 105*, where he debates with a Jew, used the 'sin exile return' theme.[56] Daube has done a study of the Exodus pattern in the Old Testament.[57]

Paschal Studies in New Testament Theology

Jeremias judged that the Passover theme was extensively appreciated by the early church and was the reason why statements such as 1 Corinthians 5:7-8 could be made to Gentile congregations without fear of the point being missed.[58] However, Jeremias did not explore the *prōtotokos* title in the light of the Passover.

Preiss is emphatic concerning Paschal influence when he says: 'The totality of the events of the Exodus centring on the Passover together with its associated ideas occupied a dominant position in Christian soteriological thought in the New Testament period, especially as Jesus Himself had instituted the eucharist in a distinctively Paschal setting.'[59]

Stott also acknowledges the importance of the Passover, even though it does not shape his theology beyond what is usual, when he

---

[52]See Wright, *Testament*, 268-73, and *Victory*, xviif, 126f, 203f. 209, 224, 234.
[53]Keesmaat, Use, passim.
[54]Johnson, 'Historiographical,' 221.
[55]Evans, 'Continuing,' 77-100.
[56]Stanton, 'Polemic,' 385-6.
[57]Daube, *Exodus*, *passim*.
[58]Jeremias, *TWNT* 5: 896-904, so also Hays, 'Imagination,' 412.
[59]Preiss, *Life*, 90.

says that the New Testament 'clearly identifies the death of Jesus as the fulfillment of the Passover and the emergence of his new and redeemed community as the new exodus'.[60] Colautti had done a study of the Passover in the works of Josephus and includes a section in which he surveys Passover material in the New Testament.[61]

Daly also sees the importance of the Passover as a source of early Christian thinking: 'Thus, growing out of a religious atmosphere in which all the important events of the past were considered to be Paschal events, and in which participation in the Paschal rite assured the individual and the nation of receiving the Salvific effects of the Pasach, and in which the eschatological end event was looked forward to as a Paschal event, it is not surprising that the New Exodus Christology is so thoroughly Paschal.'[62] And again Daly says: 'The Jewish Passover, as it was understood at the time of Christ, provided not merely the background but the very foundation of Christian soteriology.'[63]

A similar view as to the significance of the Passover is held by Moule: 'To a unique degree, Jesus is seen as the goal, the convergence point, of God's plan for Israel, his covenant promises.... The Passover gathers up into itself a large number of strands of covenant promises: to speak of "its full realisation" is to use the root we are considering in a highly significant way.'[64] Despite these statements by Daly and Moule, neither developed a Pachal Christology.

Daube studied the Gospel material comparing it to known Haggadah material. His study was limited but his conclusion nevertheless was that 'It can be shown, however, that the Passover eve expositions of the exodus current at the time exercised a decisive influence.... If we can prove certain sketches of the Gospels to be composed in analogy to last supper eve expositions, the likelihood is that the same is the case with some others as to which, owing to the loss of the original, we have no means of proof.'[65]

R.H. Lightfoot noted the Paschal influence in John's Gospel.[66] Howard fully appreciated the significance of the Passover as a major

---

[60]Stott, *Cross*, 139.

[61]Colautti, Passover, 174-84.

[62]Daly, *Sacrifice*, 203.

[63]*op. cit.* 207.

[64]Moule, 'Fulfilment,' 294 and 301.

[65]Daube, 'Structures,' 174-87.

[66]R.H. Lightfoot, *St. John, passim.*

key to John's thinking, but because he focused on the lamb, and did not explore the possibility that the Son is the firstborn victim, failed to appreciate the theme as fully as the potential offered.[67] However, Howard did recognise the connection between the Day of Atonement and the Passover in Ezekiel 45, even though he did not develop it. Howard also produced a study on the Passover theme in 1 Corinthians in which he examined 5:6ff.; 7:22ff.; 10; and 11:23ff. but he did not produce any new insights beyond those generally appreciated.[68]

Leaney and Cross argued for a clear dependence of 1 Peter on the Exodus narrative.[69] Shepherd produced a study of the influence of the paschal theme on the book of Revelation and endorsed its widespread influence.[70] Wallis has also examined this Paschal theme in Revelation.[71] However, Thornton claimed that there is no proof of a Paschal liturgy in the first century.[72]

Hockel produced a historical study on the interpretation of the title 'Firstborn of all creation'.[73] He noted that many different meanings were given to the title in the early church but did not identify the specifically Paschal meaning. He demonstrated that there was an ongoing tendency beyond the apostolic age to interpret the title ontologically, while at the same time there was a tendency to a soteriological meaning that was never put into a specifically Paschal context.

Both Moule and Perrin expressed the conviction that the Passover had been an important influence on the Christological development of the early church, but neither went beyond a general statement.[74] The Passover has been linked with the binding of Isaac and this connection has been extensively written on.[75]

While some of the scholars cited above have seen soteriological

---

[67]Howard, 'Eucharist,' 329ff.

[68]Howard, 'Christ,' 97ff.

[69]Leaney, '1 Peter,' 238ff.; Cross, *1 Peter*, 1ff.

[70]Shephard, *Paschal*, 1ff. This study also examines the influence of the Paschal theme on the Patristic writers.

[71]Wallis, *Passover.*

[72]Thornton, 'Paschal,' 21. Richardson, *Introduction*, 218, was equally adamant as to there being minimal influence from the Passover on New Testament thinking.

[73]Hockel, *Erstgeborne*, 1ff.

[74]Moule, *Fulfilment*, 318; Perrin, *Pilgrimage* 76.

[75]See chapter 11.

significance in the Passover, and a few have suggested Christological links, none has attempted to construct a Paschal Christology/theology.

Prōtotokos in the New Exodus setting

Because of the position of *prōtotokos* in Colossians 1:15, which immediately follows a New Exodus description of salvation (vv. 12-14), one would expect that some attention would be given to exploring the possibility of it having a Paschal significance, especially when it is appreciated that the introduction to a work is intended to set the framework in which the main part of the presentation is to be interpreted. Such an enquiry is wanting in New Testament studies.[76] What we do find is that the term is repeatedly related to Wisdom, despite the problems that such an association presents.

Despite the absence of a developed Paschal Christology, some statements have been made that certainly point in the direction of our enquiry, but do not appear to have been appreciated for their potential by the authors concerned. Engell, discussing how the firstborn belonged to the Lord, noted how this included the firstborn of humans. He came very close to a Paschal meaning for firstborn, but failed to explore its significance: 'Even among the firstborn males, they belonged in principle, the same way to Jehovah (Exodus 13:2; Num. 3:40-51; etc). This type of sacrifice was resorted to very rarely. Once in a while a king's son was sacrificed such as Manasseh in Judah (2 Kings 21:6). Compare this to king Mera of Moab (2 Kings 3:27). The ideological association of the king as "firstborn" is at home in this context. Something like this is reflected even in the New Testament in the question about Jesus Christ as *prototokos* ("firstborn").'[77]

Bowman also came very close to identifying the firstborn with Christ the paschal victim when he wrote: 'The death of the firstborn in Mark's Christian Jewish New Haggadah of the Passover achieves the deliverance of the people enslaved to the Law and the Temple, yes and from the Romans too – but the deliverance is not wrought by the death of the firstborn of the Egyptians, not even the death of Pharaoh's firstborn, nor at the price of the foreign oppressor, but by the death of the Saviour Himself.'[78] He further wrote: 'Just as Israel

---

[76]F.F. Bruce in private correspondence with the author wrote: 'I do not know of any commentator who links the title *prōtotokos* with the paschal event.'

[77]Engell, 'Furstfodda,' 1:714.

[78]Bowman, *Mark*, 314

was delivered at the Exodus by the blood of the lamb and the death of Egypt's firstborn, so the Messiah of the new Israel, the beloved Son of God dies as the price of freedom and is delivered by His Father whose will He is fulfilling, that He may see His seed. Mark develops not only the thought of the deliverance of the historic Exodus, but of the Covenant with Abraham, the promises to Abraham, and the sacrifice and deliverance of Isaac.'[79]

Both Engell and Bowman virtually call Jesus 'God's firstborn' in a Paschal context, but show no sign that they have appreciated that it has significant theological implications. This is similar to Heyler[80] who, while appreciating that there was a New Exodus background to the use of the term in Hebrews 12:23,[81] and that the use of the term in Hebrews 1:6 was closely linked with Colossians 1:15-20,[82] nevertheless failed to see the significance of the Passover as the setting to interpret the title.

Levenson came extremely close to identifying the death of the firstborn as a Paschal offering but he did not quite pass over the boundary of actually acknowledging that the death of the beloved son was actually an atonement for sin and that its specific setting was the Passover. Levenson did however recognise that the beloved son was sacrificed to Yahweh in recognition of His rightful claim on the costliest offering that man could make.[83]

This survey demonstrates the absence of Paschal thinking for the description of Christ being the firstborn of all creation in Christian thinking and how this absence has influenced the models used to interpret Paul and the rest of the New Testament.

---

[79]*op. cit.* 325.
[80]Heyler, 'Prototokos,' 17.
[81]*op. cit.* 16.
[82]*op. cit.* 12.
[83]Levenson, *Death, passim.*

Appendix 2

The Passover/Aqedah Motif in the Early Church

When we come to examine the writings of the early church fathers we can divide the material into three sections. First is the most ancient material that existed which was used by the apostles themselves. This section would include bodies of tradition (1 Cor. 15:3) as well as blocks of testimonia, which the Gospel writers in particular are believed to have drawn upon. Alongside this material were the Old Testament scriptures themselves and the midrashim, which the early Christian community, with its heavy rabbinic influence, would have soon been producing. This growing midrash material took the same form as the contemporary Jewish midrash, which consisted in collections of comments of distinguished rabbinic authorities on Old Testament scriptures. The Christian midrash was a similar body of comment, which was attributed either to the apostles themselves, to their associates or to the communities that they had influenced as a result of apostolic presence. Clement records how through a visit to Palestine he learnt things that he felt compelled to record for the sake of Gentile believers. By this visit he came into direct contact with a body of material and a way of understanding of which he had previously been unaware. A comparison between Clement and the epistle of Barnabas shows that parallels exist, which would suggest that either one borrowed from the other, or more likely, that they used a common midrash. What is important about this material is that it is 'characteristic of a very archaic period of Christianity'.[1]

The second body of material is the writings of the early church fathers who retain the same basic exegetical methods as the New Testament writers. These are early second-century writers and include such as Clement, Barnabas, Justin, Melito of Sardis and Hippolytus. They did not necessarily have access to all the traditions and material of the primitive church, but nevertheless they remained essentially under its influence as regards the way it tackled the task of the exegesis of the Old Testament scriptures.

The third body of material reflects growing Greek influence on the

[1]Daniélou, *Theology*, 89.

church, which led to the adoption of the exegetical methods of the
Greek schools of philosophy, as had been previously applied for the
Jews by Philo. There is no one who did this in the early church more
enthusiastically than Origen. For him, allegory was the dominant
exegetical principle. Significance was seen in everything, whether it
were numbers, colours, days or names; everything had a divinely
imparted significance, which the gifted teacher looked for in order
that his students could benefit.

The most important of these three sections for our study is
undoubtedly the first, which includes the Christian midrash. The writers
of this material were clearly influenced by extra-canonical sources in
their exegesis. Danielou sees the influence of the *Apocalypse of
Baruch* on Papias, one of the writers of such midrash. Another source
of midrash was Irenaeus, but he was not sympathetic to the extraneous
sources accepted by Papias and referred to them as 'strange teachings
of the Saviour'. He said that they had come down to Papias from
unwritten traditions and that they were statements of 'mythical
character'. Irenaeus also referred to other data which he attributed
to 'the Elders who were disciples of the Apostles'. This is a clear
reference to the same community as that from which Papias drew
his traditions. Danielou, after examining the influence of these traditions,
concluded:

> Thus internal evidence confirms the external data pointing to the traditions
> reported by Papias as a form of Jewish Christian theology. These traditions
> clearly go back to a very early date: some may come from the Palestinian
> community before 70 AD.... As will be seen later this particular stream in
> Jewish Christianity had a strong Messianist flavour....it is therefore an
> entirely new side of Jewish Christianity which is disclosed by Papias.[2]

With this material of Papias we must include that of Clement, for,
as we have mentioned, he visited Palestine personally and returned
with information of which he had been previously totally unaware.
Clement was deeply concerned to record this information, because
until then it had existed only in oral form, and he feared that it might
soon be lost to the church. He wrote concerning these sayings:

> They, preserving the tradition (*paradosis* [Gr]) of the blessed doctrine
> derived directly from the holy apostles Peter, James, John and Paul, the

---

[2]*op. cit.* 48.

son receiving it from the father (but few were like their fathers), came – thanks be to God! – to us also to sow these fertile and apostolic seeds. And well I know that what will please my readers will not be the literary form in which they are now presented, but simply the traditions which these notes preserve. This sketch, then, is the work of a soul whose only desire is to guard intact the blessed instruction.[3]

A further source of early material is the use of Greek translations of the Old Testament by the early Christian community which was clearly undertaken to bring out a particular point. While the early church both reverenced and used the LXX they were not afraid to use or make other translations if they felt that the LXX had failed to make a particular point clear.[4] The use of these translations in preference to the LXX, especially in the New Testament, ought to underline for us that the writers were anxious to clarify or emphasise a truth which the LXX was failing to illuminate adequately. These textual variations and inclusions will help us to determine better what was in the mind of the New Testament writers when they wrote.

Clement of Alexandria
It is clear that Clement saw that there existed an important relationship between Isaac and Christ. He wrote:

> Isaac is a type of the Lord, being first of all a child inasmuch as he was a son (for he was the son of Abraham, as Christ is the Son of God) and secondly a consecrated victim like the Lord. But he was not offered as a sacrifice as the Lord was; he, Isaac, only bore the wood (*duxa* [Gr]) for the sacrifice, just as the Lord bore the Tree (*xulon* [Gr]). He laughed with mystic meaning as a prophecy that the Lord would fill us with joy, we who have been ransomed from destruction by the blood of the Lord. But he did not suffer, not only leaving to the Logos, as is to be expected, the firstfruits of suffering, but what is more, by the fact that he himself was not slain he hints (*ainittetai* [Gr]) at the divinity of the Lord; for Jesus, after his burial, was raised up without enduring corruption, just as Isaac escaped the death of a sacrificial victim.[5]

It is not possible to prove on the basis of Targumic quotations whether or not the Jewish community had begun to develop its *Aqedah* doctrine. What can be claimed is that very soon after the writing of

[3] *Strom.* 1,11:3-12:1.
[4] See Ellis, *Use.*
[5] *Paed.* 1,5:23,1-2.

the last of the New Testament works, we find that the Isaac/ Christ typology is fully developed in the thinking of the Christian community. It is difficult to believe that the presence of such a theology of Isaac, especially if it is reflecting the Palestinian origin that Clement has claimed for his distinctive ideas, did not produce an early reaction and reply from the Jewish community.

Clement elsewhere says of Isaac that he 'is shown as one who possesses infused knowledge (*automades* [Gr]); that is why he is also a type of Christ'.[6] Later, commenting on the preference shown by Isaac for Jacob over Esau, he wrote: 'This ordering of things (*oikonomia* [Gr]) is also prophetic and prefigurative (*tupika* [Gr]).'[7]

Clement saw significance in the three days Abraham and Isaac spent travelling to Mount Moriah and wrote that 'the three days may also be the mystery (*musterion* [Gr]) of the seal (*sphragis* [Gr]) through which one believes in the true God'.[8]

Danielou thinks this interpretation recalls the first three days of creation in terms of the three Persons of the Trinity.[9] He sees Clement as drawing back from the total Philonic domination of his exegetical method and to be coming to terms with the method and material he has discovered on his visit to Palestine.

In a fragment from Clement's last work, *On The Pascha*, preserved in the Paschal Chronicle, we find:

> Accordingly, in the years gone by, Jesus went to eat the passover sacrificed by the Jews, keeping the feast. But when He had preached, He who was the Passover, the Lamb of God, led as a sheep to the slaughter, presently taught His disciples the mystery of the type on the thirteenth day, on which also they inquired. 'Where wilt Thou that we prepare for Thee to eat the Passover?' (Mt. 26.17). It was on this day, then, that both the consecration of unleavened bread and the preparation for the feast took place. Whence John naturally describes the disciples as already prepared to have their feet washed by the Lord. And on the following day our Saviour suffered, He who was the Passover, propitiously sacrificed by the Jews.[10]

---

[6]*Strom* 1,5:31, 3.
[7]*Strom* 11,19:95,3 .
[8]*Strom* V.11:73, 2.
[9]Daniélou, *Theology*, 241.
[10]cf. *Eusebius H.E.* vl 13.9.

Isaac is the type *par excellence* of Christ in another passage of Clement where he wrote that 'God selected for Himself Isaac in a figure as a consecrated sacrifice to be a type to us of the ceremony of salvation'.[11]

Daly lists the following features in the above passage as clearly reflecting the influence of the *Aqedah*.[12] They are: (1) The laughter of Isaac; (2) The resurrection theme; (3) The specific mention of the redeeming merits of Christ's blood; (4) The soteriological significance of the passage; (5) The conscious rejection or modification of specifically Jewish interpretations of the *Aqedah*. A major shift has clearly taken place, as in this passage there is not even a mention of Abraham on whom earlier *Aqedah* material had focused.

Justin

The same Isaac typology is found in the works of Justin. In a midrash on 2 Esdras Justin puts his case to his Jewish readers in the following way.

> From the expositions (*exaegeseis* [Gr]) which Esdras gave of the Passover, they have removed this: And Esdras said to the people: This Passover is our Saviour (*soter* [Gr]) and our refuge. And if you reflect, and the thought arise in your heart that we are to humble Him on a cross (*semeion* [Gr]), and afterwards put your hope in Him, this place will never be laid desolate, saith the Lord of Hosts. But if you do not believe in Him nor hearken to His preaching (*kerugma* [Gr]) you shall be a laughing stock of the Gentiles.[13]

This passage, which is an elaboration of 2 Esdras 6.19ff., is clearly Christian in character. The expression, 'This passover is our Saviour,' echoes Paul in 1 Corinthians 5.7: 'for Christ our Passover has been sacrificed for us.' The use of *tapeinoun*, in a variant reading that Lactantius gives,[14] links with Philippians 2.8 in the context of Christ's passion and *semeion* is normally used for the cross in the New Testament writings. It is possible that this midrash which Justin used was part of a group of testimonia on the cross.[15]

[11]*Strom* 11.5
[12]Daly, *Sacrifice*, 456.
[13]*Dial*, LXX 11,1.
[14]Daniélou, *Theology*, 102
[15]Daniélou, *Theology*, 102.

The significance of this passage is that it shows that there was a Christian/Jewish encounter taking place in the early part of the second century which challenged the Jewish community to think about the significance of the death of Christ in the light of the Passover. This suggests that the *Aqedah* doctrine will have been emerging, if not already in existence, earlier than the end of the second century, as it is difficult to believe that such goading from the Gentiles in mocking the Jews for their unbelief in the fulfilment of the Passover typology could be left without a response to explain the Passover in another way.

There are two important passages in Justin's *Dialogue* that refer to Christ as being the firstborn of every creature. The first has its setting in a debate Justin is conducting as to who was meant when the Psalmist referred to the entering in of the King of Glory. Justin argued:

> Again the prophecy which says, Lift up your gates, O ye princes, and be lifted up, ye everlasting doors, that the king of glory may come in, some of you presumptuously explain it to be said of Hezekiah, and others of Solomon: whereas it may be shown that it was spoken of neither the one nor the other, nor of any one of your kings whatever, but only of this Christ of ours; who appeared without comeliness and honour, as Isaiah and David and all the Scriptures say; who is Lord of Hosts, through the will of the Father who gave him to be so; who also rose from the dead, and went up to heaven, as the Psalm and the rest of the Scriptures shew: which also proclaimed him the Lord of Hosts, as, if you will, you may easily be convinced, even by the things that are passing under your own observation. For through the name of this very Son of God, who is also the First-born of every creature, and who was born of the Virgin, and made a man subject to suffering, and was crucified by your nation in the time of Pontius Pilate, and died, and rose again from the dead, and ascended into heaven, every evil spirit is exorcised and overcome and subdued. But if you exorcise them by every name of men who have been born among you; whether of kings or of righteous men, or of prophets, or of patriarchs; none of them will be subject unto you. If indeed any of you exorcise them by the God of Abraham, and the God of Isaac, and the God of Jacob, they perhaps will be subjected unto you.[16]

It is true that the phrase 'First-born of every creature' comes straight after the mention of Jesus being the very Son of God and

---

[16]*Dial Tryph*, 85.

therefore could be claimed to have an ontologically-oriented meaning. But that is not the only evidence in the context in which it is used. First is the fact that Isaiah's prophecy about Jesus being without comeliness and honour has been mentioned earlier in the passage and this cannot but introduce the concept of the suffering servant setting into the stream of Justin's ideas. Second, the reference to the king of glory being allowed through the gates of Jerusalem cannot but suggest the entry of Christ as he rode into the city and was hailed as the king of the Jews. He rode in to face the betrayal and suffering that were imminent. Third, Justin immediately goes on to refer to the virgin birth (Mary's firstborn) and his suffering, death and resurrection. Finally, Justin taunts the Jews over the fact that there is power in the name of Jesus to exorcise demons. That power, exhibited at the Passover when the power of the angel of death was thwarted, was a power Jesus possessed by virtue of his conquest over the forces of evil through his death.

The next passage from Justin is taken from his argument over the significance of Noah and the deluge:

> You know then, Sirs, I said, that in Isaiah God has said to Jerusalem, In the deluge of Noah I saved thee; but what God said was this, that the mystery of mankind who are saved was in the deluge. For righteous Noah with the others at the deluge, that is his wife and his three sons, and their wives, making eight persons in number, were a type of that day on which our Christ appeared when He arose from the dead, which in number indeed is the eighth, but in power is always the first; for Christ being the first-born of every creature, was also made again the beginning of a new race which is regenerated by Him through water, and faith, and wood, which contains the mystery of the cross; as Noah also was saved in the wood, being born upon the waters with his family.[17]

It is clear from elsewhere that Justin tends to use the title 'firstborn' loosely with the title 'Son of God' and that his usage tends to have the Greek-oriented idea of priority built into it.[18] But here Justin is linking the title 'firstborn' with the events of the deluge, which is a type of salvation, and he distinctly refers to the wood, which is an obvious reference to the cross. Not only this, but he also goes on to link the title with Christ being the head of a new race, i.e. the second or last Adam figure, with all of its federal representative implications.

[17]*Dial Tryph*, 125
[18]Cited by Richardson, *Library*, 1:224.

There is another text which is attributed to Justin, but is generally accepted as pseudepigraphic. It is the so-called Letter to Diognetus. It is questioned as to its authenticity because there are no Old Testament quotations (and this is totally foreign to Justin's style) and because there is no respect for philosophy. It also is different from the style that Justin uses in his authentic letters. However this may be, it is nevertheless an early document which gives some information regarding the theme we are pursuing. The text says:

> Let your heart be your wisdom, and let your life be true knowledge inwardly received. Bearing this tree and displaying its fruit, thou shalt always gather in those things which are desired by God, which the serpent cannot reach, and to which deception does not approach; nor is Eve then corrupted, but is trusted as a virgin; and salvation is manifested, and the Apostles are filled with understanding, and the Passover of the Lord advances, and the choirs are gathered together, and are arranged in proper order, and the Word rejoices in teaching the saints – by whom the Father is glorified: to whom be glory for ever. Amen.[19]

What is of interest in this passage is first the mention of the tree. Clearly it would have a twofold meaning, the tree from which Eve took, and the tree upon which Christ died. The first defiled whereas the second does not, and that is the point being made here. So the cross is to the fore in this section. Secondly, the reference to 'a virgin' is clearly referring to Mary. Immediately the passage goes on to say that 'salvation is manifested.... and the Lord's Passover advances'. It would suggest that the writer is linking the Virgin's offspring, who must be her firstborn, with the Lord's Passover.

Elsewhere Justin takes up the Passover theme, using it to illustrate the significance of Christ's death:

> The mystery, then, of the lamb which God enjoined to be sacrificed as the Passover, was a type of Christ; with whose blood, in proportion to their faith in Him, they anoint their houses i.e., themselves, who believe on Him...and that lamb which was commanded to be wholly roasted was a symbol of the suffering of the cross which Christ would undergo. For the lamb, which is roasted, is roasted and dressed in the form of the cross. For one spit is transfixed right through from the lower part to up to the head, and one across the back, to which are attached the legs of the lamb.[20]

[19] *The Epistle to Diognetus*, xii.
[20] *Dial* 40.1-3.

Once again Justin directed Trypho to the significance of the Passover when he wrote:

> For the Passover was Christ, who was afterwards sacrificed, as also Isaiah said, 'He was led as a sheep to the slaughter' (Isa. 53.7). And it is written, that on the day of the Passover you seized Him, and that during the Passover you crucified Him. And as the blood of the Passover saved those who were in Egypt, so also the blood of Christ will deliver from death those who have believed.[21]

Barnabas

We have seen how scholarship has failed to appreciate the significance of Ezekiel 45:21ff., where Ezekiel saw the merging of the feast of Passover with the sacrifices of the Day of Atonement. We provided evidence that this merger explains some of the confusion that has existed in interpreting the significance of the purpose and value of the Passover sacrifices. We see this merger of the two feasts in Barnabas. He had no difficulty in providing the typological significance of the Passover lamb. He wrote:

> The mystery of the lamb which God commanded to be sacrificed as the Passover was a type of Christ.[22]

Barnabas was able to bring other sacrificial offerings from other feasts under the same Passover motif, as is shown when he explained:

> The offering of fine flour, which it was handed down should be made on behalf of those cleansed from leprosy, was a type of the bread of the Eucharist.[23]

Barnabas quotes an ancient text which is a midrash on Leviticus 16:7-8, the ritual for the Day of Atonement. It is obvious how he allows the ritual of the Atonement to merge with the details of the passion of Christ as the following extract illustrates.

> Attend ye to the commandments which he gave. Take two goats (*trogous* [Gr]) fair and alike, and offer them, and let the priest take one for a whole burnt-offering for sins, but the other one – what must they do with it?

[21]*Dial* 40.1.
[22]Danielou, *Early*, 201-02.
[23]*op. cit.* 202.

Accursed (*epikataratos* [Gr]) upon it (*katakentasate* [Gr]), and place scarlet wool about its head, and so let it be cast into the wilderness.'[24]

Danielou points out the similarities in this passage with the passion of Christ:

> The rites mentioned at the end of the quotation may still be traditional but the manner in which they are presented and the choice of words certainly indicates a Christian origin. It has already been remarked that *tragos* replaces *ximaros* in the Epistle to the Hebrews. The word *epikataratos* echoes Gal. 3:10. The detail of the 'spitting' (*emptuoute* [Gr]) recalls the scene of the mocking in the praetorium, where Matthew uses the same verb (*eneptusan* [Gr],26.67); the goading (*katakentasate* [Gr]) reminds us of Jn.19:37 which has *exekentasan*; finally, the scarlet wool (*kokkinos* [Gr]) crowning the head of Jesus. Behind the scapegoat stands the figure of Jesus in the praetorium.[25]

Barnabas continues to quote the same source when he wrote:

> And when it is so done, he taketh the goat into the wilderness leadeth it, and taketh off the wool, and putteth it upon the branch which is called Rachia.[26]

The juxtaposition of the mention of scarlet (*kokkinos* [Gr]) and thorns would appear to be connected with the reference to the scarlet (*kokkinan* [Gr]) tunic and the crown of thorns in the praetorium scene in Matthew 27:28f. Barnabas has earlier compared the sacrifice of the goat with that of Isaac. Here we find in the clearest way the connection between Isaac/Passover/Day of Atonement and the passion of Christ. The ram immolated in the place of Isaac, hanging from a bush of thorns, is clearly 'an incident regarded as a figure of Christ at a very early date'.[27]

Melito of Sardis

Possibly the most significant of the patristic writers for our study is Melito of Sardis. This is because we have his Homily on the Passion, the most relevant piece of writing from this period of the church that bears upon our enquiry. Not only is the homily about Christ's passion,

---

[24]Daniélou, *Early*, 99.
[25]VII,8.
[26]Daniélou, *Early*, 99.
[27]Melito, *On Pascha*, 5-35.

but it was delivered on Easter day, which in the second century was the same day as the Jewish Passover. Because, like Clement of Alexandria, Melito had visited Palestine, he had been directly exposed to the unique traditions of the Palestinian Christians.

Melito's argument is that the type is only of use until its fulfilment arrives. He likens a type to a sketch that a sculptor uses. An onlooker by observing the sketch can see what the sculptor is working to produce. The sketch is of little use once the masterpiece has been produced. So Melito argues that the Passion of Christ fulfils that to which the Exodus type pointed.

Two important extracts of the homily reveal the progress that the early church was making in understanding the relationship between Isaac and Christ. The first passage shows how Melito held that the celebration of the Passover is worthy of high honour because it signified the mystery of Christ:

> When the blood of the lamb stayed the hand of the destroying angel, it was not the blood which checked him, but the type (*tupos* [Gr]) of the Lord (v. 31), and when He saw the mystery (*musterion* [Gr]) of the Lord in the death of the lamb.[28]

What is important to notice in this extract is that it attributes to the type something that it normally does not possess in typological exegesis. Types normally are nothing more than a pointer to a future event of which they are the shadow. Here, however, the very significance of the future happening actually endows the type with a power that has an effect on the outcome of the event in which it participates. This development is very much like the use of the type made in the *Aqedah*, but in the Jewish version the type does not look forward but backwards. The Passover is the type, reminding rather than anticipating, and receives its power from the offering of Isaac.

In his homily Melito regularly refers to Isaac, likening Christ's arrest to the Patriarch's binding. The references do not go beyond this incident and they are always set in the context of other types of Christ's suffering, suggesting no great significance is being put on Isaac.

> But if you look carefully at the model, you will perceive him through the final outcome. Therefore if you wish to see the mystery of the Lord, look

---

[28] *On Pascha*, 58-60.

at Abel who is similarly murdered, at Isaac who is similarly bound, at Moses who is similarly exposed, at David who is similarly persecuted, at the prophets who similarly suffer for the sake of Christ. Look also at the sheep which is slain in the land of Egypt, which struck Egypt and saved Israel by its blood.[29]

Later on in his homily, Melito again uses similar imagery, bringing together the various strands of typology under the theme of the Pascha:

He is the Pascha of our salvation. It is he who endured many things: and it is he that was in Abel murdered, and in Isaac bound, and in Joseph sold, and in Jacob exiled, and in the lamb slain, and in David persecuted, and in the prophets dishonoured. It is he that was enfleshed in a virgin, that was hanged on a tree.[30]

It is clear in both passages, i.e., 69–70 and 81–82, that Melito is unable to use the Isaac type fully. Because there was no wound, no death, the type fell short of what was required. To compensate for this lack in the typology of Isaac he brought other themes together, using the death of the Paschal lamb to convey the idea of substitutionary death. We shall see shortly that Melito did not lack appreciation for the potential of the Isaac type, but he was clearly restricted by it because of the fact that Isaac never experienced death in the context of his binding. What did exist for Melito to develop was the picture of the father giving up his son. It is this parallel that some scholars see behind such biblical passages as John 3:16, Romans 8:32 and Galatians 3:13. Later in the homily Melito speaks of Jesus as God's firstborn. In this section he seems to be accusing Israel of not living up to her name nor recognising the true Israel and of putting him to death:

O lawless Israel, what is this unprecedented crime you have committed thrusting your Lord among unprecedented sufferings. Your Sovereign, who formed you, who made you, who honoured you, who called you Israel? But you did not turn out to be 'Israel'. You did not 'see God', You did not recognise the Word, You did not know, Israel, that he is the firstborn of God, who was begotten before the morning star, who tinted the night, who lit up the day, who divided off the darkness.[31]

[29]*On Pascha*, 69-70.
[30]*On Pascha*, 81-82.
[31]*On Pascha*, 102-03.

In the setting of the homily on the Pascha in which he has been speaking of Jesus being thrust through and experiencing unprecedented suffering, reminiscent of Zechariah 12:10, the reference to Jesus being the 'firstborn of God' would have clear soteriological significance.

Another significant text occurs later in the homily where Melito writes:

> I am the one that destroyed death and triumphed over the enemy and trod down Hades and bound the strong one and carried off man to the heights of heaven; I am the one says the Christ. Come then, all of you families of men who are compounded with sins, and get forgiveness of sins. For I am your forgiveness, I am the Pascha of salvation, I am the lamb slain for you, I am your ransom, I am your life, I am your light, I am your resurrection, I am your being, I will raise you up by my right hand, I am leading you up to the heights of heaven, there I will show you the father from ages past.[32]

As has been mentioned, Isaac typology has been restrained in the homily 'On Pascha', but it is still clearly there. It is not that Melito could not develop the type adequately to bring out the full significance. It would seem it was style and purpose that restricted him. To develop the type of the *Aqedah* fully he would need to so qualify and explain the inadequacies of the type that it would have worked against the whole scheme of *On Pascha*. The force of the argument would have been lost and the power of oratory severely hindered. But we do have fragments of other works of Melito and these demonstrate both Melito's understanding of the *Aqedah* and his ability to use it.

> For as a ram he was bound [he says concerning our Lord Jesus Christ], and as a lamb he was shorn, and as a sheep he was led to slaughter, and as a lamb he was crucified; and he carried the wood on his shoulder as he was led up to be slain like Isaac by his Father, but Christ suffered, whereas Isaac did not suffer; for he was a model of the Christ who was going to suffer. But by being merely the model of Christ he caused astonishment and fear among men. For it was a strange mystery to behold, a son led by his father to a mountain for slaughter, whose feet he bound and whom he put on the wood of the offering, preparing with zeal the things for his slaughter. But Isaac was silent, bound like a ram, not opening his mouth nor uttering a sound. For not frightened by the sword nor alarmed at the fire nor sorrowful at the suffering, he carried with fortitude the model of

the Lord. Thus Isaac was offered in the midst foot-bound like a ram, and Abraham stood by and held the sword unsheathed not ashamed to put to death his son.[33]

On behalf of Isaac the righteous one, a ram appeared for slaughter, so that Isaac might be released from bonds. That ram, slain, ransomed Isaac; so also the Lord, slain, saved us, and sacrificed, ransomed us.[34]

For the Lord was a lamb like the ram which Abraham saw caught in a Sabek-tree. But the tree displayed the cross, and that place, Jerusalem, and the lamb, the Lord fettered for slaughter.[35]

Caught by the horns the Syriac and Hebrew express as hanged, which prefigures in the plainest way the cross. But the word ram also makes this explicit: it did not say a lamb, young like Isaac, but a ram, full-grown like the Lord. And just as it called the holy cross a tree of Sabek, that is of forgiveness.[36]

Irenaeus

We find Irenaeus (*c.*130-200) referring to *Aqedah* and interestingly in a way that stresses Abraham's part rather than Isaac's as is common in the older strands of the *Aqedah* material. Irenaeus views the willingness of Abraham to be the grounds upon which God was willing to give his only Son.

For Abraham, according to his faith, followed the commandment of the Word of God, and with ready mind gave up his only and beloved son, as a sacrifice to God, in order that God might be pleased to offer His beloved and only Son for all His offspring, as a sacrifice for our salvation.[37]

Hippolytus

In Hippolytus we find the Passover theme was interwoven with the sufferings of Christ to explain their significance:

And for this reason three seasons of the year prefigured the Saviour Himself, so that He would fulfil the mysteries prophesied of Him, in the

[33]*Fragment* 10.
[34]*Fragment* 11.
[35]*Fragment* 12.
[36]Cited by Dahl, *Atonement*, 150.
[37]*Fragment from the Discourse on Elkanah and Hannah,* GCS. 1, 2 (11) 122, 10-11.

Passover season, so as to exhibit Himself as One destined to be sacrificed like a sheep, and to prove Himself the true Paschal-lamb, even as the apostle says, 'Even Christ,' who is God, 'our Passover was sacrificed for us' (1 Cor. 5.7).[38]

In another passage entitled the *Refutation of all Heresies* Hippolytus links Christ explicitly with the Passover theme:

They do not, however, attend to this [Fact], that the legal enactment was made for the Jews, who in times to come should kill the real Passover, which has spread to the Gentiles and is discerned by faith and not now observed in letter.[39]

Gregory of Nyssa

Gregory spent time in his work *Against Eunomius* to explain Christ's title 'firstborn of all creation'. He first reasoned that there was a logical difference between 'firstborn' and 'only begotten', a difference that existed because 'firstborn' implied others like himself, whereas 'only begotten' clearly implied uniqueness.

Who does not know how great is the difference in signification between the term 'only-begotten' and 'first-born'? For 'first-born' implies brethren, and 'only-begotten' implies that there are no other brethren. Thus the first-born is not 'only-begotten', for certainly 'first-born' is the first-born among brethren, while he who is 'only-begotten' has no brother: for if he were numbered among brethren he would not be only-begotten. And moreover, whatever the essence of the brothers of the first-born is, the same is the essence of the first-born himself.[40]

Gregory went on to point out that 'firstborn' was used by the apostles four times. He agreed that each of these terms gave their meaning to firstborn of all creation:

In what sense then does He become 'the first-born among many brethren'? In what sense does He become 'the first-born from the dead'? Assuredly this is plain, that because we are by birth flesh and blood, as the Scripture saith, 'He Who for our sakes was born among us and was partaker of flesh and blood,' purposing to change us from corruption by the birth

---

[38]*Refutations* VIII.1. GCS 26 (111) 237, 19-22.
[39]*Against Eunomius*, Book 7.
[40]*Against Eunomius*, Book 8.

from above, the birth by water and the Spirit Himself led the way in this birth, drawing down upon the water, by His own baptism, the Holy Spirit; so that in all things He became the first-born of those who are spiritually born again, and gave the name of brethren to those who partook in a birth like to His own by water and the Spirit.[41]

What clearly is happening in Gregory's exegesis is that he is seeking a soteriological understanding for 'firstborn of all creation'. His problem is that because he does not put the title back into a Passover context he lacks the setting that would expose its full soteriological meaning. This soteriological setting is not consistently held by Gregory. In *Against Euno*mius, Book 2, he asks: 'But how can he who refers the name of "firstborn" to the pretemporal existence of the Son preserve the proper sense of the term "Only-begotten"?'[42] In other words Gregory could not help but see in the title an ontological significance which inevitably clouded the meaning of the title. Indeed he again referred to the theme in *Against Eunomius*, Book 4, and acknowledged that there was a question that naturally suggested itself regarding the title 'firstborn of all creation'. He wrote:

> They will perhaps raise a question from the very apostolic writings which we quoted, 'How could He be called "The firstborn of creation," if He were not what creation is?' for every firstborn is the firstborn not of another kind, but of its own.[43]

Gregory resolved this by accepting the adjustment on the basis that it was agreed that the whole creation is of one essence with God the Father. This then led Gregory into a discussion on the metaphysical nature of the universe and of Christ's nature. And yet Gregory was able to a degree to recover from his metaphysical excursion and came back to a soteriological context, still however lacking the decisive Passover setting.

> Of this new creation therefore in Christ, which He Himself began, He was called the first-born, being the first-fruits of all, both of those begotten into life, and of those quickened by the resurrection of the dead, 'that He might be Lord both of the dead and of the living', and might sanctify the whole lump by means of its first-fruits in Himself. Now that the character

---

[41]*Against Eunomius*, Book 2.8.
[42]*Against Eunomius*, Book 4.3.
[43]*Against Eunomius*, Book 4.3.

of 'first-born' does not apply to the Son in respect of His pre-temporal existence the appellation of 'Only-begotten' testifies. For he who is truly 'Only-begotten' has no brethren, for how could any one be only-begotten if numbered among brethren?[44]

Athanasius

Of all the Patristic writers Athanasius stands out as the champion of Christological orthodoxy. His deep concern over the widespread acceptance of the views of Arius expressed itself in a series of polemic writings as well as in his almost solitary stand following the Council of Nicaea. Athanasius was acutely aware of the value for Arius of the term 'firstborn of all creation'. It was the Achilles heel of the orthodox school. It was vital that the title was shown not to have the meaning Arius was convincing multitudes it had, i.e. the clear implication of Christ's inferiority to the Father and his beginning at some point in prehistory. How did Athanasius handle this text? Once again we will see, like others before him, he sought a soteriological setting, but never found one that was totally convincing.

> If then we are by nature sons, then is He by nature creature and weak; but if we become sons by adoption and grace, then has the Word also, when in grace towards us He became man, said, 'The Lord created me.' And in the next place, when He put on a created nature and became like us in body, reasonably was He therefore called both our Brother and 'First-born.' For though it was after us that He was made man for us, and our brother by similitude of body, still He is therefore called and is the 'First-born' of us, because, all men being lost according to the transgression of Adam, His flesh before all others was saved and liberated as being the Word's body; and henceforth we, becoming incorporate with It, are saved after Its pattern. For It the Lord becomes our guide to the Kingdom of Heaven and to His own Father, saying, 'I am the way' and 'the door,' and 'through Me all must enter.' Whence also He is said to be 'First-born from the dead', not that He died before us, for we had died first; but because having undergone death for us and abolished it, He was the first to rise, as man, for our sakes raising His own Body. Henceforth He having risen, we too from Him and because of Him rise in due course from the dead.[45]

---

[44]*Against Eunomics. Book 4.3*
[45]*Four Discourses Against the Arians.* Discourse 2.62.

Athanasius went on to try to distinguish between 'only begotten' and 'firstborn':

> But 'first-born' implied the descent to the creation; for of it has He been called first-born; and 'He created' implies His grace towards the works, for them is He created. If then He is Only-begotten, as indeed He is, 'First-born' needs some explanation; but if He be really First-born, then He is not Only-begotten. For the same cannot be both Only-begotten and First-born, except in different relations: that is, Only-begotten, because of His generation from the Father, as has been said; and First-born because of His condescension to the creation and His making the many His brethren. Certainly, those two terms being inconsistent with each other, one should say that the attribute of being Only-begotten has justly the preference in the instance of the Word, in that there is no other Word or other Wisdom, but He alone is very Son of the Father.[46]

Thus Athanasius sought to use the term 'firstborn' to speak of Christ as the origin of creation, which he argued was totally different from the title 'only begotten', which spoke of his generation from the Father. But like other Patristic writers, Athanasius clearly could not let go of the soteriological significance of the title, and later in the same work wrote:

> He is called 'First-born among many brethren,' because of the relationship of the flesh, and 'First-born from the dead,' because the resurrection of the dead is from Him and after Him; and 'First-born of the whole creation,' because of the Father's love to man, which brought it to pass that in His Word not only 'all things consist,' but the creation itself, of which the Apostle speaks, waiting for the manifestation of the sons of God, 'shall be delivered' one time 'from the bondage of corruption into the glorious liberty of the children of God.' Of this creation thus delivered, the Lord will be First-born, both of it and of all those who are made children, that by His being called first, those that come after Him may abide, as depending on the Word as a beginning.[47]

Clearly Christ's status as firstborn of all creation is being put in the context of the redeemer who will release the universe from its bondage and suffering, i.e. the firstborn in redemption. Athanasius continued in this setting when he taunted the heretics of the weakness of their arguments:

[46]*Four Discourses Against the Arians.* Discourse 2.63.
[47]*Four Discourses Against the Arians.* Discourse 2.64.

Because His coming into the world is what makes Him called First-born of all; and thus the Son is the Father's only-begotten, because He alone is from Him, and He is the first-born of creation, because of this adoption of all as sons. And as He is First-born among brethren and rose from the dead 'the first fruits of them that slept,' so, since it became Him 'in all things to have the preeminence,' therefore He is created 'a beginning of ways,' that we, walking along it and entering through Him who says, 'I am the Way' and 'the Door,' and partaking of the knowledge of the Father, may also hear the words, 'Blessed are the undefiled in the Way,' and 'Blessed are the pure in heart, for they shall see God.'[48]

Athanasius developed the salvific theme for the firstborn in the next section of the discourse:

And thus since the truth declares that the Word is not by nature a creature, it is fitting now to say, in what sense He is 'beginning of ways.' For when the first way, which was through Adam, was lost, and in place of paradise we deviated unto death, and heard the words, 'Dust thou art, and unto dust shalt thou return,' therefore the Word of God, who loves man, puts on Him created flesh at the Father's will, that whereas the first man had made it dead through the transgression, He Himself might quicken it in the blood of His own body, and might open 'for us a way new and living', as the Apostle says, 'through the veil, that is to say, His flesh;' which he signifies elsewhere thus, 'Wherefore, if any man be in Christ, he is a new creation, old things are passed away, behold all things are become new.' But if a new creation has come to pass, some one must be first of this creation; now a man, made of earth only, such as we are become from the transgression, he could not be. For in the first creation, men had become unfaithful, and through them that first creation had been lost; and there was need of some one else to renew the first creation, and preserve the new which had come to be. Therefore from love to man none other than the Lord, the 'beginning' of the new creation, is created as 'the Way,' and consistently says, 'The Lord created me a beginning of ways for His works; 'that man might walk no longer according to that first creation, but there being as it were a beginning of a new creation, and with the Christ 'a beginning of its ways,' we might follow Him henceforth, who says to us, 'I am the Way:' – as the blessed Apostle teaches in Colossians, saying, 'He is the Head of the body. the Church, who is the Beginning, the First-born from the dead, that in all things He might have the preeminence.[49]

[48]*Four Discourses Against the Arians.* Discourse 11.64.
[49]*Four Discourses Against the Arians.* Discourse 11.65.

Clearly Athanasius saw that there was a soteriological significance in the title 'firstborn' and linked it with his status in the new creation, which he was instrumental in bringing about. However, Athanasius clearly missed the New Exodus theme for the new creation. Had he not, he might have made the final step of linking the title to Christ's role as the Paschal victim.

This survey of the early church fathers shows that they had moved away from a Hebraic understanding of firstborn with the result that it created philosophical problems which they could not adequately resolve. Some clearly saw a soteriological meaning in the term, but because the original context of the expression did not determine its meaning, they failed to explore the soteriological significance of the title.

Appendix 3

The Reformed Faith and Justification

N.T. Wright argues that the Reformers misunderstood Paul, that they had confused their own debate with the legalism of Rome and read their conflict into Paul's conflict with Judaism. I have argued that it has been the other way round. It is Wright who has misunderstood the Reformers and in turn has misunderstood Paul. He has not appreciated that the Reformers did not have an exclusively forensic view of justification. This itself demonstrates that in their exegesis their eye was not on the abuse of Rome but on the biblical text. While they did not explain their doctrine in the way that I have argued in this book, they nevertheless would have had no problem in accepting that justification included entering into the covenant. The following extracts from key Reformers and subsequent Reformed theologians supports this claim.

John Calvin

First, Calvin focused on entering into the covenant as being part of the doctrine of justification. In his *Institutes*, under the heading of justification, he says that it is the same as acceptance. In other words, justification is relational and not solely forensic. Elsewhere Calvin says:

> But as the Lord wills not to destroy in us that which is his own, he still finds something in us which in kindness he can love. For though it is by our own fault that we are sinners, we are still his creatures; though we have brought death upon ourselves he had created us for life. Thus, mere gratuitous love prompts him to receive us into favour. But if there is a perpetual and irreconcilable repugnance between righteousness and iniquity, so long as we remain sinners we cannot be completely received. Therefore, in order that all ground of offence may be removed, and he may completely reconcile us to himself, he, by means of the expiation set forth in the death of Christ, abolishes all the evil that is in us, so that we, formerly impure and unclean, now appear in his sight just and holy. Accordingly, God the Father, by his love, prevents and anticipates our reconciliation in Christ. Nay, it is because he first loves us, that he afterwards reconciles us to himself. But because the iniquity, which

deserves the indignation of God, remains in us until the death of Christ comes to our aid, and that iniquity is in his sight accursed and condemned, *we are not admitted to full and sure communion with God, unless, in so far as Christ unites us. And, therefore, if we would indulge the hope of having God placable and propitious to us, we must fix our eyes and minds on Christ alone, as it is to him alone it is owing that our sins, which necessarily provoked the wrath of God, are not imputed to us.*[1]

4. Justification as gracious acceptance by God and as forgiveness of sins.

Without saying more about the term, we shall have no doubt as to the thing meant if we attend to the description which is given of it. For Paul certainly designates justification by the term acceptance, when he says to the Ephesians, 'Having predestinated us unto the adoption of children by Jesus Christ to himself, according to the good pleasure of his will, to the praise of the glory of his grace, wherein he has made us accepted in the Beloved,' (Eph. 1: 5, 6.) His meaning is the very same as where he elsewhere says, 'being justified freely by his grace,' (Rom. 3: 24.) In the fourth chapter of the Epistle to the Romans, he first terms it the imputation of righteousness, and hesitates not to place it in forgiveness of sins: 'Even as David also describeth the blessedness of the man unto whom God imputeth righteousness without works, saying, Blessed are they whose iniquities are forgiven,' &c., (Rom. 4: 6-8.) There, indeed, he is not speaking of a part of justification, but of the whole. He declares, moreover, that a definition of it was given by David, when he pronounced him blessed who has obtained the free pardon of his sins. Whence it appears that this righteousness of which he speaks is simply opposed to judicial guilt. *But the most satisfactory passage on this subject is that in which he declares the sum of the Gospel message to be reconciliation to God, who is pleased, through Christ, to receive us into favor by not imputing our sins, (2 Cor. 5: 18-21.) Let my readers carefully weigh the whole context. For Paul shortly after adding, by way of explanation, in order to designate the mode of reconciliation, that Christ who knew no sin was made sin for us, undoubtedly understands by reconciliation nothing else than justification.* Nor, indeed, could it be said, as he elsewhere does, that we are made righteous 'by the obedience' of Christ, (Rom. 5: 19,) were it not that we are deemed righteous in the sight of God in him and not in ourselves.[2]

Elsewhere Calvin says:

[1]*Institutes,* Book 2:16, section 3, italics mine.
[2]*Institutes,* Book 3:11, section 4, italics mine.

Thus we simply interpret justification, as the acceptance with which God receives us into his favor as if we were righteous; and we say that this justification consists in the forgiveness of sins and the imputation of the righteousness of Christ.[3]

Scripture, when it treats of justification by faith, leads us in a very different direction. Turning away our view from our own works, it bids us look only to the mercy of God and the perfection of Christ. *The order of justification which it sets before us is this: first, God of his mere gratuitous goodness is pleased to embrace the sinner, in whom he sees nothing that can move him to mercy but wretchedness, because he sees him altogether naked and destitute of good works.* He, therefore, seeks the cause of kindness in himself, that thus he may affect the sinner by a sense of his goodness, and induce him, in distrust of his own works, to cast himself entirely upon his mercy for salvation. This is the meaning of faith by which the sinner comes into the possession of salvation, when, according to the doctrine of the Gospel, he perceives that he is reconciled by God; when, by the intercession of Christ, he obtains the pardon of his sins, and is justified; and, though renewed by the Spirit of God, considers that, instead of leaning on his own works, he must look solely to the righteousness which is treasured up for him in Christ. When these things are weighed separately, they will clearly explain our view, though they may be arranged in a better order than that in which they are here presented. But it is of little consequence, provided they are so connected with each other as to give us a full exposition and solid confirmation of the whole subject.[4]

Again Calvin says of justification:

Let us now consider the truth of what was said in the definition, viz., that justification by faith is reconciliation with God, and that this consists solely in the remission of sins. We must always return to the axioms that the wrath of God lies upon all men so long as they continue sinners. This is elegantly expressed by Isaiah in these words: 'Behold, the Lord's hand is not shortened, that it cannot save; neither his ear heavy, that it cannot hear: but your iniquities have separated between you and your God, and your sins have hid his face from you, that he will not hear,' (Isaiah 59: 1, 2.) We are here told that sin is a separation between God and man; that His countenance is turned away from the sinner; and that it cannot be otherwise, since, to have any intercourse with sin is repugnant to his

---

[3]*Institutes,* Book 3:11, sections 21 and 23, italics mine.
[4]*Institutes,* Book 3:11, section 16, italics mine.

righteousness. Hence the Apostle shows that man is at enmity with God until he is restored to favour by Christ, (Rom. 5: 8-10.) *When the Lord, therefore, admits him to union, he is said to justify him*, because he can neither receive him into favor, nor unite him to himself, without changing his condition from that of a sinner into that of a righteous man. We adds that this is done by remission of sins. For if those whom the Lord has reconciled to himself are estimated by works, they will still prove to be in reality sinners, while they ought to be pure and free from sin. It is evident, therefore, that the only way in which those whom God embraces are made righteous, is by having their pollutions wiped away by the remission of sins, so that this justification may be termed in one word the remission of sins.[5]

Calvin defines what union with Christ is:

that union of the head and members, the residence of Christ in our hearts, in fine, the mystical union, we assign the highest rank, Christ when he becomes ours making us partners with him in the gifts with which he was endued. Hence we do not view him as at a distance and without us, but as we have put him on, and been ingrafted into his body, he deigns to make us one with himself, and, therefore, we glory in having a fellowship of righteousness with him.[6]

Martin Luther

Calvin is not alone among the Reformers in having this understanding. Luther is even clearer concerning this aspect of justification. It is true that the term 'justified' is not used in the following passage but this is not a problem. A quick comparison between this passage and the Apology of the Augsberg Confession, cited in the chapter on justification, will show that one text is dependent on the other and that the Apology is quite definitely speaking of justification, for it is headed in the confession as being such. Luther says:

The third incomparable grace of faith is this: that it unites the soul to Christ, as the wife to the husband, by which mystery, as the Apostle teaches, Christ and the soul are made one flesh. Now if they are one flesh, and if a true marriage – nay, by far the most perfect of all marriages – is accomplished between them (for human marriages are but feeble types of this one great marriage), then it follows that all they have becomes theirs in common, as well good things as evil things; so that whatsoever Christ

---

[5]*Institutes,* Book 3:11, section 21, italics mine.
[6]*Institutes,* Book 3:11, section 10.

possesses, that the believing soul may take to itself and boast of as its own, and whatever belongs to the soul, that Christ claims as His. If we compare these possessions, we shall see how inestimable is the gain. Christ is full of grace, life, and salvation; the soul is full of sin, death, and condemnation. Let faith step in, and then sin, death, and hell will belong to Christ, and grace, life, and salvation to the soul. For, if He is a Husband, He must needs take to Himself that which is His wife's, and at the same time, impart to His wife that which is His. For, in giving her His own body and Himself, how can He but give her all that is His? And, in taking to Himself the body of His wife, how can He but take to Himself all that is hers? In this is displayed the delightful sight, not only of communion, but of a prosperous warfare, of victory, salvation, and redemption. For, since Christ is God and man, and is such a Person as neither has sinned, nor dies, nor is condemned, nay, cannot sin, die, or be condemned, and since His righteousness, life, and salvation are invincible, eternal, and almighty, – when I say, such a Person, by the wedding-ring of faith, takes a share in the sins, death, and hell of His wife, nay, makes them His own, and deals with them no otherwise than as if they were His, and as if He Himself had sinned; and when He suffers, dies, and descends to hell, that He may overcome all things, and since sin, death, and hell cannot swallow Him up, they must needs be swallowed up by Him in stupendous conflict. For His righteousness rises above the sins of all men; His life is more powerful than all death; His salvation is more unconquerable than all hell. Thus the believing soul, by the pledge of its faith in Christ, becomes free from all sin, fearless of death, safe from hell, and endowed with the eternal righteousness, life, and salvation of its Husband Christ. Thus He presents to Himself a glorious bride, without spot or wrinkle, cleansing her with the washing of water by the word; that is, by faith in the word of life, righteousness, and salvation. Thus He betrothes her unto Himself 'in faithfulness, in righteousness, and in judgment, and in lovingkindness, and in mercies' (Hosea ii. 19, 20). Who then can value highly enough these royal nuptials? Who can comprehend the riches of the glory of this grace? Christ, that rich and pious Husband, takes as a wife a needy and impious harlot, redeeming her from all her evils and supplying her with all His good things. It is impossible now that her sins should destroy her, since they have been laid upon Christ and swallowed up in Him, and since she has in her Husband Christ a righteousness which she may claim as her own, and which she can set up with confidence against all her sins, against death and hell, saying, 'If I have sinned, my Christ, in whom I believe, has not sinned; all mine is His, and all His is mine,' as it is written, 'My beloved is mine, and I am His' (Cant. ii. 16).[7]

---

[7]Luther, *Liberty*.

The only thing that needs to be added to this statement by Luther is that all that he says of the bridegroom and bride is about Christ and the church, and not immediately about the individual believer. Scripture nowhere calls the believer the bride of Christ. It is a description of the relationship between Christ and his church. As a member of the New Israel the believer in the moment of conversion inherits all that the covenant community has been historically blessed with. This follows that pattern of the Old Testament where all who were circumcised entered into all that the covenant had bestowed on the descendants of Abraham.

John Owen

To these two examples of Reformation understanding, we can add the Puritan John Owen, who wrote:

> The most frequent declaration of the nature of faith in the Scripture, especially in the Old Testament, is by this trust; and that because it is that act of it which composes the soul, and brings it unto all the rest it can attain. For all our rest in this world is from trust in God; and the especial object of this trust, so far as it belongs unto the nature of that faith whereby we are justified, is 'God in Christ reconciling the world unto himself.' *For this is respected where his goodness, his mercy, his grace, his name, his faithfulness, his power, are expressed, or any of them, as that which it does immediately rely upon; for they are no way the object of our trust, nor can be, but on the account of the covenant. which is confirmed and ratified in and by the blood of Christ alone.*[8]

In another part of his thesis on justification Owen emphasises that all the blessings the believer enjoys come through being members of the covenant community. Of course, to be a member of that community is to be 'in Christ'. Owen says:

> To give the sum of these things, it is inquired with respect unto which of these considerations of the new covenant it is affirmed that it was procured by the death of Christ. If it be said that it is with respect unto the actual communication of all the grace and glory prepared in the covenant, and proposed unto us in the promises of it, it is most true. *All the grace and glory promised in the covenant were purchased for the church by Jesus Christ. In this sense, by his death he procured the new covenant. This the whole Scripture, from the beginning of it in the first promise*

[8]John Owen, *Justification*, Part 10.5, italics mine.

unto the end of it, does bear witness unto; for it is in him alone that 'God blesseth us with all spiritual blessings in heavenly things.' Let all the good things that are mentioned or promised in the covenant, expressly or by just consequence, be summed up, and it will be no hard matter to demonstrate concerning them all, and that both jointly and severally, that they were all procured for us by the obedience and death of Christ. The making of this covenant is everywhere in the Scripture ascribed (as is also the sending of Christ himself to die) unto the love, grace, and wisdom of God alone; nowhere unto the death of Christ, as the actual communication of all grace and glory are. Let all the places be considered, where either the giving of the promise, the sending of Christ, or the making of the covenant, are mentioned, either expressly or virtually, and in none of them are they assigned unto any other cause but the grace, love, and wisdom of God alone; all to be made effectual unto us by the mediation of Christ.[9]

Wherefore, if he and all the benefits of his mediation, his death, and all the effects of it, be contained in the promise of the covenant, – that is, in the covenant itself, – then was not his death the procuring cause of that covenant, nor do we owe it thereunto.[10]

we have the 'righteousness of God;' instead of being righteous in ourselves before God, he is 'The LORD our Righteousness.' *And nothing but a righteousness of another kind and nature, unto justification before God, could constitute another covenant. Wherefore, the righteousness whereby we are justified is the righteousness of Christ imputed unto us, or we are still under the law, under the covenant of works.*[11]

Stephen Charnock

Stephen Charnock, another Puritan theologian, also sees that covenant is intrinsically linked with justification:

Justification is a relative change, whereby a man is brought from a state of guilt to a state of righteousness; from a state of slavery to a state of liberty; from the obligation of the covenant of works to the privilege of the covenant of grace; from being a child of wrath to be an heir of promise. Regeneration is a physical change, and real, as when a dead man is raised from death to life; it is a filling the soul with another nature, Eph. ii. 1, 'And you has he quickened, who were dead in trespasses and sins.'

[9]*Ibid*, 19, italics mine.
[10]*Ibid*, 18.
[11]*Ibid*, 26, italics mine.

Charnock's view is rooted in the slave imagery, which we discussed in chapter four, but that does not affect his perception. Justification for him is about the change of states. In other words, it is covenantal. The following extracts demonstrate this further.

> *Justification is a relative change, whereby a man is brought from a state of guilt to a state of righteousness; from a state of slavery to a state of liberty; from the obligation of the covenant of works to the privilege of the covenant of grace; from being a child of wrath to be an heir of promise.*

Two things happened to us by the fall: another state and another nature; the regaining of the former must be equally sought with the latter, a being in another covenant by justification (for naturally we are in the covenant with Adam), and a being beautified with another image, because naturally we are deformed by the image of Adam. As long as we are only in a state of descent from, and union with, the first Adam, we are under the strictness of his covenant and the deformity of his image; when we are united to the second Adam, and spiritually descend from him, we are in his covenant of grace, and are adorned with his image. Both, therefore, must be looked after as equally necessary: Rom. v. 21, 'That as sin has reigned unto death, so might grace reign through righteousness unto eternal life by Jesus Christ our Lord.' Let us, then, look after this reign of grace; let not that be the last which should be first in our thoughts. Since our natural descent from Adam, we are born God's enemies: we must be spiritually new-born before our enmity can expire.[12]

Thomas Goodwin

A third Puritan theologian, Thomas Goodwin, also sees covenant creation to be a vital part of justification. He says:

Our believing is a receiving of Christ; it is the giving ourselves up to him as lord and husband, and it is proper for the Father to woo for him, because all other fathers have the power of bestowing their sons or daughters, and therefore God hath it much more. Hagar, though but a woman, yet had the right, and exercised the power of getting a wife for her son. To give in marriage is oft spoken of in Scripture to be by the parents, and there is here Ps xv., where Christ is represented as the husband, and the church his wife. Who is it that speaks to the church, to love her husband, to worship her husband, and to forsake all for him? It is God the Father: ver.10, 'Hearken, O daughter , and consider, and incline

---

[12]Charnock, *Discourse*, italics mine.

thine ear,' &c. This is God the Father speaking of Christ unto the church. But you will say, This is not found amongst other fathers, that they should condescend to woo the wife for their sons, but that it is enough for them to give their consents, and leave to their sons to gain the heart themselves. Thus it is amongst men, and the reasons for it among men are plain, which will not hold us to God.

1ˢᵗ, Fathers are strangers to the person whom the son is to woo, and so leave it to his liking; it is enough for him to give his consent and leave to get the person's heart. But the case here is otherwise, for every elect soul is the daughter of God, even in election, before conversion; and as he knows his Son, so he knows the soul, he knows the daughter too, not only as made his daughter by marriage to his Son, but as originally chosen by him. As Eve is said to be the daughter of God by creation, as Adam was the son of God by creation, Luke iii. 38, so it is here. Therefore he leaves it not to his Son only to speak for himself, and gain her, but he out of the same fatherly interest which he hath in the soul, as well as in his Son (though he hath interest in her as his daughter, which is a lower interest that what he hath in his Son), wooes her.

2dly, Marriages amongst men stand upon equal terms, and persons of like rank is to marry together; and the father will not condescend in that case to woo for the son; no, it ere uncouth if he should, and not proper. But the church, and every poor soul, is the unworthiest creature to be matched so gloriously to Christ that ever was. Nay, it was an enemy before, and utter enemy, utterly averse; so that it becomes a matter not only of love, but of grace and mercy, for to have this soul gained and brought to Christ. It is fulness of mercy and grace to woo such a soul, and an infinite condescension so to do, and no one greater but that of God's giving his Son to die. And since it thus belongs to grace, the Father will have the honour of it as well as the Son, for you read of 'the grace of the Lord Jesus, and the Father,' and sometimes both are put together, 2 Thes. i.12. It is a matter of infinite grace, the person being so low and unworthy? In that case, saith the Father, I will be your spokesman, for it is a matter of grace. It is not matter of pure affection, as the husband hath to a wife, but it is a matter of grace which I have to such a soul; I will therefore shew it in this my wooing such a soul. Oh this infinite condescension in the great God![13]

The Father had wrought all this while, but secretly, and had not discovered himself; and though Jesus Christ in his doctrine had taught the apostles, and instructed them about, the Father, yet alas, poor creatures, they did not understand it! They did not take it in; it was the Father that drew them to believe, and they found the work upon them to be powerful and effectual,

[13]Goodwin, 'Justification,' 156-57.

yet it was obscure to them that it was he that did it; but he tells them that the time cometh (which time must be after his ascension) when he would tell them plainly it was the Father who did it. It was the Father, though now unseen, and spoken of in parables and proverbs, that drew their souls in morning by morning; and thou wilt give all the glory to the Father one one day: 'Oh what manner of love is it' (of the Father), 'that we should be called the sons of God!' 1 John iii.1. Oh what manner of love it is that the Father should woo us herein; he 'gives us power to become the sons of God,' John i.12. It is enough for other fathers to give their consent, and leave it to their sons; but here in this case, as Jesus Christ came down from heaven to redeem and purchase his church and his spouse, so God the Father comes down into the hearts of men, and draws them, and does it immediately. I do not say he doth it by his Spirit, as if himself did not. It is true the Spirit doth join in it, and so doth the Son, but the Father does this himself immediately. Is it not a mighty thing that the Father should teach us to woo his Son, and become a tutor to us and an instructor of us.

Jonathan Edwards

Jonathan Edwards also views justification as being more than acquittal from guilt. He says:

> *But that a believer's justification implies more, not only remission of sins, or acquittance from the wrath due to it, but also an admittance to a title to that glory which is the reward of the righteous, is more directly taught in the Scriptures, particularly in Rom. v, 2, where the apostle mentions both these as joint benefits implied in justification*: 'Therefore being justified by faith we have peace with God through our Lord Jesus Christ, by whom we rejoice in the hope of the glory of God.' So remission of sins, and inheritance among them that are sanctified, are mentioned together as what are jointly obtained by faith in Christ.[13]

> But what is a still more plain and direct evidence of what I am now arguing for, is that the act of faith which Abraham exercised in the great promise of the covenant of grace that God made to him, of which it is expressly said, Gal. 3:6, 'It was accounted to him for righteousness' – the grand instance and proof that the apostle so much insists upon throughout Romans 4, and Galatians 3, to confirm his doctrine of justification by faith alone – was not Abraham's first act of faith, but was exerted long after he had by faith forsaken his own country, Heb. 11:8, and had been treated as an eminent friend of God.

[14]Goodwin, 'Justification,' 158.

But there are other texts that are even more explicit in showing that Edwards understood justification to be rooted in covenant. He says:

> What is real in the union between Christ and his people, is the very foundation of what is legal; that is, it is something really in them, and between them. Uniting them, that is the ground of the suitableness of their being accounted as one by the judge.[14]

John Murray

The following extracts show how the twentieth-century Reformed theologian John Murray understood union with Christ to be the source of salvation. His focus is the eternal decree of God in electing his people, but since the union can only exist where covenant exists, both therefore precede the application of salvation to the individual believer.

> Union with Christ is really the central truth of the whole doctrine of salvation not only in its application but also in its once-for-all accomplishment in the finished work of Christ.[15]

> Union with Christ is a very inclusive subject. It embraces the wide span of salvation from its ultimate source in the eternal election of God to its final fruition in the glorification of the elect. It is not simply a phase of the application of redemption; it underlies every aspect of redemption both in its accomplishment and its application. Union with Christ binds all together and insures that all for whom Christ has purchased redemption he effectively applies and communicates the same.[16]

> Union with Adam in his sin, condemnation and death is the pattern in terms of which by union with Christ believers come into possession of righteousness, justification and life.[17]

Arthur W. Pink

More recently the writer Arthur A. Pink has shared this same belief in a covenantal dimension of justification.

> It now remains for us to point out *the ground on which* God acts in this counter-imputation of sin to Christ and righteousness to His people.

[15]Edwards, *Justification*, passim, italics mine.
[16]Edwards, *Works*, 1:126.
[15]Murray, *Accomplished*, 161.
[16]*Op. cit.* 165.
[17]Murray, *Imputation*, passim.

That ground was *the Everlasting Covenant*. The objection that it is unjust the innocent should suffer in order that the guilty may escape loses all its force once the Covenant-Headship and responsibility of Christ is seen, and the *covenant-oneness with Him* of those whose sins He bore. *There could have been no such thing as a vicarious sacrifice unless there had been some union between Christ and those for whom He died, and that relation of union must have subsisted before He died, yea, before our sins were imputed to Him.* Christ undertook to make full satisfaction to the law for His people because He sustained to them the relation of a *Surety.* But *what* justified His acting as their Surety? He stood as their Surety because He was their *Substitute*: He acted *on their behalf*, because He stood *in their room*. But *what* justified the substitution? No satisfactory answer can be given to the last question until the grand doctrine of everlasting covenant-oneness comes into view: *that* is the great underlying relation. The federal oneness between the Redeemer and the redeemed, the choosing of them *in* Christ before the foundation of the world (Eph. 1:4), by which a legal union was established between Him and them, is that which alone accounts for and justifies all else. 'For both He that sanctifieth and they who are sanctified are *all of one*: for which cause He is not ashamed to call them brethren' (Heb. 2:11). As the Covenant-Head of His people, Christ was so related to them that their responsibilities necessarily became His, and we are so related to Him that His merits necessarily become ours. Thus, as we said in an earlier chapter, three words give us the key to and sum up the whole transaction: substitution, identification, imputation – all of which rest upon covenant-oneness. Christ was substituted *for* us, because He is one *with* us – identified with us, and we with Him. Thus God dealt with us as occupying *Christ's* place of worthiness and acceptance. May the Holy Spirit grant both writer and reader such an heart-apprehension of this wondrous and blessed truth, that overflowing gratitude may move us unto fuller devotedness unto Him who loved us and gave Himself for us.[18]

Not all Reformed theologians would see justification as relational. Eveson, for example, is quite clear that 'adoption' and 'reconciliation' are founded upon and result from justification.[19] Berkhof, however, draws a similar conclusion to that presented in this chapter. He places 'adoption' within justification and understands 'reconciliation' to be objectively achieved in the atonement, through Christ's sacrifice, and subjectively experienced as the sinner accepts the gift of justification.[20]

[18]Pink, *Justification*, passim. Emphasis mine.
[19]Eveson, *Exchange*, 33-34.

Thus, Reformation understanding of justification includes those who understand that it is not only the act of acquittal, but that it is also relational. The God who freely forgives the sinner also brings the pardoned sinner into an eternal relationship with himself in a covenant that he is totally responsible for. It is because of this divine initiative that the doctrine of justification assures the believer of his/her everlasting blessing.

---

[20]Berkhof, *Theology*, 373. I am grateful to my student Stephen Derby for pointing out in an essay Eveson's and Berkhof's position. I have used his words to describe the views of Eveson and Berkhof.

Appendix 4

Firstborn and the Claims of Wisdom

The exegesis that I have proposed, in chapter 12, of the Colossian Christ-hymn challenges the widely accepted understanding of the meaning of *prōtotokos*. While the Hellenistic setting has declined in popularity, the suggestion that the term relates to a Wisdom tradition that comes from within Judaism has achieved widespread support. This view has become prevalent as the result of W.D. Davies' *Paul and Rabbinic Judaism*.[1] Although this is a dated work in research terms, subsequent work has largely been based on the arguments that Davies presented. There has been no detailed challenge to this work and it is therefore necessary to examine its claims to see if they can be substantiated. If the argument advanced by Davies is found to be unsound, then it will bring down with it those works that have depended on it. If it should be found to be sound, then it will call into question the exegesis that I am offering.

Not convinced of the validity of the earlier Greek-orientated solutions Davies began his reconstruction of the evidence by seeking to understand Paul's rabbinical background. He began his study of Pauline thinking on the assumption that Paul carried his training in Rabbinic Judaism with him when he became a follower of Jesus. Davies pointed out that the Torah was not merely a legal code for the Jews, but a divinely appointed way of life. This way of life had been surpassed for Paul, not by another code, but by the teaching and Person of Jesus. Davies noted that 'not only did the words of Jesus form a torah for Paul but so also did the Person of Jesus. In a real sense conformity to Christ, His teaching and His life has taken the place, for Paul, of conformity to the Jewish torah. Jesus Himself – in word and deed or fact is a new torah.'[2]

Davies supported this claim that the Torah has been replaced by Jesus as the new Torah, by appealing to 2 Corinthians 3 where Paul contrasts the Christian ministry with the ministry of the old covenant. In that chapter Paul says:

[1] W. D. Davies (1955), *Paul and Rabbinic Judaism*, SPCK.
[2] *op. cit.* 146.

Our competence comes from God. He has made us competent as ministers of a new covenant – not of the letter but of the Spirit; for the letter kills, but the Spirit gives life. Now if the ministry that brought death, which was engraved in letters on stone, came with glory, so that the Israelites could not look steadily at the face of Moses because of its glory, fading though it was, will not the ministry of the Spirit be even more glorious? If the ministry that condemns men is glorious, how much more glorious is the ministry that righteousness brings. For what was glorious has no glory now in comparison with the surpassing glory. And if what was fading away came with glory, how much greater is the glory of that which lasts!

Therefore, since we have such a hope, we are very bold. We are not like Moses, who would put a veil over his face to keep the Israelites from gazing at it while the radiance was fading away. But their minds were made dull, for to this day the same veil remains when the old covenant is read. It has not been removed, because only in Christ is it taken away. Even to this day when Moses is read, a veil covers their hearts. But whenever anyone turns to the Lord, the veil is taken away. Now the Lord is the Spirit, and where the Spirit of the Lord is, there is freedom. And we, who with unveiled faces all reflect the Lord's glory, are being transformed into his likeness with ever-increasing glory, which comes from the Lord, who is the Spirit (2 Cor. 3:5-18).

Davies noted Paul's argument that the glory that shone in Moses' face, which came because he had been entrusted with the Torah of Israel, was a fading glory. In contrast the Christian minister has received a glory that is not fading because he has looked into the face of Jesus Christ and found there a new knowledge. Davies claimed that the significance of this passage is only fully realised when it is appreciated that in Rabbinic Judaism the Torah was associated with light. He summed up the use he wanted to make of the passage in these words: 'The object of the argument was to prove that Jesus, not the torah, was the true revelation of the divine glory and the divine light. This probably means that Jesus was a new torah.'[3]

Davies supported his case for Jesus being the new Torah by appealing to Matthew 18:20, where Jesus promises his presence where two or three are assembled in his name, and to Matthew 11:29 and 30, where Jesus invites the burdened to take his yoke upon them. Davies pointed to rabbinic parallels in which it is said that when Jews sit together and are occupied with the Torah, the *Shekinah* is among

---

[3]*op. cit.* 149.

them, and to the fact that taking the yoke of the Torah was an expression familiar to the Jews.[4] At this point Davies linked the concept of Christ as the new Torah to Christ being the wisdom of God. Referring to Colossians 1:15ff., he said: 'Judaism had ascribed to the figure of wisdom a pre-cosmic origin and a part in the creation of the world. It becomes probable, therefore, that Paul has here pictured Christ on the image of wisdom.'[5]

To support his thesis Davies appeals to the work of C.F. Burney who had argued that firstborn in Colossians 1:15 is a direct reference to Proverbs 8:22 where it is said: 'The LORD possessed me at the beginning of his work, before his deeds of old.' Burney argued that the term *reshith* in Proverbs 8:22 was used in rabbinic Judaism as the key to the *bereshith* that begins the Hebrew Bible. This latter *bereshith* of Genesis 1 was correspondingly interpreted as meaning 'by wisdom'.[6] Davies claims: 'It is natural to infer that when in the Epistle to the Colossians Paul calls Christ the *prototokos pases ktiseos* he is thinking of him as the reshith of creation.'[7] Davies continued to appeal to Burney's work to show the link Colossians 1:15-18 has with Genesis 1:1. Burney claimed that the Colossian passage is 'an elaborate exposition of bereshith in Gen. 1:1 in the rabbinic manner'. So Davies argued that firstborn and wisdom were synonymous terms in Paul's thought.

Davies continued his argument by considering three other Pauline passages. He argued that the reference to the rock in the wilderness in 1 Corinthians 10:4 also supports his thesis, and although he recognises that no evidence exists to show that Jewish piety attached any Messianic significance to the rock, he nevertheless appeals to Philo, who interpreted the passage on which Paul's text is based, i.e. Deuteronomy 8:15, as a reference to the wisdom of God. Philo said: 'The rock of flint is the wisdom of God from which He feeds the souls that love Him.'[8] Davies noted that this same interpretation was followed by the book of Wisdom, and he summed up the relevance of 1 Corinthians 10 for his thesis by saying that 'it is not impossible, therefore, that in equating Christ with the rock Paul was thinking of Him as the Divine wisdom according to a familiar convention of interpretation'.[9]

[4]*op. cit.* 150. [5]*op. cit.* 151.
[6]Burney, 'ARCHE,' 160-68.
[7]Davies, *op. cit.* 151-2.
[8]Philo, *Leg Alleg* 2.21. [9]Davies, *op. cit.* 153.

The second passage Davies considers is Romans 10:6 ff. where Paul argues for the accessibility of righteousness to everyone: 'But the righteousness that is by faith says: "Do not say in your heart, 'Who will ascend into heaven?' (that is, to bring Christ down), or 'Who will descend into the deep?' " (that is, to bring Christ up from the dead). But what does it say? "The word is near you: it is in your mouth and in your heart," that is, the word of faith we are proclaiming.'

Davies notes Sanday and Headlam's conclusion that this passage is not a direct quotation from the Old Testament and that it might be taken from the Book of *Baruch* where it is applied to wisdom.[10] Davies rightly decided to reject Windisch's suggestion that Romans 10:6 ff. is a reference to wisdom, for *Baruch's* passage refers to the undiscoverability of wisdom,[11] whereas Paul in Romans 10 bases his argument on the essential accessibility or nearness of Christ in order to prove that the Jews who reject him are without excuse.

The third passage is 1 Corinthians 1:24 and 30, where Paul says: 'but to those whom God has called, both Jews and Greeks, Christ the power of God and the wisdom of God.... It is because of him that you are in Christ Jesus, who has become for us Wisdom from God – that is, our righteousness, holiness and redemption.'

Davies acknowledged that the translation of verse 30 is difficult, but prefers the Authorised Version rendering, 'who of God is made unto us wisdom and righteousness, and sanctification and redemption.' By accepting this translation and interpretation of the passage Davies argues that 'Here again we see Paul's twofold emphasis in his ascription of the title wisdom to Christ – it is pre-cosmic wisdom and a morally recreative wisdom that he finds in his Lord.'[12]

Davies examines the proposal made by Windisch who thought he could easily identify the progress of Paul's thinking in arriving at his wisdom Christology. Windisch said that Paul had become convinced that Jesus was the Messiah and he would automatically regard him as the wisdom of God. Messianic speculation is the key to his Christology. His equation would be simple. Thus:

The Messiah = The wisdom of God
Jesus = The Messiah
therefore Jesus = The wisdom of God.

[10]Sanday and Headlam, *Romans*, 289.
[11]*Baruch*, 329ff.
[12]Davies, *op. cit.* 155.

Davies, after examining Windisch's evidence, dismisses it with the conclusion that *in all cases we have found the evidence unconvincing*,[13] i.e. the evidence that there ever was any identification between the Messiah and wisdom in Judaism.

Davies then sought to give a detailed summary of the significance of the concept of wisdom in the Old Testament, inter-testamental and rabbinic literature.[14] In this section Davies notes the difference between the Old Testament concept of wisdom, which was thoroughly universal, and the nationalistic view which emerged later. Davies commented:

> One fact, however, will be evident from the above, namely, that wisdom as found in the Old Testament is in no sense a 'nationalistic' figure. There is about all the wisdom literature of the Old Testament an international flavour, there is in it nothing that is specifically Israelite. It is not surprising, therefore, that there should grow up a tendency to make the figure of wisdom more distinctly Jewish. It is this that we find in the book of Ecclesiasticus. There the figure of wisdom becomes identified with the torah, wisdom takes up her abode in Israel and is established in Zion.[15]

It is from the identification of wisdom and the Torah that Davies launched his concluding argument to identify Paul's wisdom Christology with the Jewish concept of wisdom, and in turn with the title 'firstborn of all creation'. Davies pointed out that, for the Jews, the Torah was older than the creation, as was wisdom. The Torah was the means of creation, as was wisdom, and creation was for the sake of the Torah.[16] Clearly Davies had no difficulty in applying these themes to Christ himself, who is pre-existent, the means of creation, and the purpose of creation.

This, I consider, summarises the essentials of Davies' argument that Christ's title of 'firstborn of all creation' is to be interpreted in the light of the Jewish concept of wisdom. Jesus is the New Torah, the Torah being wisdom itself, which in turn was begotten before all things, and involved in creation (Prov. 8:22). So Davies explained the meaning of Paul's thinking when he used the term firstborn of all creation in relation to Christ.

---

[13]*op. cit.* 162.
[14]*op. cit.* 159-71.
[15]*op. cit.* 168.
[16]see *op. cit.* 170 for Rabbinic references.

An assessment

What are we to make of this argument? The first thing is to commend
the biblical focus in Davies' attempt to explain 'the firstborn of all
creation'. This does justice to the constant reference Paul made to
the Old Testament, especially in verses 13 and 14 of Colossians 1
which immediately precede the title. It was the Old Testament that
provided the substructure of Paul's theological thinking. But are there
any flaws in the argument that Davies has overlooked?[17] Having
acknowledged that no evidence exists to claim the Messiah was
identified with wisdom in pre-Christian Judaism, Davies has to base
his argument entirely upon the New Testament text. It is the texts
which he has mustered for his argument that we will now examine.

The first is the reference in Matthew 18:20, where Davies says
that Christ's presence is to be compared to the *shekinah*. The problem
Davies' interpretation must face is that the context of Matthew 18:20
does not suggest the believers have met for worship or for instruction,
but specifically for discipline. By seeing this instruction to be the basis
of 1 Corinthians 5:4-5, where Paul also says that he will be with the
Corinthian Church in their gathering, it is right to claim that the promise
relates to nothing more than the Semitic concept of solidarity, as Best
has suggested,[18] and not to Christ modelling himself on the presence
of the *shekinah*.

Nor does Davies' argument find support in Matthew 11:29-30,
where Christ's yoke is spoken of as being easy. By stating *my yoke
is easy* Christ is not saying that he is the yoke, but that his teaching,
as compared to the teaching of the Scribes and Pharisees, was easy
and not a crushing burden. It was not the Torah that Christ guided
men away from, but from the Pharisees' legalistic interpretation of
the Torah that was so crushing and burdensome. Davies' interpretation
of Christ being the new Torah, replacing the old, cuts across Christ's
statement that he had not come to destroy (or even replace!) the law,
but to fulfil it (Matt. 5:17 ff.).

This point is supported by Suggs in his work *Wisdom, Christology
and Law in Matthew's Gospel*. Suggs accepted that Matthew
identified Jesus with wisdom, but he went on to comment: 'We should
be very clear that in the Matthean setting what is offered by Jesus is

[17]Wright, *Messiah*, 88, claims that Davies has achieved harmony between Paul and
Judaism by remaining silent about much of the contradictory material.
[18]Best, *One Body*, 162.

not an alternative to the yoke of the torah. Jesus speaks as sophia, and in such a saying as 11:28-30 that means as torah as well. Rejection neither of the law nor of authoritative interpretation as part of the law is indeed implied in principle. Matt.11:28-30 is not polemic against the law as such.' Suggs supports this position by pointing out that in Matthew 12:1-8 (which immediately follows the 11:28-30 passage), 'Matthew clearly acknowledges here that the issue involved is one of interpretation of the torah.'[19]

There is a better explanation of the yoke than that given by Davies. Matthew is the gospel of the kingdom in which Jesus is presented as the ideal king for whom Israel has been waiting. It was Rehoboam who threatened to multiply the burden of his father when Jeroboam came to him on behalf of the people. Rehoboam rejected the advice of his father's counsellors who advised him to make himself the servant of the people (1 Kings 12:8-11). He refused to lighten the yoke that they had had to bear under Solomon and threatened to multiply it. It is this that Matthew is alluding to, for in the following chapter he presents Jesus as the true son of David (Matt. 12:3), who is the perfect servant (12:15-21). He is the one who is greater than Solomon (12:42). Matthew is not pointing to personified Wisdom, but to the true king who is wiser than Solomon, and who is the true Son of David, the true burden bearer of his people.[20] The ultimate yoke as seen by the law (Lev. 26:13) and the prophets (Isa. 14:25) was the exile itself. Such a description, within the sacred writings, could hardly be missed by first century Jews. Thus Jesus could well be referring to the freedom that he had come to bring was the release from bondage (exile).

Davies also appealed to Philo and the Book of Wisdom to establish that the rock in 1 Corinthians 10 was interpreted as, and symbolised, wisdom. If this is accepted, it follows that there is a straight equation between Christ, whom Paul says the rock represents, and wisdom. But the problem that this argument presents is that it assumes Paul to be influenced by the Alexandrian Philosophical School. This is the weakness of this point in Davies' argument. Davies acknowledged that Judaism itself never made this interpretation. The influence of Alexandria on Paul must be established rather than presupposed, and until it has been the argument presented must be suspect.

The most important of the texts to which Davies alluded is 2

---

[19]Suggs, *Wisdom*, 99ff.
[20]See Stanton, *Gospel*, 364ff.

Corinthians 3:5-18, where he argued that Paul claims that, as the revelation of Christ has superseded the Torah, so Christ is presented as the new Torah. Davies affirmed that 'The object of the argument was to prove that Jesus, not the torah, was the true revelation of the divine glory and the divine light. This probably means that Jesus was a new torah.'[21]

To arrive at this explanation Davies had to argue that Paul was equating his own ministry with that of Moses. As Moses brought the old Torah to Israel, so Paul brought the new Torah to the new Israel. Davies said: 'Here Paul, a minister of Christ, assumes that he himself is no less distinguished a person than Moses.'[22]

The first question I would raise with regard to Davies' exegesis of the passage is foundational to the whole of his argument. Does Paul really compare himself with Moses? In his first letter he has modelled Christ on Moses (1 Cor. 10:2). Can it be that within a matter of months, in a letter to the same church, he should alter his typological exegesis so radically? This point, of whether Paul is setting himself up as the fulfilment of Moses as against his previous statement that Christ is himself the fulfilment, is a point of dispute amongst scholars.[23] Clearly with such a difference of opinion amongst scholars, one ought to be careful in making this passage a cornerstone, yet that is precisely what Davies has done. What then is the essence of Paul's argument? I would suggest that he is not comparing himself personally with Moses, but all those who bear the revelation of Christ to others, as Moses had done to Israel. This is borne out in that Paul repeatedly refers in the subsequent chapters to an increasing glory or renewing, a reference that contrasts with that glory which decreased with Moses. Whilst physically Christ's servants suffer and age, yet inwardly they are constantly renewed and their contact with others imparts the same blessing (2 Cor. 4:1-12). Even death itself will not rob believers of the presence of this glory (2 Cor. 4:16–5:5), and the result of its increase will be the glory of God (2 Cor. 4:15). While the apostles are the examples of God's servants, and Paul especially so, what he is saying here is not limited to his own experience. It is true of any faithful servant of Christ.

[21]Davies, *op. cit.* 149
[22]*op. cit.* 148.
[23]Munck and Brownlee support Davies, while Bruce, Shedd, Sanders and Hays claim Paul is modelling Christ on Moses.

If we examine Davies' argument more closely we find further inconsistency. His reasoning is this: when Moses went into the presence of the Lord, he received the law. This, in Jewish thinking, is associated with light; so affected by it was Moses that he radiated glory, which he had to cover over. Paul, however, has a glory that is not the result of handling the Torah, but the revelation of God through Christ. Therefore, what the Torah was to Moses, Christ is to Paul.

This way of reasoning is thoroughly Johannine (John 1:16-17), but is it Paul's argument here? I would suggest it is imposing on this passage a pattern of thought that causes the argument to be lost. If Moses was affected by the law, why did his glory fade? After all he did not stop handling the law after his visit on to the Mount. Indeed, he handled it, through application, even more. Why did this not maintain the glory supposedly given by the Torah?

The fact is that Paul is not saying that the law was the source of the glory, rather it was the Giver of the law who was. It was when Moses left the presence of the Lord that the diminishing of the glory took place. Paul is saying that he also brings a message, and its authority is enhanced by the evidence of its effect, for it brings man into contact with God. This is not a momentary contact, but an abiding one and it is authenticated by the effect it has upon the lives of people because they are being continually changed from glory to glory, increasing not diminishing. Tasker sums up our argument perfectly when he says concerning Moses: 'The direct vision of God that he was in this way privileged to enjoy was denied the Israelites to whom he had been speaking. They had to be content with a more partial knowledge of God conveyed to them through the medium of the law. And so whenever Moses turned to the Lord he could by inference be also said to have turned away from the law.'[24] In other words, the law took away the glory of Moses, rather than being the source of it.

Are there any other points that can be raised, independent of identifying who is the anti-type of Moses? There are and these ought to help us decide on the correctness, or otherwise, of Davies' exposition. First, if Christ is the new Torah, why does Paul never say this explicitly and unequivocally?[25] If this is what Paul held, then this argument would have been his trump card in dealing with the legalism that so often threatened the infant Church. Why did he not produce

[24]Tasker, *Corinthians*, 66.
[25]See Hanson, *Wrath*, 211-12.

this argument to the Galatians? Rather than saying Christ replaces the law his argument is that Christ fulfilled the law, thus following Christ's own explanation of the relationship of his own life and work to the Torah. He had not come to destroy it, but to fulfil it (Matt. 5:17).

A further problem Davies has failed to resolve is why, if Christ is the new Torah 'in word and deed', do the actions of Christ not take on the significance such an understanding would inevitably lead to. It is true that Paul occasionally appeals to Christ's instructions directly, but nowhere is there any suggestion that the deeds of Christ had a revelatory significance which equalled that which the Jews placed on the Torah. Christ promised the Apostles the guidance of the Holy Spirit in their ministry, and it is clear that they took this to mean that they would speak with an authority equal to the One who had commissioned them. Church history testifies that what the Torah was to Israel the New Testament documents became to the Church, i.e. the written revelation of God.

While Paul clearly held Christ to be the full revelation of the Father, he never expressed it in the way Davies argued. The simple reason for this is that it would have created a new legalism that was even more intolerant than that from which it had emerged, the old Torah. The Muslim community, even though not believing Mohammed to be the Son of God, have given to Mohammed's words and deeds full revelatory significance, and the outcome is nothing less than the most rigid legalism. Williams expressed this fact when he wrote:

> The Prophet is not only the founder and legislator of the community; he is the model for Muslims. It is accepted as axiomatic that every act he made after the beginning of the Revelation was preserved by God from error; had it not been so then the Revelation itself would be cast into doubt, a thing God could never have permitted. Therefore, Mohammed's slightest act was rightly guided, and of moral value. For traditional Muslims everything the prophet did is a part of his 'sunna': his treatment of children, the way he broke his fast, how he cleaned his teeth and wore his beard, are all worthy of study and emulation.[26]

This emphasis on the significance of minute details of the life of Mohammed is completely contrary to the attitude taken by both the early Church, and the Church throughout its history. The only parallel

[26]Williams, *Islam*, 84-5.

that can be drawn is the attention Christians give to the written Word, which preserves Christ's spoken word and his significant actions that are of import to the believing community as presenting guiding principles and attitudes. Nowhere is there any evidence that Christ's deeds achieved the same significance that Mohammed's deeds came to have. This is for one very simple reason. Neither the Apostles nor the historic Church have ever seen Christ to be the new Torah in the way Davies has argued. The old Torah has been supplemented by the law of Christ (Gal. 6:2), which has not set the old aside, but filled it out so that its spirit could be both understood and followed.

This observation finds support from Machen who, answering the 'search for the historical Jesus' at the beginning of the twentieth century wrote, 'If imitation of Jesus had been central in the life of Paul as it is central, for example, in modern liberalism, then the Epistles would be full of the words and deeds of Jesus.'[27]

The last of Davies' arguments that we need to consider is that Colossians 1:15ff. is an elaborate exposition of *bereshith* in Genesis 1:1 in the rabbinic manner. Davies admits that there is no evidence that Wisdom and the Messiah were ever linked in Judaism, and his arguments from New Testament texts have not been convincing. In addition to this, the material Burney presents as evidence that there was a Rabbinic tradition of interpreting Genesis 1 in the light of Proverbs 8 is later than the third century AD. This is far too late to be used for evidence of thinking in the New Testament period. Furthermore, Davies has argued that Paul in 1 Corinthians 1:24 and 30 is speaking about 'pre-cosmic and morally creative wisdom'.[28] In fact, 1 Corinthians 1 and 2 is saturated with Old Testament quotations from the prophets, and each of them are clearly linked with the New Exodus theme. The point of wisdom in Isaiah is not of some 'pre-cosmic' existing wisdom, but that Yahweh in redeeming his people from her bondage displays his wisdom and righteousness as he achieves Israel's sanctification and redemption. Hill supports this point, when commenting on 1 Corinthians 1:30: 'The context makes it clear that it is supremely in the cross that God has revealed the true wisdom which is composed of righteousness, sanctification and redemption. It seems probable that these terms refer to three aspects of the deliverance of Christ.'[29]

[27]Machen, *Origin*, 166.   [28]Davies, *op. cit.* 155.
[29]Hill, *Words*, 147.

These considerations lead me to doubt Davies' exposition of the term *prōtotokos*. But even if he had been successful in relating *prōtotokos* to wisdom, what significance would that have had for Christology? It would depend upon whether the Jewish concept of wisdom was that it was eternal or that it was created. If created, even if before anything else was created, it would still be a creature, and therefore a contradiction of the orthodox doctrine of the eternal Sonship of Christ. This, in fact, is the very position at which Davies finished up. While he claimed that the Torah and Wisdom are pre-existent and responsible for creation, he has not arrived at a Trinitarian doctrine of the Person of Christ. It is one thing to claim pre-existence, even before the cosmos, and quite another to claim that absolute eternal oneness with the Father has been established. Without that absolute oneness we are still left with an Arian Christology. Davies, in fact, recognised that the establishing of pre-existence in itself proves very little. He acknowledges that 'There is evidence that the pre-existence of a person had no particular, or unique, significance for rabbinic Judaism'.[30] He later went on to say: 'In Judaism the conception of pre-existence was midrashic; we are to seek for no deep metaphysical truth in it. We may assume that for Paul too the pre-existence of Christ by itself had no profound significance.'[31]

Davies still seems to have assumed that the wisdom Christology of Paul is tied up with Jewish concepts which to the Jews would never have suggested a personal eternal oneness with Jehovah. If we accept Davies' interpretation, then unless we are able to go further by the help of other Christological statements, we are left with an Arian Christ.

Defining Christ in Arian terms was an inevitable consequence of leaving the Paschal model of redemption, which we have seen is so fundamental to Paul's understanding of the death of Jesus. But an Arian Christology was not part of the thinking of the apostle. The early Christians were not struggling with ontological definitions, but glorying in redemptive history. From their understanding that Yahweh himself would redeem creation, and that Yahweh himself would come to bring salvation to Israel, they were driven to recognise that God was in Christ reconciling the world to himself. This is far more than

[30]Davies, *Rabbinic*, 162.
[31]Davies, *Rabbinic*, 174.

saying that they saw Jesus as Yahweh's agent through whom he achieved redemption. The way the early church naturally and almost unthinkingly ascribed the attributes of Yahweh to Jesus shows that they were Christocentric (Trinitarian being a later designation) in their thinking. They did not even notice the later theological problems the church had to tackle. Their Biblical perspective did not demand onto-logical definitions but Biblical fulfilment. The philosophical niceties of the Greeks were problems reserved for later generations of Hellenised believers who had a far more difficult task than they should have had because they had lost their way in substituting a Hellenistic mindset for the Old Testament one that had guided the writers of the New Testament.

The problem with this model that has been developed to explain the development of Christology is that it removes wisdom material from its obvious context, and disregarding the danger of this it is used as evidence for the widespread presence of the theme. By doing this the wisdom material has been removed from its New Exodus context in which it spoke not of the incarnation of Wisdom but of the display of God's wisdom in the redemption of his people. It is the same theme that is repeatedly followed in the prophets from where much of these passages originate. In doing this, theology has been deprived of the data that ought to have helped see the existence of the New Exodus paradigm as well as being given a false paradigm that did not have the supposed evidence to support it. It has also screened that Paschal meaning of the 'firstborn of all creation' and deprived the church of a rich, New Testament based, paradigm for Christology and soteriology. Wisdom Christology, in the sense of the personification of Wisdom, is not a New Testament doctrine, but the product of fertile minds and bad exegesis.

Bibliography

D. Von Allmen, 'Reconciliation du monde et christologie cosmique. de 2 Cor. 5.14-21 et Col.1:15-20,' *RHPR* 48 (1968), 32-45.

G. L. Balentine (1961), *The Concept of the New Exodus in the Gospels*, Th.D. Thesis submitted to Southern Baptist Seminary.

K. E. Baily, 'The Song of Mary: Vision of a New Exodus (Luke 1:46-55),' *Theol Rev* 2 N°1 (1979), 27-41.

J. Balchin (1983), *The Significance of Colossians 1.15-20 in the Context of New Testament Christology*. A Dissertation submitted to the University of London for the degree of Doctor of Philosophy.

J. P. V. D. Balsdon (1963), *Roman Woman*, Bodley Head.

C. K. Barrett (1957), *A Commentary on the Epistle to the Romans*, Adams and Charles Black.

'Things Sacrificed to Idols,' *NTS* X1 (1965), 138-153.

(1973), *The Second Epistle to the Corinthians*, Adams and Charles Black.

M. Barth (1974), *Ephesians Translation and Commentary*, 2 Vols. 1-3 & 4-6. Doubleday.

J. Barr (1961), *The Semantics of Biblical Language*, Oxford University Press.

S. M. Baugh, 'Cultic Prostitution in New Testament Ephesus: A Reappraisal,' *JETS* 42/3 (199), 443-460.

G. K. Beale, 'Did Jesus and His Followers Preach the Right Doctrine from the Wrong Texts? An Examination of the Presuppositions of Jesus' and the Apostles' Exegetical Method,' *Them* Vol. 12, No 2, (Jan. 1987), 89-96.

'The Old Testament Background of Reconciliation in 2 Corinthians 5-7 and its Bearing on the Literary Problem of 2 Corinthians 6:14-7:1,' *NTS* 35 (1989), 550-81.

G. B. Beasley-Murray (1962), *Baptism in the New Testament*, Paternoster.

(1994), 'The Kingdom of God and the Christology of the Gospels' in *Jesus of Nazareth, Lord and Christ*, eds. J.B. Green and M. T. Turner, Paternoster, 32-36.

S. Bedale, 'The Meaning of Κεφλη in the Pauline Epistles,' *JTS* ns.5 (1954), 211-215.

J. J. Beker, 'The Faithfulness of God and the Priority of Israel in Paul's Letter to the Romans,' *HTR* 1-3. 79 (1986), 10-16.

L. Berkhof (1976), *Systematic Theology*, Banner of Truth.

R. F. Berkey (1982), 'Christological Perspectives: The Context of Current Discussion' in *Christological Perspectives: Essays in Honour of Harvey K. McArthur*, eds. R. F. Berkey and S. A. Edwards, Pilgrim Press, 3-23.

E. Best (1955), *One Body in Christ. A Study in the Relationship of the Church to Christ in the Epistles of the Apostle Paul*, SPCK.

M. Black (1989), *Romans*, Aliphants, 2nd Ed.

G. Bornkamm (1971), *Paul*, tr. by D. M. G. Stalker, Hodder and Staughton.

P. Borgen, 'The Early Church and the Hellenistic Synagogue' *Stud Theol* 37 (1983), 55-78.

J. Bowman (1965), *The Gospel of Mark: The New Christian Jewish Passover Haggadah*, E. J. Brill.

G. L. Bray, 'Justification: The Reformers and Recent New Testament Scholarship' *Churchman* 109 N° 2 (1995), 102-126.

D. I. Brewer (1989), *Techniques and Assumptions in Jewish Exegesis before 70 CE*. A Dissertation submitted for Ph.D. at Cambridge University.

J. Bright art, 'Isaiah,' in *PCB*, 489-515.

M. J. Brown, 'PAUL'S USE OF LOGOS XPISTOS IHSO IN ROMANS 1:1,' *JBL* (2001), 723-37.

R. E. Brown (1971), *The Gospel According to John*, 2 vols., Geoffrey Chapman.

F. F. Bruce (1961), *Second Thoughts on the Dead Sea Scrolls*, Paternoster.
(1967), *The Epistle of Paul to the Romans: An Introduction and Commentary*, Tyndale Press.
(1971), *1 and 2 Corinthians*, Oliphants.
'The New Testament and Classical Studies,' *NTS* 22 (1976), 229-242.

T. W. Buckley (1961), *The Phrase 'Firstborn of Every Creature' (Col 1.15-18), in the Light of its Jewish and Hellenistic Background*, Biblical Institute Press.

R. Bultmann (1956), *Primitive Christianity in its Contemporary Setting*, tr. R.H. Fuller, Meridian Books.

F. C. Burney , 'Christ as the ΆÑ×ç of Creation,' *JTS* 27 (1926), 160-77.

F. Büschel, 'ßλαμοò' *TDNT* 3:310-323.

W. S. Campbell (1993), 'The Contribution of Traditions to Paul's Theology. A Response to C. J. Roetzel,' in *Pauline Theology*, ed D. M. Hay, Fortress Press, 234-254.

J. Calvin, *Institutes*, http://lib329.bham.ac.uk/coreRes/reformat/maincore/rupp8105.htm

P. Carrington (1952), *The Primitive Christian Calendar*, Cambridge University Press.

D. A. Carson (1982), 'Christological Ambiguities in the Gospel of Matthew' in *Christ the Lord, Studies presented to Donald Guthrie*, ed. H. H. Rowden, IVP, 97-114.
(1994), *Divine Sovereignty and Human Responsibility*, Marshall Pickering.

J. Casey, 'The Exodus Theme in the Book of Revelation Against the Background of the New Testament,' *Con* 189 (1987), 34-43.

R. P. Casey, 'The Earliest Christologies,' *JTS* ns 9 (1958), 253-277.

R. H. Charles (1913), *The Apocrypha and Pseudepigrapha of the Old Testament*, 2 vols, Clarendon Press.

J. H. Charlesworth (ed)(1985), *Old Testament Pseudepigrapha*, 2 vols, Darton

Longman & Todd.

S. Charnock, *A Discourse on the Nature of Regeneration.*
http://www.ccel.org/c/charnock/nat_regen/nat_regen.html

A. Chester (1991), 'Jewish Messianic Expectations and Mediatoral Figures and Pauline Christology,' in *Paulus und das antike Judeatum*, eds. M.Hengel and U. Heckel, J. C. B. Mohr, 17-89.

Chilton, B. D, & Davies, P, 'The Aqedah: A Revised Tradition History,' *CBQ* 40 (1978), 534-536.

A. Cody (1984), *Old Testament Message 11. Ezekiel*, Wilmington.

F. M. Colautti (2002), *Passover in the works of Josephus*, E. J. Brill.

A. Cole (1962), *Exodus, A Commentary*, tr. J.S. Bowden, Tyndale Press.

H. Conzelmann (1976), *Corinthians. A Commentary on the First Epistle to the Corinthians*, tr. J. W. Leitch, Fortress Press.

G. A. Cooke (1936), *A Critical Commentary on the Book of Ezekiel*, T & T Clark.

J. Coppens (1968), 'Mystery in the Theology of St Paul and its Parallels at Qumran,', in *Paul and Qumran* ed. J. C. Murray-O'Conner, Geoffrey Chapman, 132-58.

C. H. Cosgrove, (1992), 'The Justification of the Other: An Interpretation of Rom 1:18-4:25,' SBL Seminar Papers, 613-34.

M. Cranford, 'Abraham in Romans 4: The Father of All Who Believe' *NTS* 44 (Jan 1995), 71-88.

H. Cremer (1880), *Biblico-Theological Lexicon of New Testament Greek*, T & T Clark.

F. L. Cross (1954), *1 Peter, a Paschal Liturgy*, Mowbray.

O. Cullmann (1950), *Baptism in the New Testament*, tr. J. K. S. Reid, SCM.

N. A. Dahl (1974), 'The Atonement. An Adequate Reward for the Akedah,' in *The Crucified Messiah and Other Essays*, Augsburg Publishing House, 146-160.

R. J. Daly (1978), Christian *Sacrifice: The Judaeo-Christian Tradition,* Catholic University of America Press.

J. Daniélou (1964), *The Theology of Jewish Christianity*, SCM.

D. Daube, 'The Earliest Structures of the Gospel,' *NTS* 5 (1958-59), 174-87.

(1963), *The Exodus Pattern in the Bible*, Faber and Faber.

W. D. Davies (1955), *Paul and Rabbinic Judaism*, SPCK.

(1962), *Christian Origins*, Darton, Longman & Todd.

'Paul and the People of Israel,' *NTS* 24 (1978), 4-39.

(1993), 'Canon and Christology in Paul,' in *Paul and the Scriptures of Israel* eds. C. A. Evans & J. A. Sanders, JSNT Sup Series 83, Sheffield Academic Press, 18-39.

V. Deane (1891), *Pseudepigrapha*, T & T Clark.

V. De Jonge (1995), 'The Pseudepigripha of the Old Testament and Early Christianity,' in *The New Testament and Hellenistic Judaism*, ed's P.

Borgen and S. Giversn, Aarhus University Press, 59-71.

A. Deissmann (1927), *Light from the Ancient East*, tr. L. R. M. Strachan, Hodder & Stoughton.

D. R. De Lacy, 'Jesus as Mediator,' *JSNT* 29 (1987), 101-21.

G. Delling, art 'αρχω' *TDNT* 5:478-489.

G. Deluz (1963), *A Companion to 1 Corinthians*, Darton, Longman & Todd.

T. J. Dennison, 'The Exodus and The People of God,' *BT* Issue 171 (Dec 1977), 6-11 and 32.

R. De Vaux (1990), *Ancient Israel, Its Life and Institutions*, Darton, Longman & Todd.

C. H. Dodd, ΙΛΑΣΚΕΣΘΑΙ, It's Cognates. Derivatives and Synonyms in the Septuagint,' *JTS* 32 (1931) 352-360.

(1952), *According to the Scriptures*, London.

(1953), *The Interpretation of the Fourth Gospel*, Cambridge University Press.

(1953), *Essays in New Testament Studies*, Manchester University Press.

J. D. G. Dunn, (1974), 'Paul's Understanding of the Death of Jesus' in *Reconciliation and Hope, Essays presented to L. L. Morris on his 60th birthday*, ed. R. Brooks, Paternoster, pp125-141.

(1988), *Romans*, 2 Vols. Word.

(1993), *The Epistle to the Galatians*, A & C Black.

(1996), *The Epistles to the Colossians and Philemon*, Paternoster.

(1998), *The Theology of Paul the Apostle*, T&T Clark.

'Who did Paul think he was? A study of Jewish-Christian identity,' *NTS* 45 (1999), 174-193.

Jesus, Paul and the Law, SPCK, 1990

J. D. G. Dunn, & A. M. Suggate (1993), *The Justice of God: A Fresh Look at the Old Doctrine of Justification by Faith*, Carlisle.

A. Edersheim (1962), *The Life and Times of Jesus the Messiah*, 2 Vols., Eedermans.

J. Edwards *Collected Works*, Vol. 1 Discourse 1, *Justification by Faith Alone*. http://www.jonathanedwards.com/sermons/Doctrine/Five%20Discourses/Justification.htm

R. Eiseneman & M. Wise (1992), *The Dead Sea Scrolls Uncovered*, Shaftesbury.

P. Ellingworth, 'Colossians 1.15-20 and its Context,' *ExpT* 73 (1961-62), 252-253.

E. E. Ellis, 'A note on 1 Cor.10:4,' *JBL* 76 (1957), 53-56.

(1957), *Paul's Use of the Old Testament*, Oliver & Boyd.

(1978), *Prophecy and Hermeneutic in Early Christianity*, Eedermans.

I. Engnell art, 'Furstfodda,' in Svensk bibliskt uppslagsverk, ed. by I. Engnell, 2nd ed., Stockholm (1963-64), vol. 1, 714.

(1970), *Critical Essays on the Old Testament* tr. by J. T. Willis, SPCK.

C. A. Evans (1999), 'Jesus and the Continuing Exile of Israel,' in *Jesus and the Restoration of Israel*, ed. C. C. Newman, Paternoster, 77-100.

P. Eveson (1996), *The Great Exchange*, Day One.

F. Fairbairn (1863), *Ezekiel and the Book of His Prophecies, An Exposition*, T & T Clark.

W. R. Farmer (1956), *Maccabees, Zealots and Josephus. An Inquiry in Jewish Nationalism in the Greco-Roman Period*, Columbia University Press.

G. D. Fee (1987), *The First Epistle to the Corinthians*, Eedermans.

(1994), *God's Empowering Presence* , Hendrikson.

E. Fiorenza, 'Cultic Language in Qumran and in the NT,' *CBQ* 38 (1976) 157-177.

B. N. Fisk, 'Offering Isaac Again and Again: Pseudo-Philo's use of the Aqedah as Intertext,' *CBQ* 62 (2000), 481-507.

J. M. Ford, 'The Son of Man Euphemism?,' *JBL* 87 (1969), 189-96.

J. Fossum, 'The New Religionsgeschichtlíche Schule: the Quest for Jewish Christology' *SBL* 1991 Seminar Papers, ed. E. H. Lovering, Atlanta: Scholars Press, 638-646.

A. Fridrichsen (1953), 'Jesus, St John and St Paul' in *Root of the Vine, Essays in Biblical Theology*, ed. A. Fridrichsen, Dacre Press, 37-62.

L. Frinkelstein (1975), *Akiba, Scholar Saint and Martyer*, Atheneum.

S. R. Garrett, 'Exodus From Bondage in Luke 9:31 and Acts 12:1-24,' *CBQ* 52 (1990), 656-80.

R.H. Fuller (1965), *The Foundations of New Testament Christology*, Fount Paperbacks,

L. Gaston, 'Israel's Enemies in Pauline Theology,' *NTS* 28 (1982), 423-34.

J. G. Gibbs (1971), *Creation and Redemption*, E. J. Brill.

L. Ginzberg (1925), *The Legends of the Jews*, Jewish Publication Society of America.

F. E. Gigor (1912), *The Book of Wisdom*, http://www.newadvent.org/cathen/15666a.htm

G. Goldsworthy (1991), *According to Plan. The Unfolding Revelation of God in the Bible*, IVP.

T. Goodwin (1985), *The Works of Thomas Goodwin*, vol. 8, Justifying Faith, Banner of Truth.

L. Goppelt (1982), *Typos. The Typological Interpretation of the Old Testament in the New*, tr. D. H. Madvig, Eedermans.

P. Grech , 'The "Testimonia" and Modern Hermeneutics,' *NTS* 19 (1972-73), 318-324.

W. S. Green (1993), 'Doing the Texts Work for it: Richard Hays on Paul's Use of Scripture,' in *Paul and the Scriptures of Israel*, eds. C. A. Evans and J. A. Sanders, JSNT Sup Series 83, Sheffield Academic Press, pp 58-63.

F. W. Grosheide (1953), *Commentary on the First Epistle to the Corinthians*, Eedermans.

R. R. Gundry (1976), *Soma in Biblical Theology*, Cambridge University Press.

A. T. Hanson (1957), *The Wrath of the Lamb*, SPCK.

R. B. Hays, 'Have we found Abraham to be our Father According to the Flesh? A Reconsideration of Rom 4:1,' *NovT* (1985), 76-98.

(1989), *Echoes of Scripture in the Letters of Paul*, Yale University Press.

'The Conversion of the Imagination: Scripture and Eschatology in 1 Corinthians,' *NTS* 45 (1999), 391-412.

M. Hengel (1976), *The Son of God, The Origin of Christology and the History of Jewish-Hellenistic Religion*, tr. by J. Bowden, SCM.

L. R. Helyer, 'The Prototokos Title in Hebrews,' *SBT* (1977), 3-28.

E. Henderson (1845), *The Books of the Twelve Minor Prophets*, Hamilton, Adams & Co.

W. Hendriksen (1947), *More Than Conquerors. An Interpretation of the Book of Revelation*, Tyndale Press.

M. Hengel (1989), *The Zealots, Investigations into the Jewish Freedom Movement in the Period from Herod 1 until 70AD*, T & T Clark.

E. W. Hengstenberg (1869), *The Prophecies of the Prophet Ezekiel*, T & T Clark.

J. Héring (1962), The First Epistle of Paul to the Corinthians, tr. A. W. Heathcote, Epworth Press.

A. J. B. Higgins, 'The Priestly Messiah,' *NTS* 13 (1966-67), 211-39.

D. Hill (1967), *Greek Words and Hebrew Meanings. Studies in the Semantics of Soteriological Terms*, Cambridge University Press.

A. Hockel (1965), *Christus der Erstgeborene. Zur Geschichte der Exegese von Kol 1:15*, Patmos Verlag, Düsseldorf.

C. Hodge (1964), *A Commentary on the Epistle to the Ephesians*, Banner of Truth.

C. R. Holloway, 'New Testament Christology: A Consideration of Dunn's Christology in the Making,' *Semeia* 30 (1984), 65-82.

M. D. Hooker (1959), *Jesus and the Servant*, SPCK.

J. M. Howard, 'Christ our Passover' A Study of the Passover-Exodus Theme in 1 Corinthians,' *EQ* 41 (1963), 97-108.

'Passover and Eucharist in the Fourth Gospel,' *SJTh* 20 (1967), 329-37.

D. A. Hubbard, 'Hope in the Old Testament,' *TynB* 34 (1983), 33-59.

A. M. Hunter (1961), *Paul and his Predecessors*, SCM.

J. Jeremias (1955), *The Eucharistic Words of Jesus*, SCM.

art, 'Ἀδαμ' *TDNT* 1:141-143.

art, 'πασχα' *TDNT* 5: 896-904.

art, 'Μωυσης' *TDNT* 4 : 848-873.

L. T. Johnson (1999), 'A Historiographical Response to Wright's Jesus,' in *Jesus & the Restoration of Israel*, ed. C. C. Newman, Paternoster, 206-224.

F. Josephus (no date given), *The Antiquities of the Jews*, tr. W. Whiston, George Routledge & Sons.

D. C. Juster (1991), *Revelation: The Passover Key*, Shipensbury.

E. Käsemann (1980), *Romans*, Eedermans.

L. E. Keck (1995), 'What Makes Romans Tick' in *Pauline Theology*, vol. 3, eds. D. M. Hay and E. E. Johnson, Fortress Press.

S. C. Keesmaat, 'Exodus and the Intertextual Transformation of Traditions in Romans 8.14-30,' *JSNT* 54 (1994), 29-56.

(1994), *Paul's Use of the Exodus Tradition in Romans and Galatians*, D.Phil. thesis submitted to Oxford University,

R. Kempthorne, 'Incest and the Body of Christ: A Study of 1 Corinthians V1.12-20,' *NTS* 14 (1967-68), 568-574.

H. A. A. Kennedy (1904), *Paul's Conception of the Last Things*, Hodder & Stoughton.

S. Kim (1982), *The Origins of Paul's Gospel*, Eedermans.

J. C. Kirby (1968), *Ephesians Baptism and Pentecost. An Inquiry into the Structure and Purpose of the Epistle to the Ephesians*, SPCK.

A. F. J. Klijn, 'The Study of Jewish Christianity,' *NTS* 20 (1974), 119-31.

M. G. Kline, 'The Old Testament Origins of the Gospel Genre,' *WTJ*, N° 1, 38 (Fall 1975), 1-27.

W. L. Knox (1939), *St Paul and the Church of the Gentiles*, Cambridge University Press.

S. H. Koi (1985), *Exodus as a symbol of liberation in the book of the apocalypse*, Ph.D. thesis, Emory University.

G. E. Ladd (1972), *A Commentary on the Revelation of St. John*, Eedermans.

A. R. C. Leaney, '1 Peter and the Passover: An Interpretation,' *NTS* 10 (1963-64), 238-51.

R. Le Deaut (1963), *La nuit Pascale. Essai sur la signification de la Pâque juive à partir du Targum d'Exode XII*, Analecta Biblica 42, Biblical Institute Press

J. D. Levenson (1993), *The Death and Resurrection of the Beloved Son. The Transformation of Child Sacrifice in Judaism and Christianity*, Yale University Press.

I. Levi, 'Le sacrifice d'Isaac et la mort de Jesus,' *REJ* 64 (1912), 161-184.

S. Lyonnet and L. Sabourin (1970), *Studies in Sin and Redemption*, Biblical Institute Press.

R. H. Lightfoot (1966), *St. John's Gospel, A Commentary*, Clarendon Press.

B. Lindars, 'The Place of the Old Testament in the Formation of New Testament Theology,' *NTS* 25 (1976-77), 59-66.

D. M. Lloyd-Jones (1972), *Romans. An Exposition of Chapter 6*, Banner of Truth.

E. Lohse , 'Christuscherrshaft und Kirche im Kolosserbrief,' *NTS* 11 (1966-67), 203-216.

art, 'υιος Δαυιδ' *TDNT* 8: 478-488.

'Pauline Theology in the Letter to the Colossians,' *NTS* 15 (1969), 211-20.

R. N. Longenecker (1970), *The Christology of Early Jewish Christianity*

(Studies in Biblical Theology Series 17), SCM.

'Can We Produce the Exegesis of the New Testament?,' *TynB* 21 (1970), 3-38.

T. Longman & G. D. Reid (1995), *God is a Warrior*, Paternoster.

M. Luther (1995), *Concerning Christian Liberty*,
http://www.lib329.bham.ac.uk/coreRes/reformat/maincore/rupp8105.htm

G. H. C. Macgregor , 'Principalities and Powers: The Cosmic Background of Paul's Thought,' *NTS* 1 (1954-55), 17-28.

J. G. Machem (1947), *The Origins of Paul's Religion*, Eedermans.

J. Mánek, 'The New Exodus in the Book of Luke,' *NovT* (1955), 8-23.

T. W. Manson art 'Romans,' in *PCB*, 940-953.

I. H. Marshall, 'The Meaning of the Verb 'to Baptize',' *EQ* Vol. 45 No 3 (July-Sep 1973), 13-40.

'The Son of God or Servant of Yahweh? A Reconsideration of Mark 1.11,' *NTS* 15 (1968-69), 326-336.

R. P. Martin (1972), *Colossians. The Church's Lord and the Christian's Liberty*, Paternoster.

(1982), 'Some Reflections on New Testament Hymns,' in *Christ the Lord, Studies Presented to D. Guthrie,* ed. H. H. Rowden, IVP, 37-49.

R. Mason (1977), *The Books of Haggai, Zecheriah and Malachi*, Cambridge University Press.

P. Mauro (1910), *The, 'Wretched Man,' and his Deliverance. Rom V11*, Samuel E Roberts.

S. V. McCasland , 'Signs and Wonders,' *JBL* 76 (1957), 147-152.

H. McKeating (1971), *Amos, Hosea, Micah*, Cambridge University Press.

R. T. McKelvey (1969), *The New Temple: The Church in the New Testament*, Oxford University Press.

R. P. Menzies (1994), *Empowered for Witness: The Spirit in Luke-Acts,* Sheffield: JPT Sup 6, Sheffield Academic Press.

M. Michaelis, art 'πρωτότωκος' *TDNT* 6:871-882.

H. Mitchell, J. M. P. Smith & J. A. Bewer (1849), *Haggai, Zechariah, Malachi and Jonah*, T & T Clark.

J. Moffatt (1938), *The First Epistle to the Corinthians*, Hodder & Stoughton.

D. J. Moo, 'Israel and Paul in Romans 7.7-12,' *NTS* 32 (1986), 122-35.

(1991), *Romans 1-8*, The Wycliffe Exegetical Commentary, Moody Press.

G. F. Moore (1927-1930), *Judaism in the First Centuries of the Christian Era*, Vols. I-III, Harvard University Press.

T. V. Moore (1974), *Zechariah* , Banner of Truth.

L. L. Morris (1984), *The Atonement. It's Meaning and Significance*, IVP.

H. C. G. Moule (1903), *The Epistle of Paul the Apostle to the Romans with Introduction and Notes*, Cambridge University Press.

Saint Melito (1979), *Melito of Sardis; Texts and Translations*, Oxford University Press.

C. F. D. Moule, 'The Influence of Circumstances on the use of Christological Terms,' *JTS* 10 (1960), 247-64.

'Fulfilment-Words in the New Testament: Use and Abuse,' *NTS* 14 (1966-77), 293-320.

(1977), *The Origins of Christology*, Cambridge University Press.

J. Munck (1959), *Paul and the Salvation of Mankind*, SCM.

'Jewish Christianity in Post-Apostolic Times,' *NTS* V1 (1959-60), 103-16.

J. Murphy-O'Connor, '1 Cor.8:6 : Cosmology or Soteriology?,' *RB* 85 (1978), 253-59.

(1996), *Paul a Critical Life*, Clarendon Press.

J. Murray (1967), *The Epistle to the Romans*, 2 Vols. Marshall Morgan & Scott.

(1954), *The Covenant of Grace: A Biblical-Theological Study*, Tyndale Press.

(1955), *Redemption Accomplished and Applied*, Banner of Truth.

(1959), *The Imputation of Adam's Sin*, Eedermans.

(1973), *The Pattern of the Lord's Day*, Tyndale Press.

M. Nanos (1997), *The Mystery of Romans*, Fortress Press.

T. R. Neuffeld (1997), *'Put on the Whole Armour of God' The Divine Warrior from Isaiah to Ephesians*, Sheffield Academic Press.

J. Neusner, W. S. Green and E. S. Frerichs (eds.)(1990), *Judaisms and Their Messiahs at the Turn of the Christian Era*, Cambridge University Press

J. Neyrey (1985), *The Passion According to Luke. A Redaction Study of Luke's Soteriology*, Paulist Press.

R. E. Nixon (1963), *The Exodus in the New Testament*, Tyndale Press.

B. Noack, "A Jewish Gospel in a Hellenistic World" *Stud Theol* 32 (1978) 45-55.

A. D. Nock (1964), *Early Gentile Christianity and its Hellenistic Background*, Harper & Row.

A. Nygren (1957), *Commentary on Romans*, tr. by C. C. Rasmuss, SCM.

P. T. O'Brien (1982), *Colossians*, Word.

W. O. E. Oesterley & T. H. Robinson (1933), *Hebrew Religion: Its Origin and Developments*, SPCK.

H. Olshausen (1849), *Biblical Commentary on St. Paul's Epistles to the Romans*, T & T Clark.

(1860)(authored by J. H. A. Ebrard), *Biblical Commentary on the Revelation of St. John*, T & T Clark.

J. C. O'Neill, 'The Source of the Christology in Colossians,' *NTS* 26 (1979-80), 87-100.

C. Von Orelli (1893), *The Twelve Minor Prophets*, T & T Clark.

G. R. Osborne, 'Christology and New Testament Hermeneutics: A Survey of the Discussion,' *Semeia* 30 (1984), 49-62.

J. Owen, 'Justification': http://www.ccel.org/o/owen/just/justification.txt

W. Pannenberg (1968), *Jesus God and Man*, SCM.

C. M. Pate (1991), *Adam Christology as Exegetical and Theological Substructure of 2 Corinthians 4:7-5:21*, University of America Press.

N. Perrin (1974), *A Modern Pilgrimage in New Testament Christology*, Fortress Press.

A. W. Pink, '*Justification*': http://www.ccel.org/p/pink/awpjstf/htm/i.htm

O. Piper, 'Unchanging Promises: Exodus in the New Testament,' *Interp* 2 (1957), 3-22.

W. C. Platcher , 'Christ Takes our Place,' *Interp* 53 No 1 (Jan 1999), 11-12.

N. W. Porteous, 'The Theology of the Old Testament,' in *PCB,* 151-59.

T. Preiss (1957), *Life in Christ*, SCM.

O. Procksch art, 'λυω' *TDNT* 4 : 328-35.

E. B. Pusey (1907), *The Minor Prophets*, Vol. 4, J. Nisbet & Co.

C. C. Richardson (1993), ed & tr. *The Library of Christian Classics,* vol. 1 Early Church Fathers, SCM.

A. Richardson (1958), *An Introduction to the Theology of the New Testament*, SCM.

H. Ridderbos (1974), 'The Earliest Confession of the Atonement in Paul (1 Cor 15.3),' in *Reconciliation and Hope, Essays presented to L. L. Morris on his 60th birthday*, ed. R. Brooks, Paternoster, 76-89.
(1975), *Paul, An Outline of His Theology*, Eedermans.

B. R. Robinson, 'Zipporah to the Rescue: A Contextual Study of Exodus 1V. 24-6' *VT* (1980) 447-61.

J. A. T. Robinson, 'The One Baptism as the Category of New Testament Soteriology,' *JJT* 6 (1953), 257ff.
(1953), *The Body: A Study in Pauline Theology*, SCM.
(1979), *Wrestling With Romans*, SCM.

J. M. Robinson, 'A formal Analysis of Colossians 1. 15-20,' *JBL* 76 (1957), 270-87.

W. Robinson (1957), *Prophecy and Prophets in Ancient Israel*, 2nd ed. Duckworth.

W. G. Rollins (1982), 'Christological Tendenz in Colossians 1.15-20. A Theological Crucis,' in *Christological Perspectives, Essays in honour of H. K. McArthur*, eds. R. F. Berkey and S. A. Edwards, Pilgrim Press, 123-38.

H. H. Rowley (1968), *The Faith of Israel*, SCM.

H. Sahlin (1953), 'The New Exodus of Salvation according to St. Paul,' in *The Root of the Vine and Essays in Biblical Theology*, ed. A. Fridrichsen, Dacte Press, 81-95.

W. Sanday and A. Headlam (1902), *A Critical and Exegetical Commentary on the Epistle to the Romans*, T & T Clark.

E. P. Sanders (1977), *Paul and Palestinian Judaism*, London.
(1996), *Paul*, Past Masters Series, Oxford University Press.

R. Schackenburg (1965), *Baptism in the Thought of St. Paul,* tr. by G.R.Beasley-Murray, Basil Blackwell.

A. Schlatter (1995), *Romans and the Righteousness of God*, tr. S. S. Schatzmann, Hendrikson.

T. R. Schreiner, 'Israel's Failure to Attain Righteousness in Romans 9:30–10:3,' *TrinJ* ns 12 (1991), 209-20.

(2001), *Paul: Apostle of God's Glory, A Pauline Theology*, IVP.

B. Schreiner, 'The Corporate Meaning and Background of 1 Cor 15.45b – ΕΣΞΗΑΤΟΣ ΑΔΑΜ ΕΙΣ ΠΝΕΥΜΑ ΖΟΙΟΠΙΟΥΝ,' *CBQ* 29 (1967), 144-61.

G. Schrenk, 'δικαιοσυνη,' *TDNT* 2:178-25.

J. M. Scott, art "Adoption, Sonship" in *DPL*, 15-18.

R. Scroggs (1966), *The Last Adam*, Basil Black.

M. A. Seifrid, "The 'New Perspective on Paul' and its Problems" *Them* 25 (2000), 4-18.

M. H. Shepherd (1960), *The Paschal Liturgy and the Apocalypse*, Lutherworth.

G. Simon (1965), *The First Epistle to the Corinthians*, SCM.

G. S. Shogren, 'Presently Entering the Kingdom of Christ: The Background and Purpose of Col 1.12-14,' *JETS* 51 (1988), 173-80.

E. W. Smith Jnr., 'The Form and Religious Background of Romans vii.24-25a,' *NovT* 13 (1970–71), 120-135.

J. M. Smith , W.H. Ward & J. A. Bewer (1912), *A Critical and Exegetical Commentary on Micah, Zephaniah, Nahum, Habakkuk, Obediah and Joel*, T & T Clark.

R. H. Smith, 'Exodus Typology in the Fourth Gospel,' *JBL* 81 (1982), 329-42.

W. R. Smith (1995), *Lectures on the Religion of the Semites*, Sheffield Academic Press.

K. R. Snodgrass , '1 Peter ii. 1-10, its Formation and Literary Affinities,' *NTS* 24 (1978-79), 79-106.

D. M. Stalker (1968), *Ezekiel, Introduction and Commentary*, SCM.

G. H. Stanton (1992), *A Gospel For a New People: Studies in Matthew*, T & T Clark.

J. R. W. Stott (1986), *The Cross of Christ*, IVP.

(1994), *The Message of Romans*, IVP.

H. Strack, and P. Billerbeck (1980), *Kommentar zum Neuen Testament aus Talmud und Midrasch III*, New York.

M. Strauss (1992), *The Davidic Messiah in Luke-Acts: The Promise and its Fulfilment in Lukan Christology*, Ph.D Thesis submitted to Aberdeen University.

M. J. Suggs (1970), *Wisdom Christology and Law in Matthew's Gospel*, Harvard University Press.

W. M. Swartley (1994), *Israel's Scriptures Tradition and the Synoptic Gospels,*

Story Shaping Story, Hendrikson.

J. Swetnam, 'Sacrifice and Revelation in the Epistle to the Hebrews: Observation and Surmises on Hebrews 9.26,' *CBQ* 30 (1968), 227-234.

(1981), *Jesus and Isaac. A Study of the Epistle to the Hebrews in the Light of the Aqedah*. Biblical Institute Press.

C. H. Talbert, 'Paul, Judaism, and the Revisionists,' *CBQ* 63 (2001), 1-22.

R. V. G. Tasker (1958), *The Second Epistle to the Corinthians*, Tyndale Press.

V. Taylor (1954), *The Atonement in the New Testament Teaching*, 2nd ed. Epworth.

C. T. S. Thornton, '1 Peter a Paschal Liturgy,' *JTS,* 12,1 ns (1961), 14-26.

T. F. Torrance, 'The Atonement and the Oneness of the Church,' *SJT* 8 (1954), 245-69.

(1965), *Theology in Reconstruction*, SCM.

(1960), *The Apocalypse Today*, SCM.

S. H. Travis (1994), 'Christ as the Bearer of Divine Judgement,' in *Jesus of Nazareth Lord and Christ* eds. J. B. Green and M. Turner, Paternoster, 332-45.

P. Trudinger, 'An Autobiographical Digression? A Note on Romans 7.7-25,' *ExpT* 107 (1996), 173-74.

V. L. Trumper (1910), *The Mirror of Egypt in the Old Testament*, Marshall Morgan & Scott.

M. M. M. Turner (1996), *The Holy Spirit and Spiritual Gifts, Then and Now*, Paternoster.

N. Turner, 'Revelation,' in *PBC* 1043-61.

B. Vawter, 'The Colossians Hymn and the Principle of Redaction,' *CBQ* 33 (1971), 62-81.

G. Vermes, 'Baptism and Jewish Exegesis: New Light from Ancient Sources,' *NTS* 4 (1957-8), 308-19.

(1961), 'Circumcision and Exodus IV 24-26', in *Scripture and Tradition in Judaism*, Leiden, 178-192.

(1961), 'Redemption & Genesis XXII. The Binding of Isaac and the Sacrifice of Jesus,' in *Scripture and Tradition in Judaism*, E. J. Brill, 193-227

(1971), *The Dead Sea Scrolls*, Penguin.

(1976), Jesus the Jew. A Historical Reading of the Gospels, Fontana.

O. W. Walker Jnr., 'The Son of Man, Some Recent Developments,' *CBQ* 43 (1983), 584-607.

W. B. Wallis (Nov 17-19, 1994), 'Passover and Exodus in Revelation,', *Evangelical Theological Society Papers* 4634, Paper presented at the 46th National Conference of the Evangelical Theological Society, Lislie, Il.

V. Warnack , 'Taufe und Heilsgeschehen Nach Röm 6,' *ALW* 111 2 (1954), 284-366.

'Die Tauflehre des Römerbriefes in der Neueren Theologischen

Diskussion,' *ALW* 2 (1958), 274-332.

B. B. Warfield (1950), *The Person and Work of Christ*, Presbyterian and Reformed Publishing Co.

R. Watts (1990), *The Influence of the Book of Isaiah on the Gospel of Mark*, Ph.D. Dissertation for the University of Cambridge.

(2000), 'Exodus,' in *NBDT*.

W. J. Webb (1993), *Returning Home; New Covenant and Second Exodus as the Context for 2 Corinthians 6:14-7:1*. JOST Sup Series 85, Sheffield Academic Press.

R. A. L. M. Wedderburn, 'The Theological Structure of Romans V.12,' *NTS* 19 (1972-73), 332-354.

S. Westerholm (1988), *Israel's' Law and the Church's Faith*, Eedermans.

D. E. H. Whiteley, 'St. Paul's Thought on the Atonement,' *JTS* 8 (1957), 240-55.

(1964), *The Theology of St. Paul*, Oxford University Press.

C. Whitehouse (no date of publication given), *Isaiah 1-39,* T. C & E. C. Jack Ltd.,

W. A. Whitehouse (1956), 'Christ and Creation,' in *Essays in Christology for Karl Barth* ed. by T. H. L. Parker, Lutterworth.

W. N. Wilder (1996), *Freed from the law to be led by the Spirit: Echoes of the Exodus narrative*, Ph.D. thesis, Union Theological Seminary.

J. Williams (1961), *Islam*, Prentice Hall.

S. K. Williams (1975), *Jesus' Death as Saving Event: The Background and Origin of a Concept*, Harvard Dissertation in Religion, No 2.

B. Winter (2001), *After Paul Left Corinth. The Influence of Secular Ethics and Social Change*, Grand Rapids.

M. Wise, M. Abess and E. Cook (1996), *The Dead Sea Scrolls*, Harper Collins.

B. Witherington III. (1994), *Paul's Narrative Thought World*, Westminster/John Knox Press.

(1995), *Conflict and Community in Corinth. A Socio-Rhetorical Commentary on 1 and 2 Corinthians*, Paternoster.

(1998), *The Paul Quest: The Renewed Search for the Jew of Tarsus*, Inter Varsity Publishing.

N. T. Wright (1980), *The Messiah and the People of God*. Unpublished Thesis submitted to Oxford University for the degree of D.Phil.

(1980) 'Justification: The Biblical Basis and its Relevance for Contemporary Evangelicalism,' in *The Great Acquittal*, G. Reid, ed. Fount Paperbacks.

'The Paul of History and the Apostle of Faith,' *TynB* 29 (1978), 61-88.

(1986), *Colossians and Philemon*, IVP.

'Theology and Poetry in Colossians 1.15-20,' *NTS* 36 (1990), 444-60.

(1992), *The New Testament and the People of God*, SPCK.

(1993) 'On Becoming the Righteousness of God 2 Corinthians 5:21' in

Pauline Theology, vol. 2, ed. D. M. Hays, Fortress Press, 200-208.

(1996), *Jesus and the Victory of God*, SPCK.

(1997), *What Saint Paul Really Said*, Lion Publishing.

(1997), 'New Exodus, New Inheritance. The Narrative Structure of Romans 3-8,' in *Romans and the People of God*, Essays in honour of Gorden D. Fee on the occasion of his 65th birthday ed. By Sven K. Sonderlund and N. T. Wright, Eedermans.

(2001), 'Romans,' in *NIC* vol X.

K. S. Wuest (1945), *Treasures from the Greek New Testament,* Eedermans.

A. S. Yahuda (1934), *The Accuracy of the Bible*, William Heineman.

S. S. Yoo (1999), *Jesus' Holy War Against Satan: The Gadarene Demonic Story*, Solomon Press, Seoul.

J. Ziesler, 'Soma in the Septuagint,' *NovT* 25, 2 (1983), 133-145.

W. Zimmerli (1983, vol 2), *Ezekiel. A Commentary on the Book of Ezekiel.* Fortress Press.

Persons Index

Abegg, M. 22, 23
Akiba 191, 192
Alford, H. 117
Allmen, D. Von 276
Arius 321
Athanasius, 321-4
Augustine, 139, 198, 199
Baily, K. E. 296
Balchin, J. 278
Balentine. 293
Balsdon, J. P. V. D. 98, 113
Barnabas 305, 313-14
Barr, James 224
Barrett, C. K. 48, 60, 72-3, 75, 159
Bauckham, R. 62
Baugh, S. M. 122
Beale, G. K. 46
Beasley-Murray, G. B. 142, 296
Bedale, S. 283
Beker, J. J. 47
Berkhof, L. 336-7
Best, E. 86, 105-6, 142, 144, 149-50,
    151, 344
Black, M. 159
Borgen, P. 175
Bornkamm, G. 80
Bowman, J. 27, 293, 296, 303-4
Bray, G. 198
Brewer, Dr. David Instone 49, 192
Bright, J. 101
Brown, M. J. 75
Brown, R. E. 242
Brownlee, W. 346
Bruce, F. F. 44-5, 91, 94, 108, 122-3,
    135, 265, 303, 346
Buckley, T. W. 26
Bultmann, R. 45, 52, 85-6, 89, 90, 94,
    95
Burney, C. F. 277, 278, 341, 349
Buschel, F. 159
Calvin, John 79, 325-8
Campbell, W. S. 354
Carrington, P. 298

Carson, D. A. 163, 202
Casey, J. 299
Casey, R. P. 277
Charles, R. H. 56-7
Charlesworth, J. H. 58-9, 60-1, 62
Charnock, Stephen 331-2
Chester, A. 66
Chilton, B. D. 257-62
Cicero 123
Clement of Alexandria 305, 306-9, 315
Cody, A. 251-2
Colautti, F. M. 301
Cole, A. 242-3
Conzelmann, H. 121
Cook, E. 22, 23
Cooke, G. A. 251
Coppens, J. 134
Cosgrove, C. H. 38
Cranford, M. 201
Cross, F. L. 302
Cullmann, O. 167
Dahl, N. A. 259-60, 318
Daly, R. J. 177, 178, 301, 309
Daniélou, J. 305, 306, 308, 309, 313,
    314
Daube, D. 27, 294-5, 300, 301
Davies, P. 257-62
Davies, W. D. 47, 60, 105, 295, 297,
    339-50
De Jonge, V. 63
De Lacy, D. R. 278
De Vaux, R. 71-2, 73, 112-13
Deane, W. J. 55
Deissmann, A. 115, 116
Delling, G. 278
Deluz, G. 136
Dennison, T. J. 296
Derby, Stephen 337
Dodd, C. H. 45-6, 49, 79, 81, 88, 100,
    108, 159, 242, 284
Dunn, James D. G. 63-4, 162, 187,
    188-97, 203, 222, 223, 229, 277
Edersheim, A. 115, 263, 266

Subject Index

Scripture Index

1 Corinthians (cont)
1:24 342, 349
1:30 147, 199, 342, 349
2 349
2:8 136
3:16 127
4:4 223
5 117, 123, 124, 136
5:1ff 122, 124
5:2 114,128
5:4-5 344
5:5 125
5:6ff 302
5:6-8 124, 297
5:7 120, 128, 171, 173,
    309, 319
5:7-8 300
5:8 208, 224
5:12 128
5:12-13 123
6 94, 121, 122, 123,
    124, 132, 133, 135,
    137, 208, 209
6:1ff 152
6:2 122, 123
6:9-10 118
6:11 128, 147, 208, 224
6:12-20 117, 288
6:12-30 117
6:13-20 114
6:14f 209
6:15 119, 126, 127
6:15-16 126, 132, 288
6:15-20 119, 124, 125
6:16 120, 121, 126, 128
6:18 116, 118
6:19 121, 127
6:19-20 93, 111, 116,
    117, 119, 132
6:20 114, 115, 120,
    121, 127, 128, 240
7:1ff 114
7:4 128
7:14 128
7:22ff 302
8:1-13 128
8:4 128
8:4-7 38

8:9-13 39
9:9 128
10 135, 144, 152, 302,
    341, 345
10–15 145-146
10:1ff 143, 297
10:1-4 37, 208
10:1-22 128
10:2 128, 152, 174, 346
10:3 128
10:4 129, 208, 341
10:5 129
10:6 129
10:14-20 135
10:15-33 135
10:17 118
11 135
11:1-16 145
11:17-33 145
11:23ff 302
11:23-26 146
11:25 164
11:29 118
11:33-34 118
12 93, 118, 119, 120
12–14 118
12:13 144-146, 147,
    152, 208
12:25-26 78
13:9-12 119
13:12 174
14 120
14:24-25 144
14:25 145
14:26-39 146
15 164
15:3 67, 146, 284, 305
15:3-8 284
15:3-20 164
15:20 103, 146, 284, 297
15:21f 267
15:22 105, 149
15:24-28 107
15:26 103
15:27 267
15:35-49 126
15:45-55 103
15:55 103

2 Corinthians
1:10 208
2:14ff 298
3 339
3–4 200
3–7 76
3:1-17 297
3:3 74
3:5-18 340, 346
3:6 76
3:7–6:18 221
3:9 209, 221
3:14 149
4:1 76
4:1-12 346
4:4 103
4:15 346
4:16–5:5 346
5:5 120
5:10 228
5:14-15 76
5:15 149
5:17 76, 120, 173
5:18-21 326
5:19 221
5:21 76, 173, 199
6 173, 200
6:1-2 77
6:7 28
6:14ff 133
6:14-18 121
6:14–7:1 298
6:16 127, 133
6:16-18 77
6:17 133
6:18 133
10–11 79
11:2 98, 114, 118, 148,
    173
12:2 149

Galatians
1:3 27, 174
1:4 225
1:10 72
1:13-14 188
1:15 76
1:22 149

Other books
of interest
from
Mentor
and
Christian Focus

MISSIONARY
PAUL
THEOLOGIAN

A Survey of his
Missionary Labours and Theology

Robert L. Reymond

Paul – Missionary Theologian
A Survey of his Missionary Labours and Theology
Robert L Reymond

'This is quite a book! It tackles a big subject and grapples with it in a big way. Scholars, ministers, theological students and many general Christian readers will find much to stimulate and instruct them here.'

Geoffrey Grogan
Glasgow Bible College

'Robert Reymond has written a useful survey of Paul's missionary life and theology. The approach to the New Testament materials reflects a high view of their divine origin and authority. Of particular note is a serious defense of the now generally abandoned view that Paul was the author of Hebrews.'

Douglas Moo
Wheaton College, Illinois

'Dr. Reymond has applied his considerable skill in systematic theology to the study of the writings of the Apostle Paul. The approach that my former colleague takes is the fascinating aspect of this study. He is not writing about Paul as the great theologian, albeit he does do that, but about him as the great missionary/ theologian.'

George W. Knight III
Greenville Presbyterian Theological Seminary

'Those who have read and appreciated Robert Reymond's A New Systematic Theology of the Christian Faith, will be delighted with this new volume on the apostle Paul. Reymond's biblical and theological exposition of particular themes, for example, on canonicity, imputation, justification and the Holy Spirit, is superb and stimulating.'

A.T.B. McGowan
Highland Theological College

The writings of Paul are a major contribution to our understanding of the doctrines of Christianity. This new study, by a world class theologian, is set to become the staple book in colleges, seminaries and mission agencies.

ISBN 1- 85792-497-5

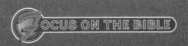

FOCUS ON THE BIBLE

Romans

The Revelation of God's Righteousness

'The deft hand of a scholar preacher is everywhere evident in the neat organization, precision, lucid explanative and warmth of this most helpful work.'
R. Kent Hughes

Paul Barnett

Romans

The Revelation of God's Righteousness

Paul Barnett

Focus on the Bible Commentary

Readable, Reliable, Relevant – the 3 'Rs' of Focus on the Bible commentaries.

"Paul Barnett's refreshing commentary on the Letter to the Romans is marked by warmth, clarity, careful exegesis of the text, and a fine grasp of the historical circumstances surrounding this letter. Throughout his exposition Dr Barnett sensitively applies the apostle's profound, yet much-needed, message to our own context. I warmly commend this clear exposition of the apostle Paul's gospel."

Peter O'Brien, Moore College, Sydney

'Paul Barnett combines a thorough going exegesis which is sane and helpful, as well as lucid and well argued, with a pastor's heart and a good eye for application. This is a brilliant commentary on a key book, which I warmly and wholeheartedly recommend. Every preacher and lay reader should have it and read it!'

Wallace Benn, Bishop of Lewes

'Distinguished New Testament historian and pastor, Bishop Paul Barnett, has given us a clearly written commentary on Romans which, while critically conversant with the present debate over the new perspective, is clear and accessible to preachers and Bible teachers.'

**R. Kent Hughes, Pastor
College Church in Wheaton, Illinois**

Paul Barnett is retired Bishop of North Sydney and Faculty Member of Moore Theological College, Sydney.

ISBN 1-85792-727-3

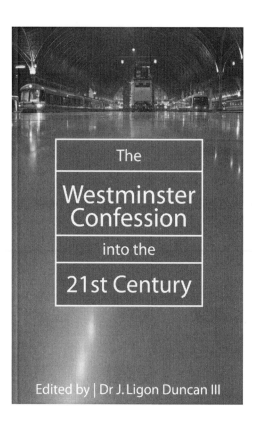

The

Westminster
Confession

into the

21st Century

Edited by | Dr J. Ligon Duncan III

The Westminster Confession into the 21st Century

Volume One

Edited By Ligon Duncan

Contributors include:
Michael Horton, Mark Dever,
Timothy George, Richard Gaffin, David F. Wright

Ligon Duncan has assembled an impressive array of contributors from a variety of ecclesiastical backgrounds. The aim is simple - to enable the 21st Century to understand the confession more fully, and so bring about the same kind of rugged, vigorous, intelligent and self-sacrificing Christianity that was the result of its initial publication over 350 years ago.

In the first of three volumes, the topics covered include:-

Baptists and the Westminster Confession
Finney's attack on the Westminster Confession
The Holy Spirit and the Westminster Confession

'...a most worthy undertaking and, to my mind, one that is quite timely not only because of the anniversary of the Assembly but also because of the clear need in Presbyterian and Reformed circles for scholarly work on the Reformed tradition and its confessions.'

Richard A. Muller,
P.J. Zondervan Professor of Historical Theology
Calvin Theological Seminary, Grand Rapids, Michigan

ISBN 1-85792-862-8

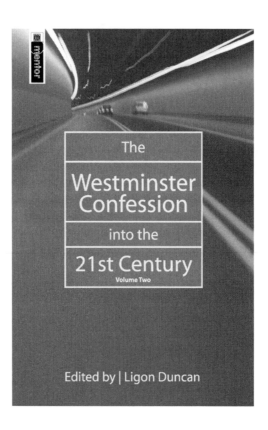

The

Westminster Confession

into the

21st Century

Volume Two

Edited by | Ligon Duncan

The Westminster Confession into the 21st Century

Volume Two

Edited By Ligon Duncan

Contributors include
Doug Kelly, Robert Reymond,
Nick Needham, Paul Helm, Joel Beeke

The Westminster Confession is a worldwide foundational document. Churches of all sizes claim it as their confession, and hold to it with varying degrees of closeness. However, countless officeholders will have vowed to abide by it with only the most perfunctory of understanding of its relevance.

Ligon Duncan has assembled an impressive array of contributors from a variety of ecclesiastical backgrounds.

The topics covered include: -
Westminster Spirituality;
Westminster and the Regulative Principle;
Old Princeton Seminary and the Westminster Standards;
The Eschatology of the Westminster Confession of Faith

'If the historic confessions are to be preserved for the future, it will take the kind of sympathetic historic description and effective doctrinal argumentation displayed in this book. It is a volume that Christians who adhere to other confessions, or those who feel that Westminster did not say the last word, should value as much as those who believe in the entire adequacy of Westminster for today.'

Mark A. Noll,
McManis Professor of Christian Thought,
Wheaton College, Illinois

1-85792-878-4

Christian Focus Publications

publishes books for all ages

Our mission statement –

STAYING FAITHFUL

In dependence upon God we seek to help make His infallible Word, the Bible, relevant. Our aim is to ensure that the Lord Jesus Christ is presented as the only hope to obtain forgiveness of sin, live a useful life and look forward to heaven with Him.

REACHING OUT

Christ's last command requires us to reach out to our world with His gospel. We seek to help fulfill that by publishing books that point people towards Jesus and help them develop a Christ-like maturity. We aim to equip all levels of readers for life, work, ministry and mission.

Books in our adult range are published in three imprints.

Christian Focus contains popular works including biographies, commentaries, basic doctrine and Christian living. Our children's books are also published in this imprint.

Mentor focuses on books written at a level suitable for Bible College and seminary students, pastors, and other serious readers. The imprint includes commentaries, doctrinal studies, examination of current issues and church history.

Christian Heritage contains classic writings from the past.

For a free catalogue of all our titles, please write to

Christian Focus Publications, Ltd
Geanies House, Fearn,
Ross-shire, IV20 1TW, Scotland, United Kingdom
info@christianfocus.com

For details of our titles visit us on our website
www.christianfocus.com